ANTI-CAPITAL: HUMAN, SOCIAL AND CULTURAL

Anti-Capital: Human, Social and Cultural
The Mesmerising Misnomers

JACEK TITTENBRUN
University of Poznan, Poland

Routledge
Taylor & Francis Group

LONDON AND NEW YORK

First published 2013 by Ashgate Publishing

2 Park Square, Milton Park, Abingdon, Oxfordshire OX14 4RN
52 Vanderbilt Avenue, New York, NY 10017

Routledge is an imprint of the Taylor & Francis Group, an informa business

First issued in paperback 2020

British Library Cataloguing in Publication Data
Tittenbrun, Jacek.
  Anti-capital - human, social and cultural : the mesmerising
  misnomers.
  1. Human capital. 2. Social capital (Sociology)
  3. Economics--Sociological aspects.
  I. Title
  306.3-dc23

Library of Congress Cataloging-in-Publication Data
Tittenbrun, Jacek.
  Anti-capital : human, social and cultural : the mesmerising misnomers / by Jacek
Tittenbrun.
     p. cm.
  Includes bibliographical references and index.
  ISBN 978-1-4094-5255-3 (hardback)
  1. Human capital. 2. Social capital (Sociology) I. Title.
  HD4904.7.T53 2014
  302--dc23

                                                                          2012039398

ISBN 978-1-4094-5255-3 (hbk)
ISBN 978-0-367-60163-8 (pbk)

Contents

Introduction

All three concepts mentioned in the title of this book have enjoyed wide currency among social scientists of all persuasions and disciplines. At first glance, there is one thing that the concepts concerned have in common – while the adjectives differ, the noun core is the same. Moreover, the origin of the term in question is in economics which somehow suggests that one of the questions considered in the present book will have to be the applicability of economic concepts outside the economy. However, this is not the only topic touched on in the book. Indeed, their range is bound to be much wider, as wide in fact as the scale of questions taken on in the human, social and cultural capital literature. The above remark on the special role played by economic concepts in the extra-economic social sciences that deal with respective varieties of capital might suggest that the author, whose one of the main academic interest is in economic sociology, is, at least potentially, well-equipped for this kind of study.

The structure of the book is linked to its tripartite title – each of the consecutive parts consists of a series of chapters devoted to the various dimensions to the main subject of a given part, that is, human, social, or cultural capital. Each of these main parts of the book contains an account of origin and definitional meaning of a given concept, as well as an analysis of chief fields of its application, be it economic, sociological, political-science, etc.

A final remark is in order; although the title of the book unequivocally suggests its critical bent, and it would be pointless to deny this, it is important to remember that the title page precedes, as is hardly surprising, the body of the text, which, though, does not mean that the content of the former preceded the content of the latter in the research process.

In other words, our critical stance is not any preconceived prejudice, but rather, it emerged from research that had been, hopefully, conducted according to the principle: *sine ira et studio*. Of course, the following analyses may not live up to this promise, but this is not for us to judge, after all.

PART I:
HUMAN CAPITAL

Chapter 1

Background

The importance of the standard concept of human capital, in contrast to social and cultural capital, is fully accepted by mainstream economists. Whilst the concept did not catch on until 50 years ago or so the very idea of human capital is far older. "Economists who considered human beings or their skills as capital include such well-known names in the history of economic thought as Petty, Smith, Say, Senior, List, von Thunen, Roscher, Bagehot, Ernst Engel, Sidgwick, Walras, and Fisher" (Kiker 1966: 481). For instance, the founder of modern economics Adam Smith introduced the notion of humans as capital in his classic *Wealth of Nations* (1776/1937). Others, such as Alfred Marshall (1890/1930) and Irvin Fisher (1906), kept the idea alive (Walsh, 1935). Notwithstanding its long history, the theory of humans as capital remained relatively undeveloped well into the 20th century.

Specifically, Smith referred to:

> The acquired and useful abilities of all the inhabitants or members of the society. The acquisition of such talents, by the maintenance of the acquirer during his education, study, or apprenticeship, always costs a real expense, which is a capital fixed and realised, as it were, in his person. Those talents, as they make a part of his fortune, so do they likewise of that of the society to which he belongs. The improved dexterity of a workman may be considered in the same light as a machine or instrument of trade which facilitates and abridges labour, and which, though it costs a certain expense, repays that expense with a profit. (1776 Book II, chapter 1)

The above passage has been cited not only for its own sake, but also because of the following commentary: "As clearly demonstrated by the above quote, the idea that part of economic activities might not be devoted to immediate production or consumption, but might rather be diverted to education, study, or apprenticeships, is well entrenched in the history of economic thought" (Coulombe, Tremblay 2009).

What is striking in the above argument is that the authors treat education as an economic activity, presumably on the grounds that education forms one's labour power which subsequently is used in the process of economic activity. And there's the rub; education may be a form of economic activity inasmuch as it is provided by some profit-seeking ventures, is organised on the private property basis. Otherwise, it is a process that can certainly have some impact on the economy, while being at the same time dependent on the latter (for schooling premises, equipment, and indirectly through taxes paid by the various economic establishments), but essentially it belongs to what, in terms of our socio-economic structuralism, is termed the ideational structure of society.[1] What this case clearly shows is the imperialistic – in an economic sense – nature of human capital theory.

Be that as it may, for much of the ensuing 200 years (after the publication of *Wealth of Nations*) economic thought largely ignored Smith's insights, and focused instead on the role of land, capital stock, and hours of labour as the crucial ingredients in economic growth (Hornbeck and Salamon, 1991: 3).

Walsh (1935) noted that prior to the mid-1900s, discussions about humans as capital were carried on "chiefly in general terms; references being made to *all* men [sic!] as capital, and to all kinds of expenses in rearing and training as [investment]" (p. 255).

In the literature several reasons are given for the delay in formulating a theory of humans as capital, and these are interesting as they introduce us into the heart of some of key controversies connected with the concept in question.

One is the difference of opinion among early theorists regarding the relationship between humans, labour, capital, and earnings. Three camps seem to have emerged. The first (represented by John Stuart Mill and Alfred Marshall) distinguished between the acquired capacities (skills and knowledge) of human beings, which are classed as capital, and human beings themselves. On the base of their profound moral and philosophical commitment to human freedom and dignity, this group of thinkers rejected the notion in question, finding the mere thought of humans as capital rather offensive. To them, humans were the purpose for which wealth and capital existed: the end to be served by economic endeavour. Marshall, for instance, argued that although it is quite possible and ethical for people to sell their labour, there ought not to be a market in human beings (Baptiste 2009: 187).

A couple of comments are in order here. The object of exchange between the worker and his or her employer is not labour itself, but labour power. Firstly, this kind of transaction would amount to selling something that does not yet exists at the moment (the worker will have an opportunity to perform his or her concrete work only upon signing the relevant contract and being assigned to the specific means of work). Secondly, the very idea of selling an activity, human action, seems odd, if not outright irrational. What constitutes the object of exchange in this case is the worker's potential labour, or labour power. Thirdly, from our theoretical point of view, the worker does not sell, but, rather, leases out his or her labour power. Why this is so? When one purchases a consumer product, one acquires full property rights to it, including its use and abuse. Nothing of the sort takes place in the relationship between the worker and her so-called employer; the latter has no right whatsoever to use the worker as he wishes; quite the contrary, he is limited to only one direction of applying his or her labour power. In addition, the owner of his or her labour power can either move to another employer or, staying at the current firm, withdraw one's labour power, for example, by means of strike action. This suggests that the relationship is rather more one of land lease wherein

---

1   More on the composition of society at large in Tittenbrun (2012).

the farmer also leases the allotment of land in the specific end, and does not hold absolute property rights in it.

Fourthly, moral condemnation or protest against economic, i.e. capitalistic realities, is futile; historically (and even today – in its underdeveloped form) capitalism proved to be perfectly compatible with the slave mode of production, and whilst morally controversial, to say the least, markets in human organs flourish nowadays in a quite considerable number of countries.

Perhaps due to this divergence between lofty moral convictions and mundane realities (despite his aforementioned objection) Marshall's (1890/1930) *Principles of Economics* includes in an appendix a methodology for calculating the private returns on investment in education that, according to Marginson (1993: 33–4), would later become the core of the theory (Schultz, 1961).

A second camp (represented by Adam Smith, Irving Fisher, and the Chicago School) argued that human beings are themselves capital, that the notion of humans as capital is not incompatible with freedom and dignity, and that on the contrary, by investing in themselves, people enlarge the range of choices available to them and so enhance rather than limit their freedom (Schultz, 1961). This group tied earnings to educational expense (capital investment), not just to productivity. Adam Smith (1776/1937), for instance, argued that "a man educated at the expense of much labour...may be compared to one...expensive machine.... The work which he learns to perform...over and above the wages of common labour will replace the whole expense of his education" (p. 101). To Smith, then, variations in educational investments (human capital) explained and justified variations in earnings.

The third position is epitomised by Karl Marx. On the one hand, he agreed with Smith (1776/1937) that greater productivity alone does not account for the higher earnings of educated workers but that the cost of education (investment in the parlance of human capital theory) also enters into the equation as part of costs of production of a given labour power in conjunction with the costs of reproduction forming the value of labour power (Marx, 1867/1976). On the other hand, Marx also concurred with Mill (1859/1956), that workers sell their capacities to labour (their "labour power") rather than themselves. However, and here is the rub, Marx conceived of the above-mentioned capacity to labour not as a form of capital but reckoned that a worker's labour power becomes capital only when it is used in the process of production (Marx, 1867/1976, 1894/1981). Crucially, this variable capital, as Marx termed it, was couched in terms of the capitalist's expenses on his or her workers' labour power which constitutes a U-turn compared to those who treat the worker herself as making those capital investments. Thus, it is rather easy to agree with Marginson (1993: 34) that Marxist economics substantially diverged from what was to become human capital theory.

According to the commentators there is another reason for the delay in developing a theory of humans as capital which is the widespread use of the Keynesian definition of consumption and investment. According to Blaug (1970) Keynes viewed consumption and investment as mutually exclusive categories:

expenditures of two different sectors of the economy, households and businesses, respectively. Keynes regarded education as largely a household expenditure and therefore treated it as pure consumption with no investment component. Consequently, as long as Keynesian economics reigned, the so-called investment aspect of education remained hidden from view (Blaug, 1970: 16–22).

The above passage also needs some comment. While the differentiation between consumption and investment is sound, it is a fallacy to treat both these activities as part of the economy. A commonplace error is committed here (whose another case has been identified above): the circumstance that X influences A, does not mean that X becomes an integral part of A. Consumer demand undoubtedly influences the allocation of capital and other processes within the economic structure, but it does not follow that it itself is a component of the economy. Such social processes could be termed economically relevant, as opposed to those which are economically conditioned. By the way, consumption, of course, is also in the latter category, and only on non-dialectical grounds one may argue that the simultaneous membership in both categories is impossible.

A third reason given for the delay is the nature of economic production prior to World War I. According to Briggs (1987), for example, prior to World War II agricultural and industrial economies did not require large numbers of highly skilled workers, and as such, there was little need for a theory of human capital. But, Briggs argued, the high-technology economies that emerged in the post-World War II era required massive doses of highly skilled workers. And this technological advancement, he believed, created some sort of demand for building a theory of human capital (Briggs, 1987: 1201–10).

To continue the present story of prehistory and history of what is often called no less than "the Human Capital Revolution" (Baptiste 2009), the articulation of a formal theory of human capital is said to begin in the mid-20th century with what has been dubbed the Chicago School (Ali, 1985; Psacharopoulos, 1988; Sobel, 1978; Walters and Rubinson, 1983).

Chicago was, of course, a centre of free-market fundamentalism and neo-liberalism which fact is not irrelevant to the shape of the theory under consideration. No one other than Milton Friedman (1962) "signaled the interest of the Chicago school economists in a human capital theory approach" (Marginson, 1993: 36). What Friedman (1962) planted, Theodore Schultz, as Baptiste (2009) puts it, watered. In his presidential address at the Seventy-Third Annual Meeting of the American Economic Association on December 28, 1960, Schultz (1961) delivered what is generally considered the inauguration of "the human investment revolution in economic thought" (Sobel, 1978: 268, footnote 2). In that address Schultz (1961) argued that much of what is commonly labelled *consumption* is really human capital investment. This investment, he stated, includes direct expenditure on education, health, and internal migration; earnings foregone by mature students attending school and by workers acquiring on-the-job training; the use of leisure to improve skills and knowledge; and so on – all of which constitute measures aimed at improving the quality of human effort and, ultimately, workers' productivity. Schultz (1961) wrote, "Although it is obvious that people acquire useful skills and knowledge, it is not so obvious that these skills and knowledge are a form of capital, [or] that this capital is in substantial part a product of deliberate investment" (p. 1). He called the body of knowledge that sought to describe, explain, and validate this phenomenon "human capital theory" (Schultz, 1989: 219).

Let us immediately note that the concept of investment with reference to the process of acquisition of what is called human capital is largely a misnomer; Human capital is not built within formal educational institutions and frameworks alone, or even predominantly. "[...] Occupational skills are learnt on the job, implicitly as well as consciously" (Schuller 2001: 22).

> Confronted with the fictitious, the vulgar economists outdo each other in propagating the trite and the banal: To derive a justification for the existence of ground-rent from its sale and purchase means in general to justify its existence by its existence. Through spotlighting such tautologies, Marx traces a decline from the peaks of classical political economy to the flatland of marginal-utility calculators: The insanity of the capitalist mode of conception reaches its climax here, for instead of explaining the expansion of capital on the basis of the exploitation of labour-power, the matter is reversed and the productivity of labour is explained by attributing this mystical quality of interest-bearing capital to labour-power itself. (McQuinn 2011)

The above suggests that there is a relationship between the concepts of human capital and labour power. Topel (2000) defines human capital as "the intangible stock of skills that are embodied in people". There are many cognate definitions, such as: "...managerial ability or human capital" (Coles et al. 2010), "human capital or more colloquially, people" (Bukowitz et al. 2004). Finally, in no uncertain terms Brown and Lauder (2002: 224) state that according to human capital theory "Workers are expected to invest in their 'employability' regardless of whether they are in employment or looking for work". The notion of "employability" refers, of course, to one's capacity to work, i.e. labour power.

And one can couch human capital in terms of labour power not only at the broadest, but also more specific levels; the following claim refers to what within our socio-economic structuralism is termed operationally particularistic labour power – the author fails to distinguish such work processes in which communication forms an inalienable and essential part of work especially, but not exclusively, in services: "Communication and teamwork skills are two of the most universally acknowledged competences for a modern economy" (see e.g. Levy and Murnane 1999). "These can be interpreted at a basic practical level, where productive efficiency requires good communication between workgroup members. [...] Human capital can certainly be understood to encompass social as well as technical skills" (Schuller 2001: 16–17).

Chapter 2
Theory and Reality

To put it in a nutshell, "the basic idea of human-capital theory is that workers invest in their own skills in order to earn higher wages, much as persons invest in financial or physical assets to earn income" (Sullivan, Sheffrin 2003). Apart from the economists already mentioned above, the main contributors to modern human-capital research are Jacob Mincer, and Gary Becker. Their ideas, focusing on investments in and returns to education and training, have provided the theoretical and empirical basis for decades of ensuing research.

The revival of interest in the human capital idea occurred at the end of the 1950s and in the early 1960s, following the growth accounting approach put forward by Solow (1957), that a substantial proportion of US economic growth was not accounted for by such traditionally conceived of as playing that role the increases in the stock of physical capital (machinery and equipment, and structures) and labour (number of people employed). It was then suggested that precisely human capital might be a good candidate for accounting for the so-called Solow residual.

The human capital concept developed, however, separately from the economic growth literature with the influential works of Mincer (1958) and Becker (1962, 1964). Mincer attempted to explain the differences in the personal income (wage) distribution by the investment in human capital. He analysed how rational agents freely determine the time they allocate to studying (or training) or working. The cost of studying is the direct cost of education (tuition fees) plus forgone labour earnings, while the return to studying comes from higher future earnings. Initially, because the return to extra years of education is decreasing, the value of future earnings exceeds the cost of studying and the individual continues to invest in education. In equilibrium, the benefit of an extra year of schooling equals its costs. This analysis – based, as it does, on marginalism – is generally regarded as the theoretical foundation of empirical labour economics (Coulombe, Tremblay 2009).

Workers invest in productivity-increasing skills through formal education and on-the-job training. Moreover, in long-run competitive equilibrium, firms hire additional labour until workers' marginal productivity coincides with their wage rate. This allows us to infer the effects of worker characteristics on productivity, which are not directly observable, from their effects on predicted wages, which can be estimated from cross-sectional data. We use such wage function estimates to value additional years of education, experience, and other forms of human capital. Applying these value estimates to the changing distributions of human capital indicators yields estimates of the growth in average worker quality.

> The critical assumption underlying our approach is that workers' wage rates
> are equal to their marginal productivity, a basic implication of the competitive
> model of labour markets. (Aaronson, Sullivan 2001)

There are, of course, models of the labour (strictly speaking, as argued above,
labour power) market in which wages are not equal to marginal products. For
example, if firms discriminate against women or minority groups or if unions or
firms exercise market power,[1] wage rates may differ from productivity. Milgrom
and Oster (1987) develop a model which implies lower returns to human-capital
investments for disadvantaged workers (e.g., "invisibles") as employers receive
rents and conceal the ability of disadvantaged workers from potential outside
employers. This concealment permits the current employer to pay high ability
invisibles less than their marginal product.

In addition, Spence (1973) argues that firms use education and other observable
human capital variables as a signal of unobservable worker ability. This can
lead workers to invest in education even when it provides no actual increase in
productivity. Finally, implicit contract models of the type studied by Lazear (1979)
suggest that in order to induce higher effort and investment in skills, firms defer a
portion of workers' compensation until later in their careers. This leads to wages
being below productivity early in workers' careers and above productivity in later
years (Aaronson, Sullivan 2001).

In basic economic theory, under perfect competition, to ensure efficiency and
maximisation of output, one needs to ensure that the workers' remuneration or real
wage rate should be equal to its marginal productivity.

> However, if the public sector, which acts as a monopsonist, at the margin
> offers real wages to its civil servants that are not in conformity with their
> respective marginal productivity, then this may lead to building distortions
> and inefficiencies into the system. If the public sector insists and continues

---

1   Overall, therefore, it is fair to refer to "the challenge that neo-Classical economists
face over the distribution of income between 'profits' and wages when they try to reckon
'capital' in the same unit as they measure the others. Their brightest and best spent decades
trying to evade this circularity before deciding that silence was the safest defence for their
'logically insecure' treatment, a censorship which they have perpetrated on generations of
undergraduates. Marxists know that the distribution of income is decided by the balance
of class forces. In the sense that capital-within-capitalism is a power relationship, all
its economic guises might be deemed fictional" (McQuinn 2011). This indeed common
amongst Marxists framing of capital and capitalism in general in power terms should be
regarded, from the perspective of socio-economic structuralism as overly narrow, one-
sidedly emphasising only one type of relations ignoring certain key others. What we have
in mind becomes clear when one draws attention to the fact that economic formations of
society are distinguished according to their distinct economic property relations, which,
of course, holds also in the case of capitalism, and, correspondingly, capital is first and
foremost an ownership relation.

to offer rigid wages not in line with the workers' marginal productivity, or if it pays far below the competitive wages, then the consequences of such rigid non-competitive wages will eventually lead to readjustments in the marginal productivities of the workers. (Haque 1998)

However, if the public sector, which acts as a monopsonist at the margin, offers real wages to its civil servants, the argument goes that:

> ...are not in conformity with their respective marginal productivity, then this may lead to building distortions and inefficiencies into the system. If the public sector insists and continues to offer rigid wages not in line with the workers' marginal productivity, or if it pays far below the competitive wages, then the consequences of such rigid non-competitive wages will eventually lead to readjustments in the marginal productivities of the workers. (Haque, 1998)

> If workers are paid the value of their marginal product, it follows that better educated workers should earn higher wages (Michaelowa, 2000)

On the other hand,

> It is commonplace for degree holders to take up employment outside their chosen disciplines due simply to a lack of fit between their chosen field of study and employment. (Mayanja, 2002)

Many of the new labour researchers frequently expressed doubts about the competitive assumption on wage pricing. Some were highly critical and considered that one of the big failures of the neoclassical theory was concerned with the wage determination, because (of) the observable declining importance of competitive forces determining wage rates, with the rising of unionisation (TeixeiraCEMPRE 2007).

Neoclassical labour market models generally assume that the former 'clear' in the sense that everyone is matched to a job commensurate with his or her human capital and preferences. [...] they reach this market-clearing result on the basis of a familiar set of assumptions. Though many contemporary economists who consider themselves within the neoclassical orthodoxy tend to relax one or more of these assumptions, the commentary I discuss below leans closer to this orthodoxy than to other theories I discuss in later Parts.

For this reason it is worth quoting:

> Neoclassical orthodoxy generally assumes that: (i) firms attempt to maximise profits, paying wages equal to the marginal productivity of each worker; (ii) workers attempt to maximise utility, and continue to supply labour up to the point where their wages equal their respective marginal rates of substitution between leisure and consumption; (iii) through competition among both firms

and workers, unregulated labour markets will 'clear' in the sense that at the equilibrium market wage, there is neither an excess supply nor an excess demand for labour; and (iv) the parties' expectations about the future are rational, in that they incorporate all existing information available, accurately weighing the probabilities of various potential outcomes given that information. From these assumptions, orthodox neoclassical models generally predict that, in the long run, a competitive equilibrium will be a Pareto-efficient one (in other words, no gains will be possible through additional transactions without making at least one other person worse off). [...] the neoclassical model predicts that a worker's eventual occupation, wages, and so on, reflect both her existing stock of human capital and endowments, and her personal preferences. Over time, of course, workers make investments in building and maintaining their human capital much as they would a set of tools. The tools may depreciate over time, or they may, as the worker hopes, lead to future returns. Not surprisingly, the neoclassical model predicts that the worker will continue to make marginal investments in her human capital until the present value of those benefits just offsets its costs. It also presumes that workers' labour market decisions reflect their preferences. (Lester 1998)

Useful and critical to a limit as this account is, it leaves something to be desired; Lucas, for instance, fails to notice that the recourse to preferences is essentially to commit the fallacy of *ignotum per ignotum;* the researcher has no independent way of determining what these preferences in the specific case are apart from observing the type of behaviour in which they are purportedly revealed. We leave aside another typical of neoclassical economics' view of preferences as fixed, not to mention its overly optimistic treatment of markets:

Thus, in making occupational choices, workers will evaluate the multiple personal trade-offs, including work as opposed to leisure, wages versus non-pecuniary considerations (such as benefits or job safety), and so on. Assuming that wages in each type of job respond to other relevant job characteristics, the worker should receive a wage which reflects the marginal worker's valuation of the costs and benefits of contingent employment. From the 'demand side', neoclassical models predict that a firm's hiring decisions will reflect its technological constraints and anticipated costs of hiring another labourer. Firms that have 'factor substitutability' (e.g., the ability to use machines instead of labourers, or vice versa) will utilise each factor until its relative cost per unit of production is just equal to the rate at which the firm can, at the margin, substitute one of the factors for another. This suggests that an increase in the price of one productive input may lead to greater use of the substitutable input. Market wages, then, would also reflect the marginal firm's technical ability to substitute factors. [...] A range of familiar critiques challenge the orthodox neoclassical prediction that labour markets clear and that equilibrium wages and employment will be Pareto efficient. For example, labour markets may fail because workers have inferior information about the features of a particular job. Also, there may be limits on workers' abilities to foresee the effects of their decisions (sometimes termed 'bounded rationality'). They may underestimate the possibility that their initial labour market investment decisions will take them down bad labour market 'paths,' leading to future disadvantage. Or they may 'choose for today', preferring high wages now and failing to see that down the road, they will require health or pension benefits. Other critics contend that even where there is full information and rational behavior, public goods problems may plague contracting, especially among nonunion workers. Thus, all workers may desire a particular employment condition, yet no individual worker has the incentive to incur the initial costs of demanding it. Similarly, signaling problems may arise. For example, even if all employees desire job security, no individual employee will demand it because of the risk that she will send a bad signal to the employer that she is the type of employee who needs it. Or employers may decline to offer job security or benefits because doing so may attract the 'wrong' kind of worker, i.e., those who are most likely to shirk or fall ill. As such, the suboptimal status quo persists. It is also commonplace to identify market power – whether oligopolies or unions – as creating a socially inefficient undersupply of good jobs. All of these arguments go to the reasons why the labour market may fail to produce efficient bargaining outcomes, contrary to orthodox neoclassical assumptions. (Lester 1998)

These all, however, are only small correction to the overall stylised picture; of course, it is far more realistic to recognise the inevitability of so-called bounded rationality, but still many key assumptions of orthodox market approach remain intact.

Neoclassical theory predicts that a profit-maximizing firm will pay workers a wage equivalent to their marginal product. Most economists believe a person's human capital is the primary determinant of personal productivity. In practice, human capital generally is treated as job-related skills and physical health. (Grossman 1972)

Of course, it is argued that the quantity and quality of a person's work may depend on their "psychological capital" as well. A person's psychological capital (to use another term from this ever-growing family) is likely to govern their motivation and general attitude toward work. Indeed, Erikson [1959], founder of the life span development theory, argued that individuals who were psychologically healthy – those with high self-esteem – would be the most productive (Goldsmith et al. 1997).

To consider some further issues involved in the theory being discussed, it is useful to acquaint oneself with the following passage, a mix of both sound and simplified as well misleading claims:

The theory relies entirely at the microeconomic level on understanding the interaction of given individuals and their labour with given quantities of capital and given quantities of technology; the income earned by each factor equal to its marginal product. This implies, practically speaking, that the income of labour (wages) is equal to the marginal productivity of the unit of labour – the infamous theory which essentially in a Panglossian exercise of benevolence declares that everyone by definition earns the wages they deserve, since wages are held to equal the extra productivity the labourer adds to the firm. Not earning enough? Should have been more productive! Now this theory does not appeal very much to anyone except the best-earning wage earners, who can pride themselves on their innate superiority, all the more since the technology being given there is not much a worker can do to improve their productivity in the workplace, except perhaps work more intensely or longer hours. (Krul 2010)

The author reveals the ideological nature of the marginal productivity theory in a really illuminating fashion, even though in his polemic zeal he goes too far: contrary to his opinion, the worker can improve her productivity by enhancing her skills, so here Krul misses the point:

But our friend, the neoclassical economist, can now produce a soothing balm for our wounded pride: in fact there is also such a thing as human capital, residing in labour, and this is also a form of capital (i.e. a means of production). Moreover, since it resides in labour itself, it can be improved by the person involved, or even by the government on his or her behalf! This sounds much nicer, indeed. The problem is stated, the solution is offered. What more can one demand of the economist?

Unfortunately, although the concept sounds appealing and has even been tempting to some of the social-democratic trend of thought because of its implications for state investment and its correlation with growth – simply put, spend more on educating your citizens and you get not just increased output, but because higher skill and education levels themselves improve technology endogenously, one can even get positive externalities from investment in education.

[…] Notwithstanding this 'left' application of neoclassical growth theory, there are good reasons to object to the use of 'human capital' as a concept altogether, and it is quite more nefarious than it may seem at first instance.

The most important thing to realise about the concept of human capital is the direct meaning of the term itself: human capital. Conceiving of skills and education as an aspect of labour in fact reinforces the understanding of labour itself as a commodity, which happens to reside in human beings individually.

This has two important effects. First, the individual human's labour has under neoclassical theory already been assumed to be a commodity, a mere instrument for the production of capital. Now, even the aspects of the carrier of labour, the human individual, which were hitherto considered to be given and outside the sphere of neoclassical capital theory are now subsumed within it. All skills, all education, in fact any number of intangibles relating to character, outlook and so forth can now be subsumed into the theory as means of production. While this is only an abstraction in theory, it reflects the very real subsumption of such attributes to capitalist production in actual life. (Krul 2010)

We are afraid the author's and our own objection to the view of labour as a commodity have little in common; in the latter case it stems from the recognition that it is labour power rather than labour as such that is involved in commodity relations under capitalism, whereas in the first instance the criticism seems to be grounded in some ultimate moral values. Krul's critical argument appears also unfair inasmuch as there are definitions to be found in the human capital literature that include into its notion only those aspects of personality that are relevant to production so that the above-mentioned charge of intended over-inclusiveness does not apply.

Secondly, although it is considered separately as a 'factor of production', the use of labour as a factor in reality only differentiates itself in that it is considered to apply to employees as opposed to employers, with the income on marginal labour therefore being wage and the income on marginal capital being profit. But it is not otherwise differentiated – each is equally seen in terms of being a means of production. This means that it is, in principle, not even necessary for such 'human capital' to reside in individual labour at all – it may as well be an attribute of society altogether, or of culture, or any number of vague and general determinants. This is in fact often the way it is viewed in growth theory, where human capital mainly shows itself in the shape of general 'stocks of knowledge'. The consequences are very clear in terms of theory:

> On the one hand, human capital production is as much as any other means of production the result of private, individual investment, even if such is done by the state. If you are poorly educated relative to the market, you have made bad investment choices; equally, if your skills are out of date, or even your character or culture is not conducive to profit, your human capital levels are by definition low, since they constitute small increases in productivity as an attribute of your labour. Even when measured in terms of years of schooling, human capital measures still weight these by productivity under the normal conditions of declining returns on investment. In other words, it's yet another form of individualizing the social processes of human life and fostering a competitive, blame the victim mentality. (Krul 2010)

Even greater importance than this, after all, rather commonplace criticism of competitive individualism driven by capitalism as its ideological aspect (although it by no means should be dismissed), has its theoretical aspect: human capital theory in emphasising an individual effort as a self-made human capitalist, ignores the cardinal fact of social production of knowledge, beginning from the institutional process of education through the official curricula to the key medium in the shape of language.

The aforementioned scholar has yet several interesting comments to make on the subject:

This is also reflected eventually in the schooling and skill-building processes themselves, which under the influence of human capital theory [...] have aimed to foster the buildup of 'stocks' of such human capital. This means in practice that they orient themselves to teaching skills which will make these units of labour, humans, more productive in the workplace. (Krul 2010)

This time round both the theoretical point (stressing the reduction to the purported lowest common denominator of two antagonistic – in class terms – forces) and an ideological one (bringing out the subservient to capitalist production character of the education system) are well taken. Interestingly enough, Krul begins the next paragraph with the notion whose lack was emphasised above:

The nefariousness of this manner of thinking resides specifically in the general failure of neoclassical economic theory to distinguish between labour and labour-power as attributes of workers. Since it does not distinguish different types of input, especially in aggregate, and reduces them all to undefined 'units' of means of production, it completely ignores the real-worldly attributes of the 'factors' it deals with. A worker can only ever sell their labour power by contract to a capitalist for a given amount of time; his labour,that is the specific, qualitative aspects of work (which exist under all circumstances and in all civilizations) is another thing. Failing to distinguish between these means in the context of human capital that those attributes seen as improvements in the qualitative nature of the factor labour are in reality 'enhancements' of labour-power. When your schooling and your skills increase your human capital, what they do in reality is enhance your abilities to produce capital, in the real and precise sense of the word, during the period in which you apply your labour-power. Any 'improved' human capital means improved from the point of view of capital, not from the point of view of the human involved. In fact, for capital it does not matter at all whether a human is involved or not as productivity is concerned, which is why its ideology, neoclassical economics, cannot distinguish human from nonhuman inputs. This raises a second issue, namely that because labour itself is done by humans, labour-power also resides in humans. The real struggles in the workplace between labour and capital take place precisely because the human and his labour are not commodities, and cannot be commodities except under conditions of actual slavery. (Krul 2010)

This claim nevertheless, shows that Krul opposes the association of the notion of commodity with that of human labour (it should read: labour power) on moral grounds; indeed, the whole difference between the slave and wage worker in relation to the commodity economy is that in the latter case it is the worker herself who comes up as the subject of a commodity exchange, thus realising benefits from it, whereas in the slave mode of production the reverse is the case – the slave labour power is the object of a transaction profit from which goes to the slaveowner's pocket.

> In the qualitative process of labour, those humans will therefore attempt to resist their labour-power being used solely to produce capital and as much as possible in as little time as possible. Far from being mere inputs into a process, to be bought and discarded at will by 'entrepreneurs' and to be 'rewarded' for their productivity in helping make a profit by a wage equal to their ability to offer such 'help', human beings resist being commodified and resist working for someone else's benefit. The concept of human capital therefore inherently passes by the class struggle and the real forms it takes in the workplace. In fact, workers can have high skills and great knowledge of production processes they are involved in at their work, but low human capital, because they are not inclined to maximally use them to help their employer make more profits! (Krul 2010)

Much as one may appreciate the high moral and ideological tone of the above remarks, their substantive character is quite another question. Employees are not inherently and automatically opposed to their class enemies – the intensity of class struggle depends on many factors, including the degree of class organisation. In addition, Krul takes issue with Marx who in "capital" argued convincingly for the capability of the capitalist mode of production effectively to subordinate workers to its needs.

The preceding has repeatedly pointed to kind of applied character of human capital theory, which is well exemplified by the following case:

> In his oft-quoted Fifth Report to the Massachusetts Board of Education (1841), Horace Mann sought to popularise the idea that education had individual as well as collective economic benefits. This report became one of the most well-known of Mann's twelve reports to the board, though Mann himself worried that such an appeal would exacerbate the materialism that he hoped the common schools would combat. In 1841, however, the Massachusetts Board was under attack from opponents of a centralised school system, and Mann thought that by showing how schooling benefited the economy he might convince the board's opponents of the value of the state's investment in public education. Accordingly, he replaced his usual arguments about its moral and civic value

with a demonstration of its monetary value to workers and manufacturers in the Commonwealth. Arguing that the key to prosperity was an educated populace, he even sought to calculate the rate of return to the state's investment in education by asking a small sample of Massachusetts businessmen to assess the difference in productivity between literate and illiterate workers.

Though Mann's argument about economic efficacy helped save the Board of Education, until the end of the nineteenth century most common-school promoters continued to prioritise the civic and moral purposes of education. Since then, however, those ideas have been eclipsed by ones like those Mann articulated in his Fifth Report, particularly about the school's role in the production of what we now call human capital. Arguments about the school's civic and moral purposes have not disappeared, of course. They appear regularly on political leaders' lists of desirable educational goals. But over the last hundred years those ideas have been increasingly subordinated to the notion that the primary purpose of education is to equip students with the skills they presumably need to improve their own economic opportunities and to make the nation more prosperous and secure. (Kantor, Lowe 2011)

These observations are fully consistent with those made earlier regarding the system of education. The authors' discussion is indeed topical and timely, as shown below:

Nowhere has the influence of this way of thinking about education been more evident than in the history of federal education policy. It is especially evident today, for example, in programs like President Barack Obama's Race to the Top, which explicitly links federal aid to his desire to restore the nation's competitive edge in the international marketplace. But the influence of ideas about human capital formation on federal education policy began nearly a century ago when they provided the chief justification for passage of the Smith-Hughes Vocational Education Act in 1917. And they have provided the main rationale for nearly all the federal government's most important educational initiatives ever since – including the National Defense Education Act (NDEA) in 1958, the Elementary and Secondary Education Act (ESEA) in 1965, and, most recently, the No Child Left Behind Act (NCLB) in 2001. Indeed, given the longstanding opposition to federal involvement in education, it's hard to imagine that these programs could have passed on any other terms.

Taken together, these initiatives helped justify the expansion of elementary and secondary education to working-class youth, immigrants, women, and people of color as well. As a result, the public high school today is inclusive – no longer the elite institution that graduated only 3 per cent of the eligible age. (*Dissent* 2011: 16)

The above passage may serve as a lesson that one must not jumped to premature conclusions – in reality, each or nearly each ideology is so rich body of ideas that it may serve a diversity of class functions. And indeed, as we shall see also below, the theory of human capital has its progressive face as well. Of course, one should not exaggerate – this progressive function has its significant limitations:

> Yet, if the programs spawned by the federal interest in developing human capital contributed to the democratization of secondary schools, they have also had less desirable consequences. They seldom provided the economic benefits their proponents promised, but operated instead to displace economic anxieties onto the schools, deflecting attention from the need for more assertive labour market policies. And, at the same time, they protected the educational advantages of the nation's most affluent and privileged citizens. This is true even though the conception of equal opportunity that has informed them has actually grown more robust over time as policy has shifted from a focus on teaching specific vocational skills to working-class and immigrant youth to a focus on equipping all students – rich and poor alike – with the cognitive skills that a more fluid, knowledge-based economy presumably requires.

> *Consider, for example,* the movement for vocational education that culminated with the passage of the Smith-Hughes Act, the first major program of federal assistance to public education. In the first two decades of the twentieth century, no other reform attracted such a broad spectrum of supporters or generated such high expectations for success. Businessmen, labour unions, social reformers, as well as many educators all argued that vocational training in schools, particularly trade and industrial education, would be an antidote to poverty, youth unemployment, and the threat of national economic decline. Yet even allowing for the rhetorical oversell that usually accompanies new programs, the payoff to investment in vocational education fell far short of what proponents assumed it would be. Not only did graduates seldom find jobs in the areas for which they had been trained, but most evaluations of vocational programs found that on average their graduates earned no more than graduates from the regular course of study. (*Dissent* 2011: 17)

Notice that such an end result undermines the logic of human capital theory. And there is even more to this than that:

> Indeed, most evaluations concluded that vocational education functioned mainly, in the words of one 1938 report, as a 'dumping ground' for working-class and immigrant youth who had been pushed out of the labour market and pulled into school by tougher enforcement of child labour and compulsory education laws but whom educators did not think were capable of doing more advanced academic work. (*Dissent* 2011: 17)

This again very expressly shows that the human capital expedients are not by themselves able to overcome and compensate for the inherent shortcomings of the capitalist labour power market. In other words, as the recent example of Spain shows vividly, it is not enough to ensure a wide access and output of to higher education, which in Spain has been in fact the highest in its postwar history, when the potential thus highly educated workforce have no chance become the actual workforce owing to high unemployment, notably youth unemployment. Even in the US and UK, graduates, for the first time since the Great Depression, have great trouble in finding a job. That the construct of human capital can be a perfect cover-up diverting attention from really crucial to secondary issues can be also seen from the following example:

> In introducing the legislation that became the centerpiece of the Great Society and the war on poverty, President Lyndon Johnson stated, 'Poverty has many roots, but the taproot is ignorance.' The solution was to provide funding to schools with concentrations of the poor in order to 'contribute particularly to meeting the special needs of educationally deprived children.' In this way the poor would be able to accumulate the human capital necessary to find employment, which would then enable them to escape from poverty.

> In addition to distracting attention from the ways labour market inadequacies contributed to poverty, there were two major problems with Title I. First, despite an initial investment of slightly more than a billion dollars, the political viability of the program depended on the wide distribution of its funds. As a result, more than nine in every ten school districts ultimately shared the money, making it impossible to concentrate significant resources in the schools and districts with the largest number of poor students. Second, the practice of Title I was governed by the conviction that poor children, especially if they were African American or Latina/o, were hampered in school because they had cultural deficits that required compensatory education; [...] Although Title the typical practice emphasized pullout programs that focused on low-level skills to make up for what students presumably lacked – and this required them to miss regular classroom instruction.

> These limitations became evident once evaluations were conducted. Early on, most of these evaluations found few positive effects. Some studies even found that the achievement of students in the program declined, though this was partly because of the wide dispersal of funding. Later evaluations, conducted once funds were better targeted to the students they were intended to help, were somewhat more encouraging, but they still paled in comparison to the program's original promise to help poor children escape from poverty. By the early 1980s, most concluded that the major benefit of the program was to keep the achievement gap between rich and poor students from getting worse.

Only modestly redistributive and built on the assumption that poor children were deficient rather than that schools were organized to hinder their capacity, Title I was a poor substitute for the more capacious view of equality of educational opportunity that integration promised. But because it distributed its funds so widely, it generated a broad constituency of support from new groups of service providers and recipients, both Republicans and Democrats in Congress and education interest groups like the National Education Association, which rallied to defend the program whenever it was attacked. As a result, Title I turned out to be remarkably resilient, despite its relatively modest impact on student achievement. It survived Ronald Reagan's attempt to turn it into a block grant in 1981, and it continues to be the chief mechanism for distributing federal dollars to the schools, which it does according to the modestly redistributive premises put in place in 1965. (*Dissent* 2011: 19)

The reader's attention may be drawn to this down-to-earth explanation of the popularity of a specific government programme amongst bureaucratic circles. As a matter of fact the author's account for the persistence of the programme concerned in terms of public choice theory which – contrary to its name, but consistent with the focus of human capital framework – concentrates on private interests, only that operating in the public domain. It is interesting to see what characteristics of human capital are manifested in a government initiative that explicitly draws on it:

Act (NCLB) in 2001 had little to do with fighting poverty. It was motivated instead by a desire to upgrade the quality of the nation's labour force and thereby increase the capacity of its businesses to compete in the international marketplace. But as with the Great Society's poverty warriors, the businesspeople, politicians, educators, and other social reformers who fretted about the nation's lagging economic performance never questioned the idea that the solution to the problems they faced lay primarily with strategies of educational reform. At the outset, NCLB did appear to embrace a more robust vision of equal opportunity than Title I of ESEA. Rather than trying to change the character of low-income children, as Title I seemed interested in doing, NCLB aimed to change the schools. By providing test score data to compare schools with students from different backgrounds and sanctioning those that did not bring all groups up to a minimum standard of academic achievement, NCLB countered the idea that low-income children and children of color were somehow incapable of achieving. Instead, it promised to offer proof that schools and educational practices, not children and their parents, were to blame for racially and economically disparate outcomes. And then it promised to press inadequate schools to address those disparities. (*Dissent* 2011: 19)

Thus, regardless of the policy-makers' motivations and goals of their policies, the latter always end up in failure, thereby exposing the drawbacks of human capital framework. Indeed, this is what the authors point out:

But this vision of reform was even more pinched than the preceding one. It rightly rejected the array of stigmatizing practices that accompanied earlier compensatory programs and that had long depressed the educational achievement of low-income children. In doing so, however, it also minimised the ideas that there was any connection between the conditions of educational provision and school achievement and that equality required the redistribution of resources. By setting uniform standards for all students and holding local schools accountable for meeting them, it sought instead to motivate teachers and administrators to raise achievement levels regardless of the often great disparities of resources available to different schools.

Over the last decade, the limits of this strategy have become all too apparent. Touted as a program to reduce the achievement gap, so that all students would have an equal chance to acquire the academic skills needed in the twenty-first-century economy, NCLB was rarely effective. Most often, it functioned to protect the educational advantages of the most privileged, just as federal policy has done so often in the past. This time, however, the familiar result didn't come about because educators formally limited access to the most challenging academic classes or because they isolated poor students in pullout classrooms. It was because teachers and administrators in inner-city schools faced the impossible requirement of annual increases in the test scores of multiple subgroups – including special education students – so that all of them attained the same level of proficiency. In order to meet this goal and avoid the NCLB's penalties for failure, these educators focused narrowly on preparation for the tests in reading and mathematics at the expense of other subjects.

Despite the authors' largely inconsistent terminology, mostly drawn from the theory of stratification rather than class, the class import of their analysis is clear enough:

In contrast, their counterparts in suburban schools, confident that their white, middle-class students could succeed on the tests without special preparation, continued to offer an enriched curriculum. In this way, the disaggregation of test scores by subgroup, which was the legislation's most progressive feature, actually worked to produce less than progressive results. (*Dissent* 2011: 20)

The summary of this useful account in which the authors contrast the repeated failure of policies drawn to a greater or lesser extent on human capital theory with the stubborn persistence of human capital idea in the minds of those designing and implementing those policies is worth reading also for its implicit reference to class:

Though the rhetoric around NCLB was all about eliminating the achievement gap between rich and poor, any program that directly attacked the sources of the educational advantages of affluent over poor children was unlikely to have won political support. As a result, NCLB focused on saving the children in urban schools while leaving the district lines that protected the suburban schools and their mostly white, middle-class students intact.

None of this long history has done much to dampen enthusiasm among policy makers today for developing human capital in schools as a way to solve the economic challenges facing the nation and to equalise educational opportunity. Economic problems, such as stagnant wages and rising income inequality, for example, have more to do with the absence of strong labour market institutions, adoption of regressive tax policies, and the social norms that enable vast accumulations of wealth for a few than they do with the quantity and quality of education students receive. Yet the commitment to addressing these problems through ostensibly better education policies not only remains unabated, but, if anything, has been enhanced by the now commonly held belief that the economy's shortcomings stem from too much government intervention rather than too little. In this environment, a 'supply-side' strategy like human capital formation has particular appeal, even to many of those who were once skeptical about it.

Some of Obama's supporters hoped he might chart a different course. But his vision of education policy has done little to alter these preferences. His call for the nation to 'out-educate' our international competitors continues to assign to the schools responsibility for solving problems that are beyond educational correction. And the policies he has adopted – such as Race to the Top – pose no challenge to the jurisdictional arrangements that have long protected the educational advantages of the affluent. Instead, following the trajectory set in motion by NCLB, they are confined to the technical problems of how to manage schools better, measure achievement more precisely, encourage teachers to work harder, and manipulate incentives to stimulate the growth of charter schools. (Kantor, Lowe 2011)

And strong words of the authors take on the notion of human capital as a panacea, severe limitations of that view being apparent under capitalism:

No less than when Horace Mann wrote his Fifth Report, Obama's strategy might be the only way in the current political climate to win backing for more spending on education. But the history of past policy suggests that we have paid a steep price for it. We should be thinking instead about how we might establish conditions both inside and outside the schools that will engage students in the kind of serious intellectual work that the Committee of Ten called for more than a century ago, rather than pursuing policies that will only add another dimension of inequality to an already unequal system. (Kantor, Lowe 2011)

Let us now revert to the marginal productivity theory of wages which posits that, in a world of efficient factor and product markets, wages and productivity go hand in hand. Is this theory, though, borne out by evidence?

In fact, most empirical studies show, at best only a sporadic correspondence between productivity and wages across sectors or countries (e.g., Van Biesebroeck 2003, Jones 2001). Hence the marginal productivity theory of wages remains for many only a theory. Moreover, there are other explanations for productivity that go beyond the employee level, to the firm or industry level, such as the extent of investment in automation (Contractor, Mudambi 2008).

One such major study is a case in point: "Using a five-year panel involving 60 countries and covering the period 1980-2000 [...] the data show that the behaviour of human capital's marginal productivity does not evolve as predicted by the neoclassical theory" (Arteaga, Cabrales 2010).

Flaws intrinsic to neoclassical economics cause that available evidence must be accounted for by some other, alternative theoretical framework. Such evidence, honestly speaking, abounds. Analysts using cross-sectional data from the Current Population Survey (CPS) have found that individuals in the United States receive earnings that are approximately 10 per cent higher for every additional year of schooling they have completed. Kenneth I. Wolpin's article on education in this special edition of the *Monthly Labour Review* shows that, over the 15-year period between ages 25 and 39, a male college graduate earns 80 per cent more than a male high school graduate without a college education, and a male high school graduate earns 57 per cent more than a high school dropout" (Frazes, Spitzer 2005).

The thing is, such facts are much better explained by the theory of labour power. Under it, the longer one's period of schooling, the greater – *ceteris paribus* – his or her value of labour power, which translates into a given employee's higher wage.

But costs of production of a given labour power may go up also as a result of training programmes initiated and paid for by its bearer's employer. Therefore, it is not surprising that "the best available evidence suggests, for example, that the wages of workers who receive employer-provided education and training are between 4 and 16 per cent above comparable workers who have not received training" (Bassi et al. 200: 336).

Being susceptible to alternative explanatory tools, this kind of evidence needs not be framed in human capital terms, which, frankly speaking, are redundant-their explanatory power is in fact only apparent, and one's opposite impression results only from their presence in the context in question, which is more exactly couched as a forceful superimposition, or theoretical violence. What underlies the above conclusion is, of course, our earlier discovery: to the extent that it is plausible to understand the concept of human capital in capital terms, it is variable capital that is at stake; otherwise, it denotes human, true, but labour power.

Chapter 3

Human Capital in the Corporation

The New Relationship: Human Capital in the American Corporation edited by Margaret M. Blair and Thomas A. Kochan (2000) is a collective volume that will serve as a frame of reference for our deliberations on a number of issues related to the topic around which the present chapter is organised. The book is a collection of papers presented to a conference on Corporations and Human Capital, which name underlines the relevance of its content to the purposes of our work.

The following statement of the book's editors may be regarded as its starting point,

> as the economic value added by corporations and other productive enterprises appears to be increasingly dependent on inputs other than physical capital. By the end of 1998, the book value of property, plant, and equipment in the publicly traded corporate sector represented only 31 percent of the total value of the long-term financial claims on nonfinancial corporations (the sum of the book value of their long-term debt, plus the market value of their equity). This compares with 83 percent just twenty years earlier, in 1978 The excess of market value over book value is, as best we understand, driven by a massive increase in the importance of intangible assets, including things like patents, copyrights, and brand names, but also including many very poorly understood assets such as organisational capital, reputational capital, and importantly, human capital – the knowledge, skills, ideas, and commitment of the employees. (Blair, Kochan 2000a)

This statement poses several issues.

The concept of value added as based on an idea of capital and labour as two factors of production receiving their respective justly deserved share of income is flawed in its own right – what has been above said on the marginal productivity theory holds for capital as well. So, an addition of a new factor named human capital only makes matters more cloudy; the term suggests its referent is a variety of capital, whereas in actual fact the concept of human capital refers to labour power, and hence has more in common with "labour" than "capital" as a factor of production.

There is another broad issue involved here. Human capital theorists are but part of a broader intellectual stream hailing the rise of a new industrial, or indeed post-industrial (and oftentimes-post-capitalist) age in the form of so-called 'knowledge economy', 'knowledge-based economy', 'information society', etc.

In the human capital literature it is held that we have moved from an industrial society, where the primary source of wealth was machinery, to a knowledge society, where the primary source of wealth is human capital. In essence, we have undergone a metamorphosis. "In the closing years of the 20th century, management has come to accept that people, not cash, buildings, or equipment, are the critical differentiators of a business enterprise (Fitz-Enz 2000: 1).

Such statements express some new tendencies in capitalism, but do so in a distorted manner. By wealth one should probably mean the sum total of use values. But modern capitalism by no means replaces fixed capital (machines) with human capital. Proclamations of human capitalists and other theorists of similar intellectual persuasion may be taken to reflect an increased role of knowledge, above all scientific knowledge, in the process of production. But this by any means reduces the role and importance of machines. Quite the contrary. Marx noted in "Grundrisse" (notebook VI):

> Direct labour and its quantity disappear as the determinant principle of production – of the creation of use values – and is reduced both quantitatively, to a smaller proportion, and qualitatively, as an, of course, indispensable but subordinate moment, compared to general scientific labour, technological application of natural sciences, on one side, and to the general productive force arising from social combination [*Gliederung*] in total production on the other side. [...] the means of labour passes through different metamorphoses, whose culmination is the machine, or rather, an automatic system of machinery (system of machinery: the automatic one is merely its most complete, most adequate form, and alone transforms machinery into a system), set in motion by an automaton, a moving power that moves itself; this automaton consisting of numerous mechanical and intellectual organs, so that the workers themselves are cast merely as its conscious linkages. In the machine, and even more in machinery as an automatic system, the use value, i.e. the material quality of the means of labour, is transformed into an existence adequate to fixed capital and to capital as such.

To return to the above-cited quote, its authors definitely make too much of the divergence of book and market value; they write about it as if the determination of stock market prices were a scientific process based on strict rules of calculation. Meanwhile, it is well-known that stock prices are largely shaped by irrational factors, speculation, etc.: "With the development of interest-bearing capital and the credit system, all capital seems to double itself, and sometimes treble itself, by the various modes in which the same capital, or perhaps even the same claim on a debt, appears in different forms, in different hands. The greater portion of this 'money-capital' is purely fictitious" (Karl Marx, *Capital*, II).

> ...fictitious capital may be re-defined as the value of ownership titles: this value is a 'pure illusion' if only because its connection with the world of commodities (and particularly with the labour embodied in them) is lost even when it does *not* consist of government bonds (Meacci 1998).

Also the following pronouncement stresses some distinct characteristics of share or fictitious capital:

> There is ready money to be gathered by gambling with the share-tokens as chips at the world's biggest casino, the stock market which is, as Warren Buffett reminds us, a voting machine,[1] not a weighing machine.

> [...] Marx stresses the difference between value and the market-price of shares as ownership titles to real capital: their money value being determined differently from the value of the actual capital that they at least partially represent; or, where they represent only a claim to revenue and not capital at all, the claim to the same revenue is expressed in a constantly changing fictitious money capital.

> That volatility happens because the shares become commodities, whose price has its own characteristic movements and is established in its own way. (McQuinn 2011)

And an attempt at the elevation of human capital to the rank of fully-fledged capital by equating it with other intangibles does not do the trick either. "Accountants and auditors conjure the mystery of fictitious capitals whenever they try to put a number on the valuation of items in company balance sheets: Brands and good-will, for instance, the closure of the *News of the World* puts a question mark over the values attributed to all mastheads, indeed, of all intangible assets" (McQuinn 2011).

The role of fictitious capital in modern corporations may be illustrated by "one News Ltd subsidiary [which] in 1996 had a capital of $190 but carried debts of $4.16bn while being owed $2.95bn by other subsidiaries" (McQuinn 2011).

The above theoretical considerations are corroborated by evidence. On the one hand, some analysts take the same position as the above-mentioned writers. For example, "the results of a recent study on human capital practices in Canada and the US (The Human Capital ROI Study, Deloitte & Touche) suggest they represent as much as 43 percent of the difference between the market-to-book value of one company compared to another" (Vicki 2003).

Similarly, "whereas in 1980 the ratio of the market value to the book value for the typical firm in the S&P 500 was about 1.2, at the end of 1998 its market value was three times its book value. Additionally, for firms listed on the NYSE, the market to book ratio has risen from about 1.1 to over 2.0 in the same period. These two pieces of evidence imply that human capital represents between one half and two thirds of the value of the typical firm" (Molina, Ortega 2002).

---

1 Although his numerous fans call him 'The Sage', this particular metaphor of the billionaire investor does not capture its empirical referent particularly well; the process of voting normally is governed by the rule "one person-one vote", whereas as between two stockholders one may have many times greater voting and purchasing power than another.

And another commentator puts the process in question in perspective: "up until the early 1980s, the book value of a company's 'tangibles' accounted for almost all of its market capitalization. At that time, a shift started to occur, and the market and book value for publicly traded companies began to deviate from past pattern and practice" (Weatherly 2003).

Still another states: "In 1982, hard assets represented 62 per cent of a company's market value on average. By 1992, this figure had dropped to 38 percent. More recent studies place the average market value of hard assets in many companies as low as 30 percent. In other words, up to 70 per cent of a company's expenses may be related to human capital" (Fitz-Enz 2000: 1).

The reader's attention may be drawn to the parasyllogism present in the above argument-from the fact that 70 per cent of a company's market value is supposedly accounted for by its tangible assets, it does not follow that human capital accounts for 30 per cent of corporate expenses. For one thing, the concept of intangible assets is far wider than what usually passes as human capital. Even more importantly, the claim concerned assumes a parallelism between capital investment, including human capital investment, and this capital's stock market evaluation, which is a far-fetched assumption. This observation prompts one to take a closer look at the studies concerned. To pre-empt the conclusions from that overview, it will be seen that "the process by which a firms human capital returns improve market and operational performance is neither well understood nor described" (Bassi et al. 2000).

One of such studies has aimed at the estimation of "...the value of the human capital assets as a proportion of the market value of the firm. The mean (median) value of this ratio was about 5% (2%). Further, the value of the human capital asset represents an average of about 16% of the difference between market and book value, and a median of about 3%" (Ballister et al. 1999). But the authors themselves insert a significant caveat when they indicate the premises of that result "...the proportion of labour expenditure that represents an investment in human capital assets, has a mean of 16%, and a median of 10%. Thus, the average (median) firm in our sample invests about 16% (10%) of total labour-related expenditures on building its human capital. This is an impressive proportion, but is probably not representative of other firms, since sample firms voluntarily disclosed labour data for a long period, presumably because it represented a significant cost for such firms" (Ballister et al. 1999).

This circumstance, together with other considerations has led the aforementioned researchers to concede that "the sample of firms we use in the study for human capital valuation represents a sample with unique characteristics, and generalizing from this sample to the larger population may well be problematic" (Ballister et al. 1999).

Human capital methodology has other problematic aspects to it, however. Lev and Schwartz (1971) argued that an employee's expected economic value to the firm corresponds to the future earnings of the employee for the remaining active service life.

Therefore, the value of the total human resources of the firm is determined by aggregating the present value of services of all employees. Ballister et al. (1999) employ a method that is not much different, and acknowledge that,

> as evident from these examples, in order to put a value to a firm's human assets these earlier models started at the individual employee level and then aggregated these values for all employees within the firm. In contrast, we start at the firm level and estimate the value of all human assets as a proportion of the total market value of the firm. Since the compensation structure of different firms varies widely and this Compustat item represents a fairly broad category of expenses, cross-sectional comparisons on the basis of this data item may not be particularly reliable. For instance, it is not clear whether items such as training costs and other long-term investments in human assets are also aggregated in this number for all firms.

This is truly astonishing confession – the researchers do not know whether the facts they are interested in are included in the available data, and despite this rather major shortcoming, they still use those problematic data.

The following statement puts its finger on the heart of the problem involved:

> The accounting system can be based on the current accounting practice of full expensing of labor-related costs, as long as it satisfies the clean surplus equation. Alternatively, an accounting system that capitalises a portion of the labor-related costs can also provide parameters (earnings and changes in book values) for the valuation equation, as long as it satisfies the clean surplus equation. Thus, an accounting system that capitalises some labour costs cannot be considered preferable to the current system based solely on its use in valuation (Ballister et al. 1999).

The preceding suggest what is at stake here; on the one hand we have a benign image of the capitalistic firm investing in its employees thereby enhancing their labour power – apparently for their benefit only as the only effect of this investment is, we are told, increased wages. It is glaringly clear that what human capital theorists present as the firm's investment in human capital refers simply to variable capital, and this is the only 'capital' aspect that the process concerned has in common with the concept of capital because viewing it from the perspective of its alleged beneficiaries one has to do with their labour power. What the foregoing implicitly refers to, however, is ownership – Who actually does benefit from the training expenditures?

Within the human capital camp the aforementioned issue is indeed highly controversial, only that – due to their failure to command an adequate notion of ownership – it remains in most part implicit. In the above-cited discussion, for instance, there was talk of the existing of expropriating either party to the relationship: "human capitalists" – real capitalists or their agents, i.e. managers.

But in another chapter of the book under consideration, its authors see the matter differently: "Workers have a stake in safeguarding their investments in human capital and in protecting future returns to these investments against opportunistic expropriation by managers or shareholders" (Applebaum, Berg 2000).

Going further, another human capital theorist begins on a somewhat uncertain note: "While some might say we could define human capital as the accumulated present value of our employee investments (salaries, benefits, training and development programs, etc., invested on behalf of the organisation), the question still remains, how would you go about putting a definitive value on that investment?" (Weatherly 2003).

Those doubts do not impede him, however, from at least tacitly implying that the question concerned should be treated from an employer viewpoint. "A company's human capital asset Is the collective sum of the attributes, life experience, knowledge, inventiveness, energy, and enthusiasm that its people choose to invest in their work" (Weatherly 2003).

Supposing such a starting point, there arises a question of not only, as noted above, how to measure corporate investments in human capital, but also-how to calculate benefits from those investments. Both questions are not easy to answer.

Measuring Corporate Investments in Human Capital

The chapter in the book on this very topic begins with, only at first glance, a noncontroversial statement. Nay, the economists concerned, it seems, should be praised for their attempt to capture the specificity of this strange entity called human capital. "Human capital is, for very good reasons, the only form of capital that modern corporations cannot buy or sell" (Bassi et al. 2000: 334).

While the distinctiveness of human capital is unquestionable, the aforementioned authors' approach to it is not. All depends on which definition of human capital out of a long list available you choose; if the choice is labour power, then according to the conventional view its bearer, but not its buyer sells it. However, it has been argued that this common not only among Marxists (only that non-Marxist economists refer to labour instead) view is wanting-it cannot account for, inter alia, an aspect of the contract in question mentioned above-namely, that the employer is not able to sell the commodity purchased by her-as opposed to all other marketable objects. None among such objects, too, can withhold its services and in general behave in the manner the employee does. And interestingly, human capital theorists are aware of this kind of special attributes pertinent to what in their terms is human capital, and under our framework-in most cases labour power. Take the following definition: "human capital – the asset that doesn't sit on the company's books at night, but goes home and has the option of whether it comes back the next day" (Johnson, Robuck 2008).

For this reason, as underlined earlier, we would rather to speak of lease instead of sale.

It is well-known in logic that from incorrect premises correct conclusions may be derived. This is also the case in the present situation:

> As a result, it is the only form of capital that does not have well-defined (if admittedly grossly imperfect) accounting and reporting requirements associated with it. This circumstance has resulted in an unhappy dearth of systematic information. Firms themselves know little about the nature and magnitude of the investments that they make in human capital, and they know even less about the effectiveness of those investments. (Bassi et al. 2000: 334; 343)

Attempting to answer what the reasons for this sorry state of affairs are, the authors concerned point to what in effect refers to private ownership relations, although they – in a manner typical of orthodox economics – generalise this reason as an instance of universal "social dilemmas":

> Under the best circumstances, a vast amount of information must be gathered and evaluated in order to gauge the relative effectiveness of investments in human capital under a variety of circumstances and in various forms of work. The collection of such a large bank of information requires common metrics and shared measurement and accounting methodologies, which, as just noted, simply do not exist. These requirements make it impossible for anyone firm or even a small group of firms working together to solve this information problem. Hence, a classic market failure results; while the information might be of great value, the market fails to produce it. For example, the estimates of how much firms spend on education and training – their most conspicuous form of human capital investment – are rough at best. (Bassi et al. 2000: 334; 343)

Nevertheless, despite the paucity and limitations of the data required, they venture to say that,

> patching together the best available evidence suggests that the average U.S. employer spent approximately 0.9 percent of payroll on formal education and training in 1995 – a figure that appears to have changed almost imperceptibly since 1983 (the only other year for which a roughly comparable estimate is available).[2] And virtually nothing is known about the investment that firms make in informal learning – although this investment is, by all available anecdotal accounts, significantly larger than that which firms make in formal learning. According to a recent report from the Bureau of labour Statistics (December

---

2   See Bassi, Gallagher, Schroer (1996: 121). This figure is based on direct costs only. Although the inflation-adjusted total expenditure estimate increased by 18 between 1983 and 1995, the labour force grew by 19 percent during that same time period (Economic Report of the President, 1996: 316), suggesting virtually no change in training expenditures as a percent of payroll.

1996), 70 percent of all training time is informal, with only 30 percent being formal. The relative cost of these two forms of training, however, is not known. (Bassi et al. 2000)

It is a 'no-brainer' that when you do not know the basis on which to calculate your profit, the latter is also an elusive magnitude. It should also come as no surprise that little systematic, high-quality information about the impact and value of firms' human capital investments exists (Bassi et al. 2000).

The authors report that in a recent review of the literature, only four serious attempts to identify the relationship between training and overall corporate performance were identified – Manufacturing firms that implement training programs increase their productivity by an average of 17 percent:

> – Participation in employer-sponsored training reduces the likelihood of an employee leaving their employer;
> – Participation in employer-sponsored off-the-job training raises workers' productivity by 16 percent and increases their innovativeness on the job;
> – Firms that downsize their work force are much more likely to increase their profitability if they train workers. (Bassi et al. 2000)

The economists in question are frank enough to admit that there is a yawning gap between this sparse evidence and the whole human capital ideology extolling the virtues of this latest, and who knows if last hope of capitalism:

> Juxtaposed with this dearth of evidence is the increasing frequency with which prominent CEOs are heard to say that 'people are our most important asset.' If this is indeed the case, and given the old maxim that 'what gets measured gets managed,' it is reasonable to expect that firms would begin to take seriously the measurement of investments in this asset and the return on that investment. (Bassi et al. 2000)

Meanwhile, for some reason managers pay only lip service to the human capital craze.

Senior management affirms the importance of the knowledge their employees bring to the firm and truly believes that knowledge can, if managed properly, lead to competitive advantage in the marketplace.

Yet, despite the stated importance of human capital and its contribution to performance revealed in these studies, it turns out that senior managers report that they do not have the measurement or management tools necessary to fully take advantage of human capital. It is capital market impressions that drive valuation. It is management belief that drives investment.

Mind you, if you are not under the spell of human capital theory, or ideology, if you will, reflect on what follows:

What do managers want? They do not want an inventory of who's working for the firm and the rate at which people leave the company. They do want a way to track the productive application of human and knowledge capital – they want to understand how the firm's people find new sources of revenues, create new revenue opportunities, increase the optionality of the firm, improve relationships with customers, and improve efficiency and decision making. Given this perspective, it seems likely that senior managers will never be interested in tracking training expenditures nor in matching the inputs of investments in people with specific cash flows to a firm. Rather, they will be much more interested in tactical tools and in measurements related to outcomes that are related to a firm's goals. (Bassi et al. 2000)

By the same token not only human capital ideology, but also human capital theory, which, after all, hinges on its practical application, has been dealt a devastating blow by this sober judgment.

Furthermore, if the above-cited experts are right, and there is no reason to doubt their expertise,[3] the results of the following survey they cite must be taken with a great pinch of salt – given that managers know so little about human capital, how it is possible that they estimate the contribution of various factors to corporate performance with such precision?

Managers say that, on average, the firm's people account for half of the firm's performance (for example, the rest of performance is explained by technological innovation, market position, access to capital, internal processes).

Despite the strong belief in the importance of this type of human capital to a firm, and in how this capital returns value to the firm, senior managers judged their firms to be underachieving in their management of human capital.

When asked what they faced as the biggest difficulty in managing knowledge in the organisation, senior managers said it was changing people's behavior and measuring the value and performance of the knowledge assets. The inability to create tactical measurements leads to bureaucracy, no reliable measure of the return on investment, and the obsolescence of ideas and loss of information. If they could, senior managers would measure:
– Revenue generated by new ideas;
– Collaboration levels in key initiatives;
– Productivity of 'knowledge' workers;
– Quality of decisions;
– Percentage of revenue from new products; and
– Employee awareness of knowledge sources. (Bassi et al. 2000)

---

3   For instance, Daniel P. McMurrer is affiliated to the American Society for Training and Development.

It is the authors' mystery how they do reconcile the conditional mode used by them to refer to the managerial knowledge with the assertion at the beginning of the aforementioned pronouncement describing the products of that knowledge which by definition are to be credible.

Anyway, the preceding makes one wonder why on earth corporate managers fail to put their action where their mouth is, so to speak. Either of the two must be true: perhaps the promised benefits of human capital are not so huge (or, alternatively, it is the rank-and-file employees who stand to reap the bulk of benefits from human capital policies) as the human capital advocates would have it, or else corporate owners do not put pressure on management to take appropriate measures, which in turn might be accounted for by the well-known phenomenon of separation of ownership and control-which, it is presumed, is wielded by management.

Either way, the puzzle remains: All the more because the writers in question paint an even more pessimistic picture depicting the quality of managers' knowledge:

> A survey highlights an important paradox. Although senior management admits that it is people who make knowledge work, senior management evinces little interest in monitoring who comes to and leaves the firm (only 2 percent) and what the skills of the employees are (9 percent interested). Furthermore, managers in the Twenty Questions survey show little interest in knowing what contributions employees are making to the organisations overall stock of knowledge (8 percent interested in the number and quality of submissions to the organisations knowledge bases). This survey reflects the opinions and experience of 431 organisations, as reported by executives in a variety of management roles. Three hundred of these executives were U.S.-based, and the rest were European. No significant difference emerged in the responses of U.S. versus non-U.S. executives or among the responses of executives in different functional areas (marketing, information services, human resources, and so on). Individuals were of uniformly senior rank, with the majority holding titles of vice president or above and reporting directly to the chief executive office or chief finance officer. Their firms averaged more $1 billion in revenues. Industry coverage was broad, ranging from aerospace to utilities. The largest subset of responding organisations fell into the category of 'general manufacturing' (13 percent). No major differences emerged in responses from manufacturing versus service-oriented firms. Equally, people in these firms viewed their businesses as 'knowledge intensive. (Bassi et al. 2000)

To be sure, a caveat should be made that, however, ought not to compromise the results to any significant degree:

> 'Twenty Questions on Knowledge in the Organisation' was a survey conducted by mail and therefore inevitably suffers some self-selection bias. The top 1,000 companies in the United States and Europe were targeted. The 431 responses

reflect about a 40 percent response rate. In sum, a self-selected sample of senior managers say that people are the source of a tremendously important asset – knowledge of why and how to achieve the firm's mission. They believe human capital leads to increased revenues (through greater innovation and customer connections) and increased flexibility. (Bassi et al. 2000)

We already know that those are just incantations not implemented, and even not meant to be implemented in practice.

What is the background to this neglect?

For one, it turns out that at least US public companies are simply not required to report any expenditures related to what is regarded as human capital.

Human Capital Reporting

Generally accepted accounting principles (GAAP) are the set of rules and regulations governing the measurement and disclosure practices of US public CORPORATIONS. These regulations are manifested in corporate financial reports, such as quarterly and annual financial statements, as well as special filings, such as prospectuses accompanying securities issues (Bassi et al. 2000).

Given what has been said above regarding the purported pivotal importance of human capital, the reader may be forgiven for being taken by surprise by the circumstance that:

As far as human capital is concerned, GAAP is silent. Public companies are not required to disclose, qualitatively or quantitatively, any aspect of firms' investment in human capital, such as expenditures on employee training.

Nor are firms required to disclose any meaningful information on the state of their human capital, such as data on employee education, training, or any other capabilities of the labour force. (Bassi 2000)

The failure to regulate this supposedly crucial sphere on the part of the US state may be read simply as a reflection of free-market spirit fundamental to the US economic system, but equally – given a wide range of advantages said to be realised by American companies – as a sign of failure of the American bourgeoisie to establish and execute, by means of their state, such a regulatory regime that would suit their class interest. On an alternative assumption, whose validity will be separately checked, it is the second megaclass,[4] under that interpretation appropriating the lion's share of the pool of benefits generated by a variety of human capital programmes, which proves incapable of instituting such a legal

---

4 Under socio-economic structuralism, the concept of megaclass refers to an aggregated cluster of classes, such as the capitalist class, or the employee class.

framework. It is true that the disclosure prescriptions in GAAP are generally perceived as minimal requirements, and firms often disclose additional, voluntary information. Indeed, a surge in the past 15 to 20 years has occurred in the amount of voluntary information provided by corporate executives. Public corporations now routinely release news about products under development, alliances, joint ventures, managerial changes and restructuring, as well as prospective information, such as warnings about disappointing forthcoming earnings. It is, therefore, possible that human capital information, though not required by GAAP, is voluntarily provided to investors (Bassi et al. 2000).

To examine the possibility that firms would voluntarily provide human capital information, the researchers under consideration focused on the enterprises that compose the American Society for Training and Developments Benchmarking Forum. In large part because of the absence of accounting standards for measuring employers' investments in education and training, a group of 18 Fortune 500 firms approached the American Society for Training and Development (ASTD) in 1992, asking for assistance in developing common definitions and measurement methodologies so that they could individually and collectively identify and benchmark these investments. As of the end of 1996 this group consisted of 56 firms. The group's procedures for measuring training and education expenditures are now well established, although some of the members (including a few of the founding members) still have trouble implementing these standards.

> Of the fifty-six Fortune 500 members of ASTD's 1996 Benchmarking Forum two members merged, eight enterprises are private, four are foreign companies, and two are subsidiaries of public companies. These enterprises do not publish financial reports in the United States (Bassi et al. 2000).

The researchers state:

> The remaining forty-one public companies constitute our sample. We have examined the annual reports of these companies for 1994 through 1996, for any information related to human capital, particularly in the management discussion and analysis section of the report (in which managers are required to discuss important aspects impacting current and past years), and in footnotes to the statements. The large majority of sample companies (for example, 32 of 41 in 1996) did not provide any human capital information in the 1994-96 annual reports (table 9-9). Of those providing some information on human capital, most (nine of forty-one in 1996) disseminated some qualitative information, while very few (four in 1995; none in 1996) released some quantitative data. Surprisingly, the trend indicates a decrease over 1994-96 in reporting about human capital: the number of firms providing no information increased from thirty to thirty-two, and those providing quantitative information decreased from 3 in 1994 to zero in 1996. (Bassi et al. 2000)

What is more, the mere presence of information on human capital does not tell the whole story. For it, disappointingly, turns out that practically all the information provided is qualitative and of such a general nature as to be almost useless for any analysis and inference. Typical statements are ones like the quotation from Andersen Worldwide in 1995. "We recruit the best people and train them to be the best professionals in the world." Or "Avon Germany implemented a new recruiting, training, and retention program in 1995." Of some interest is Caterpillar's 1995 report which states, "In Illinois alone, we are investing over $6,000 per employee per year on training." And Colgate's 1995 report informing readers, "We can actually quantify the benefits [of training] using increased employee competence and on-the-job productivity as measured". it is rather surprising, therefore, that no information is given about those measures or even their direction.

It can be concluded that, all in all, no disclosure requirement exists in the United States for information related to human capital and that public companies apparently do not have strong incentives to disclose voluntary information (Bassi et al. 2000).

The aforementioned scholars note, to be sure, some exceptions to the general rule of information gap. They indicate that "the state of Illinois (where Caterpillar is headquartered) offers a tax credit to employers, based on their training expenditures. Obviously, under these circumstances it is in Caterpillars interest to publicly disclose such information voluntarily" (Bassi et al. 2000).

But the authors immediately add, too: "Nor do they have such information readily available".

Human Capital Accounting

Human capital measurement grew out of a science developed in the 1960s called human resource accounting. Among the thinkers who established this new field are: Rensis Likert, Theodore Schultz and Eric Flamholtz. Flamholtz's book, *Human Resource Accounting*, first published in 1974 and now in its third edition, is a standard reference for those seeking to understand the topic (2). Flamholtz introduced the idea that employees contribute more to the organisation than their salary and benefits (Grossman 2005).

This is hardly an acknowledgement of the theory of surplus value, to be sure, but nevertheless represent a step in the right direction.

The next remark is also apposite insofar as it highlights the ownership role of co-operation – it is only individual, and not collective labour power that gets paid; thus, the emergent effects of co-operation the owner of the means of production receives gratis:

> In fact, the replacement cost of employees could be many times their salary and benefits, depending on the skill level and extent of inter-organisational cooperation required to perform a job. (Grossman 2005)

The author in question then recalls that:

> Some initial human resource accounting work was performed on behalf of a few
> forward-thinking organisations in the late 1970s but the movement then stalled.
>
> Why, if these ideas have been around for more than 40 years, have organisations
> been reluctant to adopt them? Primarily, for three reasons: * First, associating
> this new science with financial accounting proved to be a double-edged sword.
> On the plus side, the link with financial accounting lent power and meaning to
> human resource (HR) accounting. Any approach that aspires to become part of
> the managerial decision-making tool kit must fit with financial accounting. On
> the minus side, the link with financial accounting saddled HR accounting with
> all of the former's drawbacks – a retrospective viewpoint, an overly strong focus
> on the concrete, and a false precision that boils down sound measurement to an
> ability to count. (Grossman 2005)

This critique of calculability as the sole or most important criterion of scientificity
is certainly justified, and in it Grossman, of course, is not alone (it suffices to
mention the prominent unorthodox branch of economics in the form of Austrian
school) which, however, cannot affect the fact that orthodox economics, which
determines the prevailing paradigm of economic theory, adopts precisely such a
criterion, and therefore the apparent absence of such a possibility within human
capital framework represents a major setback of the latter:

> * Second, HR accounting required a data set that was not readily available in
> most organisations. Investing in the necessary infrastructure to produce the data
> proved too daunting.
>
> * Finally, the return side of the equation was still not well-defined or easily
> understood. The additional precision that would be achieved around costs could
> not improve decision-making without an equally robust set of information about
> return. (Grossman 2005)

The publication of Flamholtz's third edition and other HR measurement books,
most notably Brian Becker's The HR Scorecard, signals the resurgence of
interest in this topic. However, most of these new publications are targeted at HR
professionals as a way of enhancing the relevance and the effectiveness of the HR
function to the business. For human capital measurement to be truly relevant to the
business, it must be a tool in the hands of operating managers to be implemented
in their current business planning and monitoring systems, which, as we have seen
above, for a lot of reasons, is not a simple matter at all.

Many human capital analysts and practitioners emphasise the imperative to
find reliable metrics for measuring human capital as stemming largely from its
importance in knowledge-intensive companies and industries-a growing sector of

the world economy. In some industries, such as software or professional services, fixed assets are minimal; human capital (to retain in this specific context the term) makes up a substantial portion of the operating budget.

Corporate testimonies to the importance of people abound, as in "people are our most important asset." But, aside from making this statement, few companies report anything to demonstrate that this asset has an impact on the value of the enterprise. Research studies have revealed that even "best practice" companies report only a handful of people-related statistics in their public disclosures. Some, such as employee satisfaction, employee turnover, and investment in training, serve to highlight how well the organisation is managing its human capital. Other ratios, such as Revenue/Employee (or sometimes Profit/Employee) or Revenue/ Compensation serve as rather imperfect proxies for the value created by human capital – an attempt at understanding whether human capital investments are successful.

The problems inherent in linking people to value can be demonstrated by examining this latter set of metrics. Such metrics have the advantage of being obtainable from the internal financial reporting system. They are also published by most public organisations, which enables companies to benchmark against them. The problem is that individually they tell an incomplete story and do not point to any specific actions that could be taken to enhance and sustain the value-creating potential of people.

To illustrate the inadequacy of traditional human capital measures, let us first examine Revenue/Employee. This can be a useful metric when looking at the performance of the overall workforce. But it falls down when an organisation seeks to analyze what is driving performance:

> If Company A has superior Revenue/Employee compared with Company B, it is impossible to say what portion of the workforce is responsible. Is it everyone or does Company A have a better sales force? Or perhaps its RD department is innovating more rapidly. In the Revenue/Employee metric, all employees are mathematically counted as '1' in the denominator. Investment in one employee supports as much or little revenue as investment in another. Without too much thought, we can say that this formula does not reflect reality. Employees do not make an equal contribution to revenues. The most logical solution for improving performance on Revenue/Employee is to reduce the number of employees. However, we intuitively understand that 1) there is a point beyond which reducing the number of employees affects revenues and 2) revenues are affected more by some employees than others. Unfortunately, with Revenue/ Employee as our metric we have very little sense of where that point lies or which employees affect revenues more than others. (Bassi et al. 2000: 334)

It might be said that, ironically, the issue here reminds one the famous saying of a marketing executive who asked how he can distinguish between successful and abortive advertisement expenses, replied frankly that the proportion of those that are effective to ones that are not is fifty-fifty, but admitted to his ignorance which half of expenditures is which.

The authors then turn to another metric, Revenue/Compensation, which, in their opinion, more closely approximates reality by 'dollar-weighting' the investment that companies make in their employees based on compensation. While incomplete, they reckon, compensation begins to capture a missing dimension of the investment that companies make in their people:

> by sizing it according to how much is spent on individuals. Nevertheless, organisations may run into trouble when it comes to improving performance using this metric. The most logical solution is to lower the amount it pays its workforce. However, once again, this approach seems flawed because intuitively we understand that there is a point beyond which paying lower salaries results in lower-calibre employees, which can in turn negatively impact revenues. (Bassi et al. 2000: 334)

And again the scholars being cited in effect call into question the framework to which they nominally subscribe:

> The problem is that these metrics do not point us toward specific ways that we might improve the performance of human capital. In fact, the only way to improve these metrics from the human capital perspective is to cut people or their pay – measures which may help in the short run only to prove disastrous in the longer term. To improve upon our ability to understand where opportunities for improving performance of human capital might be found, we must move beyond traditional metrics toward a more finely-tuned approach that points to where cost-cutting is appropriate and where further investment is needed. (Bassi et al. 2000)

As it is extremely general, the usefulness of the above policy proposal is limited, to say the least. Bassi et al. subsequently pass to what they call, in this terrible jargon, human capital value metrics. What they have to say regarding their "metric" is quite interesting:

> ...the first hurdle that must be cleared is expanding the view of an employee's wage. Are wages a cost or are they a reflection of worth? They are both, and the Human Capital Value Metric incorporates both views in its determination of Cost and Contribution. To compute a baseline estimate of Contribution, the Metric treats wages as a reflection of value or worth determined by a series of interactions with the market. Based on this view of how wages are set, the first assumption our Metric makes is that the minimum a person contributes to an organisation can be measured by his or her Wage (Compensation, Benefits, Training & Development). The second assumption [...] is that people contribute

more than their Wage, such that organisations reap a profit from people. (Bassi et al. 2000)

What is referred to above as human capital's worth is, of course, labour power's value. And it is clear as day that should not the labour power contribute more to the employing firm than its cost to the firm, its employment would be a philanthropic activity, which in the capitalist business sector is normally present in rather rare circumstances.

And as to the aforementioned measure or index (since "metric" is horrific), the authors themselves put forward several caveats severely limiting its validity, those limitations resulting from the unavoidable dependence of an individual employee on others, and on the broader ever-changing socio-economic setting:

> ...the question of individual value is complicated by the fact that other social factors need to be considered. Not only is an individual's value a reflection of skills and competencies, but also of the particular situation in which he or she operates, interactions among individual employees will impact productivity by creating either synergies or distractions. What's more, individual value is a moving target: it changes over time as the employee gains new skills and experiences. (Bassi et al. 2000)

Needless to say, the all-important ownership issue will recur in our discussion below.

First, however, let us turn our attention to the aforementioned question of market evaluation of human capital. A commentator pronouncing himself on the matter begins on a well-known positive note, so that the reader may be forgiven for being taken by surprise by what follows: "What makes a company a blue chip investment? For most business leaders, it's really not much of a secret. From GE's former CEO, Jack Welch, to consultant Jim Collins, the message is clear: It's the value of the people and what they do. In fact, a variety of experts agree that as much as 80 per cent of a company's worth is tied to human capital" Grossman 2005).

But then the author being cited suggests that there is a flaw in this rosy picture of universal consensus:

> Somewhere along the line, however, most of Wall Street's stock analysts didn't get the memo. Because when analysts evaluate the potential worth of a company's stock – a move that can lure investors or send them running in the other direction, with resultant effects on a company's stock price – human capital plays at best a bit part. (Grossman 2005)

To be sure, there is a study whose results at first glance would suggest that the equity market takes account of at least one aspect of human capital, but it is subject to some methodological reservations.

The authors of the study in question themselves disparage its findings, calling attention to "these very small sample sizes and the range of industries represented"; given which not surprisingly, there were few significant correlations. None of the human resource practices scales (innovative training, high performance work, innovative compensation, quality initiatives, or competence training) was significantly correlated with any of the three financial outcome variables (net sales per employee, gross profit per employee, and market-to-book value). Interestingly, however, both training as a percentage of payroll and training expenditure per employee were significantly, positively correlated with 1996 market-to-book value. Furthermore, training as a per cent of payroll was significantly correlated with 1997 third quarter market-to-book value, as was percentage of employees trained (although the latter significance level was marginal) (Bassi et al. 2000: 335).

They acknowledge that:

> These are, of course, only correlations. They neither control for other relevant factors nor prove causality. Correlations between 1996 training and 1995 financial outcomes can, however, shed a bit of light on the issue of causality. Since inputs cannot possibly have an effect on outcomes in a preceding year, significant correlations (above and beyond those that would be expected to occur by chance) are either evidence of serial correlation or reverse causality. While none of these correlations are significant at the standard .05 level, three correlations are significant and positive at the .10 level and one is significant and negative at the .10 level. (Bassi et al. 2000: 335)

In their view these findings suggest either that training investments are correlated over time or that firms change their use of these practices in response to prior financial performance (although, given the one negative correlation, the direction of change is in question).

> What can be concluded with certainty is that training as a percent of payroll is significantly, positively associated with market-to-book value; in short, Wall Street values more highly those firms that make significant investments in training than those firms that do not. This could either mean that training is a part of a larger package of practices that Wall Street values (presumably because it bodes well for future performance) or that training has a direct effect on that performance. If the latter is the case, the correlations almost certainly overstate the independent effect of training.

> What is, perhaps, surprising about these correlations is that the training variables achieve statistical significance when other variables (for example, innovative compensation and high-performance work practices), which have been found to be significant by other researchers, are not significantly correlated with financial outcomes. It might be that the sample sizes are simply too small, or that these other variables are not measured with sufficient precision. (Bassi et al. 2000: 336)

On the other hand, two studies by Ernst and Young reveal that securities analysts rank the "ability to attract and retain talented workforce"[5] high in making their investment decisions but rank information about training as unimportant (Mavrinac and Boyle 1995). In discussing training, the CEO of Cummins Engine reports, "When I brief Wall Street analysts on our current earnings, sales projections, downsizing programs, and capital spending plans they busily punch all these numbers right into their laptops as I speak. When I then start telling them about our plans to invest in training and reform the workplace, they sit back in their chairs and their eyes glaze over" (Kochan and Osterman 1994: 114).

And it is well-known that securities analysts play a key role at each stock exchange. Their opinion shapes decisions of investments managers and individual punters alike, thus accounting for a large part of what passes as the Wall Street or City community.

This kind of attitude has prompted comments to the effect that "this does not seem to make sense because [...] participation in employer-sponsored training reduces the likelihood of an employee leaving. More research is necessary to understand this apparent contradiction" (O'Connor 2000: 336).

If the reader is curious what the reasons for this professional blindness might be, the commentator under consideration is as well, and, moreover, he attempts an answer to that puzzle:

> So why are analysts missing what everyone else seems to intuitively understand? There are a number of reasons, some more valid than others. For example, some point to the absence of universally accepted metrics for numerically capturing the value of an organisation's human capital. And while it's true that there is still work to be done in this area, the HR profession is considerably further along than analysts seem willing to give it credit for. (Grossman 2005)

Grossman, however, downplays this factor;

> In fact, the reasons why human capital, and the effective management of that capital, are not more widely appreciated by analysts seem to have more to do with their own particular blind spots – caused by a narrow view of corporate worth and a lack of familiarity with strategic HR – than with any shortcomings in HR metrics. (Grossman 2005)

To elaborate, he first focuses on capturing the Value of HR Successful companies that manage their human capital well (note in passing yet another misnomer in the long series: human capital is what has hitherto been called human resources, which in turn, went prior to this historic era under the simple name of staff).

---

5 It is to be noted that talent, as being an innate ability, is not covered by most definitions of human capital which lay emphasis on schooling and training.

They hire the right people and train them in the skills they need to help the company perform spectacularly.

They develop compensation systems that incent the right behaviour and performance so that the best workers stay and move up – and the worst ones move on.

These concepts are, he concedes, not new, but they do become more widely accepted and vital in a knowledge-based economy, where intellectual property and human capital account for more of a business's worth than physical capital.

Which is, of course, a circular proof – one must not prove the relevance of human capital by referring to the same human capital. To an even greater extent, nothing is proved by rhetorical proclamations of the kind of such as one cited below:

> 'Everyone understands that the quality of people is the key differentiating factor – whether they're great as individuals or because they've set up systems that work best', says Peter Cappelli, Professor of Management and Director of the Center for Human Resources at the Wharton School at the University of Pennsylvania (Grossman 2005).

And even this human capital enthusiast cannot but admit that "the hard part is how do you measure it? There aren't best practices that work across the board. It's about fitting people practices and management to the strategy. In some companies, it's smart to invest in people; in others, it may make sense to just churn them through."

But some experts, like Jim Hatch, principal with PricewaterhouseCoopers/ Saratoga, a leading source for HR metrics and benchmarking, believe that there already are important human capital keys Wall Street should be paying attention to, keys that can be useful indicators of good HR management and of potential corporate profitability.

> For instance, Hatch says that Human Capital ROI (return on investment) – the amount of money you get back in profits for every dollar invested in human capital – is a good predictor of mid- and long-term success. […] Laurie Bassi, chair of Bassi Investments Inc. in Washington, D.C., also believes that human capital keys can predict future corporate profitability – 'We're looking for firms that spend between 3.5 percent and 4 percent of their budgets on workforce development. That translates into the top 5 percent to 10 percent of the [best performing] companies within a sector,' she says. (Grossman 2005)

Grossman admits, though, that: "even as the validity of metrics like Bassi's and Hatch's gain wider acclaim, they've failed to impress most stock analysts".

"There's a big disconnect between the figures you see in a balance sheet and the market value of the company," says Steven Gates, CFA, principal researcher for The Conference Board in Paris and a former investment and securities analyst. Wall Street analysts, he says, are missing the big picture by failing to take employees into account. "How can they defend themselves," he asks, "when they're not accounting for the majority of the company's value?"

Grossman (2005) cites other interesting comments of businesspeople that shed light on the (mostly) misfortunes of human capital theory in practice. Part of the problem is that when analysts evaluate a company, they focus their attention too narrowly on a few factors – to the detriment of others, says Cappelli. "They pay attention to the immediate financials [and] the strategy story and hear from the top executives. They don't have very deep information and don't want to talk to people who might give them a more nuanced view", such as HR professionals.

Harry A. Ikenson, managing director and a senior retail analyst at First Albany Capital in New York, confirms that most analysts are not interested in the HR "nitty-gritty". "Dealing with the minutiae of how people are managed to get results is not our concern," he says. "When I visit a company, I meet the director of stores, the person in merchandising, the CEO and CFO. I want to talk to the line people – not HR. They know compensation, but aren't the best source for what's really happening."

Gates explains that what analysts are most concerned with when evaluating a company is short-term cost control, even when the way costs are managed is not good for a company's human capital or long-term financial health – for instance, with massive layoffs. "They don't care too much about how you arrived at your numbers if the financials look good", says Gates. "They react positively when you're going to fire a lot of people. Announce a major downsizing and they're happy.

The commentator concerned put his finger on, indeed, key weaknesses of capitalism, notably its Anglo-Saxon variety. But whether short-termism and corporate myopia are good for the company in the longer run or not, is one thing, and the fact that corporate executives actually suffer from those limitations-is quite another.

And this basic fact holds, Grossman's warnings notwithstanding:

> Ironically, this kind of narrow perspective may not pay enough attention to the costs of turnover, lost intellectual capital or decreased productivity that can result when large numbers of employees are let go. Analysts' fixation with costs means they also can easily miss the big picture on investments such as training, which are fundamental to Bassi's understanding of company value. Under current accounting methods, training and development costs are dumped into a company's balance sheet along with all the other expenses. Therefore, if one firm is investing a lot of money in development, to an analyst it will look like a more costly, less attractive investment opportunity than another that reports lower expenses. (Grossman 2005)

Considering that these words belong exactly to the securities analyst and not, say, some armchair academic, they must be regarded as a credible criticism of the human capital idea that in this light appears as untenable.

Final remarks presented by Grossman are not optimistic either:

> So unless a company chooses to report its workforce development expenditures
> separately – and there's no uniform reporting standard for doing so – there's
> no way analysts can get at Bassi's ratios. Gates says the fact that there is no
> standard format for reporting such data is a valid concern. 'It's not official, not
> audited, not clearly comparable from company to company,' he says. 'And there
> are justifiable doubts about the consistency of the data'. (Grossman 2005)

But there is even more to the matter than that: "But even if companies were to
report such data consistently, many analysts would be leery of going out on a limb
to take those numbers into account. Burned by the dot-com bubble and debacles
surrounding Enron, MCI and others, they are less likely to pursue new theories or
perspectives" (Grossman 2005).

There is a kernel of truth in the kind of explanation offered by Grossman, but
ultimately the latter only strengthens the former overall conclusion:

> 'Back then, analysts came up with all kinds of reasons why inflated [stock] values
> made sense,' says Jim Holinchek, an industry analyst at Gartner in Chicago.
>
> Afterward, they were criticized, he says, and 'they went back to fundamentals.'
>
> They're sticking within the safety zone, engaging in what Boris Groysberg,
> assistant professor at Harvard Business School, describes as 'maintenance
> research,' following the same quantitative formulas and analytic techniques as
> their peers. 'There's no downside to doing what everyone else does,' Bassi says.
> It's safe. But 'if you do worse because you did something different, you can be
> blamed'. (Grossman 2005)

Grossman adds still one more reason to the above list of causes of sidelining by
financial analysts of what has become a true idol for many economists which
is in his opinion their skewed view, and at the same time part of their class
consciousness:

> In addition to looking at a narrow data set, analysts can be blinded by their
> own experience – or lack of experience. While they generally have strong
> backgrounds in finance or accounting, they typically have limited exposure to
> strategic HR, which affects their ability to gauge its importance to the health of
> an organisation.
>
> 'It's like a doctor giving advice about nutrition,' says Hatch. 'If you had only one
> course in a subject, would you use it? They [analysts] don't, because they really
> don't know much about it and aren't that interested.'

Part of the reason they may not be interested in HR is that analysts aren't exactly typical of the workforce at large, which benefits from HR's efforts in many areas, including training and development. By contrast, those who survive and thrive in Wall Street's high-pressure environment tend to be extremely self-confident risk-takers who focus on winning big and are supremely motivated by their own bottom line – a fat paycheck. They don't want a handout or a hand up – which is good because it's something they won't get on Wall Street. 'It's sink or swim,' Groysberg says of the Wall Street culture. 'You either have what it takes or don't. Why spend money on training and development when it can be spent on bonuses for peak performers?' Groysberg says for the past 20 years or so, investment firms have favored nature over nurture, churning over continuity, an approach to hiring and promotion that seems to suit analysts just fine. (Grossman 2005)

The above argument involves several simplifications; the so-called quants or mathematical wizards who took Wall Street and City firms by storm are by no means product of innate talent, which may play a part in some cases, but the preponderant contribution to their professional career had their specific education. Despite such shortcomings, the argument is valuable in implicitly pointing to the class source of divergent views on human capital on the part of financial and non-financial agents. It may be added that the "bonus culture" prevailing in the so-called financial community may be interpreted to mean ownership of achievement-based labour power. In terms of compensation, there are essentially two types of labour power: one paid by concrete effects, and the other, ascriptive labour power where compensation is based on what one is rather one does or how performs. To be sure, oftentimes we are dealing with mixed cases-even in the above-mentioned finance sector, for example, there emerged a rather paradoxical institution of guaranteed bonus; bonus is by definition a reward for distinguished performance, so that one receives it regardless, it undermines the very idea of incentive pay. But leaving aside those pathological, albeit numerous cases, there remains a class distinction captured by the following passage:

So where Bassi sees a value in helping employees to develop their skills and become more effective, analysts live and breathe in an environment where top-notch performers are expected to be self-made, to pull themselves up by their own bootstraps. Little wonder, then, that Bassi's metrics have had little success taking root on Wall Street. (Grossman 2005)

Chapter 4

Human Capital and Ownership: Corporate Transparency and Ownership Distribution

As a discussant to the above-discussed essay by Bassi et al., Marleen O'Connor presents a few interesting comments which can be treated as an introduction to the headline topic that is taken on directly in the later part of the chapter.

O'Connor notes that the effort to identify and quantify investments in human capital and to track the implications of these investments for profitability and share value, are part of a larger movement under way in the accounting profession and in the international community to improve methods of measuring and reporting on intangible assets. This movement, she says, has the potential to be politically controversial if it is seen as a Trojan horse for the labour movement (Blair, Kochan 2000a).

Before proceeding, a remark is in order. The usage of the term "political" in the above passage bears a close resemblance to the case of our main heroes inasmuch as it is also a misnomer; this usage is to be justified because, firstly, the association of the term in question with conflict. But the thing is, not all social conflicts are political conflicts. The second context which is to legitimise the christening of the process in question as political has, by itself, equally little in common with the political. Trade unions are an economic organisation in that their basic function is to secure the best possible terms of lease of labour power. That unions, e.g. in the US and UK, to further their aims act sometimes on truly political actors such as political parties, parliament, etc. is irrelevant here. Or rather, it reveals a common error[1] consisting in mistaking influence for membership. The fact that A impacts on B by any means entails that the former becomes part of the latter. Concomitantly, unions may be said to be politically relevant, which, however, is worlds apart from being political structures themselves. Or, to put this argument in still more general terms, the usage under consideration attests to a non-dialectical view of society in which the basic units are not activities, as in our own framework of socio-economic structuralism, but organisations and institutions. This is not to say that under socio-economic structuralism the latter are denied right to existence or otherwise downplayed. By no means, only that our analytical framework draws attention to the fact that one and the same organisation may well have many structurally different functions, that is, activities taking part within those

---

1   The case in point is Deleuze's paradigmatic example of what he calls a rhizomatic relationship. He argues that the wasp and the orchid both evolve in the direction of the other so that the wasp can be said to be "becoming-orchid," and the orchid "becoming-wasp".

organisations may be part of a variety of distinct societal substructures. The state, for instance, is first and foremost a political body, but it can undertakes many economic activities. The same applies to religious or charitable organisations, and so forth.

Further comments put forward by O'Connor make it clear that what she means as political refers to class relations, including class struggle (which a historical parallel cited by her makes even clearer – "in the 1920s, cost accounting developments were related to the destruction of craft control of production in early factories and the advent of scientific management").[2]

She argues, namely, that the current focus on intangible assets is being driven primarily by individuals in the business community who are trying to improve their management of intangibles such as knowledge assets. O'Connor notes, however, that the movement in question has a dialectical dimension to it.

She points out that the conclusions that these business leaders are coming to bear a striking similarity to ideas promoted by social activists in the 1970s who were interested in the social responsibilities of corporations toward their workers, as well as to issues being raised today by social activists concerned about diversity in the workplace and child labour practices. O'Connor points out that greater information about workplace practices might help to protect the interests of workers, but also warns – which constitutes a nice example of dialectics in action – that such clarity could have the opposite effect: Once "it becomes known how much corporations are spending on training, for example, shareholders could pressure companies not to spend that much, especially if the link between training expenditures and profits is not clear" (Blair, Kochan 2000a).

O'Connor's final conclusion bears on our earlier discussion on the reason for the apparent indifference of shareholders to a lack of commitment of corporate managers to a genuine implementation of human capital ideas, although it naturally does prejudges the matter one way or other as this can be decided only by evidence.

The author herself clarifies that focusing, as she does, on the ramifications that the accounting development in question has for workers, she is far from suggesting that the IC movement is motivated by concerns about improving the position of workers. To the contrary, the IC movement has tended to develop as a "knowledge management" tool to aid managers in creating shareholder value in the new economy. My point, however, is that labour leaders and industrial relations experts need to explore how accounting matters affect employees.

And her perspective is even broader; she cites the business magazine Forbes' article which argues that "at best, IC will bore you to death. At worst, IC is a potential Trojan horse for those who want stakeholders, not shareholders, to

---

2 Which is not affected by the fact that there are many misunderstandings, or even popular myths over Taylorism; for instance, it is little known that the founder of the movement himself had progressive views, and he wanted his management method to better working conditions Cf: Tittenbrun (2012).

control our companies, and social agendas, not performance, to drive business decisions".

O'Connor's own agenda, however, is not that of Forbes. She argues that:

> ...specifically, accounting information is becoming increasingly relevant to workers under the new employment relationship that has developed in the 1990s in two ways. First, firms are trying to increase commitment by introducing profit-related pay and employee share ownership plans. Second, new human resource practices urge employees to focus on the bottom line by sharing an increasing amount of financial information with them.

> The IC movement has only begun to explore the influence that accounting has on the employment relationship. (O'Connor 2000: 336)

And O'Connor again demonstrates her capacity for dialectical thinking when she notes that:

> ...by providing increased transparency, the IC movement could shed light on the fundamental paradox [...]: downsizing has weakened the traditional ties of job security and loyalty that bind employees to firms; at the same time, decentralised decisionmaking and cross-functional teams increase the firms dependence on human capital. Disclosure of human resource values could substantially inform the public policy debate about this paradox in many ways. For example, much work of the IC movement focuses on the value that training has for the firm. This is significant because although many firms use the rhetoric of 'employability security,' studies show that firms are not interested in providing generic training that increases employability outside the firm. (O'Connor 2000: 336)

As we shall see below, this remark goes to the heart of the debate over the division of ownership fruits. And the subsequent comment is relevant to this issue as well: "The issue of training is particularly relevant to workers because [...] training is associated with higher wages. In this way, the IC movement could provide insight into why wages for many workers have stagnated over the past decade while stock prices have skyrocketed".

O'Connor's empirically grounded approach allows her to look with some scepticism at Bassi et al.'s claim that "although there are no guarantees that the disclosure of human capital values will ultimately advance workers' interests, this strategy is one of the most politically feasible alternatives for making managers more accountable to both workers and shareholders in the new world of global corporate governance".

She adds a note of caution:

> The IC movement has the potential to have a major impact on workers. It is far from clear, however, whether disclosure of workplace practices will work

to the advantage or disadvantage of workers. What is clear is that disclosure of human capital values will open up new categories of visibility, transparency, and accountability and offer new terms of discourse within organisations and between organisations and society. [...]However, labour leaders need to be distinctly wary. The IC movement may lead to the exact opposite result for three reasons. First, once figures for training are revealed, shareholders may take the position that too much investment in training is a bad thing and discourage companies that invest more than the norm. Second, changing the accounting practices may lead managers to try to improve earning figures by investing less money in training. Former SEC commissioner Steven M.H. Wallman explains:

'If it is true that the US economy has done better than some others because of the fact that we do invest quite heavily in these areas, part of that may well be the fact that we have had an accounting paradigm for a long time that has, in essence, contributed to that: If we were to change that, so that companies would have to take a hit to earnings on an ongoing basis, we might well find that people do the same thing that they're doing with retiree benefits – which is cut back on it, as opposed to increase it'. (O'Connor 2000: 336)

The above clearly shows that O'Connor's observations are both context- and class-sensitive, which is not that frequent, and among human capital scholars constitutes a nice surprise.

Finally, the IC movement could serve to disadvantage workers if it turns out to be just another management tool used to intensify surveillance and control of the workplace. (O'Connor 2000)

Similarly, her further remarks definitely go beyond the conventional wisdom inasmuch as she touches on, in point of fact, class issues, raising the question of class bias pertinent to capitalist accounting:

In this way, the IC movement helps us to recognise the significance of the role that accounting plays in creating perceptions of the enterprise. Specifically, once we begin to try to quantify aspects of the labour relationship, the ideological aspects of current accounting practices are dramatically highlighted. That is, accounting systems do far more than document features of financial performance. Rather, the IC movement illustrates that the current accounting regime provides a narrow picture of the economic activity of the corporate entity because, for the most part, employees and environmental matters are not represented.

While one certainly cannot make too much of O'Connor's claims, interpret them as a confession of conversion into the labour theory of value, nevertheless-drawing attention to a lack of internalisation of externalities, or neglecting by the price mechanism and cost accounting of true green costs of economic activity certainly deserves praise, as does her going far beyond the framework of orthodox textbook economics.

And further O'Connor's argument again underlines her ability to reason in socio-economic (as distinct from purely economic, divorced from the social context in which all economic relations are enmeshed) terms:

> These omissions are important because, in many ways, accounting determines the legitimate terms of debate within the organisation. What is accounted for shapes the players' ideas of what is significant by establishing the agenda and influencing how corporations function. In this way, accounting plays important symbolic roles, reflecting and reinforcing power distribution and political manoeuvring within the firm. (O'Connor 2000: 336)

Finally, she puts her argument in a historical perspective:

> By focusing on the disclosure of human capital values, the IC project picks up on an issue long promoted by social activists interested in increasing corporate social responsibility to workers. In the 1970s, Ralph Nader and others used the shareholder proposal mechanism under the federal securities laws to push firms for more disclosure about employment and environmental issues. In the 1990s, social activists have tended to concentrate their efforts on seeking information about diversity and child labour practices. Through the IC movement, the broad topic about workplace practices has resurfaced, not based on social concerns but fueled by economic motivations. As part of the movement, for example, so-called knowledge companies such as Skandia and Dow are seeking new performance measures to indicate the firm's potential to innovate and improve the bottom line in the future – as indicators of sustainable shareholder value. In focusing on human capital, the IC movement may provide much of the information that activists concerned with corporate social responsibility have traditionally sought: the breakdown of the number of workers by full-time, part-time contingent; training, turnover, diversity; violations of the Occupational Safety and Health Act, pay for performance, and employee stock ownership. Law professor Donald Langevoort, recognising this turn of events, explains:

> We should note first that there are two different kinds of arguments at work in the 'stakeholder' debate. The first, and more aggressive, is that to the extent that corporations are simply webs of stakeholder interests mediated by company managers, disclosure in the interests of other stakeholders is justifiable on the same protective grounds as disclosure for investors.

> The second argument retains investor primacy, but argues that other stakeholder-oriented disclosure is needed so that investor/shareholders can evaluate properly the governance and financial performance of the firm. Both arguments end up

at the same place, which can tempt those committed ideologically to the former to invoke the latter because of its more conventional rhetoric. (O'Connor 2000)

O'Connor takes on this important issue of different systems of corporate governance (which in point of fact refer to different modes of economic activity, or traditionally-modes of production) to which we shall return in the chapter on trust.:

> By highlighting the importance of human capital to the firm, the IC movement has the potential to promote the stakeholder concept of the corporation. This is an important development because the stakeholder concept has lost much credibility in the United States (the truth of the matter is that this model of corporate governance has never been so popular there as within the alternative capitalist system) in the past few years as the US economy has improved and outperformed those in Germany and Japan.[3] Indeed, the overwhelming normative consensus among American corporate governance scholars is that the board of directors should focus on shareholder interests exclusively and that workers should protect their interests through contract.

> The shareholder value mantra is firmly rooted in the United States and is sweeping the globe. Although obstacles to harmonisation ensure the continued diversity among national laws governing corporations, in the past few years, several factors have operated to push European countries toward the American model of corporate governance. First, the increasing globalisation of business pushes for a universal set of business measures; cross-border deals like Daimler-Chrysler will likely increase in the future and reinforce convergence trends. (O'Connor 2000)

One begins to wonder whether O'Connor is really that knowledgeable about the economy, and where her dialectical aptitudes have gone. The merger of Daimler-Benz and Chrysler was a singular failure, not a paradigm case to be followed.

> Second, the current global economic crisis is likely to create even greater demand for transparency and accountability along the lines of the American system of disclosure. Finally, one of the main drivers is US institutional investors, with CalPERS (California Public Employee Retirement System) taking the lead in

---

3   This assertion should be taken with a pinch of salt: whilst Germany is beyond any reasonable doubt the powerhouse of Europe, in the two main economies of shareholder capitalism alias Anglo-Saxon or in still other terms-free-market model, economic growth is sluggish, and it is in those two countries that the grassroots movement against blatant flaws of the latter model, on their part clearly linked to corporate governance, such as astronomical executive pay packages, achieved the greatest intensity. And debt and deficit problems plague pretty much all economically developed capitalist countries.

articulating global governance principles. Indeed, institutional investors from around the world are joining forces to promote global corporate governance efforts to make managers more accountable for creating shareholder value. Henry Hansmann and Reinier Kraakman summarise the situation: 'We now have not only a common ideology supporting shareholder-oriented corporate law, but also an interest group to press that ideology'.

One of the most influential efforts to shape global governance norms are the recommendations of an advisory group to the Organisation for Economic Cooperation and Development (OECD). The first draft of these guidelines strongly focused on protecting shareholder interests and barely mentioned the interests of workers. For this reason, the International Confederation of Free Trade Unions, trade union advisory council to the OECD, strongly objected to the first draft. As a result, the second draft of the OECD corporate governance guidelines moves away from the shareholder focus to emphasise that 'board members should act in the best interests of the company as a whole.' The OECD guidelines go on to state: 'The corporate governance framework should recognise the rights of stakeholders as established by law and encourage active co-operation between corporations and stakeholders in creating wealth, jobs and the sustainability of financially sound enterprises'.

These guidelines seek to make boards more accountable to shareholders. (O'Connor 2000)

And here we have again O'Connor at her best – suspicious of and keen to debunk the corporate law rhetoric; she is not a sociologist, but thinks in perfectly sociological terms.

Additional evidence of this trend toward convergence can be found in the voluntary corporate governance guidelines that have been recently adopted by several European countries (O'Connor 2000).

O'Connor draws attention to certain specific consequences of the said process of globalisation qua Americanisation (whose class significance is, again, crystal clear):

As corporate governance mechanisms around the world undergo convergence toward the American model, one of the most intense political issues concerns the impact that this will have on European systems of co-determination that provide workers with information and consultation rights in strategic corporate decisions. These OECD guidelines do not encourage co-determination or provide employees with the right to legally enforce the stakeholder view of the corporation. However, the OECD guidelines focus in great detail on making the board more accountable to shareholders by allowing them to vote for important decisions and voice their concerns. The obvious question raised is how the board will balance the competing interests between shareholders and employees to make the best decisions for the corporation when shareholder rights are increased with no corresponding increase in workers' influence in corporate governance. It is fine to include stakeholder rhetoric that will seek to promote the interests of a diverse group of corporate constituents, but the reality of the situation is that only the shareholders have the legal power to influence corporate governance. Because the underlying global economic reality does not pressure managers to side with employees, the rhetoric of constituency language will not do much to protect workers. (O'Connor 2000)

Much as one appreciates the class edge of these largely apposite observations, its author is here and there lacking a dialectical viewpoint, as a result of which she is guilty of an unilinear style of reasoning – the processes of convergence between the two capitalist modes of economic action do indeed occur, but they are counterposed by the processes of divergence as a result of which the systems in question largely maintain their identity and integrity.

One way the OECD provides accountability to employees is by calling for disclosure concerning "material" employee and stakeholder issues prepared according to international disclosure principles. The OECD guidelines state:

> Companies are encouraged to provide information on key issues relevant to employees and other stakeholders that may materially affect the performance of the company. Some areas in which disclosure might be considered are management/employee relations, and relations with other stakeholders such as creditors, suppliers, and local communities.… . Some countries require extensive disclosure of information on human resources. Human resource policies, such as programmes for human resource development or employee share ownership plans, can communicate important information on the competitive strengths of companies to market participants. (O'Connor 2000: 336)

Against this official background, her expertise makes it possible to pass a realistic enough judgment on the matter:

Overall, it is, however, difficult to show that information about human capital values passes rigorous tests of materiality for "quantitative disclosure," because we lack the necessary quantitative data establishing the link between workplace practices and specific financial measures. Indeed, the OECD briefly considered but decided not to promulgate voluntary disclosure guidelines for human resource values because of the need for more empirical work to establish the appropriate measures of human capital (O'Connor 2000: 336).

The foregoing discussion has been useful in yet another respect; it has shown that human capital scholarship is by any means ideologically uniform. While some of human capital theorists and practitioners are inclined to view it as a management tool, and others, wittingly or not, impede the development of class consciousness of the working class by making workers believe that they are in fact capitalists, there are also such scholars as O'Connor who do seem to believe in the possibility to employ human capital theory and practice in the interest of the working class.

However, the main aim of the above discussion has been to prepare the ground to an analysis of the issue being signalled throughout; it would be difficult to understand why the issue of human capital accounting and disclosure is such a battleground were it not for the ownership benefits from human capital investment, and the intensity of debate over the former suggests that it is the division of the latter between the parties involved that is the bone of contention.

There is a split within human capital research: on the one hand, human capital theory posits that all benefits from investment in an employee's labour power are appropriated by the employee herself, but at the practical level – particularly but not exclusively due to the fact that it is her employing firm that makes investment in her training – it turns out that there is another claimant to the benefits concerned in the form of the firm's owners. In other words, just as in the regular process of surplus value production, it is – to a proportion to be determined on an empirical basis – also the owners of real, not human capital that own the latter, sharing this property ownership with those who are in standard human capital theory considered the sole beneficiaries of that property (i.e. the firm's employees).

Human Capital Ownership and Theories of the Firm

One way of approaching the topic under investigation is too look at it from the viewpoint of the established theories of the firm. That the latter are, however, rather uncomfortable with the thorny issue in question, is evidenced by the amazement of Margaret Blair who calls attention to the seeming paradox: "To a casual observer, the relationship between a firm and its employees would seem to be a central, perhaps defining, feature of the firm itself. Yet the tendency among economists and legal theorists has been to study the nature of the firm, as well as the property rights and governance structure associated with it, separately from the structure and terms of relationships with and among the employees of firms" (Blair 1999).

The reader's attention may be drawn to this pointed identification of non-dialectical, non-relational view of corporate property. Blair claims that: the main exception has been work that focuses on one subset of employees – managers – and uses principal-agent analysis to explore the relationship between managers (understood to be the agents) and shareholders (understood to be the principals). This view is premised on an underlying assumption that "the firm" is basically a bundle of assets that belongs to shareholders but is managed for them by hired managers.

> [...] The legal debate in recent years has relied heavily on a contractarian view, which treats the firm as a 'nexus' through which all the various participants in the productive enterprise contract with each other, either explicitly or implicitly.

> Although the 'nexus of contracts' view would seem to focus on the relationships among all the participants in the firm, most legal scholars have emphasised one relationship – that between shareholders and managers – above all others. A somewhat different approach can be seen in what is known as the entity view. It holds that, under the law, a new entity, with status as a separate legal 'person,' is created when a corporation is formed. (Blair 1999)

The above account calls for some comment. Whilst the theory of agency, linked to property right approach, is, in principle at least, economic in focus, the concept of legal person is expressly juristic in nature, whereas in real social life no such fictional bodies exist;-these concepts makes sense only for legal reasons, otherwise they would create a fantastic, mystified social world populated by so-called in law physical persons and also legal persons, such as corporations, universities, churches, etc. Blair does not seem aware of those drawbacks of the concepts she, as a matter of fact, promotes it: "advocates of the nexus approach reject this idea and would analyze firms as devices by which shareholders (as principals) contract with managers (as agents)" (Blair 1999).

Blair, in fact, drawing on what she calls the new economic thinking about the nature of the firm, sets out to argue that the entity view of the firm should be brought back to center stage in the law because the legal device of creating a separate juridical person may be an important mechanism for protecting enterprise-specific investments made by all participants in the firm, including both employees and shareholders (Blair 1999).

Now it is clear that the legal guise may conceal some very real and important issues. Their relevance to the topic of the present chapter becomes even clearer when Blair's subsequent argument is considered:

> A growing body of economic theory suggests that specialised investments – investments whose value in a particular enterprise greatly exceeds their value in alternative uses – play a critical role in determining [...] the allocation of risks, rewards, and control rights within firms.

> According to the theory, such investments need appropriate incentives and protections, and in particular, there are incentive benefits that flow from assigning control rights over the assets of a firm, or over the firm itself, to parties who make such investments. Much of the earlier literature on specific investments, however, referred primarily to physical or other alienable capital.

> The exception has been in labour theory, which for decades has recognised the importance of firm-specific human capital. Nonetheless, theories of the firm have done little until recently to address the problems raised by such investments.

It is evident that, regardless of "how firm-specific investments have been treated in the theory of the firm" (which is Blair's chief interest), the question of the kind of investment mentioned above is extremely relevant to our topic of interest.

It was Gary Becker who in 1964 coined the phrase "human capital" to refer to the idea

> that much of the skill and knowledge required to do a job could only be acquired if some 'investment' was made in time and resources. Most relevantly in the present context, Becker considered the implications of the fact that some of the knowledge and skills acquired by employees have a much higher value in a given employment relationship than they do in other potential relationships. Such specialised knowledge and skills may often be productivity enhancing, he argued, and are therefore likely to be an important part of the employment relationship in practice. But, he noted, they introduce a complication into simple models of wages, investments in training, and other terms of the employment relationship. In particular, 'the labour services of employees with specialised skills can no longer be modeled as undifferentiated, generic inputs, for which equilibrium price (wages) and quantity (number of employees or number of hours of work) are determined by the intersection of supply and demand curves' (Blair 1999).

Irrespective of the overall evaluation of the conception of specific human capital, and indeed the whole conception of human capital, it must be conceded that it represents a progress as compared to orthodox neoclassical theory in which the sole, and bleak at that, trace of the labour power concept is the notion of labour as an undifferentiated factor of production.

The above-mentioned conception has other consequences as well: "Once employees are understood to have specialised skills, it matters which employee does what job for what firm. Furthermore, if a firm had paid for the specific training of a worker who quit to take another job, its capital expenditure would be partly wasted, for no further return could be collected" (Blair 1999).

This comment would suggest that – barring the above-mentioned situation, normally it is the firm (or its socio-economic owners, to be precise) who benefits from the said specific human capital. However, the commentator's further claims complicate the matter: Likewise, a worker fired after he had paid for specific training would be unable to collect any further return and would also suffer a capital loss." Where investments in specific skills are important, Becker reasoned, it is no longer a matter of indifference "whether a firm's labour force always contained the same persons or a rapidly changing group" (Becker 1964: 21).

Becker's claim is, given his assumptions, undoubtedly true, but it does not address the crucial question mentioned earlier; who ultimately bears the expenditures involved, and who benefits from them. The latter question is indirectly raised in the following excerpt:

> [...] Becker[...] introduced a concept that provides a rationale for long-term relationships between firms and their employees. Peter Doeringer and Michael Piore built on this insight to [...] argue[...] that investments by firms in specialised training encourage firms to put in place other institutional arrangements designed to stabilise employment and reduce turnover. The organisational stability that results from these practices in turn facilitates further development of specific skills. (Doeringer and Piore 1971)

Doeringer and Piore further argued that the use of mass-production technology, with its detailed division of labour, requires specialised skills and makes stable employment relationships more important. This again tips the scales in the direction of the firm; it would make no economic sense for the firm to bear those additional costs involved with the institution of the requisite arrangements were it not for the benefits secured by the latter. But the creator of the original conception was in fact more ambivalent about this. Becker argued, namely, that employees and employers would be likely to split both the costs and returns from specialised training, to provide an incentive for both parties to stay in the relationship. Hashimoto (1981) subsequently provided a formal model suggesting that the division of the costs and returns from training would be split according to a formula that was a function of the relative probabilities of layoffs versus quits, and the costs of evaluating and agreeing on both the worker's productivity in the firm and his opportunity cost, or potential productivity in an alternative firm (Blair 1999).

Not least because of the difficulty, if not impossibility, of quantifying the said productivities and opportunity costs, the whole model, with all its seeming precision, is rather problematic; it implies that the process of estimating the probabilities of layoffs and quits is scientific in nature, being somewhat akin to the use of actuarial tables by insurance companies.

Aside from the above-mentioned arithmetic or econometric problems, its key flaw lies in failing to recognise the role of class struggle as a determinant of income distribution. However, those shortcomings allegedly do not undermine the status of the above-sketched model as a relatively good approximation of reality.

It would imply that employees would typically earn less than their opportunity cost during the early stages of their employment relationship (while they were in training, for example), and more than their opportunity cost later in the relationship. An earnings pattern like this would produce an "upward sloping wage-tenure profile," an empirical regularity that labour economists before Becker had observed, and that work by subsequent scholars has documented extensively. Consistent with the "firm-specific human capital" hypothesis, labour economists have also observed that long-tenured employees typically earn quite a bit more than their short-run opportunity cost. This empirical pattern is confirmed through studies of layoffs, which show that long-tenured employees laid off through no fault of their own (as a result of plant closings, for example) typically earn 15 to 25 per cent less on their next jobs. What is more, it is contended that these are conservative estimates. Topel (1990) found that the losses of displaced workers ranged from an average of 14 per cent for all displaced workers in his study to 28 per cent for workers with 10 or more years of service (Blair 1999).

A moment of reflection, though, suffices to realise that the aforementioned conclusion is grossly premature and therefore unfounded. Even without questioning the figures given above, it is evident that they neither prove nor disprove the earlier presumption concerning the shared costs of training. Those numbers are consistent equally with the hypothesis that the costs of training are borne by employees and the supposition that they are covered by the employer. These two lines of argument are simply irrelevant to each other. Even worse for the human capital assumption, the quantitative findings indicated can as well be couched in terms of labour power. It is evident that owing to the well-known process of learning by doing, an employee of longer tenure is likely to advance higher up in an occupational hierarchy and, accordingly, earn more. It is not at all surprising, therefore, that such long-tenured employees after moving to another firm may earn much less because they must start anew from the beginning; their lateral mobility is at odds with vertical mobility.

The issue of layoffs discussed above by the human capital theorists only underlines the fundamental ownership and class division between real capitalists and those who are told they are just another kind of capitalists, as two other authors of a chapter in the above-mentioned volume at least implicitly suggest when they draw attention to the fact that "workers have no protections against layoffs and no means of enforcing any claims to a long-term employment relation" (Applebaum, Berg 2000). Exactly; the fundamental distinction between ownership of means of economic activity on the one hand and ownership of labour power (which as a misnomer shows up as human capital) is that it is the wielders of the former that lay off the latter, and not the other way round.

Similarly, in another chapter in the book its author initially embraces in good faith the concept of human capital, only to call its validity into question by her further argument drawing attention to: "the inherent conflict in interests between labour and capital that is present in the corporate form. in the biotechnology industry, an important complementarity exists between human capital and financial capital; the former cannot be attracted without the latter. This contrasts with the typical situation of financial capital serving to replace labour in production. Yet, a conflict of interests between capital and labour may still be present in an NBF [new biotechnology firm], since the suppliers of capital to an NBF must have their own incentive and governance concerns satisfied" (Porter Liebeskind 2000).

Be that as it may, the authors tacitly recognise that "human capital" has more in common with "labour" than financial, i.e. true capital.

One misnomer breeds another-in the following passage, despite their purportedly fair intentions, the authors, by means of the word "wealth" applied to wages, tend to obscure the nature of relation: capital-labour power.

> Just as the wage premium earned by workers with long tenure is rarely
> recognised as part of the wealth created by their corporate employers, the
> substantial losses in earning power experienced by laid-off workers is rarely
> counted against the gains that shareholders enjoy from corporate restructuring.
> (Blair, Kochan 2000)

Finally, the above-mentioned reasoning of firm-specific human capital theory is
a misnomer also in this sense that – even assuming, for the sake of argument,
its concept of human capital, it turns out that the latter can account for at best
a portion of the statistical results cited above; wage premiums pertinent to a
worker's employment in a given firm that may be lost after her displacement,
have actually three sources: firm-specific human capital, good job matches, or
anti-shirking bonuses – for the existence of at-risk wage premiums that are lost
when layoffs occur:

Note the underlying model of man typical of conventional economic thought;
it is the so-called X-paradigm, where a human being is perceived as lazy, driven by
the principle of minimum effort, and therefore requiring constant supervision and
stimulation for lack of inner motivation and autotelic conduct.

By underpaying new employees, but promising a rising wage in the future,
the firm can provide incentives against shirking – employees with any length of
service at the firm who are caught shirking and fired will have to start all over
again at a lower rate of pay in another firm (Schultz 2000).

The same applies to Jacobson, LaLonde, and Sullivan's (1993) findings that
earnings losses persisted, so that even six years after displacement, workers who
had six or more years of service in their previous job were still earning 25 per cent
less than comparable workers who had not lost their jobs.

The fact of the matter is, no conceptual innovation like human capital is
necessary to invoke for one to comprehend that the unemployed, notably long-term
unemployed, lose part of their qualifications, and thus the labour power owned.
Their labour power is subject to both physical and moral depreciation, and human
or other capital does not come into the picture at all. On that basis one might assert
that the human capital framework violates the principles of conceptual economy
or theoretical parsimony – the phenomena it claims to be able to account for are
explainable by an alternative theory.

And the above are not the only objection to the aforementioned argument. Jacoby
(1990), calls the above-mentioned conclusion into question. He acknowledges, to
be sure, that empirical evidence supports a shift from the late 1800s to at least the
mid-1970s toward greater job stability. He argues (p. 323), however, that "there
is little evidence that the shift resulted from a growing reliance on firm-specific
techniques or skills. In fact, the evidence suggests that the opposite was true: that
is to say, that technology and job skills became less, rather than more firm-specific
over time".

The list of criticisms is in fact even longer. According to Blair, these estimates
and others in related work suggest that the aggregate returns to investments in

firm-specific human capital could represent as much as 10 per cent or more of the total wage bill of the corporate sector, a figure that is of the same order of magnitude as all of corporate profits (1999).

There are, naturally, problems with this argument. Given how problematic is the marginalist basis of that calculation, the exact figure reproduced above is only seemingly exact. Furthermore, Blair a priori assumes that the benefits calculated accrue to the workforce only, whilst earlier she herself recognised that the two parties involved share in the costs and returns to human capital alike. And Blair herself concedes that:

> although wages do seem to rise with tenure, and wages of long-tenured employees often exceed short-run opportunity costs, this evidence does not persuade all labour economists that employees acquire substantial amounts of firm-specific human capital. Perhaps other features of the labour market could account for these empirical regularities. For example, labour market models that emphasise a process of searching for an especially good job 'match' also predict low wages at the start, which will rise if the match is a good one. Similarly, in 'efficiency wage' models, employees are induced to perform well by making it costly for them if they get laid off, generally by paying them more than their opportunity cost – that is, the wage in their next-best job. In such cases, employees have something of substantial value at risk in the firm that can be expropriated by the employer, or that can be lost altogether if the employees lose their jobs with their current employer.

These other explanations for a rising wage-tenure profile also imply that labour markets would exhibit involuntary unemployment; hence they have figured prominently in the debate about the extent to which labour markets clear.[4] Naturally, both in terms of logical, theoretical argument (market segmentation, unionisation, minimum wage and other state regulations) and on empirical basis) where the labour power markets stubbornly refuse spontaneously to clear necessitating thereby state intervention, any talk about the spontaneously equilibrating market is untenable. However, adding a caveat that the concept of human capital (as established thus far) is a misnomer (which the following passage only brings out again-note when the author refers to substantive issues, she leaves her human capital rhetoric, and talks about employees and compensation instead which phrases have certainly more to do with the concept of labour power than that of capital, human or otherwise), one may concur with Blair's contention that "this comparison of human capital to equity capital in terms of their purportedly identical structure of risk would seem to indicate that the author views the ownership of the former the same way as in the latter case, i.e. as being vested in the employees. This first-

---

4 For a summary of arguments on the efficiency of nonmarket-clearing wages, see Krueger and Summers (1988); Weiss (1990). For evidence on nonmarket-clearing wages and employment practices, see Katz and Summers (1989); Dickens and Lang (1993).

glance impression is, however, not quite correct, as it turns out. While the first of the following two pronouncements can be read in the framework of the above-mentioned interpretation, the second definitely cannot.

In addition, note that a further contribution to the fuzziness of the conceptual framework used in Blair's argument is the ambiguous usage of the term "investment" or "expense". At times it means financial expenditures, but elsewhere simply an effort required to acquire knowledge and experience, which in many instances is minimal, as in the case of learning by doing. "If the firm compensates the employee up front and fully for the costs of expending the effort, or developing and using such assets, the employee could, in principle, take the compensation and walk out the door, depriving the firm of a return on its investment" (Blair 1999).

So far, so consistent. But then the scholar under discussion makes a U-turn: "Suppose, however, that the firm does not fully compensate the employee up front, but instead pays a lower wage at first, with a promise of a higher wage later. That employee would then have a stake in the firm that is unrecoverable except as payments are made to the employee out of the economic surplus generated by the relationship in the future" (Blair 1999).

Make no mistake-the concept of economic surplus present in the above passage is not the same as one of surplus value, although the two relations in question have in common their relationship with economic ownership. However, Blair implies that although the firm is the first and immediate owner of the said surplus, the worker receives a chunk of it. According to Blair, there are some problems with the execution of that payment stemming from the fact that the employee' stake is very difficult to protect by means of explicit contracts. On one side, the firm cannot enforce a contract that requires the employee to stay and utilise those skills in the firm. On the other, because the skills and special effort in question are likely to be hard to define, let alone measure, the employee cannot enforce a contract that requires the firm to pay for the special effort expended, or the development and use of special skills (Blair 1999).

Thus, giving the author the benefit of the doubt (which is not obvious at all, suffice it to mention so-called non-competition clauses that have long been successfully implemented in a variety of capitalist economies), it would follow that the situation in question is a lose–lose one. But then another act in this roller-coaster tale follows: "In general, the lesson from labour theory has been that employee investments in firm-specific human capital cannot be well protected by explicit and complete contracts. Other institutional arrangements are needed, and those arrangements often have the effect of tying the fortunes of the employee together with those of the firm" (Blair 1999).

There the implication is that the said tying is disadvantageous for the employee, as it may deprive her of at least part of her ownership in the labour power. On the other hand, the above formulation is so general that it does not rule out the possibility of some special advantages flowing to the employee owing to her ascription to the employing firm.

Having sketched out her argument, Blair sets out to put it in the context of the theories of the firm. She first recalls the seminal contribution of Ronald Coase who sought "the reason that a hierarchical relationship, with some individuals having the authority to make decisions about how people and resources are used, might be substituted for market transactions" (Blair 1999). To put it differently, the underlying rationale for the existence of the firm is its ability to economise on transaction costs.

As Blair notes:

> From Coase's initial insight, economists took the theory of the firm in two different directions. One approach has been to focus on circumstances in which it might be less costly to organise production within a firm. A central question here is what factors might increase the 'transactions costs' of organising activities through market transactions. One answer that has been given particular attention is investments in specialised assets. The second approach stresses the importance of joint production technologies, in which the firm provides a mechanism for measuring and rewarding the productivity of interacting team members. (Blair 1999)

The former line of inquiry, associated with transaction costs economics has been developed notably by the Nobel-winning economist Oliver Williamson who has identified several features of transactions that make it costly to trade in impersonal, arm's length markets. Where these conditions hold, he suggests, it is efficient to administer such transactions through hierarchical governance arrangements (Williamson 1975: 1985). A key feature – important for its relationship with the type of human capital under consideration is what Williamson called the "asset-specificity" of investments, which refers to the degree of difficulty in redeploying assets to other uses.

As Blair notes: "Williamson's work spawned a literature on the contracting problems that arise when assets are specific" (1999).

Because of its relevance to the ownership issue, a particularly interesting argument is that by Benjamin Klein, Robert Crawford, and Armen Alchian who claimed that when two contracting parties each make investments that are specific to their relationship, either party can attempt to expropriate the returns from those investments by threatening to "hold up" the other party in the enterprise (Klein, Crawford, and Alchian 1978).

The potential "hold-up" problem, they reasoned, would encourage the contracting parties to integrate their operations vertically; that is, the supplier would acquire the customer, or vice versa. An example given by Blair will be useful. Suppose, she says, "one party owns a coal mine, and the other party owns a power plant built at the mouth of the coal mine and designed to use coal from the mine. Then the two parties would probably find themselves in frequent disputes about the price and terms on which the coal is to be sold to the power plant" (Blair 1999). Their interdependence creates the fertile ground for blackmailing or checkmating each other. In such a situation it is rational for a single party to come into possession of both the mine and the power plant because such an owner "would maximise the joint return and would not waste resources haggling over the terms of trade between the two units.

> Empirical research that has attempted to test the Williamson and Klein, Crawford, and Alchian hypotheses has generally confirmed that firm-specific investments are important in determining ownership structure and degree of vertical integration (Blair 1999).

Most importantly for our topic, this research, she notes, "…has taken an interesting twist, which implies that firm-specific investments in human capital may be a more important reason for corporate integration than firm-specific investments in physical capital" (Blair 1999).

Before passing to her further discussion, recall that the opposition in question should be couched differently-as that between variable and fixed capital. Kirk Monteverde and David Teece have studied parts production in the automobile industry to ask under what circumstances firms might choose to undertake production in-house rather than contracting production out to a supplier (Monteverde and Teece 1982a, 1982b). They argue that vertical integration might not be necessary if the specialised assets used in production of the parts include only physical capital, such as tools or dies. The hold-up problem, in this case, can be avoided if the automobile assembly company owns the specialised tools and leases them to the contractor who produces the parts. Such arrangements, which Monteverde and Teece refer to as "quasi integration," are commonly observed in auto parts production. But where the specialised investment involved in producing the parts is in non-patentable know-how and skills, the two aforementioned researchers argue that quasi integration will no longer solve the hold-up problem (Monteverde and Teece 1982a, 1982b).

As reported by Blair, "They speculate that full integration will be required to minimise the transactions costs" (1999). Similarly, Scott Masten, James Meehan, and Edward Snyder find that, in regressions in which both investments in specialised knowledge and investments in specialised equipment are used to explain vertical integration, investments in specialised knowledge have much more explanatory power (Masten, Meehan, and Snyder 1989).

Blair points out, however, that "none of these authors offer much insight into why and how organising production within a firm solves the hold-up problem associated with firm-specific investments by multiple parties, nor which of several participants in an enterprise should ideally be the "owner" of an integrated enterprise. Sanford Grossman and Oliver Hart address this issue. Grossman and Hart's model considers a situation in which participants in an enterprise must make firm-specific investments that are very difficult or impossible to define in enforceable contracts. Their model leads to the conclusion that the ownership rights in the firm should go to the party whose firm-specific investments add the most value to the enterprise but are the most difficult or impossible to contract over. Ownership rights over the firm provide some assurance to the party who must make these investments that its claim to a share in the rents generated by the investments will not be expropriated by the other participants. (Blair 1999).

Thus, even the language used confirms the relevance of Blair's discussion to the topic of this chapter.

Then Blair relates the above considerations to the theory of the firm. Lurking in the background of these transaction cost arguments for why a firm exists is the assumption that a firm is a fairly well-defined entity whose interests are simply an extension of the interests of its owners. By this assumption, employees are contracting with the firm but are not, themselves, part of it (Blair 1999).

By the same token, Blair indirectly brings out how much the whole concept of the firm as a person is flawed-she shows that the latter entails a bizarre, and profoundly asociological view in which employees are not part of their employing organisation. Of course, such a view is inconsistent not only with sociology, but also with the human capital rhetoric whereby it is recited that people are the most important asset of the firm. How can that be, if their position is reduced to that of outsiders who only at a distance enter into contractual relations with the firm?

The above question ceases to be merely rhetoric if one takes into consideration a key methodological premise of human capital theory lying in its individualism. Human capital theory posits, after all, that autonomous individuals decide on how much skill to acquire in their lifetime – guided by the cost-benefit calculation as determined by prices and by their ability to learn. The social determinants of education within an unequal economy, the social, above all class[5] conflicts over the very definition of, and access to, skill, and indeed the social character of the prevailing technology and methods of work organisation which determine skill demands, are all precluded by an individualistic framework (Ashton and Green 1996: 14–21).

Then Blair hits the nail on the head: "Under the terms of the Grossman and Hart theory, for example, firms are defined as bundles of assets under common ownership, where ownership implies control over the use and disposition of the assets" (1999).

Blair's formulation is ambiguous insofar as it is not clear if ownership only entails control, but remains a distinct relation, or if, contrariwise, control constitutes the substance of ownership. It is apparent that Blair does not feel exactly at ease as regards the notion of ownership, and her comment below only reinforces that impression:

---

5   And indeed, criticising the sister concept of social capital, it is pointed out that "that concept allows no genuine space for class conflict" (Fine, Green 2002: 91). Similarly, others charge that Putnam's definition of social capital ignores the conflictual and unequal aspects of a society divided by class and race (Portes 1998; Foley and Edwards 1997).

> Economists have not necessarily agreed on the key economic features of 'ownership.' Hart and Moore (1990), for example, emphasise that ownership implies the ability to exclude others from the use of assets. According to Wiggins (1991: 615), shared ownership means that the owners are compensated out of a common stream of residual payments that are left over after contractual payments are made. (Blair 1999)

Naturally, there is much more to the notion of ownership than the above passage implies-for a more extensive discussion see (Tittenbrun 2011), but what is most relevant in the present context is the self-contradictory character of the above-cited pronouncement. At the beginning, a definition of ownership is put forward, without realising that it is modelled upon private property; by any means all forms of ownership imply monopolisation of property-for instance, common, or – to put it in the economists' jargon terms-open-access property. So, it is not only surprising, but inconsistent that the second part of the aforementioned pronouncement refers to precisely common ownership, mistakenly implying that the above-mentioned way of sharing in the corporate income is peculiar to this form of ownership, whereas in reality it is not the case-thus conceived claims to the residual are equally pertinent to private ownership of the economic activity means.

From her perspective, Blair quite rightly notes that the tendency in the transactions cost literature has been to recognise that firm-specific human capital raises similar questions, but then to sidestep the implications of these questions for corporate governance (Blair 1999).

Thus, Williamson identifies features of organisations, such as team accommodations, informal process innovations, and knowledge of codes and procedures, that tend to make incumbents more valuable to employers than workers hired on spot markets might be. He points out that "transactions in which investments in specific human capital are important must include some sort of safeguard for those investments […] lest productive values be sacrificed if the employment relation is unwittingly severed" (Williamson 1985: 242–43).

However, complaints Blair, Williamson then devotes little attention to identifying the "protective governance structures" that should exist in relationships between employees and firms that employ them. To be sure, he mentions severance pay and forms of job security as possible mechanisms for encouraging and protecting worker investments in firm-specific skills, and pensions as a mechanism for providing incentives that discourage employees with specialised skills from quitting. He also points out that collective bargaining through unions and "internal governance structures" (such as grievance procedures and pay scales) can help in providing a protective governance structure for idiosyncratic investments in skills by workers, although he notes that unions, with their bent toward egalitarianism, may not be the best institutions for arranging pay structures that will differ across workers according to their degree of firm-specific human capital (Williamson 1985: 246–47, 254–56, 265).

Still, Blair is not happy with Williamson's proposals; "it is something of a leap – she reckons – to assume that these protections are fully adequate to protect employees who make firm-specific investments. This assumption is implicit, for example, in Williamson's analysis of the transactions cost benefits of corporate governance arrangements that give the right to elect board members only to shareholders, rather than (or in addition to) other constituents: "Stockholders as a group bear a unique relation to the firm," he asserts. "They are the only voluntary constituency whose relation with the corporation does not come up for periodic review…Stockholders…invest for the life of the firm, and their claims are located at the end of the queue should liquidation occur" (Williamson 1985): 304–05.

But Blair has some powerful counter-arguments. This line of thinking follows in the tradition of labour theorists, discussed earlier, that makes a hermetic separation between labour market relationships and corporate governance. But firm-specific investments in human capital cannot be redeployed (by definition), and thus employees too are invested for life. Employees can deprive the firm of their firm-specific skills, but they cannot benefit from doing so, since these skills (by definition) have less value elsewhere. Those who make firm-specific investments in human capital are presumably expecting to be compensated from the future productivity of those investments; that is to say, from a share of the future "residual" income, or economic surpluses, of the firm. Despite their reliance on the continuing relationship with the firm, however, employees have no explicit future claim on the firm – at least not solely by virtue of their employment relationship, though employees may also be shareholders, and in Germany, employees' pension claims may be tied to the long-term success of their firms (Blair 1999).

What is missing in this argument is that this tying of the employee's fortunes to his or her firm's prosperity is a double-edged sword, it is all very fine as long as the company makes healthy profits. But it may well go bankrupt as well, leaving its employees with titles to its assets worth on paper perhaps even some considerable amount, but in reality virtually nothing.

> Although we do not have precise estimates of the aggregate value of investments in firm-specific human capital, it is surely large, and possibly of the same order of magnitude as the aggregate value of equity capital. (Blair 1999)

If this does not seem shocking, this is because the reader has been apparently, and unfortunately, socialised to believe in the validity of human capital theory, whereas – from our perspective – the above comparison is like comparing apples to oranges – human capital is actually a misnomer, and even if conceived of as variable capital, one still speaks about incommensurate magnitudes.

> This recognition of the potential importance of firm-specific human capital, soon followed by an implicit denial that it should have anything to do with actual corporate governance such as voting for board members, has been echoed by

numerous legal scholars, especially advocates of a contractarian theory of the firm. (Blair 1999)

As stated, regardless of how one assesses the credibility of such estimates, it turns out, for the second, or even third time in row, that a human capital scholar sides with the underprivileged class. It is logically possible that from an incorrect premise one derives a proper conclusion, and – at least from our standpoint – this precisely is the case of the aforementioned researcher.

It is striking that she retains this class perspective in assessing the second major theory of the firm.

A second main justification for the existence of the firm is to organise team production, that is, one in which, amongst other things, not all resources used in team production belong to one person (Alchian and Demsetz 1972: 779). As reported by Blair, the problem raised by team production, according to Alchian and Demsetz, is one of metering output (where the output of any one individual is not separable from the output of teammates), and issuing rewards in ways that will motivate team members to exert effort (Blair 1999).

It is remarkable that even a scholar challenging many important assumptions of human capital paradigm, abstains from doing the same regarding the key individualistic assumption – speaking all time of team members, team-work, she fails to take into account various well-known collective systems of compensation, such as collective piece-rate, or a system based on targets for attainment of which the whole team is responsible. Her subsequent comments are nothing new to readers of Smith, Marx, Durkheim, to name but a few:

> Advantages arise from team production if the team members can accomplish more by working together than by working separately. If this extra productivity exceeds the cost of monitoring and motivating team members to exert effort, then team production will be chosen over individual production methods. Alchian and Demsetz go on to argue that, where team production is preferred, the metering and reward problem can be solved by having one team member specialise in monitoring, and by giving that individual both the authority to hire and fire team members, and a claim on the earnings from the enterprise net of payments to providers of other inputs, who are assumed to be paid their opportunity cost. (Blair 1999)

Remarkably, and refreshingly for the reader used to the ready-made offers of conventional textbook economics, Blair remains unconvinced:

> This story purports to provide an explanation for capitalist ownership and control of firms. Taken by itself, however, it offers no particular reason why the membership of the team could not change from day to day, or hour to hour. In fact, Alchian and Demsetz state that 'long-term contracts between employer and employee are not the essence of the organisation we call a firm.' They

argue, rather, that the relationship between firm and employee is equivalent to a series of short-term contracts: 'The employer is continually involved in renegotiation of contracts on terms that must be acceptable to both parties'. But in large corporations, fairly long-term relationships are the norm rather than the exception. So their story seems, at best, incomplete, for explaining the actual way that large corporations typically operate.[6] (Blair 1999)

From her perspective, Blair wants to contribute somewhat to the above account:

> The original Alchian and Demsetz story can be improved by allowing for investments in firm-specific human capital, or other factors that might make it advantageous to keep a particular team working together. Demsetz himself has moved in this direction in more recent work. An important aspect of the 'nexus of contracts' that make up a firm, he says, 'is the expected length of association between the same input owners....Do the contractual agreements entered into contemplate mainly transitory, short-term association, which in the extreme would be characterised by spot market exchanges, or do these agreements contemplate a high probability of continuing association among the same parties? The firm viewed as team production exhibits significant reassociation of the same input owners (Demsetz (1991: 170).

Demsetz goes on to define a firm as "a bundle of commitments to technology, personnel, and methods, all contained and constrained by an insulating layer of information that is specific to the firm, and this bundle cannot be altered or imitated easily or quickly. Team production with specific human capital, then, the human capital is worth more when applied together with the human capital of the other team members than it is when applied alone, and the productivity of a particular individual depends not just on being part of a team, but on being part of a particular team engaged in a particular task (Blair 1999).

It is all very well, but an awkward question arises – what has human capital to do with all this? Blair depicts simply the role of co-operation in the work process, and the phrase "input owners" in that context only highlights that it is the labour power that is at stake; the said input is presumably a concrete labour, but labour cannot be property, only labour power can.

It is ownership as well, albeit of another kind, that is touched on by Blair in what follows:

> If it matters who is on the team, this complicates the original Alchian and Demsetz story, because it is no longer clear that team members who invest in specialised skills and who know they are especially valuable when deployed with this particular team will be willing to accept only their (short-run) opportunity

---

6 And this contention remains valid despite of the current much-trumpeted causalisation or individualisation of work.

> cost in wages. Hence it is no longer obvious that the monitor will be able to
> collect all of the economic surplus from the enterprise. (Blair 1999)

Although the above argument cries for framing it in terms of class struggle, the
conclusion itself seems correct, only that it could be arrived at also from another
starting point-that of specific labour power rather than human capital. Meanwhile,
Blair emphasises in what respect her argument differs from that of Demsetz:
Jensen and Meckling argued that organisations "are simply legal fictions which
serve as a nexus for a set of contracting relationships among individuals" (Jensen
and Meckling 1976: 310).

As an exponent of a sociological point of view, it is obligatory to call attention
to the phrase "legal fictions" to describe the nature of corporate bodies. On
the other hand, from the same viewpoint it is another legal fiction to speak of
contractual relations as comprising the corporation. The said contracts are valid
in, and relevant for the law, for the sociologist-the firm is a complex of social
relations, and the problems Blair discovers and complaints about in the received
theories of the firm are in no small part result of failing to take the social fully into
account.

To put it differently, the aforementioned theorists are out of the frying pan into
the fire inasmuch as they criticise some "legal fictions", only to fall prey to another
kind of one.

With remarkable consistency, Blair brings out the ideological, or class
significance of the above-mentioned seemingly purely academic considerations:

> Jensen and Meckling are thus generally credited as the source of the view of
> the firm as a 'nexus of contracts,' and their notion of firms has been taken into
> the legal literature on corporate governance in support of a contractarian (rather
> than an entity) theory of firms. More important for the present discussion, it has
> often been imbued with normative status, as a statement about whose interests
> managers are supposed to serve. In recent years, principal-agent models have
> also been influential in research on labour relations in firms. But the corporate
> governance and labour relations literatures have typically remained rather
> separate.
>
> The economical principal-agent problem involves a transaction between two
> parties, one of whom must take an action that affects the other. For some reason,
> however, the principal cannot compensate the agent directly for the action itself,
> perhaps because the action itself is not observable to the principal, or perhaps
> because the principal does not have the information or knowledge necessary to
> evaluate the action.[7] It must also be true that the consequences or observable

---

7 This fairly trivial, it seems, observation, was nevertheless hailed as a milestone
in economics (which by itself speaks volumes about the quality of that discipline whose
pretensions far supersede real achievements).

output of the agent's action is not a determinate function of the action taken by the principal; otherwise, it would be possible for the principal to infer the action taken by observing the consequences.

Instead, in the principal-agent problem, the output is assumed to be a stochastic function of the agent's action, or it is assumed to be measured with error. Since the principal cannot pay the agent for the action, the problem for the principal is to base the fee schedule on the observable factors in a way that gives the agent incentives to choose actions that benefit the principal. [...] With a risk-averse agent, the optimal incentive structure will share the risks between the agent and the principal; for example, the principal might agree to pay a minimum wage regardless of the outcome, plus some fraction of realised output. The sharing of risks gives a risk-averse agent higher utility than if the agent bore all of the risks, but because the agent is receiving only a fraction of output, the incentive of a risk-sharing contract is less powerful than would be the case if the agent received all of the output. Another device that can be used to induce effort by the agent is a flat fee, accompanied by a threat of termination if the agent is caught shirking. (Blair 1999)

Those considerations are useful inasmuch as, Blair argues, in some ways the problem raised by investments in firm-specific human capital is analogous to the principal-agent problem. The employee must take some action – for example, acquire some skills, accumulate some special knowledge, exert some special effort, develop some special relationships with co-workers – which the firm cannot directly measure and for which it cannot directly compensate the employee. The firm can only observe (perhaps imperfectly) the outcomes of such investments. As Kenneth Arrow has noted, "The employment relation in general is one in which effort and ability acquired through training and self-improvement are hard to observe" (1985: 39).

Well, yes and no; on the one hand that the effort as such is not observable is trivially true, but in order to cope with that problem there have been devised a range of incentive pay systems. But this is not the end of the story, because one should also differentiate between the various types of labour power, which the above formulation does not. For instance, as regards the possibility of observation and measurement, there is a definite difference between a material worker paid by the piece, and, say, a conceptual employee, holder of an intellectual labour power whose (pre-material) work outcomes become visible only after some, often quite a long time. This is in part related to the necessity to differentiate between ascriptive and achievement-based labour power.

However, even if the above distinction is sometimes implicitly recognised in the literature under investigation, this recognition becomes obscured due to what in effect is an undifferentiated notion of labour – the following argument is meant as universal, without any reference to the various types of labour power and corresponding types of work:

Dual moral hazard is defined as follows: "An opportunistic firm may renege on a promise to give its worker a higher wage, by claiming that the worker has not acquired the required skills even when she did; anticipating this, a worker has of course no incentive to collect firm-specific skills. Most solutions to this problem rely on discrete incentives and internal labour markets: wages are linked to jobs rather than performance, and diligent employees are rewarded through assignments and promotions." (Sinclair-Desgagne and Cadot 1997: 2).

Also Steven Wiggins stresses the similarities between the principal-agent problem and the problem of firm-specific investments: whenever "one party performs first, he effectively makes an investment specific to the trading relationship; he invests in a specific asset. After investment, he relies on the other party to perform. The problem is that the second party can only make limited commitments to follow through" (1991: 604). Blair, however, draws attention to the fact that: "the economical principal-agent problem is different from the firm-specific investment problem in a critical way: it is asymmetric. In the [ec[onomical principal-agent problem, there is an implicit assumption that, once the fee schedule has been determined, the actions of the principal have no further effect on the outcome of the variable to which the fee schedule is tied. The outcome is realised, the fees that were promised to the agent are determined as a function of that outcome, and the agents are promptly paid.

> Thus some strong assumptions about the credibility of the parties and the enforceability of the arrangement are embodied in the simple principle-agent story. (Blair 1999)

Note the direction of critique in what follows where Blair not only employs the perspective of action (which among economists is characteristic only of the Austrian school), but moreover uses the concept of rent that in our own socio-economic structuralism expresses the very essence of economic ownership as gratuitous benefit (elaborated in: Tittenbrun 2011; 2012). Meanwhile, "in the case of firm-specific investments actions of both parties can affect the payoff from the investment. The employee takes an action that affects the payoff for the firm, but the firm, in turn, can take actions that not only affect the fee that the employee gets, but that affect the stream of rents and quasi rents generated by that action. For example, the firm can decide to close the plant where the employee works, and suddenly there is no opportunity for the payoff to be realised" (Blair 1999).

The point Blair makes is a good illustration of the legal fiction that posits equivalence of both parties to a contract, which upon contextualisation to a concrete social situation such as one above, reveals all its fictitiousness-the capitalist firm is a mechanism of class power. Similarly, a further example given by Blair refers to the realities of capitalistic economy-"or the shareholders can sell the firm to someone else who can fire the manager or dismantle the firm" (Blair 1999). And her further discussion has a definite ownership dimension to it; namely, Blair indicates that her "point is also close to that made by Shleifer and

Summers (1988) in their critique of hostile takeovers, arguing that such takeovers may create value for the new owners by breaching the implicit contracts with employees and other stakeholders put in place by previous management. Although Shleifer and Summers do not appeal explicitly to investments in firm-specific human capital, such investments would be one explanation of the quasi rents that are supposedly up for grabs in their story" (Blair 1999). And further on she makes such a reference explicitly: "Firm-specific capital is indeed central to theories about the nature of the firm. [...] Although considerable thought has been given to how ownership structures might be arranged to protect investments in firm-specific physical capital, less has been said about how contracts might be drawn up or other institutional arrangements might be made to protect firm-specific human capital.

Much has been made of the idea that the corporate form facilitates a division of labour in which managers specialise in decision-making and outside investors specialise in risk-bearing" (see e.g. Fama and Jensen (1983).

And again there is a clear class edge to Blair's counter-argument, all the more interesting to us for its reference to ownership of – in our terms – labour power:

> This approach, however, essentially ignores the risks borne by employees with firm-specific human capital. An investment in firm-specific human capital can be risky not only because of potential hold-up problems and the associated risk of expropriation, but also because a particular skill may no longer be as useful in a given firm, or the firm itself may do poorly while the economy does well, or the entire economy may do poorly. Outside shareholders might be able to draw up contracts that can protect employees to some extent from some of these risks, but surely not from all of them. Employees, inevitably, will also bear some of the enterprise risk. (Blair 1999)

Blair would have surely been surprised to hear that by the same token she has made a valuable contribution to the theory of specific labour power. She sticks to her terminological framework although by each argument of hers it should become clearer that she is in fact referring to labour power rather than capital. Capital is something which the other side of the class equation possesses and takes advantage of, as she has in effect showed above.

Blair should be praised for her fairness-she tries to do justice to the position she is criticising:

> Numerous scholars have argued that employees are protected from the risks of expropriation by the fact that the firm must be concerned about its reputation for fairness. A good reputation enables it to contract on favourable terms with other employees in the future. Oliver Williamson writes:
> > Employers who have a reputation for exploiting incumbent employees will not thereafter be able to induce new employees to accept employment on the same terms. A wage premium may have to be paid; or tasks may have to be redefined

> to eliminate the transaction-specific features; or contractual guarantees against
> future abuses may have to be granted. In consideration of those possibilities,
> the strategy of exploiting the specific investments of incumbent employees is
> effectively restricted to circumstances where (1) firms are of a fly-by-night kind,
> (2) firms are playing end games, and (3) intergenerational learning is negligible.
> (Williamson 1985: 261)

Under the realities of capitalism, however, the list of exceptions to what Williamson
considers the normal rule is much longer than the list of cases showing the rule
in question in action, the latter boiling down, by and large, to those firms who
seriously treat the so-called corporate social responsibility. Not that such firms
are non-existent, but the basic truth is that under stockholder capitalism at least,
the corporation is focused on and primarily obligated to the maximisation of
shareholder value. And when (which is essentially permanent in capitalism which
somehow cannot dispense with the reserve army of labour, to use Max's phrase)
the labour power market is a "buyer's market", i.e. when there is unemployment,
all Williamson's talk about the corporation's inducements to play fair means little
because in such a situation the priority of the firm would certainly be not its care
for reputation amongst prospective employees. Blair finds some weak spots in
Williamson's argument as well:

> In practice, employees are also not given significant protections against the risks
> of decline in the value of their firm-specific skills. It is difficult to imagine how
> such protection could be provided in any company over an extended period of
> time, as long as the company retains ultimate power to deny wage raises or to
> terminate employment altogether. Indeed, it is much harder to enforce 'fairness'
> in an employment agreement whose terms can be renegotiated as business
> conditions facing the firm vary. As Paul Milgrom and John Roberts note: 'The
> firm's management may be tempted to exaggerate financial difficulties in order
> to justify paying lower wages to workers'. (Blair 1999)

This once more points to which party to "the contractual relation" is superior –
after all, it is the firm that leases the worker's labour power, not the other way
round.

On the other hand, Blair warns that:

> totally insulating employees against risks might discourage them from doing the
> things that are under their control to pull resources out of lower-value investments
> and move them to higher-value investments, by retraining, for example. Some
> of the disincentive effects of mechanisms that shelter employees from the risks
> inherent in making specialised investments could possibly be counteracted with
> intensive monitoring. But the monitor must focus on the measurable dimensions
> of performance, which might lead employees to focus on those 'monitored'
> dimensions to the exclusion of nonmeasurable dimensions that may also be

important to productivity. Ultimately, attempting to monitor investments in firm-specific human capital would present such severe problems of measurement, verification, and evaluation that it would probably be ineffective. (Blair 1999)

Fair enough. But it is not the end of the story.

Yet another contracting problem raised by investments in human capital is how to understand and quantify all of the forms that the returns to those investments can take. Whereas the returns to physical capital investments can generally be measured in monetary terms, some of the returns to investments in human capital may take other forms. For example, human capital may not depreciate with use, but may, instead, appreciate. Knowledge and skills that are used may build on themselves and become more valuable. If so, the returns to tenure may go well beyond just the returns from skills accumulated up to a particular point in time, and by extension, the losses from premature job separations may be even larger than that implied by immediate losses in workers' incomes. An employment relationship may include a component that is like an option. If the employee stays with the present employer, the employee will have an opportunity to acquire skills tomorrow that build on the skills acquired through today. Those skills would generate an additional stream of returns on top of the stream of returns from the skills accumulated through today. If the employment relationship is prematurely severed, that option value is lost (Blair 1999).

Assuming Blair's characterisation of what she terms human capital is correct, it should make her think twice about her terminological choice; why one should persist to use the term when what she in effect is arguing is that human capital has little in common with other types of capital. In addition, the comparison to option is rather misleading and unfortunate, since it prejudges what has in no way been established-that human capital is a genuine capital, and its holders are true (not metaphorical) capitalists-just as option holders are part owners of equity capital. And as if reading our thoughts, Blair concedes that the complex nature of the returns to human capital may make it impossible, Milgrom and Roberts note, "to identify any individual or group that is the unique residual claimant [in a firm], or, indeed, to identify the benefits and costs accruing to any decision and so compute the residuals" (1992: 315). By the same token, the scholar acknowledges that her own earlier usage – in at least some context taking for granted, or at least making such an impression, that it is definitely the employee who benefits from human capital investments is at least problematic, even leaving aside who shall be treated as the "investor".

And the chief reason why the issue of distribution of the aforementioned benefits must not be treated as a purely technical question, dependent merely on solving some relevant econometric hurdles is the all-important factor of class struggle decidedly intervening in this distribution. And Blair talks as if she were aware of this fact:

> The difficulty of computing and assigning residuals complicates the problem of bargaining between any employee and the firm over the allocation of residual claims, or over any scheme of payments that might be devised to encourage both parties to the relationship to take into account the impact of decisions by one on the other. In sum, work on theories of the firm also tends to imply that explicit contracting cannot be used effectively to protect firm-specific investments in human capital by employees. (Blair 1999)

What is the solution to the aforementioned problem? Blair's following brief discussion is of interest, to be sure, not so much for the effectiveness of the solutions proposed, but for their relationship, if any, to a key issue of our interest, i.e. economic ownership. We should, however, draw attention to the author's shift in perspective; Blair considers the topic from the standpoint of the firm, assuming it is the latter who benefits from human capital. And her further argument appears to be a result of deduction rather than induction inasmuch as it glosses over the current spread of part-time, temporary and suchlike forms of employment:

> Long-term relationships also encourage the development of reputations. After all, good reputations are more valuable the longer the time-horizons of the contracting parties, so that in a longer-term relationship, both sides to any given transaction within that relationship will have stronger incentives to perform fully. Career paths and job ladders are said to be important mechanisms for encouraging employees to make investments in firm-specific human capital and for ensuring that the firm shares the rents generated by those investments with employees. (Blair 1999)

From a common-sense point of view it is incomprehensible why the firm should want to share instead of monopolise the said rents at all, given that it is the employee who makes the relevant investments. The only sensible explanation seems one that Blair and scores of other economists are reluctant to embrace-the uncomfortable fact that the firm, as a collective capitalist, is the prime owner of surplus value, and thus profit from any investment made in the firm, which implies that human capital is in actual fact (in capital terms) variable capital.

And again, seniority is a concept applicable not to any capital whatsoever but to labour power:

> Seniority rules are a related mechanism that provides some protection for employees from the possibility that the firm will renege on its implicit agreement to compensate the employee for his or her firm-specific investments by paying them a higher wage during their later years, perhaps even a wage that exceeds their productivity during those years. Seniority rules protect the high-tenured worker by requiring the firm to lay off low-tenured workers first. Both seniority rules and job ladders help ensure that the employee will be appropriately compensated for making firm-specific investments over time. Of course, such

promises would have no incentive benefit if employees did not believe that the employing organisation would continue to exist over the relevant period. So these mechanisms are not useful by themselves but must be embedded in a relationship that is understood to be for the long term, with an entity that is long-lived. (Blair 1999)

Blair's legal background makes itself felt here-the corporation, being a legal entity, may potentially last forever, as opposed to so-called natural or physical persons, which alone, however, does not determine its economic fortunes.

It is to Blair's credit that she tries – as far as her analytical lens allows for – to take account of social relations, and does not, by and large, divorce them from economic relations but, conversely, views them as interwoven, whose another example is her discussion of unionisation. Her account is balanced, that is, she does not take the widespread among economists negative view of the organisations dealing with the terms of leasing employee labour power:

One effect of unions is to protect employees from actions such as dismissal (except 'for cause'). Other terms in the typical collective bargaining agreement in turn help prevent firms from driving out unwanted employees without actually dismissing them. These take the form of rules designed to safeguard wages, benefits, and job assignments, as well as to protect against layoffs. However, these sorts of protections impose rigidities that can have negative implications for efficient adaptation to changed circumstances. (Blair 1999)

Blair, however, is not prone to the mantra of corporate flexibility, at least not at all cost. She points out that "these costs must be weighed against incentives for long-term investment in firm-specific capital (and other benefits) that union agreements may provide" (Blair 1999). She continues with a discussion of "hostages" or Performance Bonds. She explains that: a "hostage" is something of value that is pledged by one party to a transaction and that will be forfeited to the other party if the first party fails to perform according to the contract". A case in point is to her mind as follows: "workers accept wages that are lower than their opportunity cost in the early years of their employment relationship, and this serves as a commitment by the worker to stay with the firm and to be repaid later with wages that are higher. Another version of the hostage argument is the 'performance bond', in which an employee posts a bond upon being hired that must be forfeited if the employee were to leave or to underperform" (Blair 1999).

This is a clear and lucid analysis as far as it goes; what – from our point of view – is missing is ownership implications. These are double-edged; on one side the fact that an employee is tied to his or her employer means that to that extent he or she loses ownership of his or her labour power. The less pronounced is this effect of ascription to the firm, the more prominent becomes an aspect of job ownership (noted by, *inter alia*, Weeber, only that in slightly other terms).

Meanwhile, Blair draws attention to the fact that: the administration and enforcement of performance bond agreements, however, requires that third parties be able to observe and verify certain measures of performance and certain triggering events. Hence performance bonds by themselves seem to be poor candidates for solving the contracting problems presented by the accumulation of specialised human capital unless they are embedded in institutional arrangements that also foster trust or that make reputations valuable. Hostages provided by the employer include severance pay commitments and their gilt-edged cousins, golden parachutes; these make it costly for the employer to sever the employment relationship. Penalties for certain kinds of changes in the contract terms may perform a similar function. Milgrom and Roberts (1999) argue, for example, that employment contracts might be designed to impose a penalty of some sort on the employer for invoking a claim of hard times in an effort to negotiate lower wages, so that the employer will not be tempted to use this claim frivolously in negotiations.

Already those considerations, and even more so what follows is concerned in fact with the problematics of corporate governance and, in particular, the various institutional paradigms of running the firm. The most important distinction here is between stockholder capitalism on the one hand, and stakeholder capitalism on the other. And what is critical about this distinction is that it refers to economic ownership relations, as shown, *inter alia*, in Tittenbrun (2012).

Blair uses other terms: she speaks of corporate Culture, Norms, and Goals. She argues that:

> 'workable principles and routines...create shared expectations for group members,' as Milgrom and Roberts note. The advantages of such principles are that they 'help guide managers in making decisions,' provide 'a set of clear expectations for everyone in the organisation,' and 'provide a set of principles and procedures for judging right behavior and resolving inevitable disputes'. to David Kreps, these aspects of corporate culture may serve as 'focal points' around which participants in the firm can arrive at stable patterns of interacting that are Pareto superior to patterns they might lapse into without the benefit of the common norms. Hence corporate culture can help support investments in firm-specific human capital by fostering trust. (Blair 1999)

And indeed, trust constitutes a key attribute and advantage of stakeholder capitalism. It is important not to restrict oneself to its perception as an aspect of culture, but to notice its dependence on and the entanglement in the relevant ownership relations which, not obliterating their respective peculiarities, have much in common as between Japan and Germany, for instance-to cite those two examples of typical countries of what is meant by stakeholder capitalism. That the term "culture" in relation to the phenomena under consideration is not adequate, seems to be realised, in her own way, by Blair as well, as she says that:" Corporate culture, itself, can also be seen as part of the firm-specific capital of the firm, the organisational capital, as it were." (Blair 1999).

The notion of organisational capital is extensively discussed in my forthcoming book entitled "Karl Marx's Posthumous Revenge? The Proliferation of Capitals Across the Social Sciences" (Brill), and the concept of cultural capital is, of course, the subject of the present book. It is no accident that the following argument does not provide any proof of the validity of the concept just introduced by Blair:

> Richard Nelson and Sidney Winter argue that the knowledge of how to do things is often implicit in the routines that make up the daily activities of the people in the firm. As such, this knowledge is neither articulable nor alienable but is embodied in the people and in their relationships to each other. Another similar mechanism, Sanford Jacoby writes, is the 'socialisation at the workplace itself, which relies on consensual methods of inculcating norms and goals, such as ideologies or authority that must be seen as legitimate if they are to be persuasive. (Blair 1999)

This is all very well, only that Blair fails to notice that her argument lacks consistency; if the kind of tacit knowledge referred to in the first part of the above-cited passage may be regarded as part of human capital because albeit most definition of the latter emphasise formal education and training as its components, at least some definitions take account of learning by doing, which notion best fits the everyday work experience related to the aforementioned knowledge in question., the same does not apply to ideologies mentioned in the second part. The thing is, by no means all knowledge held by a worker can be included in his or her labour power (human capital theorists would substitute there their conceptual favourite), one's labour power involves only those pieces of knowledge that are actually applied in the work process; one's general world-view, religion, ideological beliefs, etc. are devoid of this kind of effectivity.

The subsequent paragraph is of great interest, as Blair deals here directly with the question put in the title of the present chapter:

Yet another non-contractual mechanism for protecting specific investments is "ownership", or "property rights". Oliver Hart and others remind us that "ownership" involves possession of "residual" control rights, the rights to make all decisions (at least those that have not been delegated to others by contract) and receive whatever is left over after all payments specified by contract have been paid (Milgrom and Roberts 1992: 334).

Now this conceptualisation of ownership is unsatisfactory in that it combines two distinct relations: control and benefit. When the two aspects are combined in one person's hands, the problem this definition encounters may be less apparent, but in an opposite situation there arises an immediate question-which of the two: the beneficiary or controller should be deemed the true owner? Nor is the solution the attribution of ownership to both because, as it will be seen immediately below, the scholars concerned reserve the term "common ownership" to other kind of relations. On the other hand, it appears the concept of benefit is sidelined, and that of control-prioritised.

In particular, Hart has noted, "ex post residual rights of control will be important because, through their influence on asset usage, they will affect ex post bargaining power and the division of ex post surplus in a relationship. This division in turn will affect the incentives of actors to invest in that relationship". On these grounds, Hart has argued that "co-specialised" assets should be owned in common. If they are not, then the separate parties who own each asset will have reason to fear that the other parties will expropriate an unduly large share of the rents earned by the assets and will tend to underinvest (Hart 1989: 1757–74.

Still, whilst there is no denying that a specific decision may affect the distribution of income, this by itself does not demonstrate that it is this right to make decisions that constitutes ownership. More broadly, if a phenomenon A affects B, it does not follow that they merge into each other. Conversely, if one aims scientifically to investigate the impact in question, a strict differentiation of the objects concerned must be maintained. How does Blair extricate herself from this conceptual trap? She has difficulty doing so, which stems from her underlying assumption treating private property with its attributes such as monopolisation and exclusion, as an exemplary model of property in general. Hence, when the situation under investigation lacks those features, she is lost:

But, of course, neither the firm, nor any other participant in the enterprise that the firm directs, can "own" the human capital that may be co-specialised with the other assets of the firm. Where firm-specific human capital is important, then, arguments about the role played by property rights might in some cases point toward employee control of the enterprise, or at least participation in management, rather than capitalist ownership and control. In noting the advantages of the partnership form of organisation, for example, Milgrom and Roberts point out that "human capital is not easily tradable, and if the residual returns on that capital belong to the humans who embody it, then the usual arguments about ownership rights suggest that the residual control should be assigned to them, too (Milgrom and Roberts 1992: 523).

Several comments are needed. Firstly, at least initially Blair deploys private property as a model on which other types of ownership are moulded – this is evident from her assertion to the effect that what she calls co-specialised, complementary assets cannot be owned by anyone in the firm, the latter included. If ownership is understood as benefit, then the aforementioned relationship does not prevent the objects involved from being a property. All this is the more odd that in the second part of the argument it is precisely that conception of ownership that is deployed-it is stated that control should follow ownership conceived of as benefit. And the final problem concerns the notion of human capital adopted in the above-cited passage. The assertion that it is not tradable prompts two sorts of comment-it is, for one thing, inconsistent with the usual view of labour in neoclassical economics which otherwise functions as the underlying foundation of human capital theory. For another, granted that the observation cited in the above passage is correct (which is inconsistent also with the view that human capital ultimately boils down to labour power), then it should make one rethink the status of "human capital" as capital due to the former's lack of a key attribute of the latter. Those reservations aside, there is no doubt that Blair's discussion has been very useful; and there is yet more to it: "There are several possibilities for assigning a share of ownership and control rights to labour, ranging from equity ownership by employees to labour participation in management to direct labour ownership of firms" (Blair 1999).

Unfortunately, this recommendation is, again, unclear as to what ownership in essence is-both benefit and control as its distinguishing features are deployed in the above pronouncement.

> Compensating employees with equity stakes in corporations might foster and protect investments in firm-specific human capital. Equity ownership by employees serves as a kind of hostage, helping to make the firm's promise to share in the rents credible. It also gives employees some control rights (by virtue of their equity holdings rather than by virtue of their status as employees), while at the same time helping to align their interests with those of outside equity holders. And if equity claims are substituted for the wage premium that firm-specific human capital supposedly earns, the wages will come closer to reflecting opportunity cost and thereby send the correct economic signals to decisionmakers within the firm to guide hiring and firing decisions. There is substantial evidence that the use of equity-based compensation systems is growing in US corporations, although no definitive empirical studies have linked employee ownership in publicly traded firms to investments in firm-specific human capital. (Blair 1999)

And that's one point; the other is that the topic of employee ownership, stock ownership included, is too extensive and complex to be reducible to a few brief comments. Blair continues her argument to point out that: "direct labour participation in management is more common in Japan and Europe, where corporate governance systems seem to feature institutional arrangements that provide mechanisms by which employees are given a direct voice in management. Japanese scholars, especially, have credited these arrangements with providing incentives and protection for employee investments in firm-specific human capital" (Aoki 1988).

Germany's codetermination system has also attracted attention in this regard. As an empirical matter, employee-controlled industrial firms remain rare. One could argue that partnerships, which are a common organisational form in law, accounting, consulting, advertising, and other professional services, are a type of employee-controlled firm. An interesting question for corporate governance scholars is why firms in such fields are typically organised as partnerships, whereas industrial firms are typically organised as corporations.

Well, the reason is not overly difficult to find; capital requirements are totally different in the respective fields of economic activity; and it is not only ownership relations of capital that make the difference-accountants, lawyers, etc. hold a highly skilled labour power that is by far the most important factor of competitive advantage. Such shortcomings, however, do not detract from our high evaluation of Blair's discussion overall who probes the topic ever deeper:

> However, a number of scholars were inspired by the Yugoslavian experiment with labour-managed firms in the 1960s to consider the advantages and disadvantages of organising production in this way. This produced a lively academic debate in which some neoclassical economists argued that employee-controlled firms would be inefficient for a variety of reasons: for example, such firms would supposedly maximise net revenues per worker rather than profits, would not have the right incentives to maintain their physical capital adequately, or would be inefficient because hierarchies are needed for efficient processing of large amounts of information. Other scholars have answered these criticisms by pointing out that, in each case, the supposed inefficiencies are a product of peculiar modelling assumptions made by the critics. But absent obvious legal restrictions against such firms, economists generally take their rareness or absence to mean that this form is not economically viable for a variety of reasons. For example, Henry Hansmann has argued that the disadvantages of collective decisionmaking by heterogeneous employees might easily outweigh the advantages of common ownership of the capital and labour inputs. According to others, the fact that capitalists have more wealth and better access to credit markets than workers do, and the fact that capitalists can diversify risks better than workers can, also argue against employees having a sizable share of their personal wealth in equity stakes in the firms where they work. (Blair 1999)

It is a pity that Blair has failed to notice the apparent circular reasoning involved in the claim reproduced. Capitalists' wealth is a product of the same ownership relations which it is attempted to explain on the basis of the former. Access to credit, or more general – finance also is a matter of particular institutional arrangements which even within capitalism can be rearranged. And one more comment – Blair's narrow, US-centred horizon does not allow her to notice the thriving co-operative sector[8] whose experiences are most relevant in the context discussed above.

Meanwhile, on the basis of her discussion Blair makes the case for a new thinking about the theory of the firm.

While she admits that "the idea that the firm is a nexus of contracts was a significant insight that helped get scholars thinking about the terms of the relationships among the various participants in firms", she nevertheless deems it necessary to plead in the employee class' (one may shrug at our use of the term in the context of Blair's argument in which the term of class is absent – this is true as far as it goes, but this objection does not take account of the actual presence in the

---

8   The combined membership in co-operatives, according to the International Co-operative Alliance, is more than 800 million people (Jones, Kalmi 2009).

very argument of concepts of class and class interest, only without naming them as such) favour:

> But in probing the nature of corporations and corporate governance it is not enough to look only at relationships between shareholders and managers and to assume that employment relationships are a separable topic. The role played by investments in firm-specific human capital and the problems raised by that role suggest that the nature of the employment relationship is central to the nature of the institutional arrangements that are the essence of modern, large corporations. Economic theorists are now beginning to acknowledge the complex nature of the way employees participate in firms. Hence a few have even defined firms as institutional arrangements developed to elicit contributions by employees to the joint productive effort of the enterprise. If the full range of contributions needed could be adequately elicited through market relationships or explicit contracts, perhaps they would be. But the very fact that they cannot is what calls forth complex organisational forms such as modern corporations. (Blair 1999)

Well put, and this point justifies an introduction of the concept akin to those of market or government failure, namely-corporate or private ownership failure. Blair discusses several ways of going about the problem:

> Holmstrom and Milgrom view firms as systems of incentives. They propose a multitask principal-agent model to address the problems that arise when the tasks the worker is supposed to do are multidimensional, and performance is difficult to measure in some or all of those dimensions. When agents must perform a number of tasks, and their choices about effort and allocation of their time can affect many dimensions of the firm's performance, high-powered incentive structures that reward performance in some dimensions, but neglect performance in other dimensions, can greatly distort the behavior of the agent. (Blair 1999)

This is a pretty common-sensical example of armchair deliberations; from an empirical point of view the above account neglects certain types of labour power whose performance is intrinsically difficult, if not impossible, to measure, such as conceptual employees, performers of pre-material work whose case, as involved in the production of intellectual means of work should be of prime interest to human capital theorists. More broadly, the spread of ascriptive labour power that by definition is not compensated according to performance is much wider. And to round off this brief commentary, in our terms the above passage refers to combined labour power. Blair, referring to the above-quoted passage, writes further:

> Of course, a key feature that distinguishes agents who are 'in' the firm from agents who are on the outside and merely contracting with the firm is the structure of the compensation agreement. Their model explores why 'the

attributes of an employment relationship differ in so many ways from the attributes of a contractor relationship.' Compensation for contractors generally provides for task-specific payments, with all risks of nonperformance borne by the agent, whereas with employees, such risks are generally pooled and borne collectively by the firm itself, so that the agent is paid a regular wage or salary for the duration of employment, regardless of the actual tasks performed. The Holmstrom and Milgrom model implies that, under certain conditions, an optimal incentive structure 'may require the elimination or muting of incentives which in a market relationship would be too strong.' Thus, they conclude, 'the use of low-powered incentives within the firm, although sometimes lamented as one of the major disadvantages of internal organisation, is also an important vehicle for inspiring cooperation and coordination'. (Blair 1999)

The aforementioned distinction refers to a class one – between the employee and autocephalous (traditionally known as the petty bourgeois) class. In addition, Blair's notion of "regular wages/salaries" is consistent with our earlier comments pointing to the need for differentiating between two basic systems of compensation and the respective types of labour power. Interestingly enough, Blair's following ruminations on the distinction mentioned above conclude with a further criticism of human capital theory:

> In comparing the terms on which in-house insurance sales agents typically operate to the terms on which independent sales agents typically operate, for instance, Holmstrom and Milgrom note that employment relationships typically involve lower-powered incentives (such as a fixed base salary and lower commissions), ownership of key assets by the employer (rather than by the employee), and more restrictions on the mode of operation of the employee. They find that the choice between structuring the relationship as an employment one, versus structuring it as one of an independent contractor type, appears to be driven by the relative ease or difficulty of measuring key aspects of performance, more than by the extent of investments in firm-specific human capital. (Blair 1999)

Blair, and very rightly so, draws attention to the diversity of actual working situations, and corresponding compensation arrangements:

> But it seems unlikely that this factor drives this choice in all occupations. Consider production line workers. Assembly line workers who work on large, highly capital-intensive automated assembly lines are typically paid hourly wages, and a variety of other institutional arrangements are used (such as pension funds and collective bargaining) to discourage turnover. By contrast, workers in garment factories are more likely to be paid piece rates, turnover rates are often high, and there are fewer institutional arrangements designed to reduce turnover. In other words, apparel workers are often compensated and treated more like subcontractors than employees. (Blair 1999)

Blair's accounting for the state of affairs described above refers in fact to an important distinction between particularist and universalistic operational labour power – in the garment factory, individual workers can set their own pace at separate sewing machines, whereas in large automated factories, individual workers must learn to function at a pace set for them by the machines and by the other members of the team. Meanwhile, the aforementioned scholar reckons that:

> Holmstrom and Milgrom's model might be used to test the hypothesis that the differences in compensation systems and institutional arrangements between, say, auto factory workers and garment factory workers, are accounted for by the fact that workers on automated assembly lines must make a higher level of investment (that is, exert more 'effort') in learning to work with the particular equipment in the factory and with the particular teammates on the assembly line. (Blair 1999)

This explanation is scarcely convincing; rather, it may be interpreted as a drawback of the human capital theorist who is used to her specific analytical framework and accordingly endeavours to put the facts under consideration in it, even if it means, as in the present case, squeezing them into the incongruent straightjacket.

Hers is essentially the perspective of property rights theory, as the following passage shows as well:

> Holmstrom and Milgrom show the importance of considering the whole mix of incentives facing employees. Instead of seeing firms as 'bundles of assets,' they look at them as constellations of institutional arrangements designed to provide appropriate incentives where cooperation and coordination are especially important.
>
> Their modeling approach falls within the principal-agent paradigm, however, and, as is generally the case with principal-agent models, it does not take into account the incentives facing the principal to renege on the promised payment scheme, or to alter the job design in ways that reduce the payoff to the agent after firm-specific investments have been made. The model also does not explain two other features that distinguish the employment relationship from the independent contractor relationship, features that have been cited as evidence that investments in firm-specific human capital are important. These are the longevities typically observed in the employment relationship in relation to independent contracting relationships and the wage premia associated with tenure. (Blair 1999)

Thus, although she departs in some respects from the principal-agent model which on its part is included within the broader property rights framework, Blair retains the essential features of that approach, including an ambiguous notion of ownership Perhaps more to her liking will be an approach where the notion of the specific figures prominently.[9]

According to Raghuram Rajan and Luigi Zingales, a firm should be defined not as a nexus of contracts, but as a "nexus of specific investments." Rajan and Zingales use an optimal-contract model that is similar to, and builds on, the approach used by Grossman and Hart discussed earlier. Their approach is reminiscent of that used by Aoki, who defined the firm as "an enduring combination of firm-specific resources" and argued that firms should be regarded as combinations of specific labour and capital, and that management should be viewed as mediating between these two interests in making decisions about output levels, investments, and the sharing of firm-level rents.

The authors define a firm as "a collection of commonly owned critical resources, talents, and ideas, and also the people who have access to those resources" (p. 405).

The definition cited by Blair is an example of ideological fiction; at best it registers the fact of the corporation being a group private property, i.e. owned by the body of shareholders. Another aspect of collective ownership present in this context is collective ownership of labour power that may or may not exist within a firm.

In the Rajan and Zingales model, the enterprise requires a physical asset that is specific to the enterprise and two individuals. The total productivity of the enterprise will be maximised if both individuals make specific investments in human capital. But each individual must have access to the physical asset in order to "specialise." If either individual fails to specialise, an non-specialised outsider can be substituted for that individual without loss of total productivity.

Rajan and Zingales distinguish between "ownership" and "power." In their model, "ownership" of the enterprise gives the owner the right to exclude other individuals from access to the physical asset and the right to sell the physical asset to some third party. These rights give the "owner" significant "power" in bargaining over the eventual distribution of rents. But participants can also acquire "power" in another way. Investment by either individual in firm-specific human capital also gives that individual bargaining power in the relationship, because his investment in human capital means that there will be more total rents to share if he stays in the coalition and uses his human capital in the enterprise (Blair 1999).

There are a number of problems involved in the above treatment of ownership. Firstly, it confirms our earlier conclusions regarding Blair's view of the relationship between ownership and control. As if that picture were not sufficiently unclear, the author adds a new dimension in the form of power, which concept, to be frank, adds little to the picture in question. Power to exclude others from the use of one's property is an element traditionally included under the definition of private ownership, and one's ability to sell a given property constitutes indeed one of the two fundamental components of economic ownership. However, further remarks about employees as possessing a kind of countervailing power, to use

---

9   For a more extensive analysis see: Tittenbrun (2011; 2012).

J.K. Galbraith's term, are ill-conceived, look as an attempt to fishing for facts that might be put forward as supporting the view of workforce as an equally powerful side of the corporate equation. At best, Blair's claims might be treated as a clumsy rendering of the fact of high capacity to produce surplus value pertaining to owners of scientifically educated labour power:

Other economists have argued that ownership of the physical asset increases the incentive for the owner to make the optimal investments in human capital. But, Rajan and Zingales point out, ownership of the physical asset also enables the owner to sell the asset, or to share in the rents from the enterprise even if he fails to make firm-specific investments. Hence ownership rights over the physical asset have a doubled-edged effect in this model. They increase the owner's bargaining power and therefore increase his incentive to "specialise" by assuring him that his share of the rents generated by the enterprise will not be expropriated. But they also raise the owner's opportunity cost of specialising, since the owner can extract rents even without specialising.

Well, one would think that to notice the existence of rentiers one need not be a rocket scientist; but Blair apparently thinks otherwise:

> If the negative effects of ownership by either individual dominate the positive incentive effects, Rajan and Zingales show that the optimal investment decisions and production levels cannot be achieved if either of the two potential 'specialisers' owns the physical asset. But remarkably, if the physical asset is owned by an otherwise passive third party, optimal investment decisions and production levels can still be achieved. In this situation, the two individuals who want to participate in the firm would form a coalition and bid collectively for access to the asset, and the right to use the asset in production. Third-party control over the physical asset helps encourage both individuals to make the optimal firm-specific investments, because it, in effect, enables the two individuals to make binding commitments not to use control over the asset strategically to extract rents from the other individual.[...] Their third party is assumed to get an arbitrarily small fraction of the total rents, and the party's only task is to select from among multiple coalitions bidding for access rights to the physical assets. The third party naturally selects the coalition that will produce the highest total rents, the bulk of which go not to the third party monitor (as in Alchian and Demsetz), but to the coalition members who have invested in specialised human capital. (Blair 1999)

The above-cited argument is a typical example of deductive reasoning-given some definite premises, specific conclusions follow. But the problem is, how these abstract propositions match the real world of capitalist economy peopled, as opposed to this modern Robinsonade, not by some elusive dyads of partners confronted with an equally abstract "third party", but very concrete holders of collective or individual, and many other types of labour power, takeover artists, pension fund managers, private equity firms and so on, and so forth. And Blair in what follows also draws attention to the empirically problematic quality of premises the theorists under consideration embrace:

> Rajan and Zingales interpret their 'third-party owner' as providing an explanation for 'ownership' of firms by passive outside investors, or shareholders.

> But this is a highly implausible interpretation. The third-party 'owner' in their story is restricted to receiving an arbitrarily small return because that party does not provide anything critical to production. That role could be played by anyone except, notably, any of the active participants in the enterprise, or any participant who contributes something critical.

> Instead, the role of the third party is to keep control of the assets out of the hands of any of the active participants in the firm, precisely so that those active parties will not use control over the assets to gain strategic advantage for themselves at the expense of the other participants and thereby cause the coalition to fall apart. An alternative, and more plausible, interpretation of Rajan and Zingales's work might be that it provides insight into the role played by creating a separate legal entity under the law (the corporation), which acts as the repository of all the property rights over assets used in production, and over output, and assigning decision rights over this legal entity to an independent board of directors with fiduciary obligations to their firms. (Blair 1999)

The above assertion goes too far inasmuch as Blair imperceptibly oversteps the line dividing the economic and the legal-ownership, as stressed over and again throughout this book, is not a legal relation. Blair goes on to say that:

> Rajan and Zingales have taken a significant step toward integrating models of the employment relationship and the associated incentive issues raised by investments in firm-specific human capital into a theory of the firm. But their model is still limited by the fact that it follows the two-period structure. [...] From the perspective of repeated games, each act of self-restraint on the part of participants in the firm can be seen as a 'firm-specific investment' whose value can be realised if the coalition stays together, but not if it falls apart. (Blair 1999)

The above argument demonstrates again how elastic and dilutable human capital framework can be-given such a concept of investment, regular work performed by those who produce surplus value, and thus the source of investment in the firm, and typify variable capital, which is a form of investment itself, might be classed as an investment, this time on the part of a given employee.

Blair's further conclusion touches on our earlier considerations about the various types of capitalism. For it should be emphasised that albeit an intuitive presumption assigns the varieties in question to different regions of the world, such as continental Europe and Asia on the one hand, and the Anglo-Saxon world on the other, it is not adequate, since what is at stake is the two different modes of economic activity that may be present also in those parts of the world where the alternative system predominates. Thus, trust, which is prominent in stakeholder capitalism, may well play a considerable role in some, say, Australian firms:

> The cumulative result of a large number of such acts of self-restraint could represent a sizable investment in a type of firm-specific human capital that one might call 'trust' or 'culture.' The firm can be viewed as a nexus of these investments, and for the full value of the investments to be realised, key participants in the firm must be kept involved. Moreover, it may be necessary for the 'firm' that comprises this coalition of individuals and specific investments to have a permanent legal status separate from any of the participants, to be the repository of the reputational capital and the key property rights. (Blair 1999)

Blair's terminological choice above should be considered unfortunate-whatever one means by culture, and an extremely general character of the term does not make this task easier, trust can be regarded, if anything, as part of the former, and not its equivalent.

This criticism does not mean that one should treat equally critically the argument by Blair cited below in that it rightly brings out some questionable aspects of neoclassical orthodoxy (which e.g. posits the completeness of markets):

> Scholarly work on the theory of the firm, both in law and in economics, has perhaps fixed too long on one particular relationship (between shareholders and managers) and on one approach to modelling corporate relationships (the principal-agent approach). The implicit assumption behind this approach has been that a firm is a bundle of assets that belongs to shareholders, so that the only relationship that matters is that between the owners of the assets and the managers hired to manage them. More sophisticated analyses have acknowledged the importance of other relationships but have overlooked their significance for corporate governance questions by assuming that they are all governed by nice, neat, complete contracts, contracts that effectively motivate participants to contribute their ideas, or skills, or effort, and either protect them from risks in the enterprise or completely compensate them for the risks that they bear. Interest is now turning to actual contracting difficulties and alternative models that address more directly the complexities of the human input into corporations. These models have provided rich insights into many noncontractual institutional arrangements used to govern the relationships among a variety of participants in firms. Although these models have had little influence on legal scholarship to date, arrangements for governing the relationships among employees, and between employees and the firm, can no longer be treated as something separate from corporate governance.

In particular, contractarian legal scholars need to recognise that certain kinds of multilateral and multidimensional relationships and agreements among individuals may only be possible in a legal environment that grants separate legal status to the entity that serves as the repository of the specific investment involved in the relationship. It may be necessary for the law to assign fiduciary responsibilities to the individuals whose job is to govern this entity, whether as directors or as managers. In other words, contractarians should reconsider the merits of an older school of legal scholarship that emphasises that a corporation is a separate entity, and more than the sum of its parts. Under the entity view of the firm, a corporation is something apart from each of its participants, something that cannot protect itself through contract, but that needs to be protected by fiduciary duties and corporation law from possible predatory behavior by any of the parties. With a better understanding of the full and complex dimensions of the contracting problem involved in organising production, it should be possible to develop a renewed appreciation of the 'entity' view of firms in the law. (Blair 1999)

It is not our aim to interfere in legal debates, but as a sociologist of the economy, those willing to follow Blair's recommendations, are well advised to remember about the fictitious quality of the concept concerned.

The issue of ownership is so pivotal that it is worthwhile to consider also Blair's another paper in which she deals with it, since it will possibly give rise to a few novel insights.

Marx and Engels' argument that the emergence of joint-stock company brought out the redundancy of shareowners, since it showed that a company can function without them playing any effective role in its management is well-known. What is less known, or overlooked, however, is a cognate argument put forward in the ground-breaking treatise by Berle and Means (1991), who argued that the separation of ownership and control, by unbundling the traditional attributes of ownership, deprived stockholders of their sole claim to corporate profits and entitled the people to demand that corporations be managed in the interests of workers and "all society" (1991: 312).

Blair is apparently inspired by not only the famous Berle and Means' thesis concerning the collapse of traditional legal concept of property, but also by its normative implications mentioned above. What she overlooks, however, is a contradiction in Berle and Means' argument-if one argues that the breakdown of property brought about the divorce of ownership and control, then either the first or the second part of the proposition can be true, but not the two at the same time; if ownership ceases to exist, then it makes no sense to speak about its divorce from control. As a result of this omission Blair embraces such two-pronged definition of ownership, glossing over its ambiguity: "Ownership is the right to an asset's residual returns and to control over the asset" (Blair 1995: 277).

The ambiguity here lies in the fact that the two relations identified above may not converge in one subject (which precisely constituted the substance of Berle and Means' thesis) in which situation one has to decide which of them to use in order to indicate the owner.

Blair argues that shareowners are not a corporation's sole residual claimants and therefore should not be deemed its sole owners and granted exclusive control. Because many employees embody firm-specific human capital, they too are rewarded with a share of the firm's residual returns (Blair 1995: 15–16, 230–32). Again, this claim is not free of ambiguity inasmuch as it is not entirely clear if it is simply a statement of fact, or rather a normative proposition referring to a desirable – but not yet existing – state of affairs. For Blair argues both that workers who have firm-specific skills often already share in residual returns, and, on the other side, that such workers should share in both residual returns (perhaps through stock ownership) and control (Blair 1995: 15–16, 326).

Blair's starting point is her acknowledgment of a nearly universal consensus among scholars that a corporation's primary goal is to maximise the value of the stockholders' shares (Blair 1995: 12, 95–115, 122). Under shareholder capitalism, this is indeed deemed a corporation's proper purpose because shareholders bear the residual risk and, accordingly, "receive the residual returns from the firm's business" (Blair 1995: 15, 228–9). Others who deal with a company, including employees, protect their interests by contract (Blair 1995: 210). The above-mentioned exposure to risk gives the former group the greatest incentive to monitor the company to ensure that it maximises profits. Thus, the company should be focused on enhancing stock value. Blair calls into question this majority view on efficiency grounds, drawing on the work of economists who have long recognised the existence of firm-specific human capital.

Holders of such firm-specific skills, she argues, like shareholders, share (or ought/are able to-this is not clear) in the firm's residual returns (Blair 1995: 230–32). Firm-specific human capital is valuable only to the firm at which the workers have obtained it through training and experience. Once the workers develop such capital, therefore, they are in a position to bargain for compensation higher than the market value of their general human capital; as such workers are valuable to the firm benefiting from their enhanced productivity and thus keen on retaining them, the firm has an incentive to pay them such higher compensation, effectively sharing the quasi-rents generated by the firm-specific human capital (Blair 1995: 251, 256–7). Blair argues that such compensation represents sharing in residual returns, since it is contingent on the success of the firm (Blair 1995: 231, 257). Whether one does like Blair's stance towards corporate governance or not, it must be acknowledged that – on the capitalistic logic at least – her conclusion that workers' exposure to their employers' varying fortunes mandates giving them a share in ownership and control hardly follows, to which we shall return below. From a certain point of view, paying a portion of workers' compensation in corporate shares exposes them to an even bigger risk than that which they normally have to bear; in the second case, if the company goes bankrupt, they lose jobs, in the former-an additional financial loss. And it is hard to believe that giving the workforce one or two seats in the supervisory board or board of directors can prevent such developments.

Be that as it may, on the basis of her argument above, Blair argues that managing a firm so as to maximise only the residual gains to stockholders leads to inefficiency in the event that the firm's revenues suffice to provide returns to firm-specific human capital but not to equity. Here again, Blair falls into contradiction-she forgets that among those equity holders are also employees who by virtue of possessing firm-specific human capital are entitled to participate also in equity capital-both as a reward and a protection. It is evident that a great deal of the theorist's problems stems from her misrecognition of labour power (and variable capital) as human capital. If the former concepts were used, it would be much harder to conceive of employees as equal business partners, as it were, of (true) capitalists.

> This critique does not detract from Blair's sincerity in her attack on existing legal and business doctrine as one that encourages management to fire workers or even discontinue operations, squandering human capital that should remain productively employed (Blair 1995: 256–7).

Yes, activities of asset-strippers, corporate predators, and the like remain harmful irrespective of how one conceptualises its victims: as human capital, or labour power holders. Which, naturally, does not alter the fact that even policy recommendations one submits to corporate governance lawyers would gain enormously in clarity and consistency if they were cleansed of misnomers.

> And Blair's policy recommendations are that directors should recognise a duty to maximise returns to firm-specific human capital as well as equity (Blair 1995: 239–40, 324–6).

This postulate might be rendered in terms of what in fact is a clash of two alternative capitalist modes of economic activity: stakeholder capitalism and stockholder capitalism. Blair, however, is neither a revolutionary, nor a radical.

Although she hints at changing "[t]he law and the culture of the boardroom" (Blair 1995: 239), she advocates no major changes in corporate law; rather, she favours increasing employee ownership and control under existing laws. She urges firms to experiment with various ways of achieving this goal, such as employee stock ownership plans (ESOPs), worker-management committees, and corporate pension-fund investment in employees, own firms (Blair 1995: 328–37). She also urges a change in boards' conception of corporate purpose. Whether or not workers own stock, she argues, those with firm-specific human capital should be deemed stakeholders with rights to share in control of the firm and in its residual returns (but she does not clarify whether directors, duty to non-stockholder workers should be legally enforceable by some form of fiduciary duty transcending the employment contract) (Blair 1995: 326).

Such moderation on the part of the human capital scholar' in question may stem from the fact that existing corporate law, as she notes, does not, strictly speaking, compel boards to act solely to maximise stockholder value (Blair 1995: 93, 211–23). A corporation may be chartered to pursue any lawful purpose), and many a US corporation complements its unrelenting pursuit of profit maximisation with some social goals. During ordinary operations, directors owe fiduciary duties to the corporation and are free to weigh competing claims of employees, stockholders, and other constituents within the mantle of the business judgment rule (Blair 1995: 56–8). Even when a bidder for a firm offers stockholders a premium for their shares, the target board has some discretion to weigh the interests of stakeholders such as employees in deciding whether to resist the offer. In practice, however, this margin of freedom is limited: in the midst of the 1980s takeover wave, the Supreme Court of Delaware, the leading state of incorporation for large firms, held that target boards could consider takeover bids, impact on constituencies other than stockholders in deciding whether to resist offers. The court, though, soon limited this aspect of board discretion, holding that once a firm is for sale, its board may consider other constituencies, but only to the extent such consideration is rationally related to benefiting stockholders. Furthermore, and more importantly, anti-takeover stakeholder statutes do not create enforceable rights for workers. Even more significantly, the prevailing attitude informing corporate law, let alone its practical implementation, remains that corporations are to serve the stockholders by maximising share value. Accordingly, only stockholders may legally enforce directors, fiduciary duties, while employees are left to their contracts. Widespread corporate layoffs, even in profitable firms at a time of economic growth, glaringly show how precarious is the situation of labour power (alias human capital) owners under existing law.

As hinted above, however, Blair's argument that workers should share in control and residual returns suffers from several weaknesses. First, as she admits, economists have yet to devise a reliable measure of firm-specific human capital (Blair 1995: 263), Since (as Blair acknowledges) workers are compensated for their general skills by their contractual pay and benefits (Blair 1995: 230, 263–5), the inability separately to measure firm-specific skills undermines her claim that appropriate shares in residual returns and control, commensurate with firm-specific skills, can be determined.

The following argument, apart from its critical function in relation to Blair's thesis, serves to illuminate the divergence between regular capital and what passes as human capital:

> Financial capital is homogeneous and quantifiable, so it is simple to apportion both votes and dividend and liquidation rights among stockholders. Human capital, by contrast, is difficult to measure, diverse, and often not attributable to any particular employee or group of employees. (Chandrasekharb 1996)

Realistic enough, the only trouble being that the above observation is out of kilter with the whole idea of human capital. The aforementioned assertion acknowledges the inalienable in the modern industrial firm role of co-operation, in other words, in terms of socioeconomic structuralism – collective labour power.

Accordingly, it is held that teamwork skills are one form of firm-specific human capital; even more to the point, Benjamin Klein (1985: 199, 207–8), argues that firm-specific team expertise not attributable to individual or small group capable of withholding it is owned by equity owners of the firm.

In socio-economic terms, the above contention is valid to the extent that co-operation normally enhances productivity whose effects may be appropriated by the aforementioned shareowners.

In turn, Ronald J. Gilson and Robert H. Mnookin (1985: 313, 357, 368 (1985) note (fully consistent with the misnomer logic, shifting and extending the meaning of the term under consideration) that: "such firm-specific human capital as reputation and client relationships often resides in firm as a whole". Along somewhat similar lines, Chandrasekharb 1996: 28) points out: "Giving workers control rights with which to appropriate a share of a firm's profits risks overcompensating them relative to their productivity. Making firms answerable to different groups with diverse, sometimes hostile interests (such as investors and various categories of workers) would also impose substantial management costs as participants struggled to set policy and allocate rewards among themselves". Blair acknowledges this problem (Blair 1995: 326),

> but her sanguine acceptance of the fragmentation of corporate boards into rival factions representing labour and capital is unpersuasive. Corporations with conflicting goals and divided boards would surely be less efficient than those devoted primarily to seeking profits and directed by boards answerable to one group alone. (Chandrasekharb 1996)

If Chandrasekharb considers Blair's argument unpersuasive, his own is much less so-it utterly ignores especially German experiences of co-determination which indicate, to the contrary, that such a mixed along class lines composition of boards is not only economically, but much more important, socially, efficient inasmuch as it materially contributes to class peace, which on its part (costs of industrial action) contributes to the bottom line. Besides, this kind of argument is kind of ideologically and politically dangerous; how come that political democracy ought not to be extended into the economic sphere? Whilst in the political realm modern Western Democracies better or worse implement the principle of representative rule and universal vote, the business firm is still largely a matter of oligarchic and hierarchic rule which most often has no resemblance to democratic systems at all. This creates the systemic, or formational, if you will, divergence between the two structures under consideration, and thereby raises the question of legitimacy of the whole capitalist democracy. On top of that, Chandrasekharb ignores the well-known problem of collective action encountered by what only seemingly is a single and unified body of shareholders ; the point is not profit as such, since its accumulation, or reinvestment is an essential precondition of corporate survival, and thus of interest also to the workforce. The crux of the matter is how this profit is to be distributed, i.e. what is the concrete shape of property relations.

Therefore, more interesting – from the viewpoint of our central question regarding ownership – is the above-mentioned economist's next argument:

> Finally, Blair's argument that workers with firm-specific skills should be given new rights to control their firms and share in profits does not adequately acknowledge that such workers already are rewarded for their firm-specific skills, and that there are important reasons for using arm's-length bargaining rather than employee ownership to determine worker compensation. [...] To the extent that compensation for firm-specific skills is not fixed but contingent, such pay is better understood not as an attribute of ownership, but as a form of bonding to control the moral hazard of shirking and as a bargained sharing of the profits generated by such skills so as to maintain the relationship between workers and firm. This is advantageous to both sides because workers with such skills are more productive at their current employer both than they would be elsewhere, and than new hires lacking their skills. Protecting workers' interests in such contingent compensation by means of a share in control, rather than by means of the ongoing, incomplete contract between workers and the firm, would vitiate the compensation's bonding effect and impair the firm's flexibility when changed circumstances reduce the skills' value. (Chandrasekharb 1996)

The class significance, and one would add here – bias of this argument is crystal clear, of course. Indeed, in that sense it fits better in the broad human capital framework whose main –intentional or not – class function is the imposition of false class consciousness on the working, and more broadly-employee class, talking them into the acceptance of self-identity as capitalists. But the above-cited passage involves some theoretical issues as well. Compensation on the basis of qualifications applies to the holders of ascriptive labour power. On the other hand, by itself making employee wages and salaries contingent on the firm's profits, that is to say, the effect of joint labour of the workforce indeed does not need to express capital ownership, but it refers to collective labour power. However, under specific conditions, such a share in profits may indeed represent not a transformed form of wages, as in the former case, but genuine ownership of capital. This, however, depends on the magnitude of benefits received by employees, and not on the mode (through collective bargaining or not) such benefits are secured.

Chandrasekharb's remark underlining the bonding effect of ownership allegedly pertaining to employees as holders of human capital is also of interest; one may sympathise with Blair's progressive views, yet it is her critic's more sober assessment that is much nearer the truth given the realities of stockholder capitalism.

And, by the way, it is fully realised by other human capital theorists as well. The authors of another chapter in the book under discussion argue that "job incumbents often have more skill and knowledge than new recruits, so the departure of these employees would impose significant search and training costs on the firm.

This can lead the firm to offer stock ownership and deferred profit sharing, which tie current actions to future benefits and thus provide an incentive to workers to protect their investments by acting on behalf of the firm's long-term interests" (Avner Ben-Ner et al. 2000). And in yet another chapter its authors point to what in effect is a degree of real, socio-economic (as distinct from formal-legal) curtailment of such plans' beneficiaries' labour power ownership: "when a significant portion of pay is at risk, allowing workers to share in the rents earned by the firm makes it costly for workers to leave since the high degree of firm specificity of their skills makes it unlikely they can earn similar rents elsewhere. Importantly, these pay arrangements also signify a partial recognition that workers have ownership claims on the firm" (Appelbaum, Berg 2000).

Whether such contingent, inclusive of equity-based, forms of compensation do involve ownership of not only labour power, but also of capital, does not depend on the juristic or quasi-legal recognition of a given relationship, but, as noted above, on very definite socio-economic realities. It is also on the latter that the extent of limitation of one's ownership of labour power hiding behind the seemingly benign term "bonding" is dependent.

Specific and General Human Capital

The concept of specific human capital, prominent in the discussion in the previous section, owing to its relevance to the pivotal question of ownership deserves a more extensive discussion.

The concept of firm-specific capital was originally developed by Gilson and Mnookin according to whom, the paradigmatic example of firm-specific capital is IBM's relationship with Cravath, Swaine, and Moore, which transcended any loyalties to individual Cravath lawyers (1985: 354).

This usage of the concept in question is not exactly typical for reasons that are not difficult to grasp; the notion of capital is here extended to cover non-employees of a given firm. Under a more common approach, it is posited that a worker's productivity in the labour market is determined by his stock of general and specific human capital (Becker, 1975).

The difference is that investments in general human capital, which increase worker productivity in a variety of jobs (thus referring to our concept of general labour power), typically take the form of formal or informal education, including vocational training. The presumption is, the costs of acquiring general human capital are borne by the worker, an explanation being that a firm has no incentive to fund training that increases a worker's productivity at competing firms. Accordingly, under this standard framework, the worker reaps the benefits in terms of higher wages. Equally relevant to ownership relations are investments in what is termed specific human capital which are acquired on the job, and which increase a worker's productivity in the firm in which the training occurs, but not at other firms. According to human capital theory, the costs and benefits of firm-specific training are shared between workers and firms. The firm pays the worker part of the increased productivity associated with investments in specific human capital, because it needs to retain the worker to recoup its investments, but not all benefits go to the worker, which is purportedly justified by the fact that his or her productivity in other firms is based only on her general human capital (Oi, 1962).

Ownership relations in the form of distribution of gains from an enhanced through training-on-the-job labour power (firm-specific human capital, in terms of the theory under investigation) is one thing, the concrete shape of specific labour power, quite another, and very important, too, as it determines a worker's functioning on the labour power market, or his/her occupational, and lateral socio-economic mobility.

To begin with, as opposed to what the phrase "firm-specific human capital", might suggest, recent evidence shows that specific skills might be tied more to an occupation than to a particular firm. Several studies have shown that the coefficient on firm tenure in a wage regression declines if one controls for occupational or industry tenure (Gibbons et al., 2006; Kambourov and Manovskii, 2002; Parent, 2000). Similarly, evidence from displaced workers demonstrates that wage losses are much lower if workers return to the sector of their pre-displacement job (Neal, 1999).

But even if one relaxes the aforementioned standard assumption to concur that human capital and related job search models might be built on the assumption that specific skills are tied either to a firm or an occupation, this does not save those conceptions from criticism either. The above-mentioned "assumption implies that specific skills are fully lost when an individual leaves that particular firm or occupation" (Gathmann, Schönberg 2006).

The last sentence justifies our interest in the conception of specific human capital from the standpoint mentioned earlier-it refers, in our terms, to a reduction of ownership in a given individual's labour power. The core concept concerned, however, may not be precise enough.

In contradistinction to the common in the human capital literature assumption to the effect that "labour market skills are either fully general or specific to the firm", the aforementioned two scholars have used patterns in mobility and wages to analyze how portable specific skills are in the labour power, or in their terminology-labour market. Using data on tasks performed in different jobs along with a large panel on complete working histories and wages, they found that labour market skills are partially transferable across occupations. Specifically, they found that "individuals move to occupations with similar task requirements" (Gathmann, Schönberg 2006).

To illustrate, "…based on the task data, the skill requirements of a baker and a cook are very similar. In contrast, switching from a banker to an unskilled construction worker would be the most distant move observable" (Gathmann, Schönberg 2006) in their data. All in all, their key finding is that "individuals are much more likely to move to similar occupations than suggested by standard turnover models" (Gathmann, Schönberg 2006).

Similarly, another researcher points to "the importance of skills that are not truly specific to given industries, but rather specific to a set of jobs that are associated with the intersection of certain occupations and industries. Future research in this area must confront the task of defining job categories that capture important skill specificities" (Neal 1995: 669–70).

Two economists pick up on this kind of observation to argue that there is a growing trend away from skill development that can be categorised as strictly either industry or occupation-specific – witness the growing importance of computer literacy across a broad range of jobs and industries. To the extent that this is the case, quasi-specific human capital is becoming a more and more important element of the human capital accumulation process. (Novos, Waldman 1997)

The aforementioned scholars clarify their conceptual innovation. They recall that Becker's 1962) considered seminal human capital article drew attention to the polar cases of general and specific human capital. They also point out that Becker himself (1962: 17) recognised that "much on-the-job training is neither completely specific nor completely general..." such intermediate cases – a key one of which they propose to term quasi-specific human capital – have received rather little attention.

> In the simplest intermediate case, all alternative employers value the productivity increases associated with human capital identically, with the valuation falling between that for fully general and fully specific human capital. [...] Since the value of a worker's human capital does not vary across alternative employers, the amount of human capital which would be lost in a move is uncorrelated with whether, in fact, the worker moves (Novos, Waldman 1997).

They point out that:

> in reality, however, the increase in productivity associated with human capital often does vary across alternative employers. This paper focuses on a form of human capital – which we call quasi-specific – which captures this idea. In particular, we consider environments in which the value that alternative employers place on human capital is high for some firms and low for others. Job search thus becomes relevant because a worker might not, in any specific period, receive an offer from a firm that places a high value on the worker's accumulated human capital. (Novos, Waldman 1997)

Further, they specify the relationship between their conceptual proposal and the pair of concepts most commonly used in that context:

Industry- or occupation-specific human capital is general human capital if a worker will never move outside the industry or occupation. If the probability of such a move is greater than zero, however, then industry-or occupation-specific human capital should be regarded as quasi-specific (Novos, Waldman 1997).

The two writers concerned justify the need for their concept, which justification constitutes at the same time a critique of the received human capital literature which, neglecting this concept, shows significant gaps and flaws:

The concept of quasi-specific human capital is useful for a number of reasons. It explains job transitions which cannot easily be explained by recourse to general, firm or industry-specific human capital. [...]in a world in which job search is a relevant aspect of labour markets, the presence of quasi-specific human capital has interesting methodological implications for both returns to tenure and the extent to which human capital accumulation is specific. Because the amount of human capital lost by workers who move is less than the amount which is specific for similar workers who stay, there is a downward bias in estimates of the return to tenure, according less importance to specific human capital than is warranted. (Novos, Waldman 1997)

The Authors under consideration illustrate their conceptual innovation by:

Lou Gerstner's move from being the CEO of RJR Nabisco to being the CEO of IBM. He had no IBM or industry-specific experience, [but] the human capital he had accumulated elsewhere was central to what IBM needed in a chief executive. To quote James Burke, who led IBM's search: 'What I didn't understand as much as I should have, and what IBM didn't understand enough, was the rate of change in this industry. I don't think any of us understood [...] how much smaller, entrepreneurial companies can exploit that rapid pace of change. They move quickly and they love to take risk. And I see those qualities in Lou.' [*NY Times*, 27 March 1993, 1]. According to Burke, Mr. Gerstner had acquired human capital which was not valued equally by all firms, and was particularly highly valued by firms operating in environments characterised by rapid change. In turn, Mr. Gerstner's move to IBM can be seen as an example of our description of the job transition process when human capital is quasi-specific. [...] Quasi-specific human capital fits neatly into Sicherman and Galor's theory of career mobility. In their framework individuals [...] would not want to accumulate only firm, or even industry, specific human capital, but human capital appropriate to their desired career paths. Quasi-specific human capital is exactly the type of human capital such people would be interested in accumulating. (Novos, Waldman 1997)

Without questioning the validity of Novos and Waldman's point, it is important to draw attention to their human-capital bias-they impute that employees move to other firms and jobs in search of a new human capital, which is, of course, even leaving aside an otherwise fundamental fact that the core concept is a misnomer, a gross over-interpretation – occupational and job mobility is driven by a rather more mundane motivation to get higher wages, or better working conditions, and by no stretch of imagination this can be superseded by the quest for elusive human capital. In the case of managerial class such moves may indeed have something in common with capital, but understood as equity – executive stock options, or "golden hellos", are merely some of the relevant examples.

Ironically, the point just made is implicit in Novos and Waldman's case for quasi-specific human capital as being central to empirical studies estimating the return to tenure:

> Consider Apple Computer's hiring of Gil Amelio as its chairman and CEO in February 1996. Mr. Amelio, who was hired away from a similar position at National Semiconductor, received a significant increase in remuneration from Apple. The computer industry certainly had other CEOs with similar backgrounds, who, in February 1996, would have been interested in a job switch. Invariably, however, unless they received a sufficiently attractive offer to move we wouldn't have learned about their desires. Assume for the moment that among this group of CEOs there existed a CEO, Mr. X, demographically identical to Mr. Amelio and with a similar earnings history, and earning what Mr. Amelio earned at National Semiconductor. Assume further that the best alternative employment offer Mr. X received in his search was significantly below what he was then earning, and that he thus decided to stay where he was. The observable data – Mr. Amelio earning more than Mr. X, but at a new firm – would suggest that most of the human capital was general. The observable data does not capture the fact that Mr. X didn't move because he couldn't find a sufficiently good match for his accumulated human capital.

> This story captures exactly what we have in mind. Workers who switch employers, like Mr. Amelio, will need on average to sacrifice little human capital.

> As a result, one might easily conclude that most human capital is general, since the observable data indicates that little human capital is lost when workers switch employers. This, however, is an incorrect conclusion. Workers who do not switch employers, such as Mr. X, frequently only stay because moving would result in a significant sacrifice of human capital. (Novos, Waldman 1997)

And regardless of a number of reservations one entertains towards some of the specifics, the thrust of Novos and Waldman's argument is sound, and useful, too, as it points to some shortcomings of orthodox human capital framework. Under socio-economic structuralism, its theory of labour power stipulates the direction and distance of occupational and social mobility between previous and next job by interpreting those positions through the prism of the three main types of labour power: intellectual, affective, and manual, the thesis being that an employee moves to a job most close to the profile of his or her previous one. It is assumed that each job, or, more exactly task, is characterised by some mix of all of three components, but typically one of them will predominate, acting as kind of occupational magnet.

PART II:
SOCIAL CAPITAL

If the advocates of the concept of human capital could at least attempt to make the case for their favourite on the grounds that its applications concern largely the economic, which likens it to its truly economic original, in the case of social capital such an argument would be more difficult to make-because of its much wider, and predominantly non-economic at that, area of application. This claim alone, in conjunction with a reminder that in the former case even that economic focus has not proved sufficient to prevent the concept in question from being a misnomer, may prompt a suspicion that the same classification applies to social capital. And indeed, the first section of this chapter endeavours to prove this is the case.

Chapter 5
Social Capital as Civic Engagement

That the concept concerned is a misnomer can be gleaned even from the very circumstances of its birth alone.

Although its origins are claimed to go back to classic authors such as Adam Smith and Montesquieu (Sturgess 1997, Woolcock 1998, Schuller et al. 2000), it was an otherwise obscure writer going under the name of Lyda J. Hanifan who introduced the term into use in "The Community Center", published in Boston in 1920:

> In the use of the phrase social capital I make no reference to the usual [understanding] of the term capital, except in a figurative sense. I do not refer to real estate, or to personal property or to cold cash, but rather to that in life which tends to make these tangible substances count for most in the daily lives of people, namely goodwill, fellowship, mutual sympathy and social intercourse....
> (Hanifan 1916)

The reader's attention may be drawn to the aforementioned author's awareness of metaphorical nature of the concept in question, which has been somewhere along the way lost is by its subsequent users.

Specifically, Hanifan's notion of social capital is, as she herself makes no bones about, built on the metaphor of economic capital. Her guiding metaphor was very specifically "...the joint stock Corporation [...] She was, after all, writing at just the time when capitalism was reaching its maturity in the vertically integrated joint stock Corporation (Chandler 1962) – and at a time when that same system of capitalist production heaped up greater and greater concentrations of plant, housing, and work force in its signature creation, the industrial city. For more conventional observers, the industrial city was a social pox – a magnet for the unwashed, a clattering disturbance of nature's slow rhythms, a profit-turning evil from which the bourgeoisie should take the money and run" (Fishman 1987).

Apart from other failings of which below, one wonders, without regressing to any idealisation of lifestyle in the countryside or other small communities, how one can consider the subject without ever mentioning some classic distinction known in the history of sociological thought, such as *Gemeinschaft* and *Gesellschaft*, and an array of similar ones, whose significance is inconsistent with the judgments put forward by the prophets of industrialism. Take Simmel, for instance. He was far from condemning the modern epoch and capitalism or money economy in general, but his view was dialectical throughout – he precisely saw that the very merits of the commodity-money economy produced at the same time a plethora of its grave economic, and notably social ills, so that the reader of Simmel has, frankly, a somewhat strange feeling hearing to what heights had been elevated Putnam's work (to be discussed later) which, in terms of a metaphor (at least in the present author's view) occupies the ground floor, while Simmel's treatise, the top floor of the same skyscraper.

But take the following statement: "For all its smoke and noise, the industrial city was a dynamo for the production of capital – most obviously economic capital, but also social capital" (Rey 2002: xii).

The above claim is a clear case of logical fallacy going under the name of *petitio principii* – the conclusion appears as a logical derivation from the premise, but the latter is not substantiated separately from the argument itself, so that the conclusion adds nothing beyond what has been already assumed in the premise. To put it in simpler terms, any substantive claims concerning social capital hinge upon the specific definition of the latter, which, given that the term (at least in this usage) is new, is a stipulative one, that is, neither correct nor incorrect, not able of being proved or disproved. In still other words, the above-mentioned definition of social capital is a convention that the author wants to impose, which is fine on the condition that one keeps in mind this, its conventional quality, and does not confuse the latter with substantive reality. Rey points out as well that:

> Several others, including urbanist Jane Jacobs, have since independently discovered this idea, and Robert Putnam has made it part of the ordinary language with his Bowling Alone. But the importance of this idea owes a great deal to its historical origin, so it is worth taking the time to situate [it...] the historical moment that provoked Hanifan's spark of insight.

> When she wrote her essay, Hanifan was State Supervisor of Rural Schools for the very rural state of West Virginia. Like Putnam eight decades later, she looked at her human environment through the lens of social capital and saw its absence: 'That there is today almost a total lack of such social capital in rural districts throughout the country need not be retold. ...Everybody who has made either a careful study or close observations of country life conditions knows that to be true' (Hanifan 1916, 131). Hanifans task was defined by the question, 'How could these conditions be made better?':

> In community building as in business organisation and expansion there must be an accumulation of capital before constructive work can be done, In building up a large business enterprise of modern proportions, there must first be an accumulation of capital from a large number of individuals. When the financial resources...have been brought together...they take the form of a business Corporation whose purpose is to produce an article of consumption – steel, copper, bread, clothing – or to provide personal conveniences – transportation, electricity, thoroughfares. The people benefit by having such products and conveniences available for their daily needs, while the capitalists benefit from

the profits reserved to themselves – Now we may easily pass from the business Corporation over to the social Corporation, the community, and find many points of similarity. The individual is helpless socially if left entirely to himself. Even the association of members of one's own family fails to satisfy.... If he may come into contact with his neighbors, and they with other neighbors, there will be an accumulation of social capital, which may immediately satisfy his social needs and which may bear a social potentiality sufficient to substantial improvement of living conditions for the whole community. The community as a whole will benefit by the cooperation of all its parts, while the individual will find in his associations the advantages of the help, the sympathy, and the fellowship of his neighbors. (131).

Both merits and the very necessity of human co-operation are indeed uncontroversial, what is disputable whether it does need any new label, which, in addition, has the weakness of being historically specific-since capital appeared in the history of humanity much later than co-operation. Rey does not see any contradiction between his appraisal of Hanifan's "insight" and his own underscoring the historicity of her original:

Hanifan's explicit model is the joint stock Corporation, and her implicit trope is, of all things, the dense neighborhood of the industrial city – dense in people, dense in social connections, dense in civic associations, dense in retail proprietorship, dense in ward politics. Unlike the patchwork isolation of the countryside, where neighbors are too distant for neighborliness, and where lives are lived so diffusely that trust is limited to family, the city is a great factory for social capital. Hanifan sees the absence of dense connectivity as a great disadvantage for rural places – and, by implication, a great advantage of urban places. […] urban density of the sort which prevailed in Hanifan's day generates and sustains 'networks that bind and lubricate interactions. (McLean, Schultz, Steger 2002)

The reader then learns that:

Hanifan saw the absence of social capital in cross-section, looking from the countryside into the city; Putnam saw it in historical perspective, looking backward at the twentieth century. They were both seeing the same story, which consists in the process by which capitalism first built the socially dense city and then dismantled it. (Rey 2002)

Rey's subsequent illustrations are worth citing as well because they illuminate the meaning of social networks, interaction, etc.:

By the World War I era, these cities were at their midsummer's day with immense economic energy and exceedingly dense patterns of social interaction. New Haven in that period may serve as an illustration, […]

- Retail density in the neighborhoods so great that more than 600 groceries served a city of about 160,000, one store for every 270 people or about 90 households.
- A 'civic fauna' of fraternal and sororal associations, athletic teams, churches, temples, and neighborhood associations roughly ten times denser than what exists today. [...]
- A poverty of indirect, electronic communication, encouraging close face-to-face interaction.
- The near-total absence of broadcast media. (Rey 2002: xvi)

And Rey further argues, and rightly so, for the historically-specific conjuncture of developments that gave birth to the above-mentioned phenomena:

this depended on an historical accident, a concatenation of technological, institutional, and cultural forces that had begun to unravel even before Hanifan's writing. (Rey 2002)

Conditioned by several important chiefly technological developments, with a great deal of encouragement – prodding, manipulation, even bribery – from capitalist enterprise, the great majority of American households have rejected the dense urban neighborhood, with all of its challenges. In our millions, we have moved away from urban density toward the suburban cul-de-sac, away from the club hall to the living room, away from the local athletic team and its besplintered bleachers to the safe and comfortable isolation of the TV and upholstered chair.[...]
- Where once retailing was very local, and closely integrated with place, it is now dominated by large outlets, owned by distant multi-nationals.
- Religious congregations to one side, the civic fauna of many cities has all but collapsed (Hall 1999).
- Political participation in local politics, to say nothing of national, has fallen steadily. (Putnam 2000.
- Face-to-face communications have been supplanted in many cases by indirect, unidirectional, and asynchronous media such as the telephone, broadcast media, and the Web.

Taken together, these changes are the mainspring of change in the twentieth century, and the idea of social capital is important because it responds to them. (Rey 2002: xvi)

To what extent the picture painted above is true, is one question, but the author's justification of the relevance of social capital does not – for the same reasons as those noted above – follow.

It is beyond question that these changes are real, that they are of immense importance in everyday life, and that they leave us as a nation with no direct model of the sort which Lyda Hanifan saw in urban life at its peak. We have lost that model, and in its place we have an idea. And an idea of this kind is no small resource. (Rey 2002: xvi)

Rey, as can be seen, has rather strong views about both the plausibility of his story and its alleged conclusion underlining the need for the social capital concept:

Attempts in the late twentieth century to deal with the loss of community, the passing of the industrial city, the withering of old neighborhoods have been at once superficial and expensive. Dollars are easier to find than ideas in coping with our cities and their regions in the early years of a new century. In the hands of scholars like Putnam […] the idea of social capital will be refined, and may very well become a critical element of the way we seek our future as a society in coming generations. (Rey 2002: xvi; 2002)

These kinds of predictions are safe to make since by definition it is impossible to verify them at a given moment. On the basis of our findings in this study, however, the reader should be able to determine whether such a historic role of social capital is plausible, as well as desirable.

To pass such a judgment, it is indispensable to know precisely what one is talking about. The reader of a cluster of texts assembled in the volume under consideration will have little doubt as to the primary, if not exclusive, referent of the concept involved. We are told that:

today's civil society enthusiasts argue that democratic political institutions depend on voluntary associations in civil society for their stability and vigor. In civil society we learn to cooperate with one another, trust one another, and create a shared respect for fellow citizens.

Robert Putnam's catchy metaphor for civic disengagement in America, 'bowling alone', represents the most recent phase of the new fascination with civil society. His concept of 'social capital' networks that bind us and lubricate our interactions offers a potential measure of the vitality of civil society. In his research, Putnam purported to show that the nation's stock of 'social capital' has measurably declined since the 1950s. He notes that while more Americans than ever are bowling, they are no longer organised in networks of leagues, as was common during the 1950s. […] In like manner, membership has declined in a vast array of voluntary associations. […] Gone are the Norman Rockwellian days when Americans joined clubs by the scores, regularly attended PTA meetings, and participated wholeheartedly in league sports such as bowling. Our image-driven, postmodern world is increasingly characterised by solitary television watching, alienation, declining membership in school and after-work functions, and forms of civic engagement. (McLean, Schultz, and Seger 2002)

The validity of Putnam's diagnosis is a question which will be have to be considered below. But more important for our purposes at this juncture is another point – social capital appears as simply another name of civic engagement. Thus, the author of one of numerous books on social capital states that: "Putnam's definition of social capital objectifies the concept into participation in activities that foster a sense of shared community. Social capital becomes a commodity like the skills set of 'human capital' that can be acquired through networking or community involvement. Following the attention in policy circles given to Robert Putnam's (1995) work, the term was transformed into a metaphor for civic participation" (Schneider 2004).

Another example of the aforementioned peculiar reification may be provided by the following statement: "In a bid to understand persistent differences in economic growth and other measures of well-being, social scientists are increasingly broadening their analysis beyond traditional variables to include human capital, social capital and institutions, and the interaction among these three components of civil society. The potential impact of these three components of civil society on economic growth has attracted a great deal of attention" (Coté 2001: 28).

To cite one more claim of a key exponent of the notion in question who extolls the merits of social capital by pointing out that "people›s engagement in civil society not only improves a community›s economic performance, but also has a significant impact on the quality of democratic governance" (Putnam 1993, 117, 152). And the editors of a collective volume on social capital introduce the reader, inter alia, to "four different efforts to focus more closely on the actual workings of civil society at the grassroots, and in the global system. These chapters not only represent interesting studies of community, but they also stand as critiques to Putnam's approach to civic engagement" (McLean, Schultz, and Steger 2002). For instance, Levi (1996) has highlighted the poor explanatory power of the construct of social capital. She argues that Putnam has failed to explicate the mechanisms whereby high levels of involvement in voluntary associations and networks, and the allegedly associated relationships of trust, reciprocal help and support, lead to more effective local government.

To reiterate, whether anxieties over its dramatic decline in America's social life are justified is quite another question. But the main issue is this: what is the point of inventing a new term for something that already has its well-established name. What is more, that expedient is far from being innocent; on the contrary, its inherent economic connotation is misleading, makes it a poor tool with which to explore the aforementioned dimension of social life which by no stretch of imagination can be framed as an economic phenomenon.

The latter point is overlooked by an otherwise cognate to our own one critique (that by the same token undermines the claim that "the concept is intuitive enough to be mediatisation in a world in which new ideas are at a premium [Thrift 1999: 33]):

the set of processes encompassed by the concept are not new and have been studied under other labels in the past. To call them social capital is, to a large extent, just a means of presenting them in a more appealing conceptual garb. (Maloney, Smith, and Stoker 2002: 225).

Not all commentators, though, view the nomenclature in question in such benign terms:

the term social capital arises from an explicit analogy with the way the word capital has figured in economic analysis for hundreds of years. The primary meaning of the word capital thus comes from the way it has been used in economic analysis. This meaning is irretrievably linked to capitalism, individualism, competition, the market, and the acquisition of wealth, things that most political discourse views as opposed to those aspects of community that discussions of social capital typically value. The tension, conflict, and contradiction between capital and community are obscured by the term social capital because it strongly suggests that it, financial capital, and human capital are merely different species of the same genus, capital. Moreover, given the historic and primary meaning of the word capital, to use the term social capital to describe the virtues of community and the prerequisites of democracy is to facilitate a view of civic engagement and democratic participation as a kind of economic transaction, thus further obscuring important distinctions. Finally, to urge all of us to be social capitalists, as the last chapter of Bowling Alone so unabashedly does, is to becloud the historic meaning of the word capitalist. Such beclouding euphemises many of the longstanding meanings of the word capitalist, helps legitimise capitalism, and impedes thinking about noncapitalist ways of organising society. (Smith, Kulynych 2002)

One cannot agree more; that social capital writers are prepared to go to any lengths to make their point, may be illustrated by the following exceptionally unfortunate use of economic jargon: "the competing demands of social capital exchange from individuals' community networks" (Schneider 2004: 191).

Thus, as a matter of fact, if in our view (to be expanded on below) the term "social capital" is a misnomer both in its adjective and noun part, we are not alone. "Social capital seems to be different from other types of capital as described by economists. While this need not be a problem for the concept if it is coherently explained in relation to other forms of capital, or as a complementary part of the family of capitals, its difference to the convention notion of capital has been acknowledged but rarely interrogated" (Haynes 2009a).

While we strongly disagree with the first point – a misnomer is one, after all, and nothing can change this fact, Haynes's point about the incongruity of social capital and real capital is well taken, as is his comment on a general neglect of this issue. There are some exceptions, however: According to Kenneth Arrow (1999) whose name was mentioned in Part I, the word "capital" implies three elements:

extension in time; an intended sacrifice for deferred benefit; alienability. He points out that the concept of *social* capital lacks each of the three elements required to be a genuine capital, which means that there is no reason for "*adding* something called 'social capital' to other forms of capital" (Arrow 1999: 4). Inherent in the concept under consideration confusion with the meaning and functions of other types of capital has been condemned by Samuel Bowles who even – not denying that the concept "social capital" might describe important relationships – contended, however, that the term itself and the way it is conceptualised in the literature, is so unlike other forms of capital that the term "social capital" should be abandoned:

> 'Capital' refers to a thing possessed by individuals; even a social isolate like Robinson Crusoe had an axe and a fishing net. By contrast, the attributes said to make up social capital – such as trust, commitment to others, adhering to social norms and punishing those who violate them – describe relationships *among* people. (Bowles 1999: 6).

Again, while to apply the concept of capital to a "social isolate" is to indulge in a methodological Robinsonade, as Bowles, a Marxist political economist, should know, the thrust of his argument is sound. For a member of this school of thought, it is also rather odd to put forward a conception of capital as a thing, given that according to the said theoretical stream capital must be conceived of as a social relation rather than simply a thing or assemblage of things. Indeed, from that perspective the term "social" as an adjective to the word "capital" is superfluous, amounts to an imposition of another layer of misnomer, as capital is really a socio-economic relation, and there is no need to characterise it as "social" in addition to its intrinsic attributes. In somewhat similar terms this matter is viewed also by Fine who argues That "social" is attached to capital to mark a distinct category is indicative of the failure to understand capital as social in its economic, putatively non-social form (2002: 797).

> In this way, the 'social' element of social capital is therefore supplementary, adding to and replacing the features of capital such that it undermines the concept of capital itself, for example capital is characterised as being depleted by utilisation; however, social capital is depleted by *not* being utilised. In this way, by introducing new forms of capital – social, human, knowledge – to fill in gaps in the concept, the meaning of the concept as a whole is actually eroded.

Highly critical of "social capital" is another well-known economist, Robert Solow, who implicitly deems the concept in question a misnomer in arguing that it is based on a bad analogy. He believes this is easily demonstrated by asking simple questions to develop the analogy (e.g. what it is social capital a stock of? What is its rate of return?) as a result of which it breaks down. He explains that the aforementioned simple expedient: "is the quickest way to explain why I doubt that 'social capital' is the right concept to use" (Solow 2000: 7). And from the perspective of this study, one should fully concur with his conclusion: "I do not see how dressing this set of issues in the language and apparatus of capital theory helps much one way or the other" (Solow 2000: 9).

Along similar lines, Claude Fischer argues that,

> the term 'social capital' is unnecessary as other clearer and simpler terms, such as membership, trust and sociability, serve, perfectly well on their own. Indeed, even the supporting concepts of social capital, such as 'bridging' and 'bonding' fit better with a different metaphor, such as ties or association, while many of the reasons for using the term are based on conjecture, for example that trust norms are closely related to networks. A further danger is that the argument becomes susceptible to a slippery slope argument, i.e. that other features able to alter productivity are also a form of 'capital'. (Fischer 2005: 157)

And indeed in the course of our analysis we did, or will note, the peculiar ability of all the three concepts under consideration to swell or extend beyond their already ill-defined limits. And the aforementioned commentator's further criticism is fully in line with the subtitle of the present book:

> Even before the content of the concept is examined, then, the use of the word 'capital' is a hindrance that must be addressed and its meaning fully unpacked:

> the phrase itself is a problem. It is a metaphor that misleads: Where can I borrow social capital? What is the going interest rate? Can I move some of my social capital off-shore? (Fischer 2005: 157)

These are, without a doubt, rhetorical questions, but they amount to a powerful criticism of what is a respective deplorable misnomer.

It may seem paradoxical, but actually it is simply the other side of the coin that this economistic frame of reference is accompanied by the failure to recognise real, not notional, importance of economic relations in social life.

In his study of social capital in Italy one of its most famous exponents argues that vertical relations in the southern region, (characterised by a concentration of power by landowners, less social participation and a more individualistic allocation of opportunities), led to social inequality. Putnam traced the roots of this development back to medieval times and concluded, "communities did not become civic because they were rich...they became rich because they were civic."

Notice how the notion of economic conditions has been reduced in his final statement to that of material standard of living, whereas he has disregarded his own observation concerning ownership of land; and ownership relations, it can be contended, are a more fundamental and deep-rooted dimension of the economy than the level of GDP or suchlike.

As to the US: "While Putnam sees political parallels between the community challenges of the 1890s and today, he does not extend the comparison to the economic transformations occurring in both periods. Great transformations in economic life have far-reaching effects on political and social life, and set the stage for movements that seek to revitalise the spirit of community" (McLean, Schultz, and Steger 2002).

Foley and Edwards (1997: 551, 553) find social capital theory flawed in three main ways: "First, in general social capital is under-theorised and oversimplified. Second, contemporary writings have under-emphasised the conflictual nature of civil society. Third...these (mis)understandings conjoin in the suppression of the economic dimension of contemporary social conflict".

As a result, Putnam's fellow American can contend:

> *Bowling Alone* neglects [...] the most important cause of this country's declining civic vitality: neoliberal globalisation. [...] As globalisation tendencies strengthen, societies become more and more dominated by unbridled market forces that damage people's social relations and discourage civic engagement. In a world organised around the notion of individual liberty understood primarily as unrestrained economic entrepreneurship, traditional communal values of cooperation, solidarity, and civic participation are trumped by competitive market norms. Like its nineteenth-century predecessor, today's era of neoliberal globalisation represents an experiment in unleashing the utopia of the self-regulating market on society. After a successful start in its respective countries in the 1970s, the phalanx of dominant Anglo-American globalist forces has been turning the entire world into its laboratory. Following Polanyi's analysis, one would expect the social costs of this free-market experiment, that is, declining social capital worldwide, to be staggering. (Steger 2000: 268)

Perhaps contrary to the aforementioned commentator's intentions, the juxtaposition of two "social" words highlights the poverty of the social capital construct, which is too poor in content to be able to capture, let alone analyse social costs of capitalism, whether in the era of primitive accumulation, or globalisation. And the above-mentioned Putnam critic's further argument in fact bolsters our view:

> Putnam's remarks (2000) regarding the potential correlation between neoliberal globalisation and declining civic engagement in the United States are limited to a one-page discussion of the role of 'big business, capitalism, and the market' (Steger 282–3).

While grossly inadequate in scope and depth, his musings on globalisation are nonetheless sufficiently revealing 'to offer the reader a glimpse of his overall rationale for recommending a swift dismissal of this particular "suspect" (Steger 2000: 268).

It is surely worthwhile to get to know Putnam's deliberations, but let us first note how surprising it is that Steger has somehow managed to reconcile this rather harsh critique of the leading figure of social capital school with the high evaluation of the concept itself mentioned above. Well, perhaps it is the matter of the adjective mentioned in the subtitle of our study.

To be sure, Putnam acknowledges that social critics have long emphasised the tendency of capitalism to erode interpersonal ties and social trust by devaluing human ties to the status of mere commodities. But, for Putnam, the problem with such "generic theories of social disconnectedness" is that they "explain too much." As he emphasises, "America has epitomised market capitalism for several centuries, during which our stocks of social capital and civic engagement have been through great swings. A constant, he points out, can't explain a variable" (282).

The reader may be forgiven for *not* being surprised by Putnam's critic's reaction:

> But is American market capitalism really a 'constant'? I submit that the answer to this question is, 'No.' The list of academic authors who have documented the passing of qualitatively distinct phases of capitalism in the United States is far too long to be reproduced here in its entirety. [...] Indeed, acknowledgments of the changing face of American capitalism appear as matter-of-fact statements in introductory textbooks on American politics. It is hard to imagine reasons other than those intended to avoid a critical discussion of contemporary neoliberalism that would prompt Putnam to turn distinct phases of capitalism into an easily dismissable 'constant.' By admitting that capitalism is not a constant but a variable, Putnam would have to concede that changing economic dynamics are potential causes for the rise and fall of social capital in the United States. [...]
>
> In his brief discussion of globalisation (282–3), Putnam presents his readers with an extremely narrow understanding of globalisation. (Steger 2000: 271)

And a class-bias, too:

> Putnam reduces the topic of globalisation to a brief inquiry into the possible 'decline in civic commitment on the part of business leaders'.[...] Having thus absolved business interests from any significant involvement in the 'killing of civic engagement', [...] Putnam disregards more substantive developments suggesting a link between globalisation and disappearing social capital. For example, neoliberal globalisation contributed to growing social inequalities, the need to work longer to stay afloat, and a shrinking middle class. This, in turn, leads to what Putnam calls 'time pressures'. The widening gap between the rich and poor is also a prime candidate responsible for the growth of insular neighborhoods as well as the breakdown of associations linking social groups. (Steger 2000: 271)

As different Putnam's view of the main reasons for the putative demise of social capital in the US is, it manifests with a vengeance the aforementioned disregard of their actual socio-economic underpinnings and context. This actually holds both for his account of the present and the past:

> Advocates of improved civic engagement, such as Putnam (2000), harken back to the golden age of the World War II generation when patriotism and civic engagement were high. Putting aside for a moment the very different pictures of society in the 1940s and 1950s painted by civil rights historians, let me end by examining several features of this time period that meant very different social capital resources for members of that generation. First, the war created opportunities for decent employment, for many different populations, that have rarely existed in this country. Women and people of color were offered jobs in primary-sector workplaces during the war that quickly disappeared as soldiers returned. The GI bill, which offered unprecedented class mobility to returning veterans, removed some of the potential employment pressure after the war. More people had opportunities to participate in generalised prosperity throughout their careers owing to a combination of the wage and benefit agreements established between government and employers during and after the war. The GI bill and the expanding economy created economic opportunities for that generation very different from those for more recent generations. Economic stability meant more leisure to participate in voluntary organisations and other civic activities. (Schneider 2004: 361)

Meanwhile, Putnam's key argument is that the rise of civic disengagement in the US can be attributed to the remarkable influence of television. Connecting this argument to his claim that generations born after 1940 are socially less engaged than their parents and grandparents, Putnam identifies younger people as members of an intensely private, socially disconnected, and passive "TV generation". He sums up his findings on this topic in the following way: "Americans at the end of the twentieth century are watching more TV, watching it more habitually, more pervasively, and more often alone, and watching more programs that were associated with entertainment, as distinct from news)". Importantly, according to Putnam "the onset of these trends coincided exactly with the national decline in social connectedness, and the trends were most marked among the younger generation..." (246).

According to Putnam's critic, it is not the facts as such, but at best gaps in their interpretation that may be at issue:

> Putnam is surely right on the first point. There is little doubt that Americans have become more hooked on televised entertainment than ever before. The daily average viewing time spent per TV home has increased from 5 hours and 56 minutes in 1970 to 7 hours and 26 minutes in 1999. In 1999, TV household penetration stood at 98.3 percent, with 73.9 per cent of TV households owning

two or more sets. […] Putnam also correctly points to a steep increase of shallow 'entertainment shows' at the expense of more informational and educational programs. Perhaps he is even right in his controversial claims that excessive television watching is mildly addictive, causes anxiety, irritation, and depression, undermines physical health, encourages lethargy and passivity, steals valuable family and community time, obstructs civic enlightenment, provides merely pseudo-personal connections, and replaces social awareness and neighborly concern with asocial entertainment values (238–46).

Yet, nowhere in *Bowling Alone* can one find a critical analysis of the politics of television placed within the context of neoliberal globalisation. (Steger 2000: 272)

What is in our view disputable, is not so much Steger's questions and answers amounting to an apt critique of Putnam's analysis of social capital, as some of their aspects, notably the persistent use of the term "political" which is supposedly to strengthen his argument, but in fact is, sorry to say, largely a misnomer. Media corporations' policies, and other processes that Steger is talking about (except the moves of the state), are part of the economy, and not the polity. The fact that Putnam himself is a political scientist does not matter. The aforementioned misunderstanding is actually quite widespread; Wacquant (1998), for instance, argues that unequal power relations are fundamental to continued poverty. Applying social capital involves first understanding the power relations inherent in the concept. Successfully altering individual career paths and changing social welfare policy involves paying attention to the power structures inherent in existing social and cultural capital. This kind of argument involves either the non-legitimate "politicisation" of non-political relations, or misinterpretation of ownership, as the foundation of class – the most fundamental of those social relations – in terms of power or control.

The ambiguous relationship of power to social capital is compounded further in the face of claims such as the following one: "Within social units, social capital creates power and influence" (Cook et al., 1983). Now it is totally unclear whether the kind of social relationships that are defined, one way or other, as social capital are conditioned by the power relations, the latter are, conversely, created by the former, or alternatively, those power relations are simply one type of relations included in social capital, and, should the latter be true, how one is to reconcile that view with the notion of social capital as voluntary relations based first of all, if not exclusively, on trust.

This is not to say, as suggested above, that Steger's criticisms are without merit:

What are the social and political forces that have fueled the expansion of what political theorist Benjamin Barber (1996, 60) has called the "infotainment telesector"? What are the political and economic interests that are driving the proliferation of entertainment programs on television? Putnam (2000: 245) correctly refers to "the encouragement of materialist values" as "another probable effect of television." But he remains silent on the principal causes of the commercialisation of television, thus failing to explore the political forces and shifting social conditions behind these developments. In fact, Putnam speaks of "the rise of electronic communications and entertainment as one of the most powerful social trends in the twentieth century" (245) – as if the commercialisation of television was a natural phenomenon that "just happens", like bad weather or an earthquake.

Communications scholars Edward Herman and Robert McChesney (1997) have pointed out that the same powerful phalanx of social forces behind neoliberal globalisation are also responsible for the creation of a global commercial media system. The dissemination of TV images around the world is controlled by a small number of super-powerful, mostly US-based transnational media corporations that also dominate global markets for other types of entertainment such as radio, publishing, music, theme parks, and cinema. [...] Even some defenders of globalism like Christopher Dixon, media analyst for the investment firm Paine Webber, concede that the recent emergence of a global commercial-media market amounts to the "creation of a global oligopoly [...] (cited in McChesney 2001,2). [...] the global media system "works to advance the cause of the global market and promote commercial values, while denigrating journalism and culture not conducive to the immediate bottom line or long-run corporate interest" (McChesney 1997, 11). Not necessarily linked by a conspiratorial intent but by the pursuit of profits, the mainstream media in the United States nonetheless share a neoliberal worldview that results in the creation of remarkably similar TV programmes.

While these facts may seem more or less well-known, the reader may be forgiven for thinking that this also applies to the scholar under consideration:

> Unfortunately, Putnam has no comment on the explosive growth of advertisement 'clutter' on television and radio. As media specialist Matthew P. McAllister (1996, 24–5) points out, TV clutter has increased since the early 1970s in a number of ways. First, today there exist more television outlets that carry ads. Second, the major networks try to squeeze in more commercials, especially in popular entertainment and sports shows. [...] advertisement clutter on radio and network television reached new record levels in 2000. ABC and NBC averaged over 15 minutes of commercials per prime time TV hour, not including cutaways for local ads (Mass Media News 2000). The daytime level of advertising on major TV networks increased to 20:53 minutes per hour. These remarkable figures indicate that today's TV stations and advertisers have more power than ever to transmit consumerist images and values to the viewing public. (Kaufman 2000)

These data are extremely useful not only for sociologists of the media, or culture, but of society in general. Note that in the following comments the framework of ownership is being used, which stands out amongst standard social science analyses: "TV clutter increased as a result of the shift to neoliberal deregulation. In the area of communications, this means that the barriers to commercial exploitation of media and to concentrated media ownership have been relaxed or eliminated" (McChesney 2001). "The 1996 deregulation of the telecommunications industry fundamentally weakened public control over the dissemination of sounds and images in the United States. Yet, Putnam is content to discuss only the final effects of this chain of political developments leading back to the rise of neoliberal globalisation in the 1970s. [...] In order to present the reader with a comprehensive genealogy of these 'uncivic' effects of television – as measured in the depletion of social capital – Putnam would have to offer a critical analysis of the political forces behind these commercial interests" (Steger 2000: 276).

However, there are good reasons to believe that it is not in politics but in a quite another societal structure, as stressed above, that an inalienable ingredient of social theory in general, and thus also social capital theory, whatever that misnomer, if anything, might mean; this much is suggested also by the following commentators:

> In sketching the six areas that 'deserve special attention from aspiring social capitalists: youth and schools; the workplace; urban and metropolitan design; religion; arts and culture; and politics and government' (404), the book does not discuss how economic inequality affects prescriptions in any of the areas, except for a brief mention in the discussion of politics and government. [...] the omission is a crucial one because the scant attention paid to economic issues in the agenda for social capitalists reflects an approach to current social problems including civic engagement that is so one-sided as to be deeply misleading, if not wrong. The attempt to describe the workings of community life and civic engagement in the language of capital muddles both the extent to which the workings of financial capital have undermined community and civic engagement as well as the extent to which the rejuvenation of community and civic engagement has involved challenges to the operation of capitalism. (Smith, Kulynych 2002)

Well, if the authors expected to come across a fiery revolutionary, or at least single-minded activist, they must have been disappointed. Putnam is, rather, an exponent of a quite fashionable "declinism" – the idea that human society is in decline.

This kind of neglect lies also behind Putnam's peculiar thesis that the placid 1950s were the height of civic America and that the politically turbulent 1960s were the period of social capital's decline. Boggs (2002) argues that this counterintuitive conclusion stems from the limits of Putnam's methodology, namely, his focus on traditional, mainly unpolitical associations favoured by older Americans.

Joining the Rotary or Elks club, singing in choir ensembles, competing in sports leagues, and going to dinner parties may indeed have furnished some element of solidarity for many people, but these could be categorised as mostly safe, conformist, traditional community activities favoured by the older generations and, within those generations, by largely middle-class or upper middle-class strata; "politics" scarcely entered into such forms of participation, or did so in only the most limited, conventional fashion. The old voluntary organisations Putnam cherishes went into decline precisely because they lost their *raison d'etre* as their goals became outdated, mostly reflective of a small-town America that, itself, was in the process of vanishing. Likewise, earlier cohorts may have been more willing to work for political parties, turn out for elections, sign petitions, and write letters to government officials or newspapers, but such expenditures of time and energy were viewed as peripheral, even wasteful, by newer generations that – for many justifiable reasons – became increasingly suspicious of a political system riddled with scandals, corruption, official deceit, and ideological convergence of the major parties and their candidates (Boggs 2002).

Finally, according to Boggs, the deterioration, if any, of public activity cannot be understood without taking into consideration historical shifts of economic factors. "Indeed, Putnam viewed capitalism as a constant and downplayed the momentous growth of the Corporation in American life" (McLean, Schultz, and Steger 2002).

Before expanding on this point, though, let us focus on two important issues that, as a matter of fact, have been already touched on above. The first of these has to do with class.

Researchers such as Verba and Nie (1972), Parry, Moyser, and Day (1992) and Verba, Scholzman, and Brady (1997) upon an examination of extensive data found that the more economically prosperous participate to a much greater extent than poor or disadvantaged groups, with the result that policies may be skewed in favour of 'the particular participant groups and away from the more general "public interest"' (Verba and Nie 1972: 342). Although the researchers concerned do not use the language of class, their findings are fairly easy to convert into such terms. Much to the point, Verba, Scholzman, and Brady (1997) argue that debates about declines in civic vitality and civic participation have missed – arguably – the key issue: the focus should not simply be on the amount of civic activity but its distribution, that is, who within the citizenry takes part and who does not. According to this view, differential civil participation rates should be conceived of as a key dimension of social – and political – exclusion of central concern to the social capital debate. Hence, "...for scholars such as Putnam who are concerned about the health of democracy and the decline in 'civicness', their critiques and remedies might be better aimed at identifying the causes, consequences, and possible cures for facilitating the meaningful engagement of the politically, socially, and economically disadvantaged" (Maloney, Smith, and Stoker 2002: 225).

While a specific researcher and his work are in the general scheme of things more or less occasional, and whereas the word "class" is by some regarded as a four-letter word, as it were, there is another recently popular concept to be used by the adherents of social capital: "social exclusion".

In a similar vein, other critics argue that the body politic cannot draw and rely on social capital to develop a cohesive society precisely because social capital involves defining boundaries among small groups against others outside of their social networks. Various subgroups within this society – it is stressed – are very effective at mobilising social capital in support of their own needs (Portney and Berry 1997; Wood 2002).

According to this line of criticism, in the majority of cases, social capital functions actually as a mechanism to exclude outsiders lacking connections from jobs and other social resources (Waldinger 1995; Stepick et al. 1997).

Identifying some problems raised by Putnam's conception, the three commentators of his work inadvertently draw attention to an even more pivotal issue. Surely, Putnam is correct in emphasising that democracies require citizen activism and involvement if they are to thrive (Dahl 2000). Yet, there remain open questions about social capital and civic engagement, including whether those social resources are really being depleted. In fact, some of Putnam's most vociferous critics are not convinced by his arguments at all, raising serious questions regarding the role voluntary associations play, or ought to play, in American society (McLean, Schultz, and Steger 2002).

As a result and manifestation of those controversies, despite the amount of interest in a possible decline of US social capital, scholars have not reached a consensus on the trend. Putnam has claimed that social capital is in decline while others (e.g., Ladd 1996) have argued that social capital has remained stable over time.

According to one commentator, this lack of clarity should be largely accounted for by the fact that "there is a large gap between the concept of social capital and its measurement. Previous studies provide little rationale for how their measures of social capital connect to the theoretical definition of social capital. [...]The lack of an obvious link between theory and measurement has, in some cases, led to the use of questionable indicators of social capital. [...] Many different measures can be and have been posited as indicators of social capital. Without strong ties to theory, however, researchers can choose among many pieces of data that provide contrary pictures of the health of social capital in the United States. Also, using measures from a variety of different sources means that assessment is difficult due to incomparability in sampling designs and question wording" (Wuthnow 1997).

Finally, by using single observed variables, researchers cannot account for measurement error, which we would expect to find in the survey questions used to assess social capital. "[...]The problems with previous assessments of social capital indicate that current debate over social capital in the United States amounts to a great deal of arguing over selective pieces of information, drawn from different sources and analyzed with weak statistical techniques [...]" (Paxton 1999: 89).

Apart anything else, the above review suggest that the name "the theory of social capital" is overdone – the analytical apparatus is not linked to its theoretical framework, the central concept lacks operationalisation, there is no consensus as to even the elementary set of propositions stemming from the theory. This does not bode well for its scholarly status. And this is still not the end of its troubles: "Largely unquestioned in the academic debates on Putnam's empirical measurements, however, were the normative implications of his social capital theory. The Harvard scholar leaves little doubt that America experienced a decline in some face-to-face forms of participation in the last forty years" (McLean, Schultz, and Steger 2002).

Although this is by no means the main thrust of the three commentators' argument, they nevertheless indicate what, from our viewpoint, is another major form of misnomer pertinent to social capital. Not only it turns out that the concept concerned is a misleading name of community involvement, but the attribute "social" is in fact illegitimate, as "social" is another misnomer, meaning "sociable" instead, and sociability is just one aspect of sociality, or, to put it differently, face-to-face interactions are but one form of social relations, contrary to what is suggested by such definitions as the following which, by default, consider them the only form: "social capital is broadly defined to include interpersonal relationships that affect efficiency of the economy" (Omori 2001). And, we hasten to add, the above-mentioned one is by any means the only, or exceptional statement of similar import in the social capital literature. Here is how three scholars couch the basis of social capital's merits: "the direct social link between people is taken to be crucial to engendering tolerance, accommodation and mutual understanding" (Maloney, Smith, and Stoker 2002: 221).

It follows that the merits of social capital and interpersonal relations are merely two sides of the same coin:

> [The] principle that we live by entering into relations with one another, provides the basic structure within which all human experience and activity falls, whether individual or social. For this reason the first priority in education...is learning to live in personal relation to other people. Let us call it learning to live in community. I call this the first priority because failure in this is a fundamental failure that cannot be compensated for by success in other fields; because our ability to enter into fully personal relations with others is the measure of our humanity. For inhumanity is precisely the perversion of human relations (McMurray 1958, quoted in M. Fielding (1996: 162).

This is, of course, a grossly exaggerated view; the history of science and humanities abounds in "lone wolves" without whose work the entire education system could hardly function; moreover, their solitary work has often been the condition (and at the same time-price) of their scientific, scholarly or academic or literary achievements. To call them inhuman, is an insult. Nevertheless, it is the aforementioned particular form of human relations that has captured attention of social capital theorists.

In stating, for instance, that, "associations between individuals fall into two types. Individuals can be informally connected to others through friendship choices and other types of network ties, or individuals can be connected to others through formal group memberships" (Paxton 1999: 99), she ignores the presence and relevance in society of many diverse indirect social relations, i.e. mediated by a variety of material and ideal objects.

An influential creator of perhaps the greatest number of various capitals defines social capital this way: "The aggregate of the actual or potential resources which are linked to possession of a durable network of more or less institutionalised relationships of mutual acquaintance or recognition" (Bourdieu 1985: 248). As hinted above, Putnam (1995: 2000) traces back the demise of social capital in the United States to the fact that people now have fewer opportunities for face-to-face interactions in which to work together to improve conditions in a locality. Another leading social capital theorist, "Coleman portrays social capital as instrumental relations that come from face-to-face interactions" (Schneider 2004). Applications of Coleman's model also focus on face-to-face relationships (for example, Teachman et al. 1997). Another writer "understands social capital [...] to consist of three components: 1) Social networks/interactions and sociability; 2) trust and reciprocity; and 3) sense of belonging/place attachment" (Schaefer-McDaniel 2004). Yet another theorist of social capital associates it with "networks of personal contact" (Szreter 2002) and his fellow social capital theorist explain the meaning of the latter defines in no uncertain terms: "individuals have relationships with other individuals. That is, individuals have a social network. Relationships (ties) can be of many different types, including friendship or other emotional ties; transfers of material resources, or exchange relationships; proximity in space, such as neighbors or office mates; and kinship relations (Wasserman and Faust 1994). They can also be directional or non-directional, valued or dichotomous, and uniplex or multiplex (see Wasserman and Faust [1994, chapters 1–2] for a discussion of network terminology).)" (Paxton 1999: 99); this otherwise impressive typology, however, fails to include intermediate social relations. And so on, and so forth – the list can go on and on.

For this reason alone one cannot concur with the contention that "social capital opens up the way for different approaches to modelling social relations, which address some of the moral and technical complexities of their protean character" (Schuller, Baron, Field 2000).

Such sweeping assertions lose all their plausibility in the face of serious problems the concept encounters even on its own native terrain. In particular, this core assumption is self-defeating, undermining social capital theory's core conclusions, as shown, *inter alia*, by the following critic:

> Social capital is comparable to the notion of collective efficacy – the linkage of mutual trust and the willingness to intervene for the common good. Just as individuals vary in their capacity for collective action, so too do neighbourhoods vary in their capacity to achieve common goals. When the horizontal links among institutions in a community are weak, the capacity to defend local interests is weakened. Many communities exhibit intense private ties among friends and kin and yet still lack the institutional capacity to achieve social control. To achieve social order must have interdependence among informal social control and formal institutions such as police. In areas of economic distress the incentives for participation in the social aspects of community life are reduced. Studies have found that the neighbourhood socioeconomic status and joblessness interacted to predict adolescent outcomes. The absence of affluent neighbours is a better predictor of poor outcomes than the presence of low-income neighbours. This supports the theory of collective socialisation. (Sampson 1999)

Numerous scholars have protested at Putnam's assertions regarding the civic health of the United States (Rich 1999; Portes 1998; Ammerman 1997). People in the United States participate in many forms of joint activity. More important, the homogeneous communities envisioned as the recent past in this country never existed (Lynd and Lynd 1929).

Putnam focuses on the decline of "classic secondary associations", such as: sports clubs, trade unions, professional associations, which is accompanied by the growth of what he terms "vertically ordered", "tertiary associations" – exemplified by staff groups, mail order groups and protest businesses. Such associations are, as a rule, organised on a hierarchical basis because membership simply entails the payment of dues. The ties that exist are to 'common symbols, common leaders, and perhaps common ideals, but not to one another' (Putnam 1995a: 71). These organisations are seen as taking advanced democracies closer to mass societies (Hayes 1986). They are 'a symptom of a sick society in which individual citizens choose to abandon true democratic participation where persons meet and debate face-to-face. Instead, they select ersatz political participation in which the electorate responds only to a national elite that communicates through direct mail' (Topolsky 1974, cited in Godwin, 1988: 4–5). Ultimately, the argument goes, these processes lead to depletions in social capital resources because within social capital framework the direct social link between people is taken to be crucial to engendering tolerance, accommodation and mutual understanding.

However, not all agree. Specifically, Putnam et al., as suggested above, regard horizontally organised networks to assist social capital, while vertical relationships were thought to inhibit its formation. "Intense horizontal interactions...are an essential form of social capital... . A vertical network, no matter how dense and no matter how important to its participants, cannot sustain social trust and cooperation" (Putnam et al. 1993: 173–4). However, in his later writings, Putnam opts for shortening the list further to include only certain types of horizontal networks. Compared to secondary groups where members have frequent face-to-face contact, tertiary and mailing-list organisations are far less able to generate social capital (Putnam 1996).

Putnam's preference for horizontal organisations has not gone unchallenged, however. A critic has pointed out that it is not at all clear how in practice one determines whether an organisation is vertically or horizontally organised. The Boy Scouts, for example, are a hierarchically organised group, yet they seem to be favourably regarded by most social capital analysts. On the other hand, "militias and other nationalist organisations", excluded in most accounts, "do not appear to be much more vertically or hierarchically organised than other types" that get added in to social capital. (Berman 1997a: 567).

Schneider (2004: 13) states: "I differ from Putnam because I do not see face-to-face ties as essential for developing bridging social capital. Instead, institutional networks can serve the same function, developing bridges that extend to individuals who may not know one another but trust the common bonds created through organisational connections."

Schudson (1996: 18) has argued that checkbook participation may be a highly efficient use of civic energy. The citizen who joins may get the same civic pay-off for less personal hassle. This is especially true if we conceive of politics as a set of public policies. The citizen may be able to influence government more satisfactorily with the annual membership in the Sierra Club or the National Rifle Association than by attending the local club lunches (Maloney, Smith, and Stoker 2001: 221).

Likewise, Godwin (1988: 50) argues that if checkbook participation stimulates and motivates the public to pay attention to important issues and the actions of their representatives, then it could be perceived as strengthening democracy. Robert Wuthnow reckons that what is really under way is changes in forms of participation rather than a decline, with shifts from bureaucratic structures to more ad hoc ways of participation, which have manifested themselves in many forms that social capital research has scarcely picked up on (Wuthnow 1998).

In turn, Whiteley (1999: 30–31) has hypothesised that social capital can or may be generated "by membership of 'imaginary (or abstract) communities', that is communities which individuals identify with, but which they never actually interact with on a face-to face basis." Imaginary communities are large and geographically dispersed and individuals within them can socially interact only with a very small fraction of the group. In spite of this 'social barrier', Maloney (1999: 116) argues that 'individuals within these groups can develop very strong levels of group identification: "joining like-minded people" in pursuit of a cause may develop a sense of "community" or belonging. Membership of these groups may not be as detrimental to the generation of social capital as the Putnam/ Tocqueville model suggests.

It will be seen that apart from its substantive aspect, this kind of criticism involves a sound methodological point, also evident from the following argument: "Like the 'imagined communities' of ethnic nationalism, social capital relies on reference to known networks through cultural symbols (Anderson 1983). Individuals gain access to resources through reference to a recognised individual or organisation and displaying appropriate cultural behaviours, not simply through face-to-face interaction" (Schneider 2004: 13).

In addition, empirical investigations carried out in other countries indicate that, contrary to Putnam's thesis, horizontally shaped networks do not necessarily reveal the presence of higher social capital. A study of variations in economic growth for 29 countries over a three-year period, 1980–1982 by Knack and Keefer (1997: 1284) has concluded that while trust and civic cooperation are associated with stronger economic performance, associational activity is unrelated to trust. "Horizontal networks – as measured by membership in groups – are unrelated to trust and civic norms….Promoting horizontal associations through encouraging the formation of and by participating in groups may be counterproductive."

To complicate the matter further, other empirical investigations indicate that in addition to the shape of social networks (horizontal vs. vertical) other aspects such as the composition of the membership might also matter. Stolle and Rochon

(1998: 47–62) show, for instance, that all horizontal voluntary associations are not alike with respect to social capital. Studying the effects of associational membership in three countries, Sweden, Germany and the United States, they conclude that associations that are more diverse, "whose members bridge major social categories" are "more effective in fostering generalised trust and community reciprocity." "Homogenous associations are less likely to inculcate high levels of generalised trust and reciprocity among their members".

A separate debate is waged, however, on this issue of homogeneous vs. heterogeneous organisations.

That the internal heterogeneity of groups matters both for social capital as well as for economic welfare has been independently verified by Narayan and Pritchett's (1997) study of Tanzanian villages and also by Grootaert's (1998) study of Indonesian villages. In each case, a household-level index of social capital – constructed by multiplying together numbers of associational memberships with internal heterogeneity of associations and their span of activities – was found to be positively and consistently related with household economic welfare. More heterogeneous associations are better in terms of social capital.

Another group of scholars derive the opposite conclusions, however, thereby confounding consensus on even this issue. Drawing on data gathered from five American cities, Portney and Berry (1998: 636, 642–3) conclude that compared to social, service, self-help and issue-based organisations, it is "participation in neighbourhood associations [that] is more strongly associated with a high sense of community" and civic engagement. All else being the same, more homogenous neighbourhoods are more likely to have more effective neighbourhood associations. In a separate analysis related to understanding collective efficacy at the neighbourhood level, Sampson et al. (1997) show that among different neighbourhood associations the more effective ones are less highly stratified in terms of income and concentration of immigrants. Diversity and heterogeneity are counterproductive in this reckoning. Homogeneous associations do better by way of social capital.

The above might suggest that the issue should be viewed not in absolute, rigid, but context-related terms – "each type of group matters for some contexts more than for others" (Krishna, Shrader 2002: 5).

This is, in fact, the conclusion which Stolle supports in her later work. "Groups with high diversity levels in homogenous cultures [such as Sweden's or Germany's] are much more trust producing...These relations look different in countries with more diverse populations...In the United States [with a more heterogeneous culture] homogenous groups generate more generalised trust, and not the ones that accommodate people from diverse backgrounds" (Stolle 1998: 28–9). "Her work suggests that selecting an appropriate network measure for social capital will depend upon the country or culture that one is studying" (Krishna, Shrader 2002: 5).

That ahistorical generalisations about social capital are widely off the mark is shown, *inter alia*, by Rose's (1998) study of groups and associations in contemporary Russia which has found that trust is not associated with all types of networks, even those that are horizontally organised or which have a heterogeneous group of members. In the Russian context of institutional involution, some (but not all) informal networks are more closely associated with trust and trustworthy behavior. "Trust", conclude Jackman and Miller (1998: 59) after reviewing a range of empirical evidence, "is clearly not isomorphic with group membership." The context of group membership is as important, they submit, as its density or structural form.

The upshot of this discussion about concept specification and empirical referents can be stated briefly as follows. While social capital was defined and measured originally in terms that related entirely to density of horizontally-organised social networks, subsequent investigations have resulted in complicating any such straightforward measurement. What sorts of norms are associated with which types of networks cannot be assumed in advance but it must be verified independently for each separate social context (Krishna, Shrader 2002: 6).

The restricted focus discussed above, even not counting other weaknesses of the notion, makes it also unfit for the role of an instrument of socialising economics prescribed for it by many social scientists.

It is true indeed that orthodox textbook economics based, as it does, on methodological individualism, is inherently asociological. It does not follow, however, that it is the notion of social capital that is capable of changing this state of affairs, as indeed even some economists realise; for example, Hannan (1999) in his empirical study of the role of social factors influencing unemployment exit rates explicitly has rejected the concept of social capital as an analytical tool, pointing out that confusion over its conceptualisation hindered an understanding of the effect of social context in this instance.

To be sure, some other economists' ideas for improving the concept under consideration are of little help, since they are heading in an altogether wrong direction, as in the following example of a totally misguided conviction of a scholar to the effect that "...the introduction of identity provides an empirically grounded alternative to the slavish following of norms entailed in an oversocialised theory and makes real progress in the socialisation of social capital" (Fevre 2002). It is a misconceived attempt, since it rather than socialises, psychologises further the concept of social capital, as evident from, e.g., the following formulation: "The idea of linking identity to self-transformation is clearly derived from the sociology of Mead" (Fevre 2002: 101), which, of course, leaves the above-identified weakness unaltered.

It is a no-brainer that such an interactionist perspective neatly fits in an individualistic framework actually adopted by Putnam and other social capital theorists. In the former, for instance, social capital is viewed as more of a psychological or attitudinal factor than a structural force. By that, "civic engagement seems to produce individual attributes in specific individuals that are lacking in persons who do not get involved. Therefore, those who opt to watch television have less social capital than those who do not" (303). Similarly, those engaged in religious or other forms of participation have a greater sense of trust, honesty, voluntarism, and philanthropy than those not engaged. Social capital thus is conceived something that individuals can acquire via personal investment (323, 388).

Second, and related to the first point, social capital in Bowling Alone no longer appears to be a social attribute, if by social one means "a shared or collective good." Though Putnam contends that social capital has a collective aspect (2000, 20), his definition of a collective aspect is discussed in terms of how it individually benefits someone, or in how it enhances the productivity of the individual (20, 323). Moreover, in distinguishing two forms of social capital – bonding and bridging – both are really individuated forms of social capital. Bonding capital provides "social and psychological support" to individuals and it helps with providing real capital, such as financing, in the marketplace (Schultz 2002: 81).

Leaving at this point all other things aside, what is interesting in the above passage is the inadvertent acknowledgement that social capital, whatever it is, is not a real capital. Exactly so. There are a number of other statements to the same effect, willy-nilly recognising the distinction between "social capital" and economic capital. Here is one example: "SOCIAL capital enhances entrepreneurial activity thanks to the use of flexible and informal social networks, making it relatively easy to find personnel and capital" (Light, et al., 1999).

The same interactionist perspective cannot but narrow Putnam's purview generally – as Michael Shapiro (2002) points out, stressing Putnam's romanticisation of "face-to-face" associations confining him to nineteenth-century neo-Tocquevillian assumptions about civic space and association owing to which he overlooks that new technologies alter the frame of social agency and transform traditional notions of territory, association, and citizenship and point toward a civic renaissance.

The perils of the interactionist and economistic (in the sense of conventional economics) notion of social capital are illustrated by not only what Putnam does not, but in fact also what he does say:

"If Putnam is correct that 'face to face' associations are necessary for a vibrant civil society, then shouldn't the family – the first and most powerful of all face-to-face associations – be the logical place to look for the source of civic decline? After all, the percentage of households made up of a married couple with children has been dropping to its historic low of below 25 per cent in 2000" (Schmitt 2000).

Moreover, Putnam demonstrates that "family connectedness" is changing, and he points the disappearance of the customary family evening meal as the starkest example (2000, 100). Family attendance at religious services and even families watching television together has declined, as households increasingly have multiple television sets (2000: 101).

Yet, given his critical acclaim and wide readership success, the reader may be forgiven for being surprised that Putnam's evidence does not support the idea that changes in families are the key to civic decline across generations. Changes in the family are relatively continuous, whereas generational analysis presumes a sharp break between one generation and another. After analyzing his evidence, Putnam says "family instability...seems to have an ironclad alibi for what we have now identified as the critical period, for the generational decline in civic engagement began with the children of the maritally stable 1940s and 1950s... . Similarly, working mothers are exonerated by this re-specification of our problem, for the plunge in civicness among children of the 1940s, 1950s and 1960s happened while mom was still at home" (Putnam 2000, 267). In fact, Putnam points out that people who are married, with children, attend fewer club meetings than demographically similar unmarried people (2000, 278). "Apart from youth and church related engagement, none of the major declines in social capital and civic engagement that we need to explain can be accounted for by the decline of traditional family structure" (2000, 277, 279, emphasis in original).

Moreover, even if Putnam did have evidence of strong correlations between changes in family life and changes in civic engagement, it would run counter to the basic assumptions of his social capital concept. For him, we join groups and informally socialise with friends in order to "benefit our own interests" (Putnam 2000, 20). Emotional bonds or loyalties are often treated with suspicion or relegated to the private realm. Putnam thinks social capital best applies to a range of formal and informal associations, from political parties to poker nights. While these kinds of associations can plausibly be described in instrumental terms as "bridging" social capital, Putnam has difficulty with associations typical of "bonding" social capital. There, instrumental interests seem to disappear, and group identities play a greater role in behavior. Sometimes, such groups are so powerful in reshaping and defining identities of the members that it becomes nearly impossible to say that people belong to them out of "interest". Putnam barely considers such groups "civic" at all, since their members see their membership less as something chosen and more as something they are "born into" (McLean 2002).

What is more, the aforementioned interactionism is responsible for many methodological problems encountered by Putnam and other social capital researchers. Attempting to develop a unit of analysis small enough to capture the effects of social capital in facilitating the dissemination of resources to groups or individuals, has limited data collection to a reliance on methods such as questionnaires, which provide data with which it is difficult to make the distinctions between outcomes of social capital with forms or indicators of its presence (Haynes 2009a: 11).

Durlauf considers that:

> social capital can be researched but it cannot permit the type of analysis with the clarity and precision that the advocates in the field claim:
> The empirical social capital literature seems to be particularly plagued by vague definition of concepts, poorly measured data, absence of appropriate exchangeability conditions, and lack of information necessary to make identification claims plausible. These problems are especially important for social capital contexts as social capital arguments depend on underlying psychological and sociological relations that are difficult to quantify, let alone measure. (Durlauf 2002: F475)

It does not come as a surprise that even social capital analysts themselves begin to wonder whether "Should only small face-to-face groups be considered, or are large multi-regional and multi-national organisations also instrumental in promoting coordinating and cooperation for mutual benefit"? (Minkoff 1997, Oliver and Marwell 1988).

As to the aforementioned normative bias of social capital literature, its blatant illustration is provided by Nancy Rosenblum's (1998) recent claim to the effect that "...all voluntary associations – even those banding together neo-Nazis – are valuable in that they impart social capital".

Meanwhile, it is useful to compare this over-optimistic, to say the least, view of civic virtues purportedly pertaining to social capital with one held by the thinker whose role in the tradition of debate over civic and democratic institutions in America cannot be over-estimated.

When Tocqueville spoke of voluntary associations, he did not seem to be referring either to bowling leagues, chambers of commerce, or economic corporations. His voluntary associations were public-regarding entities that fostered civic-mindedness within the context of an overall economic and political equality of conditions. Similarly and perhaps more significantly, voluntary associations were important not simply in terms of the individual attitudes they fostered in citizens, but because they functioned to improve, nurture and help organise institutions such as juries, administrative decentralisation, manners, mores, and the laws (Pope 1986, 51–2).

Thus, Tocqueville's views on voluntary associations differ from that of the pluralists in that he would not have considered all interest groups to be of equal value in the maintenance of a democratic spirit (Schultz 2002).

An otherwise adherent of social capital doctrine offers nevertheless a mild criticism in noting: social capital 'may indeed generate valuable goods and services...but we should not assume that it does, and we should not include such goods and benefits as part of the definition' (Newton (1997: 578).

And indeed, as suggested above, the social capital literature adopts a biased, one-sidedly positive view of social capital. Meanwhile, each of the three key factors underlying its putative beneficial social function – source of social control, source of family support, source of benefits through related networks – can be easily converted into "hindrances to effective decision making through imposing obligations, implying restrictions or exclusion, and entailing unintended consequences and uncertainty" (Haynes 2009a: 16).

Putnam approaches the issue in terms of his distinction into two fundamental forms of social capital; he suggests, namely, such problems can be the result of an imbalance of bonding and bridging social capital inasmuch as "bridging social capital can generate broader identities and reciprocity, whereas bonding social capital bolsters our narrower selves" (Putnam 2000: 23). The problem with that explanation, however, is that as in the case of the account of civil society in general, "the notion of 'balance' is used in a tautological way" (Haynes 2009a: 13).

It is symptomatic of the quality of social capital theory that even taking within its framework a purportedly more balanced position apparently cannot be done without exposing another downside – this time, of the theory of social capital specifically.

What is social capital in one context can be unsocial capital in another. The Church that supports brotherhood and peace in one context becomes a forum for armed militancy in another. Unions that may promote coordination and cooperation with the state in a corporatist context can wage bitter confrontation in another context (Krishna, Shrader 2002: 6).

Note the tendentious selection of examples that puts on an equal footing very diverse phenomena, and, first and foremost, targets unions as a potential trouble-maker. This is directly related to the drawback discussed below.

Another pivotal gap in the theory of social capital is a corollary of the following musings: "Has it become impossible to rebuild a civic society? If citizens tried to revive the old patterns of American civic culture, would the country really be better off? If so, for whom and in what respects?" (McLean, Schultz, and Steger 2002). The question: *cui bono?* is critical here, for it brings out the glaring gap in the theory of social capital–social class. Meanwhile, social capital scholars, with few exceptions such as Bourdieu (leaving aside the issue of quality of his class conception, which leaves very much to be desired), in viewing social differentiation restrict themselves to ethnic and gender divisions, while reducing socio-economic disparities to the issue of poverty.

But the poor, of course, are not a social class, and any talk of societal divisions along the lines poor–rich only serves to cloud the real, deep-seated source of such disparities. It is interesting to note that in this regard there is a striking difference between contemporary social capital theorists and the godfather of the whole tradition of deliberations on the state of civil society and democracy in America, i.e. de Tocqueville, who warned against concentration of wealth because the wealthy bourgeoisie would tend to pursue private interests and abuse their economic and political power (Boesche 1987, 78, 83). In a bourgeois society, excesses of wealth destroy public life by atomising it and isolating people. Should wealth control or rule in America, popular participation, which Tocqueville described as important to the maintenance of a public life, would be threatened (121–2). In addition, he states "private citizens, by combining together, may constitute great bodies of wealth, influence, and strength, corresponding to the persons of an aristocracy" (Tocqueville 1960, vol. II, 387). And accordingly, in Democracy in America, the French thinker describes the new manufactures in negative terms, saying that its aim was to "use" citizens and that it tends to create a private-spirited "aristocracy" (1960, vol. II, 193).

Meanwhile, the contemporary self-styled heir to this grand tradition neglects what, amongst other writers, Schlozman, Verba, and Brady note: the "inequality of civic engagement is unambiguous" (1999: 457). Putnam apparently thinks otherwise, as suggested by the book's 96 figures which highlight a wide range of data and findings but, interestingly enough, not one of the figures provides any breakdown of individuals' civic engagement even by their income or wealth, let alone social class. Only the careful, nay, meticulous reader will be rewarded by stumbling upon observations such as one, drawing on Wilson's work on Chicago's black ghetto, that "social networks are absent in precisely the places where they are needed most" (Putnam 2000, 321). Even so, *Bowling Alone*'s discussion of Wilson's work as a matter of fact only brings out again the one-sidedness of Putnam's emphasis on social capital. Calling Wilson "the nation's leading urban sociologist" and his book *The Truly Disadvantaged* a "classic", Putnam cites it as part of a discussion of how the "decline in neighborhood social capital – community monitoring, socialising, mentoring, and organising – is one important feature of the inner-city crisis, in addition to purely economic factors" (Putnam 2000, 312). In fact, however, as his critics note, "The words "in addition to" are deceptive because they put the decline in social capital on a par with "purely economic factors" and imply that the two are largely independent of each other." But while *The Truly Disadvantaged* repeatedly emphasises that the problems of inner-city black ghettoes have a range of inter-related causes, it also makes clear that economic factors have played a decisive role within this multi-causal web. For example, prior to summing up the chapter on "Social Change and Social Dislocations in the Inner City," Wilson writes: "The increasing social isolation of the inner city is a product of the class transformation of the inner city, including the growing concentration of poverty in inner-city neighborhoods. And the class transformation of the inner city cannot be understood without considering the effects of fundamental changes in the urban economy on the lower-income minorities, effects that include joblessness and that thereby increase the chances of long-term residence in highly concentrated poverty areas" (1987, 61–2).

Such criticisms are valid independent of whether Putnam's thesis itself is valid or not. And it may be noted, first and foremost because these weaknesses are significant as stemming in the last analysis from the flaws inherent in social capital theory, that the said thesis has attracted a range of criticisms. And, again, these objections need to be taken into consideration quite independent of whether one sympathises with the following judgment and its ideological bent: "civic revival will have to contend with a larger political and cultural system that promotes the pursuit of self-interest and political indifference" (McLean, Schultz, and Steger 2002).

Whether one concurs with such an evaluation of capitalism or not, its purported consequence in the form of civic disengagement is not such a clear-cut issue as the above statement seems to imply.

One critic, for instance, distinguishes between exclusive and homogeneous networks and heterogeneous forms that create links across boundaries of class, race, ethnicity, etc. He gives examples: congregation-based community organising, civic environmentalism, and so on. This framework enables the critic in question to pinpoint a flaw in Putnam's thesis of declining social capital to the effect that quantitative decline does not tell the whole story; some of the decline may have in fact been in exclusive/homogeneous forms of social capital, which in his judgment is actually a positive development. Also decline in overall numbers, the critic stresses, may not be as significant as Putnam argues because some associations may now be more proactive in terms of dealing with social problems than they were when their numbers were larger (Civic Practices Network).

Another sceptic, in turn, questioned whether group memberships and civic activities are actually on the decline, or whether they are merely being replaced by new activities in smaller, less formal groups (Ladd 1999). As Nicholas Lehmann put it, referring to the hallmark of Putnam, we may be bowling alone, but we are also "kicking in groups" as soccer leagues have reached new heights of popularity in America (Lehmann 1996).

In Putnam's terms, bowling leagues embody "bridging" forms of social capital and are more conducive to strengthening liberal democracy than associations like the Ku Klux Klan, which represent "bonding" types of social capital. The problem, though, is, Putnam's theory does not explain how societies can generate bridging capital necessary for vibrant bowling leagues while at the same time also accumulating bonding capital that encourages the formation of such illiberal, to put it mildly, associations as the Klan or Militia groups. Be that as it may, the generation of more social capital does not necessarily lead to a flowering of the "good aspects" of liberal democracy. The reader not versed in dialectics may be forgiven for being surprised by Peter Berkowitz (1999) and Michael Edwards' (2000) observations pointing to the fact that social capital can be put to many diverse uses, some of them undemocratic.

In general, Putnam's evidence offers very little in the way of explaining why an increase in social capital should necessarily lead to more democratic participation in the political realm (Barber 1998; Fukuyama 1995; McKnight 1995; Rosenblum 1998).

This weakness to his argument is closely related to another one – ahistoricity that, after all, often goes hand in hand with its metaphysical, or anti-dialectical side; Putnam's analysis testifies, frankly speaking, to rather parochial horizons of its author, as it "misses the fact that civil society is historically amorphous and has an ambiguous relationship with order, revolution, and democratic politics" (McLean, Schultz, Steger 2002). Similarly, globalisation is conspicuous by its absence in Putnam's discussion. As a result of which his "...analysis of trends in American society remains incomplete without a comparative dimension that captures the significance of these burgeoning interconnections around the world" (McLean, Schultz, Steger 2002).

The aforementioned charge of ahistoricity is closely linked to that of asociologism which, in turn, is related to economism – not surprising to us, as we have repeatedly stressed social capital theory's connection to economics, evident from its very name. Putnam's analysis is grounded in a rational-choice individualistic framework alluded to above. Likewise, it is from rational choice theory that Coleman's draws his general view of social processes as created by the free will of individuals. As regards specifically social capital, for Coleman (1988), it is created by rational, purposeful individuals who build social capital to maximise their individual opportunities.

He therefore sees social capital as a form of contract made between individuals unconstrained by underlying economic factors. Social capital here has an "economic rationalist" flavour where individuals freely choose to build networks to further their self-interest (Pope 2003).

Pope also emphasises that "The key component of Coleman's definition is that individuals must have trust that others will reciprocate their actions". And indeed, economists within the rational choice tradition view social capital as informal norms produced as a private good in order to facilitate co-operation. According to this perspective, social capital emerges spontaneously out of interactions of individuals who behave like those participating in prisoner's dilemma games. To cut the long story short, in such a game, the purported rational strategy of humans is to defect, not to cooperate. Robert Axelrod (1984) argues, however, that repeating this game over and over with the chance of meeting the same players again leads to a rational strategy of reciprocity, one in which cooperation is rewarded with cooperation, and defection punished by defection – thereby cooperation begets more cooperation from players in reiterated prisoner's dilemma. As individuals interact repeatedly over time, their rational self-interest induces them to "... develop a self-interested stake in having a reputation for honesty, reliability, and trustworthiness. Hence, we supposedly achieve an individualistic explanation for social mores" (McLean, Schultz, Steger 2002), one which does not, and need not, invoke any altruistic motives of behaviour.

From a sociological point of view, though, for which the aforementioned argument is a modernised version of well-known 'Robinsonades' (after all, Robinson had his Friday) it is easy to concur with the above-cited commentators who find such rational-choice interpretations of social capital and civic engagement severely flawed because they are remarkably ahistorical and contextless. Ultimately, the rise and decline of social capital cannot be explained by rational-choice games alone. After all, many of society's norms and values are lodged in hierarchical structures of authority such as religion and traditional institutions. People tend to obey these norms and remain loyal to them, not out of enlightened self-interest, but for non-rational reasons such as identity, faith, and feelings of duty. Norms from these sources do not come about from bargaining patterns but are passed down from generation to generation through processes of socialisation and habit. They change slowly, unpredictably, and often because of unforeseen developments such as war or dramatic economic change. Tradition – or "path-dependence" as Putnam prefers to call it, sometimes means that norms that are "suboptimal" for individuals can persist for a very long period of time in society. Hence, civic connections in institutions tend to precede individuals in time, rather than follow from their rational choices in a market (or politics).

To be sure, traditional norms are socially constructed, often by accident, but some of these values are more durable and more stubbornly held than others (McLean, Schultz, Steger 2002).

It is precisely the erosion of those forms of civic participation that rely on a sense of faith and moral duty, rather than on economic self-interest or state coercion, which are said to be in decline (Wolfe 1998). "A civic culture cannot simply be 'reinvented', no matter how much social capital theorists such as Putnam would like to see that happen. Thus, to the extent that economistic assumptions are built into the social capital paradigm, it is difficult to see whether attempts to build up more social capital can successfully revive American community." (McLean, Schultz, Steger 2002).

Other critics, as if referring to our headline slogan, accused Putnam of being caught in a "logical circularity" where social capital is theorised as both a cause and effect of civic action (Cobb et al. 1995; Edwards and Foley 1998; Portes 1998; Tarrow 1996). Specifically, it is charged that social capital "definitions do not really differentiate what social capital is from what social capital does, or what are the sources and the consequences of social capital. To confuse the sources of social capital with the benefits derived from them leads to circular reasoning because the presence of social capital is often inferred from the assets that an individual or group acquires" (Veenstra 2001). To use Portes' example, when Putnam argues that a town is "civic" because it has civic participation and "incivic" if it doesn't, it explains nothing since: "equating social capital with the resources acquired through it can easily lead to tautological statements" (Portes 1998: 5). Social capital scholars should take on board that – given the complex, to say the least, nature of their subject – untangling the causes, effects, correlations and conjunctions is a difficult task when dealing with complex, interdependent structures, i.e., networks and their ramifications, "and bold claims should be based on theory, a mechanism, excellent case studies or other solid empirical findings, preferably triangulated with other data" (Haynes 2009a: 9). And yet it is exactly the bold, largely unsubstantiated or outright faulty claims made on behalf of social capital that are gaining it currency (DeFilippis 2001: 801), claims based on co-location (Fischer 2005) "the product of many additional factors that are difficult to reduce to mere resources" (Haynes 2009a: 9).

Still others point out that Putnam neglects the crucial role played by public authorities in the creation of social capital (Maloney et al. 2000).

Along similar lines, Schultz points out that "Putnam's view of democracy is incomplete, seeing it as one that is the sum of the individual attributes and attitudes of its members, while lacking a structural component. In short, Putnam lacks a theory of the state and the role it plays in fostering the conditions that make it possible for voluntary associations to form, exist, and interact" (2002). And indeed, other commentators agree that "the lack of state agency is one of the major flaws of Putnam's explanatory model" (Tarrow 1996).

Some of his fellow theorists go even further, explicitly wishing to restrict the role of the state – along the laissez-faire lines – to that of night watchman, like in this Fukuyama's claim, akin to a well-known view by the otherwise very different thinker, F. Hayek of an Austrian persuasion, according to which the state interferes in the spontaneous production of order at its peril.

Such a stance attracts a lot of criticism. It is emphasised that in the social capital literature "the complex forms of interaction between public bodies and institutions of civil society have not received the attention they deserve" (Maloney, Smith, and Stoker 2002). The aforementioned scholars point out that "it is necessary to take a wider and more contextual perspective on social capital, and not only to focus on numbers and activities of voluntary associations but also to take into account the relationship between different voluntary associations and political institutions". Meanwhile, many "…accounts in the social capital debate imply that influence flows only in one direction – civil society to state – rather than reciprocally" (Maloney, Smith, and Stoker 2002).

This impact may show up both in the presence and absence of relevant effects, as attested to by an investigation of recent attempts to improve social circumstances in poor housing estate areas in Sydney (Randolph et al. 1999). The authors conclude that the community development effort in Waterloo failed because a more substantial "all of government" approach was needed. They argue that jobs, welfare policy, education, skills training, health and social services are required to bring disadvantaged households back into the mainstream.

Meanwhile, as Tarrow (1996: 395) notes, Putnam generally perceives the state as an exogenous factor, which neglects the role played by political structures and institutions in shaping the context of associational activity and hence, as follows from the preceding, the creation of social capital. The above-mentioned commentators "…argue that political institutions have a significant role, at least in helping to sustain civic vibrancy and probably also in stimulating its growth. Public authorities are deeply implicated in the shape and activities of voluntary associations" (Maloney, Smith, and Stoker 2002). For example, Maraffi (1998: 16) argues that the vibrancy of associational life he found in north-eastern and central Italy 'is not so much the result of spontaneous, horizontal, "bottom-up", social activity; rather it is the result of purposeful activities to mobilise the population…. The presence of voluntary associations in a given area is a complex phenomenon as to its genesis and development'.

Skocpol (1997: 16) states that "recent research by historians underscores the enduring importance of the US federal government in promoting a vibrant civil society". Walker's (1991: 49) data show, on the other hand, that one of the most important reasons for the rapid expansion of the citizen groups sector in the US was the growth of patronage. His 1980 survey found that 89 per cent of citizen groups had received financial assistance from an outside source in order to start its operations. Regarding the UK, Hall (1999: 443) reports that: 'not only have British Governments made substantial efforts to ensure that voluntary activity flourishes, they have also adopted an approach to social policy that makes extensive use of volunteers, alongside professionals, for the delivery of social services. This commitment has been accompanied by large public expenditures, via grants and fees for services, to the kinds of associations that mobilise voluntary action on the local level.'

Thus, the state does matter; "all the indications are that these government policies have made a major contribution to sustaining the kind of associations that augment the level of social capital in Britain" (Maloney, Smith, and Stoker 2002).

At the local level, Lowndes et al. (1998: 16) have argued that encouraging participation is an everyday element of English local government practice. Their 1997 study found that local government in the UK was engaged in a wide range of public participation initiatives "…such activities on the part of political institutions cannot be ignored and may well have important effects on the creation or enhancement of social capital" (Maloney, Smith, and Stoker 2002).

According to the aforementioned scholars, their field research on civic associations demonstrates that Putnam's approach overlooks the level of inter-penetration of public authorities and voluntary and community associations.

This aspect of social capital theory is criticised even by social capital themselves; the following criticism is useful in that it points to a key source of the above-mentioned failings consisting in a too narrow focus of the theory discussed above:

> The author argues for keeping theoretically distinct three elements of social capital: norms, networks, and consequences. Social capital, in his opinion, encompasses values and attitudes that encourage citizens to trust and cooperate with each other. Social networks are, according to this view, a critical part of social capital because the ability to mobilise personal social contacts is important to a functioning society. It is not clear, however, whether trust according to the conception under consideration must exist for social networks to form or if the networks foster trust. On his part the theorist in question suggests that social capital should not be defined by the social goods that it is assumed to produce, rather, one should pose the question: Does social capital help generate collective goods and services and, if so, under what conditions? He also, importantly, criticises the Tocquevillean (1968) approach, which suggests that democracy is generated by face-to-face interaction in formal voluntary organisations. He suggests that researchers must instead address the question of what sorts of organisations are best at generating what forms of social capital (Newton 1997).

If the very account of social capital condition in the US by Putnam is disputable, no less doubts are raised by his explanation of the developments concerned. Putnam dismisses such factors accounting for the decline in civic participation, as frequently indicated in the literature: increased mobility, suburbanisation, pressures on time and money, generational change, and women entering the work force – he instead points to television watching as the "main culprit" in the erosion of social capital.

While from the viewpoint of sociology of knowledge it is understandable that people who themselves deal with ideal products, overplay the role of the ideal compared to material in social life, this tendency as such, naturally, by no means validates particular claims to that effect. Trapped within his interactionist–individualist, and thereby anti-structuralist perspective, Putnam "fails to appreciate forces in the polity and economy that cause civic indifference. We may be bowling alone, not by individual choice, but as a result of the vast growth of corporations and interest groups since the 1950s" (McLean, Schultz, Steger 2002).

And there is even more to this than that; Putnam's analysis exhibits problems with logical circularities (Portes 1998), historical flaws (Sabetti 1996) or internal contradictions (Lemann 1996).

To reiterate, however, the chief conclusion from our discussion above is the possibility of substituting the term of civic engagement for the term of social capital. This conclusion might be drawn on the basis of other pieces of social capital literature as well.

In another work, for example, a study is being reported that uses a Coleman/Putnam-derived definition of social capital as a productive and positive resource: "social capital refers to those stocks of social trust, norms and networks that people can draw on to solve common problems. Networks of civic engagement, such as neighbourhood associations, sports clubs and cooperatives, are an essential form of social capital" (Civic Practices Network).

Besides, in our conclusion we are not alone. Others may arrive at a similar conclusion in quite different contexts, as the following example shows.

Schuller (2001) suggests that, although social capital lacks an agreed upon definition and measurement approach, it is useful as a policy concept because it provides a wide focus and foundation for policy analysis, it, Schuller insists, allows for the issue of social cohesion to be addressed in economic decision making and it inserts a longer term perspective into our policy decisions.

From our analysis, however, it may be suggested that utility of a misnomer as a practical policy tool is bound to be rather limited, to say the least.

This is reflected, inter alia, in the critique made by structural scholars who argue – pointing thus implicitly to the said nature of the concept in question, as not referring to any capital or resources in the real sense – that it is access to economic resources that underlies impoverishment, not lack of social capital. In a similar vein, it is noted that "there are real dangers in seeing top-down programmes to 'enhance social capital' as a quick fix for the unwanted effects of market economics. If people need jobs, a living wage, better housing, a better diet, more autonomy, more self-respect and less stress, then tinkering with their social relations is unlikely to make the vital differences" (Wilkinson 1999).

And more broadly,

> there is little ground to believe that social capital will provide a ready remedy for major social problems, as promised by its bolder proponents. Recent proclamations to that effect merely restate the original problems and have not been accompanied so far by any persuasive account of how to bring about the desired stocks of public civicness. (Maloney, Smith, and Stoker 2002: 225)

To focus again on a specific area:

> the concept of social capital has generated much enthusiasm in health promotion circles, but also many criticisms, with even its most enthusiastic supporters pointing to its shortcomings. Baum (1999) warns that in its present state of

development the concept is vague, slippery, and poorly specified, and in danger of 'meaning all things to all people' on both right and left of the political spectrum. As such it urgently needs clarification. Gillies (1998) emphasises that social capital is a descriptive construct rather than an explanatory theory, and that much work remains to be done in accounting for the mechanisms underlying the alleged health-community link. Other less sympathetic critics argue that those who seek to import social capital into the field of health promotion research are simply reinventing the wheel, and that most of the so-called insights the concept would allegedly bring to health promotion are already well established in both research and practice in this field. (Labonte 1999)

The most strongly articulated criticism is that the concept of social capital has been so enthusiastically grasped by health professionals, ranging from local and national government representatives to overseas development agencies, because it points towards a convenient justification for a retreat from expensive welfare spending. Cynical critics point out that despite the abundance of strong research linking material deprivation and health inequalities, such as Gordon et al. (1999), social capital proponents prefer to place their emphasis on the, as yet only hypothesised, link between health and social capital. Critics suggest that social capital is popular because its implications for policy – for example, that ordinary people should be encouraged to participate in the local civic community in the interests of improving community levels of health – are cheaper than the goal of reducing income inequalities.[1] They also argue that such thinking potentially incorporates an element of victim-blaming, implying that poor people are unhealthy because they do not devote enough energy to participation in community activities (Muntaner and Lynch 1999).

And, as hinted above, even social capital proponents are forced to admit that empirical research into the health–social capital link is still in its infancy. However, a preliminary analysis of existing health survey data in England (Cooper et al. 1999) suggests that material living conditions and socio-economic position remain stronger predictors of adverse health than various indicators of social capital (Campbell 2002: 184).

Along similar lines, Gillies, Tolley, and Wolstenholme (1996) emphasise that the primary cause of health inequalities is poverty and that the economic regeneration of deprived communities is essential for reducing such inequalities.

---

1   More broadly, the reason for which social capital has become so fashionable amongst politicians is shed light upon by Brown and Lauder (2002: 225). "At a time when there seems little hope of expanding public provision, social capital seems to provide a panacea for underwriting new forms of social solidarity at little extra cost to the exchequer". And, as might be expected, the aforementioned critics are not fond of this fad: "The fundamental concern with the way the term 'social capital' has been converted into political currency is that it is being used to rationalise cheap remedies for problems which require new ways of thinking" (Brown, Lauder 2002: 255).

What lies at the heart of "capitalisation" of social relations subsumed into the term under consideration is revealed by the following contention: "Social capital reduces the cost of coordination and, consequently, impacts directly on the boundaries of the firm, by placing them in a better position than their competitors to outsource and specialise still further, and to appropriate the excess rents flowing from the resulting deepening of the division of labour" (Maskell 2002: 117). A grain of truth in the label concerned comes from its association with economic ownership – as manifested in the above quote by the use of the word "rents". However, and there lies the rub, "social-capital" relations only indirectly contribute to the acquisition of rents; as the aforementioned author admits, they stem from the division of labour.

In a similar vein, one report discussing application of social capital theory to non-profit organisations using The Benevolent Society (Australia's oldest non-profit) as a case study suggests that the term social capital is confusing and intimidating – so for the purposes of the case study the term 'community engagement' was substituted (Hampshire and Healy (2000).

Chapter 6
Social Capital as a Multi-Misnomer

The situation is actually far worse than the former section might suggest. The point is, the Protean (as aptly noted above) term of social capital may refer to a plethora of diverse phenomena, thereby proving to be a misnomer in plural.

Thus, the above-mentioned focus on interpersonal networks within community associations leads to a misnomer whereby the new label is being imposed on an old notion – particularism, or one of Parsons' pattern variables: "Each family must access systems through particularistic social capital mechanisms" (Schneider 2004: 195).

However, as distinct from the understanding discussed above, an author of an essay on social capital notes in its concluding remarks: "In the present essay, social capital has been treated as an analytical category [...] independent of civic society and democracy" (Maskell 2002: 121). And Schneider (2004: 219) is even more explicit: "social capital means relationships that help people find resources to meet their needs, not civic engagement". Likewise, Paxton (1999: 98) refers to "the conflation of social capital with its outcomes (civic engagement)".

Another social capital scholar has this to say regarding his subject:

> Some authors who have used this term are concerned with institution-building, democracy, effective service delivery, political and administrative accountability, and ideas about citizen participation. Others are concerned with even broader issues in societal integration, and with the differences between those for whom a political system works and those whom it might be said to fail, and who fail to thrive in it. (Loizos2002: 125)

As a consequence, even some social capital scholars willy-nilly bring out the problems its definitions pose:

> Social capital has emerged in some articles as an overarching phrase for a range of concepts, which researchers have cited as elements reflecting the presence or the absence of social capital. Some of these include 'social connectedness', 'social cohesion', 'community competence', 'social networks', 'social inclusion', 'social support', 'social isolation' and 'social exclusion'. Debates have ensued about their various definitions, discriminating characteristics and their relationships to social capital. (Pope 2003)

And this is not the end of the story.

Social capital is used in a myriad of ways in the literature: as "family and kinship connections; social networks or associational life related to groups or organisations; cross-sectoral linkages or networks of networks that link organisations of state, market and civil society around problem-solving tasks; political capital, the informal relationships and norms that link civil society and the state and which determine levels of social control over the state; institutional and policy frameworks regulating public life; and social norms and values which influence societal functioning" (Fevre 2002).

And, typically for the social capital literature, there immediately appears an addition and correction to the above treatment: "identities are a third, neglected component of social capital, neither norms nor networks but intimately tied to both" (Fevre 2002).

According to another all-encompassing definition, social capital should be referred to as "those expectations for action within a collectivity that affect the economic goals and goal seeking behavior of its members, even if these expectations are not oriented toward the economic sphere" (Portes and Sensenbrenner 1993: 1323).

As if in response to the criticism of too narrow a scope of the concept of social network, a social capital scholar avoids this weakness at the expense of stretching the concept in question beyond all sensible limits, couching it as "the ability of actors to secure benefits by virtue of membership in social networks or other social structures" (Portes, 1998: 6); the reader is told in this connection that "it is important to note that, by this definition, social capital is not limited to its network forms, but includes broader social structures that facilitate certain action of actors – whether persons or corporate actors – within the structure" (Coleman 1988: S98).

Another writer goes even further, as a result of which in this breadth competition the definition cited below comes up certainly as a leading contestant: "we conceptualise social capital as the ability to secure benefits by virtue of membership in social structures, an ability that is qualified by the cultural practice within the social structures" (Lin 2007).[1] This qualification does little to narrow the extreme scope of the concept so defined, since the term "cultural practices" is just as general as that of "social structures".

If anything, even more inclusive is the following definition offered by an author of an essay: "The definition offered by this paper is that social capital is a resource to collective action leading to a range of outcomes" (Stone 2001).

---

1 Interestingly enough, the researcher in question puts a rather scornful judgment on a cognate ["human resources (defined as the total pool of human capital under the control of the firm (McWilliams et al. 2001)]) term, failing to measure his own concept by the same yardstick; he dismisses human resources as "The fancy word for 'people'. The human resources department within an organisation, years ago known as the 'personnel department', manages the administrative aspects of the employees" (Lin 2007).

Small wonder that operating on such a broad platform, many definitions arrive at so wide a scope that their *definiens* becomes nearly identical to society; "Social capital manifests in formal bodies such as the core judicial, democratic and governance institutions, to disseminate and reinforce social values and expectations. It is also embodied in the less formal institutions of sports, religion and fashion" (Asadi 2008).

Along the same lines, it is held that in terms of constructing social capital, there may be three pathways (Fox, 1996): state society convergence when government insiders use their power and influence to support disadvantaged communities, 'co-production' which refers to collaboration between local and distant civil society organisations, and grassroots group formation and mobilisation (Bebbington, Perreault 1999).

A still broader approach to social capital is represented by the following definition: "the social processes of groups that bestow advantage on individuals" (Pope 2004: 9). This definition, as well as certain others, loosely alludes to ownership, but because it does it in a cryptic way and without any clear notion of ownership, the said under-articulation with ownership makes it, if anything, a poor analytical tool. As they say in Poland, they know that the bell rings, but they don't know in what church.

A broad conception of social capital is also espoused by a prominent scholar in this field of study who defines its subject as follows: "It is not a single entity but a variety of different entities, with two elements in common: they all consist of some aspect of social structures, and they facilitate certain actions of actors.... within the structure.... Like other forms of capital, social capital is productive, making possible the achievement of certain ends that in its absence would not be possible" (Coleman 2000: 16).

Putnam attributes numerous benefits of social capital, including facilitation of voluntary and spontaneous cooperation, the ability to maintain credit associations, and other forms of social commerce (McLean, Schultz, Steger 2002).

Other social capital writers, however, disagree, insisting that not only spontaneous co-operation counts. There are two mechanisms through which people pursue social capital: reciprocity transactions and enforceable trust; individual's disciplined compliance with group expectations (Burt, Yasumoto 1998). But one can easily point to such treatments of social capital which definitely distinguish it from trust – "social capital is economically superior to built trust" (Maskeill 2002).

Another researcher, noting an aspect that has been identified above, referring to "the Tocquevillean (1968) model, which suggests that democracy is generated by face-to-face interaction in formal voluntary organisations", reports that "Putnam has been criticized for over-emphasis on the role of voluntary organisations without considering the role of formal institutions in creating social CAPITAL" (Warner 1999). Still another commentator notes that in the literature concerned "much attention has been given to the role of voluntary associations while the roles of families, schools and firms have been less researched" (Coté 2001).

Social capital has also been measured across units of analysis ranging from the individual to the nation. To cite but one example, "Robert Putnam has alternated between emphasizing social capital as a private good for individuals and a public good for groups" (McLean, Schultz, Steger 2002).

Colem (1988: S95–120) argued that social capital exists within levels or scales as one feels belonging to family, community, profession, country, etc., simultaneously. Adler and Kwon (2002: 17–40), however, noted that although social capital was originally conceived as a community-wide concept, it should be observable at the individual level.

Given that, for example, "Bourdieu identified it at the individual level and Putnam since at the community level" (Asadi 2008), Asadi attempts what is not exactly a Solomon's judgement:

The general consensus in the literature is that social capital is identifiable from the individual level to the level of the nation however it is clear that social capital is evident at any level where there is identification and belonging. Rather, the fact of the matter is that in the social capital literature "the distinction between an individual or a collective level of definition of social capital, i.e. social capital is a resource which facilitates ends for individual or for a social group" is persistent and very much evident. "However, collective social capital cannot be simply the sum of individual social capital. If social capital is a resource available through social networks, the resources that some individuals claim come at the expense of others" (Veenstra 2001).

This conceptual confusion is inevitably reflected at the level of measurement of social capital. Macinko et al. have reviewed the different indicators of social capital, finding out that the labelling of apparently the same criteria varies extensively from one study to another (e.g. social trust, mistrust, civic trust, interpersonal trust). A second problem arises because of the aforementioned lack of consensus on the level of aggregation at which social capital measures should be assessed (individual, community, state). Most of the studies have been quantitative and have used proxies, when trying to measure a per capita membership in voluntary groups and levels of interpersonal trust. Concepts such as 'trust', 'community' or 'networks', are intrinsically difficult to quantify. Some of the more recent work on social capital has *expressis verbis* recognised the difficulties in measuring social capital as a single explanatory variable. Kawachi, for instance, has concluded that because of the methodological problems in measuring social capital, findings concerned with the role of social capital should be interpreted with a good deal of caution.

Another social capital scholar notes that

> indicators of social capital include outcomes based on its core components of networks, trust and reciprocity. The outcome of civic engagement has been measured by counting memberships in voluntary associations. Other more

indirect indicators of social capital in the literature include: life expectancy, health status, suicide rates, employment rates, growth in GDP, etc. (Stone 2001).

His apposite critical conclusion that "these approaches have led to confusion about what social capital is as separate from what it does" (Stone 2001) should, however, be extended to include the observation that in fact the said confusion is of much wider nature, since on the basis of the above-mentioned enumeration one can scarcely distinguish social capital from society at large.

Thus, amongst problems the measurement of social capital encounters, there are undoubtedly at least some that cannot be resolved by the following statement, otherwise quite dialectical and correct in its implicit criticism of crude positivism or form of mathematical idealism according to which "to be or not to be" should be understood as "to be quantifiable or not"; not quantifiable things simply find themselves beyond the confines of cognizance, and this unavailability for cognition, for all intents and purposes, equates to non-being:

"Social capital may be a prime illustration of the *importance/measurability* dilemma: the important may not be measurable but this does not stop the measurable from becoming important. However, this is a paradox of despair. In almost any sphere the question is not the binary one of whether or not something is measurable, but to what extent (as well as under what conditions and at what cost)" (Schuller 2001: 17).

> This all-encompassing nature has led to criticisms of the concept as being too flexible and therefore meaningless (Woolcock 2001).

It is fair to say that Robert Putnam contributed significantly to this semantic dilution; on the banners of the French Revolution was inscribed a triad of ideals – liberty, equality, and fraternity. Fraternity, as the French democrats intended it, was another name for what I term "social capital" (Putnam 2000: 351).

This claim has provoked, and deservedly so, an acrimonious comment on the part of some stunned commentators:

> Although 'Bowling Alone' is replete with statements about the wondrous qualities of social capital, few are as grandiose as the claim linking it to one of the most famous, lofty, and inspiring slogans in Western political history. Given the grandiosity of the claim, it is made with surprising nonchalance. No evidence, historical or otherwise, is offered for the putative equivalence of social capital and fraternity. Rather, it is presented as if self-evident (Smith, Kulynych 2002).

And the critics show that actually this is far from being the case: "any claim of the synonymy of fraternity and social capital conflates what the French revolutionaries considered two very different worlds of meaning – one associated with community and the other associated with the pursuit of economic gain" (Smith, Kulynych

2002). And the fact of the matter is that "Even if the sansculottes' antipathy to capital in the traditional meaning of the term is set aside, fraternité had a meaning for them that simply cannot be comprehended by the term social capital" (Smith, Kulynych 2002), for in those years of the Revolution, the term referred to a "relationship which ought to exist between all citizens as members of a national community of equals, and its realisation is both demanded and praised" (Roberts 1976: 334). The following three social capital writers recommend their favourite by distinguishing no less than precisely three approaches to the construct under consideration: "The concept has an immediate intuitive appeal, [...] The first limits itself to those writings which use the term explicitly; its scope is then defined by what emerges when 'social capital' is entered into the search engines available to us. The second takes the key elements, such as trust or networks, and reviews the literature relating to these. The third, most extensive, kind would include all the theories which seem to be related in some way to social capital, even though they make no explicit reference to the concept itself" (Schuller, Baron, Field 2000).

With such a wide purview, the reader may be forgiven for being surprised to hear that also no other than Emile Durkheim turns out to be one of the founders of not only modern sociology, but also theory of social capital – "social capital has a long history in sociology: it may have started when Durkheim, in 1901, identified a relationship between the rate of suicide and the level of social integration (Veenstra 2001; see also, Schuller, Baron, Field 2002: 33).

This intellectual misappropriation is, in all probability, based on Durkheim's interest in social cohesion (e.g. Campbell (2002) uses interchangeably the terms: "social capital or community cohesion"), which, naturally, adds yet another meaning to an ever-lengthening list – as social cohesion, albeit related to some of the previously cited definitions, is nevertheless a concept in its own right.[2]

The French classic finds himself at that in the company of rather strange bed-fellows: "it is impressive how wide is the collective range of intellectual pedigrees adduced to social capital. Many of the classic figures of social science appear – Ferguson, Smith, Marx, Durkheim, and Douglas, to name only some. Sometimes the lineage identified is surprising: for instance, the inspiration provided by John Dewey" (Schuller, Baron, Field 2002: 33).

Small wonder that from such a broad perspective, it is argued that "the preoccupations of the social capital approach have been the preoccupations of classical sociologists and anthropologists. They have been 'social capital theorists' since the early days of their discipline because of the centrality of their concern with

---

2   Which, as a matter of fact, by no means prevent it from being a misnomer in another, ahistorical sense; ahistoricity of human and social capital approaches has been repeatedly identified in the body of the text, and this very flaw plagues also definitions of social cohesion such as the following one: "Social cohesion has been described as 'a reconciliation of a system of organisation based on market forces, freedom of opportunity with a commitment to the values of solidarity and mutual support which ensures open access to benefit and protection for all members of society'" (Ritzen 2000).

core social institutions and with the constitution of society: that is, with kinship and the family, with marriage, with local political and religious organisations, and with friendship through the concepts of exchange and trust in all its forms between equals and between unequals. The functionalists, from Durkheim and Malinowski, were preoccupied with the way in which social systems bound their members into something more than the pursuit of individual interests.[...] their interest in factors promoting coherence and integration have entered into the collective thinking of the discipline" (Loizos 2002: 125).

And social capital advocates themselves cannot deny that even in the first sense of the three mentioned above, that is, in the area of explicit definitions, the unity of meaning seems a distant dream. Take, for instance, A work published by the Royal Commission on Canada's Economic Prospects under the title "Housing and Social Capital" which defines social capital in terms of 'schools and universities, churches and related buildings, hospitals, roads and streets, airports, sewer and water systems, and other buildings and installations appertaining to public institutions and departments of government' (Dube, Howes, and McQueen 1957: 1–2). Social capital, in this formulation, is the public physical infrastructure of a nation, and, by the way, while at first glance because of this very physical connotation, the label of capital seems in the above-mentioned case appropriate, in fact this is not the case; the use of "capital" is proper only with reference to the private sector, whereas streets, government buildings, and so on even do not belong in the economy.

Even setting aside such rarer[3] definitions, the preceding fully corroborates the charge of all-purpose nature of the concept (Portes 1998). Thus, it should be made clear that this kind of critique is by no means original; to cite but one example, two critics cannot hide their astonishment engendered by "the sheer breadth of phenomena that are being potentially claimed for social capital" (Fine, Green 2002). No wonder that armed with such an inclusive concept, one can make grossly exaggerated claims about its importance: "networks of civic engagement are[...] seen by many interested scholars as having direct policy relevance in areas such as health, crime, welfare, economic growth, the performance of political institutions, and the development of effective and democratic governance (see Coleman 1988a; 1990a; Fukuyama 1995; Halpern 1998; Putnam 1993a; 1995a, b; 1998b). Grootaert and Van Bastelaer (47) assert that social capital has a profound impact in many different areas of human life and development: it affects the provision of services, in both urban and rural areas, transforms the prospects for agricultural development, influences the expansion of private enterprises, improves the management of common resources, helps improve education, can

---

3   In a sense, however, they are not that rare in that they overlap a cognate category of a more conventional character, as exemplified by the following notion of "public health and other social infrastructure investment" as involved with "a classic social movement of social capital building in Britain's new industrial towns, spending increasingly on their environments and local social and health services" (Szreter 2002).

contribute to recovery from conflict and can help compensate for a deficient state. Moreover, "social capital is critical for poverty alleviation and sustainable human and economic development" (Dolfsma, Dannreuther 2003: 405–13). It also turns out that "outcomes of social capital "are so wide-ranging, that they "include: life expectancy; health status; suicide rates; teenage pregnancy; crime rates; participation rates in tertiary education; employment and unemployment rates; family income; marital relationship formations and dissolutions; business confidence; job growth; growth in GDP; and balance of trade" (Spellerberg 1997: 43–4). In slightly different terms, "the level of social capital in a community has direct impact on business, children, neighborhoods and health. Social capital leads directly to individual and community prosperity" (Bay Area Community Council 2002). Social capital proponents will go to any lengths to pay homage to their idol, even indulge in tautologies, as in the following contention, where it is rather self-evident, after all, that social capital accumulation cannot dispense without social capital: "Social capital is multifunctional. It embraces essential factors of economic production, provides a basis for collective action within society and is in itself an essential input factor of social capital accumulation" (Asadi 2008).

Small wonder that many social scientists still remain unconvinced, being sceptical of the "panacea for all ills" school of thought (Berman 1997; Foley and Edwards 1997; 1998; Maloney, Smith, and Stoker forthcoming; and Portes 1998). For example, Portes (1998: 2) rather dismissively points out that: 'Despite its current popularity, the term does not embody any idea new to sociologists. That the involvement and participation in groups can have positive consequences for the individual and the community is a staple notion" that dates back to the work of Durkheim and Marx.'

Indeed, and hence, for instance, Asadi's (2008) conclusion drawn from, inter alia, Ostrom's seminal research that "Enhanced social capital can improve environmental outcomes through decreased costs of collective action, increase in knowledge and information flows, increased cooperation, less resource degradation and depletion, more investment in common lands and water systems, improved monitoring and enforcement" refers to some real enough socio-economic phenomena, but fails to notice that the only ground for his claim that it is social capital that gives birth to them is his own subsumption of the latter into the former, which, needless to say, violates canons of valid explanation. Likewise, his claim that "where social capital is well-developed, local groups with locally developed rules and sanctions are able to make more of existing resources than individuals working alone or in competition. Social capital indicates a community's potential for cooperative action to address local problems" (Asadi 2008) is a tautology, since if one defines social capital as a capacity to co-operate ("As Fukuyama notes social capital refers to the ability of people to work with each other in groups." [Asadi 2008]), it is hardly a startling inference that social capital enhances co-operation. To break this vicious circle it would be necessary for him to identify the real underlying source of this collective spirit, which is common ownership. Suffice it to mention Jodha's (1988) argument that in many traditional cases of rural resource management, farm and village families had a strong community stake in the resource base on which they have long been so heavily dependent, over which they had effective local control of their integrated management system and of which they have had close functional knowledge of the subtleties of sustainable management (including coping with climatic variability). Given a self-sustaining nature of those resource management systems as based on common ownership, He argues that contrary to the received wisdom it is not poverty per se that leads to actions and decisions leading to resource degradation but rather externally generated changes to the managerial environment of the community.

Such sober and sobering observations seem, though, to do little to reduce the number of claims pointing out the alleged efficacy of social capital: "A society's endowment of social capital is critical to understanding its industrial structure, and hence its place in the global capitalist division of labour" (Fukuyama 1995: 325); or, "large stocks of social capital are probably also among the reasons why low-tech firms can continue to prosper in high-cost regions and even dominate the economy of most countries in western Europe" (Maskell and Tornqvist 1999). Nay, we are told that it is social capital which nowadays constitutes a virtually sole competitive advantage and reason for the divergence in the rates of national economic growth.

Recent level accounting exercises have [...] shown how a large variation across countries in output per worker with seemingly similar levels of physical capital and educational attainment must indicate the existence of factors crucial to economic performance residing outside the realm of mainstream economics (Hall and Jones 1999).

Many labels have been put on the residual. Abramovitz (1986) coined the expression 'social capability' to describe the aptitude to make institutional changes leading to divergence in growth rates. Hall and Jones (1999) talk of 'social infrastructure'. Others have discussed the significance of 'social fabric' or emphasized the role of national or regional 'culture' favourable to innovation and change. In spite of such difference in focus and terminology the studies signify a growing awareness and recognition of non-monetary factors significance for economic growth. But what we would really like to measure: not only the effect or outcome of social capital, but the input: each community's stock of social capital (Maskell 2002: 117).

Note the paralogism involved in the argument cited above. Its author himself acknowledges and lists a number of terms referring to what he defines as social capital. What he fails to recognise, though, is that his conclusion does not follow; whether the researchers cited by him are right or not, they by any means refer to "social capital". Conversely, they apparently have had good reasons for not using this catchword. This does not restrain the economist under consideration from paying tribute to the alleged merits of social capital bolstered by an array of half-truths and outright untruths (location of business is still relevant, labour and other costs are vastly different in the various regions of the globe and may constitute a major competitive advantage or handicap, cutting-edge technologies are only seemingly easy to copy, as their implementation requires duly skilled labour force whose availability in many economies cannot be taken for granted, all foreign companies investing, e.g., in China would be astonished to hear that a large domestic market has no appeal, and so on (Dierickx and Cool 1989, Prahalad and Hamel 1990).

What follows is equally interesting, but – for reasons considered below – controversial: "Firms cope with this problem of former important inputs converted to ubiquities by basing their competitiveness on unique in-house competencies and capabilities gradually developed over time and supplemented with any remaining heterogeneous input. In order to contribute to the competitiveness of firms, such an input must be valuable and difficult to imitate, replicate, or substitute (Barney 1991). Social capital is such an input. It is increasingly valuable as globalization progresses. It is not abundant in all communities. It cannot be bought or acquired. And, most significantly, it is impossible to imitate, replicate, or substitute" (Maskell 2002: 118).

Elsewhere the same advocate of social capital argues that "social capital enables firms to improve their innovation capability and conduct business transactions without much fuss and has, therefore, substantial implications for economic performance" (Maskell 2000: 111).

Interestingly enough, the author of this bold assertion with disarming frankness concedes that "we still know very little about the process by which social capital is produced and accumulated" (Maskell 2000: 114). How to reconcile the above-cited sweeping statement with this kind of ignorance is a puzzle. It is also a puzzle how Hans Westlund and Elin Nilsson (2005) can reconcile their claim to the effect that there are grounds to believe that there are connections between an enterprise's investment in social capital and its growth, and their even more truly stunning confession that "when the available research is examined in more detail, it is found to include advertising sponsorship and internal entertainment among the main types of investment in social capital".

That supposedly universally valid, ahistorical claims on the importance of social capital lose much of their generality when properly contextualised is exemplified by the next conception which begins with the following bold declaration: "'attitude' has the potential of being the crucial cognitive social capital for the development of any society" (Prasad 2007). Upon closer scrutiny, however, it turns out that the strange creation named "cognitive social capital" refers largely to co-operation (which, naturally, implies communication, which may be, if one wishes, term "cognitive" aspect), and moreover, to its specific variety tied to common property management. The writer concerned explains (note, adding yet another term for social capital, as though the existing list were not enough): "Attitude influences action. It can work as the crucial cognitive social capital for the sustained management of any common property resource. Social capital for managing water for irrigation although used chiefly in regions with annual rainfall of less than 20 ins (51 cm), it is also used in wetter areas to grow certain crops, e.g., rice. as a common property resource in a western Tarai village, Nepal. Such capital is also widely known as 'social subjectivity' in the literature of contemporary development" (Prasad 2007). The word "capital" in this context, social or whatever, is a misnomer if only because the concept in question is inextricably connected with private property relations.

Some proponents of social capital, acknowledging the all-encompassing character of the concept, attempt, nevertheless, to defend its raison d'etre on rather peculiar grounds. Thus, the three aforementioned social capital scholars recognise "the breadth and protean character of the concept", while at the same time admitting that the criticisms levelled against it on that count "are serious ones and carry weight, Yet" they reckon that the fact that those criticisms may at one level be 'valid' does not necessarily undermine the case for using the concept", for "it reflects the fact that a concept that has such breadth is bound not to be a perfect fit for all, or even many, of the cases where it is applied" (Schuller, Baron, Field 2000). This, of course, begs the question, since it is exactly the very breadth of the concept that is at issue.

And, as a matter of fact, many commentators agree on this point; "The term of social capital has been widely criticised because the concept has been stretched and modified to cover a wide range of relationships at different levels" (Veenstra 2001).

As an inevitable consequence, social capital is, according to an apt criticism, "a fundamentally elusive concept, explaining almost any social science phenomenon with a "capacity to draw uncritically on any handy analysis" (Fine 2002: 796). From this perspective, "the multiple perspectives invoking social capital in support of a wide range of phenomena" (Haynes 2009a) by any means do attest to the merit, rather than weakness of the concept under consideration. Even the aforementioned social capital scholar, after all, acknowledges "the flaw in identifying the concept too closely with functionally different notions" (Haynes 2009a). And the consequences are ominous; if it is a Herculean task to explain anything on the basis of a misnomer, a multi-misnomer's explanatory power is, without a doubt, non-existent. Upon a comprehensive review of the relevant research literature, Michael Woolcock concludes "that a single term is inadequate to explain the range of empirical situations demanded of it" (Woolcock 1998: 159) on the basis that a range of perspectives conceptualise the concept in different, and conflicting, ways: "If social capital can be rational, pre-rational, or even non-rational, what is it *not?*" (Woolcock 1998: 156).

And indeed, as though referring to the title of the present chapter, he points out that the concept's original sin lies in "trying to explain too much with too little" (Woolcock 1998: 155), noting: "Ordinarily, a theory's parsimony i.e., its capacity to explain the most with the least is a desirable property; in this instance, however, a single term is being adopted indiscriminately, adapted uncritically, and applied imprecisely" (Woolcock 1998: 196).

As a result, it explains nothing.

Linked to the above-mentioned criticism of *ex post* explanation or circular reasoning is "the problem of the direction of causality. Changes in social capital and changes in communities, even if they are related, it is difficult to show which direction causality originated" (Haynes 2009a: 10). While circumstantial evidence suggests that social capital, as measured in terms of active participation in associations that knit society together is associated with perceptions of decline in the community (see Putnam 2000), then – assuming the two are causally (which itself is a rather heroic assumption, given that correlation by no means implies causation) – the problem of direction of the latter has not been resolved, as Steven Durlauf notes: "Do trust-building social networks lead to efficacious communities, or do successful communities generate these types of social ties? As far as I know, no study has been able to shed much light on this question." (Durlauf 1999: 3).

It is true that a number of more recent studies have attempted to provide a causal relationship using different methods (see, for example, Rose 2000; Mohan and Mohan 2002; Landry, Amara, and Lamari 2002). Most importantly, their failure can be traced back to the fact that the concept employed as an explanatory tool is a multiple misnomer.

However, even these results are far from conclusive. The lack of precision concerning the causes and effects of features associated with social capital is a direct consequence of operating a multiplicity of concepts under the same umbrella term:

> The importance of trust, social support and social exchange depend on different mechanisms and the nature of the interdependencies and feedback mechanisms that exist between these factors in different circumstances is not clarified by grouping them together as homogenous components. The complex nature of the interdependencies and feedback dynamics implies that linear descriptions of causality are unenlightening at best and in danger of presenting inappropriate policy instruments, and yet the literature, while acknowledging this challenge, neither address it, nor challenge the conventional direction of causality (Haynes 2009a: 10).

> Attempts to operationalise social capital in explaining innovation illustrate that once unified, the concept explains very little even when identified as a contributory factor (Haynes 2009a: 15).

For example, using data from a regional survey, Landry, Amara, and Lamari (2002) examine the relationship between innovation and six forms of social capital, five structural (business network assets, information network assets, research network assets, participation assets, and relational assets) and one form of cognitive social capital (reciprocal trust). Their conclusions, based on statistical regression, seem to suggest that marginal increases in social capital "contribute more than any other explanatory variable to increase the likelihood of innovation of firms" (Landry, Amara, and Lamari 2002: 695), which is surely "a conclusion far weaker than the hype that surrounds the concept would suggest. Indeed the findings are robust and based on excellent research practices but do not explain the processes that social capital was supposed to explain until it is separated into a number of component parts" (Haynes 2009a: 15).

And the aforementioned critic has an excellent point in attributing the existing problems with employing the concept under consideration as an explanatory and even descriptive tool to its multi-misnomer nature. Haynes argues, namely, that not only ones discussed above, but also other attempts to operationalise the concept (Tsai and Ghoshal 1998; Yli-Renko, Autio and Tontti 2002; Molina et al. 2008) provide some potentially interesting ideas, but these ideas seem more profitably explored as individual features, for example in examining how different cultures of trust in Spain and Italy contribute to different modes of innovation (Molina et al. 2008: 96–101).

This, however, is at odds with the basic assumption concerning social capital as a concept: "social capital is more than the sum of the various kinds of relationships" (Adler and Kwom 2002: 36) and that rather than reveal features of reality, actually conceal a range of individual practices by attempting to reduce them to a single homogenous category (Haynes 2009a: 15).

The above "basic assumption" only seemingly is a proclamation of methodological anti-individualism. As a matter of fact the thrust of the said assumption is not its holism, but its anti-, or rather seemingly dialectical nature whereby, in an *ad hoc* manner, the above-mentioned individual components do not weigh much because on an almost case-by-case basis you can produce such a content of the concept under consideration as you like.

Summing up our analysis in this chapter, it is fair to say that it has fully corroborated the fact of misnomer nature pertaining to the social capital concept. In such a way, only in slightly other terms, the following critics argue that to a "large extent social capital is "just" a powerful renaming and collecting together of a large swath of network research from the social support literature to social resource theory" (Borgatti and Foster 2003: 993).

Alejandro Portes, in his analysis of the various applications of social capital in sociology, has concluded that social capital as a rebranding exercise only gives the range of processes a more in his opinion attractive image under a unified concept (1998: 21). And the crux of the matter is, making a misnomer, and a misnomer to the n power at that, is not inconsequential:

> This rebranding gives the impression that the concept engages both the economic and the social dimension of association. While it might be true that social networks have economic value to participants, as a generalisation it hides as much as it explains. This is because by treating the concept as though it were a coherent whole and separated from the themes through which its meaning is derived, researchers will fail to explain how the specific mechanisms of trust, community, reciprocity, interpersonal relationships and networks impact on the features they are investigating (Haynes 2009a).

Chapter 7

Trust

One of those phenomena to which social capital supposedly refers is the subject of a study by Francis Fukuyama who – as far as the social capital, and social science literature in general, is concerned – has done most for popularising the notion (although trust is also emphasised by, inter alia, Putnam 1995; Brehm and Rahn 1997).

Fukuyama's famous, or notorious, if you will, thesis arose, it is important to remember, as a reflection of the collapse of "real socialism" in Central and Eastern Europe, as well as the apparent triumph of twin free-market doctrines of Reaganomics and Thatcherism undermining the postwar welfare state institutions. That grandiose claim proclaimed the arrival of humankind at its final form of society: "liberal democracy is the only legitimate ideology left in the world, an end of history in the Marxist-Hegelian sense of History as a broad evolution of human societies towards a final goal" (Fukuyama 1995: 3). With no competing macro-economic systems to market capitalism, and "with the competitive advantages of location or technological innovation being rapidly diminished through globalization, Fukuyama seeks to explain the relative success of national economies in terms of culture" (Schuller, Baron, Field 2000: 16). Apparently in keeping with his anti-statist bent, Fukuyama asserts that circumstances conducive to success are found among communities "formed not on the basis of explicit rules and regulation but out of a set of ethical habits and reciprocal moral obligations[1] internalised by each of the community's members" (1995: 9). According to the prophet concerned, "virtually all serious observers understand that liberal political and economic institutions depend on a healthy and dynamic civil society for their vitality" (1995: 4). "The field of social capital is thus elevated to being the crucial factor, forging the only viable forms of economy and polity" (Schuller, Baron, Field 2000: 16).

Fukuyama holds that 'a nation's prosperity and competitiveness hinge upon a single, pervasive, cultural trait: the level of trust present in the society and this depends on "the crucible of trust" – social capital' (1995: 7, 33). He goes on to distinguish between societies characterised by high trust or low trust and, consequently, between forms of solidaristic organisation which are "older, economically harmful or inefficient" and those which are "wealth creating"

---

1   To couch trust as a social phenomenon in ethical terms is to overstate the incidence and relevance of the moral in society, as, amongst other things, Luhmann (1979) implies in pointing out that to not trust in its broadest sense would prevent an individual from rising in the morning. He calls this type of trust "confidence" (Luhmann 1988).

(1995: 159). Trust is defined as 'the expectation that arises within a community of regular, honest, and co-operative behaviour, based on commonly shared norms, on the part of other members of the community...these communities do not require extensive contractual and legal regulation of their relations because prior moral consensus gives members of the group a basis for mutual trust' (1995: 26). It is instructive to learn how those notions match real-world situations. Now, examples of high-trust societies for Fukuyama are Japan, Germany and the United States characterised by the development of large-scale corporations out of family firms through the medium of "rich and complex civil society" (1995: 130). Low-trust societies are those of China, Italy and France, the first two characterised by the restriction of trust, and thus enterprise, to the 'family'; the latter by the destruction of a rich civil society by a centralising state. "The test criterion for distinguishing between high- and low-trust, and between inefficient and efficient, forms of solidarity is in each case 'economic progress', necessarily unanalysed as it is assumed to be the universal of human societies" (Schuller, Baron, Field 2000: 17).

> Japan is hailed as the contemporary nation with the most appropriate form of 'spontaneous sociability'. (Fukuyama 1995: 159)

The social capital enthusiast argues that in economic life, group co-ordination is necessary for one form of production, but when technology and markets change, a different type of co-ordination with perhaps a different set of group members becomes necessary. The bonds of social reciprocity that facilitated production in the earlier time period become obstacles to production in the later one...social capital can be said to be obsolete and needs to be depreciated in the country's capital accounts (Fukuyama 1999: 18–19).

As capitalism moves towards more flexible forms of labour discipline than those appropriate to Fordist organized capitalism, "Worker discretion becomes increasingly central to the smooth running of production and a new form of discipline is required, a form which is internalised and self-maintaining. "Trust" between workers and managers, with the shared goal of efficient production, replaces the 'rule book'.

With only one economic and political system thought viable, Fukuyama is thus enabled to restrict his conceptual field to fine-tuning heaven: the basic structures of – a certain self-image of – the United States of America are taken as universal, with the only problems remaining being to ensure maximum conformity of human factors to this inevitable moral and economic order. Fukuyama thus envisages an untrammelled "capitalism seeking 'friction-free economies' (1995: 149) in which the primacy of profit is not questioned by a trusted and trusting workforce, dedicated to the enterprise" (Schuller, Baron, Field 2000: 17).

There are, though, many reasons for questioning Fukuyama's historiography. Ahistoricity of his thesis is self-evident, if he wrote in the present century, in the period of deep, not only cyclical but structural, crisis of capitalism, above all its[2] Anglo-Saxon variety, he would have to eat his words. Contrary to his view, it is not trust, understood as a cultural phenomenon, that underpins economic relations, but the reverse is true – trust relationships are an outgrowth of underlying economic relations. Japan and Germany are examples of stakeholder capitalism, while the US epitomises shareholder capitalism. It is rather odd on the part of Fukuyama to lump together the US with the two former economies, and on the grounds that are contradicted by another social capital scholar, Putnam who made his name on the thesis exactly opposite to Fukuyama's premise – that of declining civil society. More important, however, is the aforementioned direction of causation pointing to the fundamental role of economic, above all ownership,[3] relations in conditioning extra-economic phenomena.

The following account is sound, only that the author fails to contextualise it – the web of inter-relationships underpinned by a multitude of mutual ownership stakes within Japan's groupings termed keiretsu, or similarly close ties between German companies and banks make the best fit: "Social capital has mainly been seen as contributing to economic performance by reducing inter-firm transaction costs, that is, search and information costs, bargaining and decision costs, and policing and enforcement costs. Lower search and information costs improve the efficiency of resource allocation. Reduced costs for bargaining and decision making facilitate the coordination of diverse activities between firms and enable an even further division of labour" (Richardson 1953; 1972). "Diminishing costs of policing and enforcement free up resources to be used in more productive ways" (2002). It is ownership relations that account for competitive advantages enjoyed by stakeholder capitalism not only in the inter-firm relationships, but also at the workplace. The German system of co-determination coupled with generous fringe benefits and Japanese system of lifetime employment grounded in a similar safety net both express in fact ownership of jobs on the part of employees. This ownership underpinning also accounts for what Haruo Shimada (1988) christened with a new term "human-ware" as distinct from hardware and software. He meant that the basic reason for the strong competitiveness of Japanese automobile companies was the cooperative attitude of the workers. He quoted a Japanese worker as saying: "In a US company, each worker is eager to make his individual success, and unwilling to tell what he knows to his colleague. But here, everybody is willing to tell what he knows as much as possible to the colleague. This is because he believes that he can make a success only as a team, not on his own" (p. 61).

The workers are co-operative thanks to Japan's (mutually dependent) employment system and labour power market. In an economy where long-term

---

2   At the time of writing, when the problems of the Eurozone seem to overshadow those of other regions of the world, it is worth remembering where and how all this mess had begun. And with respect, neither Greece nor Spain has enough clout to bring about the end of the world financial and/or economic crisis

3   More in (Tittenbrun 2009a; 2011; 2012).

employment is dominant, and thus one's current job and job prospects (due to a pre-established and clear path of promotion) it is worthwhile to work for the success of the whole team. Because others have a similar attitude, there is created a virtuous circle of self-reinforcing social pressure. Another result is the prevalence (at least amongst this core employee class, as by no means all employees enjoy lifetime employment) of company-specific labour power. Rather than general labour power typical of job-changers and job-seekers.

> Cooperative behaviour among firms is also thought to have aided the development of Japan's manufacturing sector, especially in the consumer durable sector. In drafting a design of a new car, for example, Japanese car producers took full account of the views of parts makers, as well as those of the retailers, and tried to find the best match of cost reduction and consumer satisfaction. This was possible only based on the mutual trust, which was strengthened by strategies such as cross holding of equities and temporary exchanges of workers between firms. Such long-run relationships and mutual trust were helpful in reducing informational costs, not only in designing a new product but also in making contracts. It was often the case that contracts were just broad agreements and specific conditions were discussed later on. [...]What was perhaps equally important was the trustworthiness of [...] infrastructure, i.e. the low defect ratio, punctuality of railways and postal service, reliability of electricity and telephone networks (Omori 2001: 5)

Thus, it is not an elusive quality called social capital, as Adler and Kwon (2) would have it, that transforms individuals from self-seeking and egocentric agents with little sense of obligation to others into members of a community with shared interests, a common identity and a commitment to the common good, because those characteristics indeed distinct from ones built-in in the free-market capitalism flow from distinctive ownership relations pertaining to stakeholder capitalism.

The ownership peculiarities discussed above mean that the two systems concerned are actually two distinct capitalist modes of economic activity, and, while they possess a geographic connotation, this does not preclude their appearance in other regions of the world. This does not validate, of course, Fukuyama's ahistorical position who in another work views social capital as "both disposable and infinitely renewable", decreeing on that basis that people must be left simply alone and social capital will be created, particularly where people are making money. Social capital and capitalism have under this conception something of a mutually beneficial, reciprocal relationship. Accordingly, the role of market relations and capitalism is never questioned: they "only cause good, For example, "market exchange promotes habits of reciprocity that carry on from economic life into moral life" (Fukuyama 1999: 261). Without closer examination of the underlying economic relations, the mere acknowledgement of their social efficacy, of course, is not good enough, nay, it distorts the picture of relationships between the economy and the non-economic sphere of society.

In a similar vein, for the British industrial sociologist Alan Fox trust does not develop out of thin air. Fox is of course not the only writer who realises the causative power of economic relations; to cite an example, "Social capital is at the same time in part accumulated as an unintended and even unanticipated consequence of economic activity as people often spend more of their waking hours 'bowling' with their workplace colleagues than with their family and friends. Norms, codes, trust, solidarity and other vital elements of social capital are built and reinforced when sharing a common goal or a mutual fate even in the most hierarchical economic structures imaginable, like the globally operating multidivisional corporation, and not just when people mingle, organize and achieve with peers in their spare time" (Maskeill 2002). Fox's treatment is, though, more elaborate. While he concedes that trust may be thought of in purely personal terms, he nevertheless focuses on what he terms "institutionalised trust". From his point of view, trust and distrust "are embodied in the rules, roles and relations which some men impose on, or seek to get accepted by, others" (Fox 1974: 67). Rules include both formal and informal understandings, whilst relations are construed in terms of interdependence, communication, supervision and authority. Fox is thus concerned not with personal feelings between people as individuals, but with relationships which are structured and institutionalised.

In addition, he conceives of high- and low-trust situations as dynamic, and usually self-reinforcing. "The essential feature of all trust relations is their reciprocal nature. Trust tends to evoke trust, distrust to evoke distrust" (Fox 1974: 66). This reciprocation, according to Fox, can be measured along two dimensions: long-term to short-term, and – in terms of Parsonian pattern variables – specific to diffuse. Accordingly, the point of lowest trust is characterised by short-term specific reciprocation, while the point of highest trust by long-term and diffuse (Fox 1974: 72). Fox insists that this typology can be employed in the analysis of employment relations at different levels.

Furthermore, the sociologist concerned distinguishes between vertical and lateral trust. In this context he – in contradistinction to the stylised ideology of social capital –draws attention to the fact that These relations may be in conflict with each other, for example where high levels of lateral trust take the form of workers' solidarity in opposition to management. "High vertical and low lateral trust comes with ideologies of competitive individualism, with highly differentiated levels of individual reward. Fox's view of employment relations is one of inherent conflict" (Schuller, Baron, Field 2000: 18); as a result he observes that "those who enjoy high-trust relations both vertically and laterally are exceptionally favoured" (Fox 1974: 79).

Schuller, Baron and Field point out that Fox's focus is on industrial relations, but this does not detract from the general relevance of his analytical framework to the discussion of social capital. They rightly point out that "the focus on institutionalised relations challenges those analyses which rely on individual level data, most prominently in the form of personal responses to questions about trust. He reminds us of the need to build in awareness of underlying structures of power and inequality as major factors in shaping trust relations, foreshadowing the critiques of social capital offered by such commentators as Edwards and Foley (1998). Nay, not sharing his radical conclusions, even some prominent social capital theorists are very critical as regards the type of methodology on which social capital studies usually rely. For instance, no other than Francis Fukuyama admits that a significant downside of the concept of social capital is the lack of consensus on how to measure it. He reports on two main approaches: counting groups and group memberships and using survey to collect data on trust and civic engagement. Both methods are in his judgment inadequate and imprecise (1999).

Let us dwell on this issue of methodology in somewhat more detail. It is fair to say that, abstracting from Fukuyama who has special interest in trust, its prominent place in the social capital research stems from its role in another leading social capital theorist's framework.

Under Coleman's model, the contract between individuals requires the trust that acts by individuals will be reciprocated at some time in the future. Trust is usually ascertained from a question in a social survey such as the World Values Survey or the General Social Survey in the US. Examples include, "Generally speaking, would you say that most people can be trusted or that you can't be too careful in dealing with people?" or "Do you think that most people would try to take advantage of you if they had a chance or would they try to be fair?" These questions may be supported by additional questions that attempt to expose attitudes towards reciprocity or fairness, such as "Would you say most of the time people try to be helpful or that they are mostly looking out for themselves?" (Cox 2003).

This methodology is indeed faulty in that it yields, if any, a superficial and shallow knowledge about social life. The survey designers are not aware that the said research technique is actually an experimental one, that is to say, one of an uncontrolled experiment in which survey questions function as stimuli inducing subjects to certain types of behaviour, in this case verbal behaviour, that otherwise in all probability would not have taken place. In other words, particular answers to a questionnaire's question may well be an artifact whose coming into being results merely from an experimental situation. To put it in still other terms, experimentally elicited opinions may have a widely diverse ontological and epistemological status. Some of them may express a respondent's genuine stance, but in most cases they will correspond, if any, to a skin-deep, epiphenomenal layer of consciousness whose artificiality and superficiality mean that it does not bear on real actions of a given individual, and those elements of consciousness or sub-consciousness, if you will, that are not relevant to real-world behaviours do not matter from a sociological point of view.

For example, to use a favourite term of social capital scholars, if a citizen duly pays his or her taxes, it – for all practical purposes – means that she places trust in the US government On the other hand, the same individuals, and individuals in general may not have a high opinion about the trustworthiness of the government. But such opinions, beliefs, etc. that do not come up as motives, stimuli, or other component of real-world actions are sociologically irrelevant.

On the other hand, in an example given by Paxton (1999: 89) exactly such a non-epiphenomenal notion of trust seems to be implied: "when a potential trustor is embedded in a group, he or she may assign the other members of that group a level of trustworthiness that is higher than the trustworthiness accorded to the average person, due to the presence of norms and sanctions against those who break trust", provided that this does not necessarily mean that a given individual holds his or her corresponding attitude out of fear of group sanctions; all what is necessary is the presence of his or her behaviour that attest to that trusting attitude. It is also to this action-relevant, socially efficacious sense of trust that Paxton (1999: 102) refers when accounting for "the recent rise of gated communities and the increased use of private security guards. It could be that our trust in one another impacts how we organize our lives and how we choose to spend our money (or how much money we spend"). Upon perusal of the social capital literature, a few other examples of such an approach can be found, i.e. Actions associated with a display of confidence in others treated as an outcome of a norm of trust (Onyx and Bullen 2000), as well as reciprocal acts or exchanges seen as an outcome of a norm of reciprocity (Rose 1999).

However, this is not how social capital researchers generally approach the issue under consideration. And the problem is further compounded due to usual sociological procedures. Curiously enough, it is an adherent of the research perspective in question who openly admits that "there are signs of statistical techniques being applied in ways which are poorly matched to the quality and the robustness of the data. This is particularly true where the data consists of comparative attitudinal surveys, for example on declared levels of trust, using highly ambiguous terminology. Quantitative analyses which relate these, and through them levels of social capital, to general measures of economic performance, need very severe health warnings" (Schuller (2001: 17). Moreover, the same author identifies a specific dimension to the aforementioned problem related to the nature of what is investigated in such surveys: "There are some curious possibilities relating to the *impact of measurement.* In the natural sciences, the impact of the observer on the observed is taken for granted. Social capital may be an extreme example of this in the social field. For where trust becomes the focus of attention, this may cause it to wither as much as to flourish; some relationships, norms and networks are strongest when they are not exposed to constant examination. On the other hand, it has been well argued that if we are moving towards[4] risk societies, and proactively managing risk rather than passively coping with it, so we should be moving from the passive valuing of trust to its active maintenance"(Schuller 2001: 21).

Even putting aside this kind of caveat, the credibility of knowledge provided by sociological surveys can be called into question." survey questions can be interpreted differently by respondents in two time periods. If respondents relax their interpretation of trust between 1975 and 1985, we could see a change in

---

4 Well, not all, including the present author (Tittenbrun 2012) agree with such an appraisal of the risk society notion.

measured trust even if there was no change in the actual level of trust over the 10-year period" (Paxton 1999: 89).

In addition, social capital studies have been subject, inter alia, to the following methodological criticisms:

1. Social capital indicators lack clear definition

Attempts to measure social capital have been widely criticised because the defining concepts, such as 'trust' and 'networks', are vague and ambiguous. It is consequently unclear which determinants are being measured in social capital research. (Pope 2003: 6).

This lack of definition is well rendered by the following witty account by Labonte (1999): "There is 'something' going on 'out there' in people's day-to-day relationships that is an important determinant of the quality of their lives, if not society's (communities?) 'healthy' functioning...it is the 'gluey stuff' that binds individuals to groups, groups to organisations, citizens to societies'. What exactly this 'something' is remains moot'." Lomas (1998) stresses that "There are few known and validated ways to measure such things as community competence, social cohesion, or a sense of worth at the level of the community". Along similar lines, Leeder and Dominello (1999) argue that, "Champions of social capital have several kilometres to travel before a definition emerges that will render it a practical matter for policy development".

Portes and Landolt (1996) have also argued that a distinction needs to be made between the sources of social capital (network, etc.) and the resources or advantages that derive from them. To illustrate this point, they put forward the case of two tertiary students in need of money for tuition. One has acquired the money from parents while the other has a highly supportive social network that cannot meet the expense. Whilst both have stocks of social capital which could be measured using an indicator, the social capital of these individuals has resulted in different outcomes. Anthropologists studying inner city and ghetto areas in the US have also demonstrated high levels of social capital in some areas, with many people relying on friendship and kin networks for survival, but the assets obtainable through these networks are not enough to remove people from poverty (Stack and Fernandez-Kelly in Portes and Landolt, (1996)). The definition of social capital is again critical to an understanding of what is being measured and how social processes lead to the acquisition of resources.

2. Collective social capital is not the same as individual social capital

A second criticism of social capital research is that it confuses its unit of measurement by aggregating information about individual social capital (such answers from social surveys) to a measure that claims to represent a broader collective unit. This conflation of analytical levels results, in the final analysis, from a concentration on a microstructual approach[5] discussed above which makes it difficult smoothly to pass onto a higher level.

Thus, Portes and Landolt (1996) criticise Putnam for making individual social capital, the property of groups or even nations. They state "collective social capital.. cannot simply be the sum of individual social capital".

The sources and benefits of social capital available at the individual network level ('the gluey stuff that binds individuals to groups) may be very different from those available at the social level of institutions and governments ('the gluey stuff' that binds citizens to institutions). For example, very different ideas of trust may be evoked in Coleman's network of Jewish diamond traders if they are asked about the network through which they are deriving social capital, or society as a whole. The two reveal different types of information about social relations and both may be lost in the process of aggregation. (Pope 2004: 7).

Coming back to Fox, the stress on the dynamics of the relationships is in his view fundamental. In particular, "it should help us avoid reliance on static cross-sectional approaches which purport to measure stocks of social capital without accompanying these with a sense of trajectory. The temporal dimension is essential" (Schuller, Baron, Field 2000: 18).

Finally, the lateral-vertical matrix addresses exactly the issues raised by the debate over whether social capital inheres in horizontal associations, or is to be found also in hierarchical relationships.

Lastly, for their anti-individualistic, structuralist perspective, it is worth citing Fox's concluding remarks regarding a perceived lack of commitment to the exercise of discretion in work organisations:

> Lack of ambition, fear of responsibility, and the absence of talent are usually offered as possible reasons but these beg questions rather than answer them. Within a society [...] where ambition is apt to be an individualistic thrust towards personal achievement, recognition, and success, there need be no surprise that many fail to clear these definitional and practical hurdles, especially when to them is added the inequalities of life chances which so patently inhibit or frustrate aspirations. Social structures and work arrangements are, however, theoretically conceivable which would invite and promote high-discretion contributions in

---

5   One more example of which is provided by Bourdieu's (1983: 248) definition: "Social capital is the aggregate of the actual or potential resources which are linked to possession of a durable network of more or less institutionalised relationships of mutual acquaintance and recognition – or in other words, to membership in a group". Social capital requires more than just a network of ties, however. Bourdieu stresses that social capital also involves "transforming contingent relations, such as those of neighborhood, the workplace, or even kinship, into relationships that are at once necessary and elective, implying durable obligations subjectively felt (feelings of gratitude, respect, friendship, etc.)" (1983: 249–50).

a setting where no premium was placed on individualistic ambition and self-assertion; where men ready to offer their involvement, judgement and discretion were not deterred from doing so by the prospect of being drawn out to a fine point of 'success' or 'failure'. (Fox 1974: 365)

Recall, too, that Fox dispenses with the concept of social capital, and his views have been considered for their opposition to the mainstream social capital literature.

In the contrasting work of Fukuyama and Fox 'trust' is seen as a central dynamic of the workplace and, in the case of the former, of the whole of civil society. Fox's knowledge of work relations permits him to view trust not as a personal attribute but as a structural characteristic.

Fukuyama, with only one socioeconomic system possible, offers a straightforward, and tautological, functionalism: differentials of power, status and reward are those 'necessary' for the system, and trust is the mechanism by which such unequal individuals unite around the shared objective of economic progress. For Fox, such inequalities militate against trust. This contrast foreshadows something of the contemporary debates about whether social capital is an essentially conservative notion built around an assumption of consensus and social unity (Schuller, Baron, Field 2000: 18).

Chapter 8

Human Capital and Social Capital

The aforementioned chameleon-like nature of the concept under consideration causes it to invade the territory of its neighbour from Part I.

Becker (1996) has expanded his treatment of human capital to include various other forms of capital such as personal capital, imagination capital, and, last but not least, social capital. Significantly, Becker views an individual's social capital as part of his (her) total stock of human capital, where social capital is the relevant past actions by peers and others in an individual's' social network and control system. Similarly, as Schneider (2004: 14) notes, Fukuyama describes social capital as "the component of human capital that allows members of a given society to trust one another and cooperate in the formation of new groups".

In turn, Schuller (2001: 14–5) sees the relationship between the two concepts the other way round: it appears that in his view social capital is a variety of human capital, as he defines the former by contending that "it gives greater prominence, for example, to informal modes of learning, and the skills acquired through learning-by-doing".

In the following claim social capital and human capital overlap: "Looked at from a social capital perspective, the direct impact of training may be as much in the strengthening of networks and information flows as in the acquisition of individual competencies or improving productivity" (Schuller 2001: 14).

Another social capital scholar not only apparently views social and human capital in similarly overlapping, if not identical terms, but moreover renders the former as a misnomer in yet another – (identified elsewhere in this book) infrastructural –sense (which he somewhat manages to reconcile with the "civic" definition):

> it was not until the 1940s that the long, slow process of raising the level of investment in human resources from the slough of despond into which it had fallen in the early and mid-nineteenth century had finally been formally completed. As T.H. Marshall pointed out in his essay, the conditions he identified for a full participatory citizenship were not in fact formally fulfilled until after 1945, reflecting a history of extremely sporadic and halting development of extensive social capital in Britain. By the end of the 1940s this had finally produced a set of facilities, in terms of health, social security, and education (Szreter 2002: 74).

The later decades of the twentieth century saw a massive swing towards the view of human capital as the royal road to economic success and social cohesion. This was based on rather simplistic linear models, which imply that investing in education yields returns in the same way as investing in stocks or bonds, with measurable, tangible results. This view is being challenged by recognition that more complex processes are at work, with multiple interactions between different social forces, and with the possibility that not all learning is individually or socially beneficial in a straightforward, aggregate fashion. In particular, we cannot simply tot up the numbers of people achieving educational qualifications and assume that we are progressing – or not – towards a 'Learning Society'.

> Our argument is that social capital offers one way of apprehending and analysing the embeddedness of education in social networks (Glaeser 2001).

He reminds the reader that education has been consistently identified as the most robust correlate with social capital. He defines social capital using an economic lens as "the set of social resources of a community that increases the welfare of that community". He also contends that, when measured at the individual level, social capital is very close to human capital. He develops an investment model that suggests that social capital is like a stock variable that yields "market" (social skills and connections that help one with employment) and "non market" (something like happiness) returns. Older or more mobile people may be less likely to invest their time in social capital producing activities. Individuals can use their social skills to invest in social capital producing activities that benefit the community as a whole or in activities that benefit only themselves" (Glaeser 2001).

Fukuyama explicitly asserts: "educational institutions [...] are a primary location for social capital creation".

While Coleman proposed the concept of social capital as the key generic tool in his wider project of integrating rational choice theory with an understanding of social structure, his empirical studies were largely concerned with pupil performance at school. Indeed, Coleman frequently provided definitions couched precisely in the language of schooling. In an early essay, subsequently reprinted, Coleman proposed the following:

> What I mean by social capital in the raising of children is the norms, the social networks, and the relationships between adults and children that are of value for the child's growing up. Social capital exists within the family, but also outside the family, in the community...in the interest, even the intrusiveness, of one adult in the activities of someone else's child (Coleman 1990c: 334).

In his late attempt at a theoretical synthesis, Coleman virtually restated the position: 'Social capital is the set of resources that inhere in family relations and in community social organisation and that are useful for the cognitive or social development of a child or young person' (Coleman 1994: 300). Education represented, for Coleman, not simply a neat example of a general proposition, but rather the strongest expression of the resources generated by the relationships, values, and trust that constitute social capital.

Coleman's work in this field has been particularly influential, not least because it appears to offer a useful communal and value-dependent counter-weight to the individualism and narrow instrumentalism of human capital theory. Coleman himself, however, drew no such direct opposition. Rather, his account explicitly seeks to establish a direct and causal connection between the two forms of capital, as is clear in the title of his paper, which refers to 'social capital in the creation of human capital'. Social capital, Coleman suggested, deserves attention precisely because it helps us understand the nature of human capital (Coleman 1988a; among replication studies see Teachman, Paasch, and Carver 1997; on relations between sociology and economics, see Granovetter 1985: 507). Indeed, Coleman treated social capital, which parallels the development of financial, physical, and human capital in economics, as a central factor in the formation of human capital. The chief difference from the point of view of economic theory is that whereas financial, physical, and human capital are normally private goods, according to Coleman, social capital is mainly a public good; it followed that somewhat different policy approaches might be appropriate in order to bring about increases in social capital (Coleman 1988a: 116). Moreover, social capital is not completely fungible; for many purposes it may be impossible to transpose the benefits of social capital across different contexts (Coleman 1994: 302). For Coleman, social capital is highly distinctive, and the idea that it is a form of capital is not simply a helpful metaphor; rather, it defines the substance of the concept.

Coleman's treatment of social capital has been subjected to widespread discussion and critique. We wish to focus here on three areas where, we think, his use of the concept is inadequate, and requires development. The first concerns the variable value of social capital; while Coleman rightly emphasised the contribution of social capital to equity and justice, he wrongly downplayed the ways in which social capital may also serve to underpin social hierarchies and create new sources of inequality – Bourdieu's work, by the same token, is vulnerable to the reverse criticism: namely, that he downplays how social capital can indeed contribute to greater social equity (Bourdieu 1997). Second, Coleman placed too much emphasis upon primary connections such as kinship, and too little upon secondary connections such as social networks and civic engagement – here, Putnam may be vulnerable to the reverse criticism. The downside of social capital as embodied in such networks was not addressed by Coleman, especially how it may act to constrain and limit individuals. Third, and very much in connection with the weight that his theory places upon family relationships, Coleman appeared to be blind to highly specific forms of inequality such as gender and disability. Below we consider the implications of the concept for women and for a group – adults with learning disabilities – that tends to be marginalised within the labour market, and is largely neglected in human capital theory.

Concerns for equity stands at the core of Coleman's work on education. An able advocate and practitioner of public policy research, he frequently emphasized the ways in which social capital can help counter racial and social inequality. Perhaps as a result, the schooling literature has rarely acknowledged the effects of inequalities in the distribution of social capital (but see 246 Field, Schuller, and Baron; Edwards and Foley 1997: 677). As Stanton-Salazar and Dornbusch have suggested in their studies of Mexican-origin students in US high schools, this may point to a flaw in Coleman's formulation. Their studies found that the level of association between social capital and students' grades and aspirations was generally positive, but relatively weak. They attribute this to the nature of the social capital available to Mexican-origin students, which may be good at transmitting some types of information highly effectively, but is relatively poor when it comes to providing information on college admission or school qualifications. They conclude that Coleman's work overplayed 'the "role-modelling" and "cheer-leading" influences of significant others'. They advocate instead a 'network-analytic approach' that draws attention to the 'inequitable transmission of tangible institutional resources and opportunities', as well as toward the difficulties for some groups in 'forming relationships with institutional agents' who are able to negotiate access to those resources and opportunities (Stanton-Salazar and Dornbusch 1995: 116–19). Below we explore how forms of social capital may act similarly to exclude people with learning difficulties from many of the benefits of contemporary Scottish society.

A second flaw in Coleman's work is that it privileges one site of social capital. Empirically, Coleman usually treated family structures, defined in terms of parental presence and numbers of siblings in the household, as a proxy index of levels of social capital.

Let us dwell for a moment on the question of methodology, since it provides a good illustration of problems involved in the measurement of social capital that are discussed also elsewhere in the book. In his analysis of the role of social capital in the creation of human capital, Coleman focuses upon parent-child relations and uses measures of the physical presence of adults in a household and attention given by adults to children as empirical indicators of such relations. Ultimately, however, the 'strength' of family relations is measured by Coleman on the basis of a ratio of parents to children.

Coleman's methodological approach is striking in its crudity.

Using the ratio of parents to children in a household as a measure of social capital is questionable, [...] as no account is made of relationship quality, such as through measures of norms of trust or reciprocity. As well, Coleman takes no account of non-resident parents, and quantitatively treats the presence of siblings as deleterious to the quality of any parent-child relation, rather than as having social capital potential, by extending networks of relations in a household (Stone 2001).

But his view of the family was not just as a convenient statistical indicator, but also as a key set of relationships. Coleman regarded what he calls 'primordial' relationships, with their 'origins in the relationships established by childbirth', as the most robust source of social capital, as distinct from 'constructed' forms of social organisation that come together for a single purpose or narrow range of purposes (Coleman 1991: 1–3). With the erosion of primordial social relations, Coleman believed that with them would vanish the 'social capital on which societal functioning has depended' (Coleman 1991: 9). Coleman largely discounted 'constructed social organisation' as a source of social capital.

This led Coleman to value close networks, and to praise 'intergenerational closure' in particular, by which he meant the extent to which all parties to the relationship, children, parents, community leaders, teachers, were communicating regularly and effectively with one another (Coleman 1988a: 103–4). But intergenerational closure may also be a powerful force for conservatism, and can be perceived by actors as inhibiting rather than facilitating their development. In certain circumstances, intergenerational closure can, as we suggest below, support 'downward levelling pressures' (Portes and Landolt 1991: 19). Equally, social capital can serve as a defensive or coping device, inhibiting innovation and preventing goal-oriented forms of reciprocity, as Kolankiewicz notes in his comments on the 'amoral familism and clientelism' that underpin network reciprocity in post-communist societies (Kolankiewicz 1996: 438).

These reservations might apply with equal force to Putnam and Bourdieu. Emphasising as he does the importance of civic engagement in creating trust, the former could well be accused of understating the place of family in his analysis of social capital in southern Italy (Putnam 1993a). While he has briefly noted that social capital can be used for undesirable purposes as well as desirable ones (Putnam 1993i: 18), his overwhelming message is that social capital serves the common good, ignoring the possibility of social capital being used by one group or individual at the expense of others (Portes and Landolt 1991: 19). In his more recent work, Putnam has considered evidence that social capital has a 'dark side', but concluded that in general social joiners and civic activists tend to be more tolerant and inclusive, and make a greater contribution to equity and choice for others, than their more stay-at-home neighbours (Putnam 2000: Ch. 22). But this then requires, as Putnam tentatively acknowledges, a more differentiated understanding of social capital.

In a more individualised and fluid society, increasing weight may be placed upon what Mark Granovetter (1974) has called 'weak ties'. Like Coleman, Granovetter was interested in promoting a convergence between sociology and economics; as an economist, he acknowledged the force of Weber's view that economic action is one special, if important, category of social action (Granovetter 1985: 507). His work upon the value of weak ties originated in a study of youth labour markets, which showed the value of social networks in helping young Americans build a career. His approach was subsequently developed through an analysis of trust in modern industrial society which in many ways foreshadowed the later, lengthier book by Francis Fukuyama (Granovetter 1985; Fukuyama 1995).

Responding to the debate among economists over the levels of trust and avoidance of malfeasance required to maintain economic activities in the context of imperfectly competitive markets in modern industrial society, Granovetter argued that it was not necessary to resort to blanket explanations such as functionalism or generalised morality. Rather, trust was generated, and malfeasance discouraged, through the operations of 'concrete personal relations and structures (or "networks") of such relations', which enabled actors to indulge their 'widespread preference for transacting with individuals of known reputation' (Granovetter 1985: 490). However, Granovetter emphasized that close relationships could not of themselves provide guarantees of trustworthiness. First, the very existence of personal trust provided opportunities for new forms of malfeasance such as embezzlement; and fraud itself became easier the higher the level of trust among the thieves. Second, personal trust could never be general, but was bounded in its working, creating further potential for conflict between those outside any particular, given relation of trust. Granovetter noted the emergence of the ideal-typical Weberian bureaucracy as a means of solving this problem; ironically, though, large hierarchical organisations with well-defined internal labour markets and elaborate promotion ladders were characteristically vulnerable to 'co-operative evasion' and 'malfeasance generated by teams' (Granovetter 1985: 501).

In a highly fluid and open social system, Granovetter argued, high levels of personal trust can be economically dysfunctional. As a counterweight to the influence of close ties, Granovetter stressed the contribution of 'weak ties' in allowing actors to place a degree of trust upon one another, without necessarily having the same tight bonds as might be found among kin or neighbourhood relationships. In similar vein, Ray Pahl and Liz Spencer have argued that strong ties can also constrain social behaviour and relationships. While the 'inward-looking, strong ties of family' may help children form a 'healthy personality', they can also prevent adults from learning how 'to cope with a risk society and gain full opportunities from a flexible labour market' (Pahl and Spencer 1997: 102). Where Granovetter merely states the value of weak ties in general, Pahl and Spencer stress the role of 'bridging ties' that stretch between different communities of interest, and may be vital in accessing resources that are unavailable on the basis of strong ties alone. Below we explore these issues further in terms of bonding social capital's limiting of the ability of people with learning difficulties to negotiate a 'risk society' (Beck 1992).

Putnam and the World Bank have become increasingly concerned to address the balance between bonding and bridging, as a matter of policy as well as theoretical debate (for example Narayan 1999; Putnam 2000). The advocates of situated learning similarly emphasise that a 'community of practice' is not necessarily based upon co-presence or even 'socially visible boundaries', but may be defined as much by the existence of shared activity systems with common frameworks of understanding (Lave and Wenger 1991: 98; Eraut 2000).

Third, Coleman's interest in equity issues was combined with a curious blindness to gender, ethnicity, and disability. Much the same might be said, of course, about Putnam and Bourdieu, who have little to say on these dimensions. Yet by defining primordial relations as primary in the creation of social capital – relations, that is, that are ultimately 'established by childbirth' – Coleman's concept is unusual in the weight that it places on activities and structures that are highly gender specific.

Moreover, his view of the family's importance in social capital is couched in highly traditional terms. Deficiencies in social capital, be they internal or external to the family, are harmful to the cognitive development of young people, and thus to the creation of human capital. Internal deficits do not solely refer to lower levels of parental involvement in schooling – for example, lack of interest in homework – but also such factors as single parenting. External deficits might include a low level of interaction between parents. Generally speaking, these parents are, in practice, mothers. It is mostly mothers who chat by the school gates, who care for a child without a live-in partner, or read with the child. In expressing concern over rising levels of maternal employment, Coleman (1988a) acknowledged this indirectly.

Subsequent attempts to test Coleman's own analysis, using child-mother data from the National Longitudinal Survey, found that early maternal employment appeared to have only 'minimally negative effects' on verbal capacity and no effects on behavioural problems among three- to six-year-olds (Parcel and Menaghan 1994: 997–9). Maynard and McGrath (1997: 136), in an extensive review of the relationship between family structure and child welfare, found that the main impact of divorce and single parenthood was the loss of income and material support, more than the absence of one parent. Empirically, then, Coleman's own propositions seem dubious (Field, Schuller, Baron 2000).

Those claims, as well as those by his followers, are dubious in another respect as well. It turns out that they all have difficulties with not only concepts of social and human, but also economic capital. An author of a study of high school students states that "Family background, Coleman (1988), is analytically separable into at least three distinct components: financial capital, human capital, and social capital. More specifically, physical resources that aid achievement, which is commonly measured by the family's wealth or income, are considered as financial capital. Human capital, which constitutes the potential for a cognitive environment that is conducive to children's learning, is usually measured by parents' education. Social capital is the least tangible as it exists only in the relationships among persons and is defined by its function" (Chew 2002).

If the possession of a refrigerator, or earning even a minimum wage would be sufficient to make one a capitalist, the world would be awash with capitalists, which, it is rather plain to see, it is not.

Highly imprecise is the contention of another "member of the pack" according to whom "for Bourdieu, economic capital accrues from property and money" (Dolan 2002).

The aforementioned ignorance is in some cases combined with other, if anything, more weird claims, like that by Looker (1994), who considers it vital to make a distinction between passive capital (e.g., money and books) and active capital (e.g., encouragement, help with homework, contacts with school officials). In order to activate the latter type of capital, parents must act and interact.

In other words, in the social capital literature the understanding of real capital seems as muddled as that of their favourite capital variety and its relationship to other capitals.

Overall, it is difficult to comprehend how the conflation of social capital with its human companion may be drawn upon in order to defend the rational of the former concept, as the following social capital scholar does:

> With criticism coming from a variety of perspectives, the phrase, though, remains appealing to the degree that there is a reluctance to concede the concept just on the basis of a stretched metaphor. This is because the use of the term 'social capital' has been strategically useful, identifying its function as a factor of production by associating the term with other (contested) concepts, such as human capital and intellectual capital. (Haynes 2009a)

In point of fact, however, the concept is being associated also to another conceptual neighbour, so to speak. Moreover, this is, again, another case of colonisation by social capital of a substantive area coming under other capital concepts.

In the following passage, for instance, all three capitals figuring in the title of this book are mixed up in ways that make them virtually indiscernible. The scholars in question consider "the phenomenon of a career path for women – one in which significant numbers of women systematically acquire the social and cultural capital and experience to lead a substantial economic organisation"…, "concluding that the benefit of globalization for women in developing countries is more likely to be captured by those who have the social capital, perhaps by virtue of birth into an educated or elite family. This social capital may provide these women with skills and qualities that make them attractive to global organisations as managers, and thereby enable them to participate in the world economy" (Shipani et al. 2002).

Similarly, on the basis of the following Fukuyama's (1999) pronouncement it would be difficult to tell social capital from cultural capital, as the former is defined exactly in cultural terms: "Social capital is important to the efficient functioning of modern economies, and is the *sine qua non* of stable liberal democracy. It constitutes the cultural component of modern societies, which in other respects have been organized since the Enlightenment on the basis of formal institutions, the rule of law, and rationality".

And indeed, Schneider (2004: 14) notes, referring, inter alia, to Fukuyama:

> A number of scholars recognize the links between social and cultural capital, but some substitute cultural capital for social capital or subsume cultural capital under social capital. Coleman (1988) includes mores and norms of the group as part of social capital. Fukuyama (1995: 90) uses social capital to refer to the culture of particular societies, stating that social capital depends on 'a prior sense of moral community, that is, an unwritten set of ethical rules or norms that serve as the basis for social trust.' The same mixing of social and cultural capital occurs in the literature on welfare reform and charitable choice. For example, Sherman (1997: 130) confuses social capital with a combination of human and cultural capital when she states that social capital refers to 'training

I received from my parents, peers, schools, and church that has equipped me with some valuable life skills'. To cite but one more example,'social capital refers to the social relationships and patterns of reciprocal, enforceable trust that enable people and institutions to gain access to such resources as social services, jobs, and government contracts. It includes two ingredients: 1) trust-based relationships with people or organisations with access to resources and 2) knowledge of cultural capital cues that indicate that an individual is a member of a group and should be given access to those relationships. The same definition applies to both organisations and individuals. Social capital enables organisations to gain government contracts, place their program participants in jobs, and find people to serve' (Schneider 2006).

While the definition laid out above is, in a manner typical of social capital, both too narrow in relation to other ways of defining the concept and too broad in that it encroaches upon the territory of cultural capital, the latter point permits us smoothly to pass to the next chapter.

PART III:
CULTURAL CAPITAL

In the previous part of the book the reader's attention has been drawn to the contested borders between social capital and human capital, which concepts do at least in part overlap. The central figure of the present part is engage in similar border conflicts as well.

Chapter 9

Cultural Capital as Overlapping Social Capital and Human Capital

What the following assertion refers to as cultural capital, might be equally well defined – remaining within the capital vernacular – as social capital "For many traditional college students, the home is a valuable resource for support and counsel. Traditional college students draw on this resource to guide them through the higher education experience. [...] many nontraditional students do not have this form of cultural capital available to them" (Valadez 2008: 37).

What the author being cited terms "a supportive home environment" (Valadez 2008) others would call social or family capital.

As a facet of the latter might also be regarded the following new form of capital that, according to its advocate in question is a variety of cultural capital: "professional-class parents who are anxious about their own prospects for continued success in a risky economy turn toward emotional capital as a necessary supplement to educational and extra-curricular success to ensure inter-generational transmission of advantage. The goals of emotional competence [...] replicate the mechanisms of control to which elite parents are subjected in professional careers and therefore represent an important form of cultural capital in the reproduction of class advantages" (Rutherford 2011).

Therefore, it is difficult, if not impossible, to figure out which capital the following claim refers to, not to mention the fact that the relationship established may well be spurious, being accounted for by some unmentioned factor: "ethnic minority families display less enthusiasm for investing in education for their children. This may be attributed to differences in educational investment behavior among families with different cultural backgrounds" (Baicai, Jingjian 2010).

Another statement attributes to cultural capital this kind of role in society at large that social capital writers would certainly ascribe to their own object of study: "It is [...] possible to examine culture from a social perspective and see it as the capital that holds communities together and helps them adapt to change" (Centre 2001).

Small wonder that a desperate cultural capital researcher disarmingly confesses regarding the two constructs involved that "these concepts are hard to disentangle. Therefore, this study, similar to past research (Croninger and Lee, 2001; Perna, 2000), simultaneously observes social and cultural capital, such that the variables I use as proxies for social and cultural capital are not necessarily assigned to one type of capital or the other" (Wells 2008). The scholar in question apparently is not aware that by the same token he has dealt a fatal blow to the concept concerned if one cannot differentiate between cultural and social capital, then the concept of cultural capital as having no separate subject matter of its own makes no logical and analytical sense. And the phrase "fatal blow" probably overstates the issue; cultural capital adherents are very well, thank you very much, which is manifested in, inter alia, an unending stream of definitions conforming to the pattern outlined above, i.e. at least partially overlapping, as in the following example where cultural capital is defined as consisting of "networks with other parents, an understanding of the schooling process and teacher jargon, and contact with school personnel" (McNeal 2011).

The following writer of multiple capitals school cautiously refrains from expressly pointing out whichever capital – social or cultural – his statement: on "access to capital through social networks; it is often not extremely difficult to find 'free' money or private loans, which is cultural tradition in some ethnic groups"(Lattas 2011) refers to. Others, though, are not so self-restrained. A cultural capital researcher states: "social class provides parents with unequal resources to comply with teachers' requests for parental participation", and she adds that "characteristics of family life (e.g., social networks) also intervene and mediate family-school relationships". From this she draws the conclusion that "the social and cultural elements of family life that facilitate compliance with teachers' requests can be viewed as a form of cultural capital. The study suggests that the concept of cultural capital can be used fruitfully to understand social class differences in children's school experiences" (Lareau 1997). How come, one could ask when the alleged tool of that fruitful analysis is a mix of two separate concepts, each of which is a misnomer in its own right?

Similarly, the reader is told by another scholar of the said persuasion that:

> For Bourdieu (1985; also see Portes, 1998), social networks are not a natural given but a result of deliberate investment of cultural as well as economic resources. Norms (e.g., reciprocity) and sanctions are considered a major source of social capital (Coleman, 1988; Portes, 1998). However, norms are culturally constructed (Hofstede, 1980), and as such, 'networks are best seen as primarily cultural phenomena'. (Curran et al.)

This peculiar justification implies an untenable view of causation wherein on the basis of an influence exerted by certain forms of what is considered culture it is inferred that the object of that influence thereby itself becomes cultural in nature. "…heavy drinking sessions when other directors were present as a way of shoring up his cultural capital and right to be chairman" (Lattas 2011). In this case "cultural capital" definitely refers to connections that on their part perfectly fit the definition of social capital.

A researcher investigating "how well religious, family, and cultural social capital influenced 8th and 10th grade student aspirations, future plans, and prior academic experience"(Al-Fadhli 2010), as can be seen, without further ado subsumes cultural capital into social capital.

The degree of intellectual derangement and spread of "anything goes" policy is glaringly shown by the following statement: "In general terms, social capital (socio-cultural capital, cultural capital) refers to a society's capability to deal with social, economic and environmental problems and be active in shaping the development of the overall system. It consists of socio-cultural values and norms, learned preferences, human capital and labour force, local knowledge of the environment, social competence and institutions, human health and life expectancy, as well as cultural and social integrity and social cohesion" (Berks, Folke 1994: 128–49).

The above statement – for all its incredible breadth – reveals that social capital is not the only neighbour of cultural capital whose territory is exposed to infringement on the part of this self-styled conquistador, as the following quotation, involving not two but all three forms of capital, clearly shows: "Social capital combines with cultural capital to influence individual outcomes For example, compare Maria, Martha, Chrystal, Anna, and Sandy, all of whom had completed solid clerical training" (Schneider 2004: 193).

> Most examples of social capital formed through congregations involved links to cultural capital. People were not only referred to jobs but also taught ways to behave. The trusting environment of the church helped Mary develop work skills (Schneider 2004: 264).

It is perhaps paradoxical, but in fact typical of the (not only) cultural capital literature that it can go from one extreme to the other. Thus, whilst the starting point of Pereira et al. (2006) is perfectly valid: (we've ourselves made an analogous point above): "Though some researchers consider cultural capital to be a form of social capital, we heed criticisms of ever-expanding notions of social capital", their inference has an opposite flaw: "We define *cultural capital* as family-mediated values and outlooks that [...] facilitate access to education" in that it limits the background of cultural capital to the family setting". What of those children whose primary socialisation takes place in an orphanage? Not accidentally, the situation regarding cultural capital is thus parallel to that of social capital where both overly limited and overly stretched definitions have been identified. One more example of the latter comes from Botma (2008) who admits that "scholars ascribe a host of meanings to the term 'cultural capital' – including the processes and products of education and creating prestige, status, art, culture, taste and (body) images in society".

Another cultural capital scholar says that "companies nurture and support the "cultural capital – non-monetary skills, knowledge and relationships generated outside the workplace" (Sharrod 2005), which could be subsumed into both social and human capital.

This very overlap has been also noticed by McNeal (2001) who admits that "If you examine what is typically thought of as parent involvement, the term itself seems to be a lay term for various elements of social and/or cultural capital...".

Indeed, the dimensions of parent involvement used in this research (e.g., parent-child discussion, parent involvement at school (e.g. PTO), parental monitoring of a child's behavior, and parent involvement directly with the educational process) are clearly components of cultural and social capital as conceptualised by Bourdieu (1977), Lareau (1989) and Coleman (1987, 1991). In terms of a unique classification, the slight overlap between cultural and social capital is likely shared by parent-child discussion; social capital is represented by parent involvement in the Parent-Teacher Organisation and monitoring; cultural capital is represented by direct parental involvement in the educational process".

Whether one does or not agree with particular attributions suggested by McNeal, it is hard to escape the conclusion of ambiguity and vagueness plaguing cultural capital theory and research.

Regarding the relationship of the form of capital considered in the present part of the study to that discussed in Part I, the reader may be, inter alia, referred back, for instance, to Wang' Human capital deliberations above in which human capital has been deemed a form of cultural capital.

A tacit relationship of the same sort seems to be implied by the following statement: "Nearly all the consumer informants possessed limited amounts of economic capital and institutional cultural capital in the form of formal education" (Adkins, Corus 2009).

Another cultural capital analyst directly equates Cultural Capital and Educational Attainment (Viinstra 2007).

In the same vein, a researcher refers to "high levels of educational attainment (cultural capital)" (Sanks 2007), whilst yet another one, "working with Pierre Bourdieu's notions of capital, social fields, and markets, [...] argues that immigrant students found a meaningful way to acquire the cultural capital of the dominant society (i.e., good grades, educational credentials, entree into higher education, and access to middle-class and upper middle-class professions" (Goldstein 2003). That cultural capital is in fact a misnomer, referring instead to labour power is equally evident from the following statement: "scientific knowledge formed the cultural and economic capital of the country's rising urban middle class, which is comprised of physicians, engineers, lawyers, teachers, architects and other modern educated persons"(Schayegh 2007).

Likewise, Yamamoto and Brinton (2010) acknowledge that "cultural capital is mainly exerting an effect through the enhancement of children's human capital", which, naturally, makes it difficult to pin down what this invisible, yet potent force consists of.

It only adds to our concept's ambiguity when, just as in the case of social capital, some authors identify it not with the outcome of education but with some of factors that might affect it, as in the following definition: "The term cultural capital represents the collection of non-economic forces such as family background, social class, varying investments in and commitments to education, different resources, etc. which influence academic success" (Hayes). It might be noted that the above definition reveals an important source of theoretical weaknesses pertinent to the cultural capital approach; in framing social class as a non-economic factor, it manifests a reified, non-sociological view of the economy. When one ignores that economic relations, including capital, are social relations, that owing to the economy being embedded in its social setting, all economic relations should be viewed as socio-economic rather than purely economic, then it is only natural that such a reductionist concept of capital is being applied to non-economic phenomena, yielding their picture that is equally skewed as in the former instance.

In those attempts, their authors follow, as might be expected, Bourdieu's footsteps:

> Bourdieu and Jean-Claude Passeron first used the term in 'Cultural Reproduction and Social Reproduction' (1973). In this work he attempted to explain differences in children's scholastic outcomes in France during the 1960s. It has been further elaborated and developed in terms of higher education in *The State Nobility* (1996).

> In *Distinction*, forms of capital are presented as real entities: 'the overall volume of capital, understood as the set of actually useable resources and powers – economic capital, cultural capital and also social capital' (Bourdieu 1984: 114). In this formulation 'also' is the key word as social capital effectively drops from Bourdieu's vision, being subsumed under economic and cultural capital. (Field, Schuller, Baron 2000)

Now the truth of the matter is, this kind of conceptual relay or musical chairs, if you will, betrays without exception, an extreme conceptual flexibility and adaptability – but not to the exigencies of reality but one's own theoretical discourse imposed by some initial presuppositions. Above all, such possibilities of shifting both the meaning and role of particular concepts within one's framework glaringly shows that they have not been adequately defined; otherwise, such shifts would be not feasible; had their substantive content been firmly attached to their terminological labels, to shuffle them as one sees fit depending on circumstances would not be that easy.

> [In] 'Language and Symbolic Power', a series of essays written between 1977 and 1982 (Bourdieu 1991b), social capital appears along with economic capital, cultural capital, and symbolic capital as the principal fields which combine to constitute the social position of any particular person, but the inter-relation of these concepts is not explored. The elaboration of forms of capital continues in *Homo Academicus* (Bourdieu 1988), with social capital now appearing alongside yet new forms of capital such as academic capital or the capital of services rendered. Social capital, however, is also highlighted in the text in that it constitutes half of the domain from which the highly orthodox, explanatory quantitative variables are drawn (Bourdieu 1988: Table 1, Appendix 1).

> The evocative use of the concept 'capital', with its promiscuous proliferation
> of varieties, was reined in by Bourdieu in 1983 in an essay on 'The Forms
> of Capital' (Bourdieu 1997). While acknowledging the primacy of economic
> capital in his previous work, Bourdieu had tended to stress cultural capital, with
> social capital a very distant third. In a subtle shift of position Bourdieu posits a
> unitary capital which 'can present itself in three fundamental guises' (1997: 47),
> economic, cultural, and social. (Field, Schuller, Baron 2000)

Another adherent of the notion under consideration elucidates its meaning by
pointing out that "cultural capital is most closely associated with individual
identity in the shape of embodied dispositions such as discriminations of taste,
accents, and mind sets, and through the consumption of goods and services,
especially those which can be institutionally formalised through education and
qualifications" (Dolan 2002).

And, as much as we disagree with Becker in many respects, it is difficult –
given the common definition of human capital – not to concur that "Musicians, for
example, are more likely than the general public to share the critics' high opinion
of Beethoven's string quartets. In other words, differences in human capital
account for some differences in tastes between artists and critics on the one hand
and the general public on the other" (Stigler and Becker 1977).

Similarly, it is immensely difficult, if not impossible, to figure out what the
difference between the two capitals mentioned would consist in; the authors
themselves point out, after all, that the knowledge relevant in their opinion to
cultural capital is just as an outcome of the education process, as professional
qualifications in the narrow sense of the word are, and, as may be inserted, the
respective dimensions of knowledge can be couched in terms of different aspects
and/or types of labour power. Specifically, they treat:

> schools as affording members of a society opportunities to learn and
> develop skills and capacities to compete in labour markets and to participate
> meaningfully in society. Indeed, a basic purpose of schools is imparting [...] the
> skills and capacities necessary for [...] society to survive and for the individual
> to survive within it. This socialisation through schooling aims at development
> of productive members of society and at the reproduction of culture. (Bourdieu,
> 1990; Boocock, 1984)

In fact, principal motivations for attending school include acquiring skills to "fit in"
or navigate within the wider society, particularly as regards obtaining employment
and increasing earning potential. As Ballantine (1997: 60–61) points out, "in the
United States, the expectation is that we can improve our life position with good
education and hard work, that all members of society have an equal opportunity
to experience upward mobility. Those with higher levels of education have more
chances at a better job and salary and occupational mobility have long been principal
goals expressed as educational motivations, i.e., for acquiring relevant "human

capital," or a person's stock of skills and productive knowledge. Operationalised as educational achievement, human capital has been measured as levels of schooling, rates of school completion or graduation, test scores, and the like.

Moreover, successful socialisation through schooling also leads to the accumulation of "cultural capital" by individuals. Cultural capital, i.e., the general cultural background, knowledge, skills, and dispositions passed from one generation to the next, is central to the process of cultural reproduction (McNeely, Figueroa 2003).

Before turning to the most relevant to our current line of argument inference from the above passage, let us dwell for a moment on another quite important point. With this whole talk of the researcher's possibility to operationalise the concepts under consideration, in reality they turn out to be a mix of ideological and substantive considerations, and before any application in a scholarly investigation, one need, as a precondition, identify the two components and proportions they occupy. For whilst Bourdieu lays stress on the system of education as by no means ensuring an equal access to it, and its effects also deepen rather than mitigate class disparities. It is true, to be true, that the claims in question refer to different countries, France constituting a typical example of continental stakeholder capitalism. But it does by any means follow that a simple contextualisation in that sense will do the trick. This would some chance to work if the data concerning both countries in question were correct. France is another story, but what the reader is told above regarding an educational version of "American dream" is laughable.

To return to the question of dangerous and ambiguous liaisons of cultural capital with the rest of "capital" family, however ethically improper it might sound, according to the above quotations, the most hotly contested borderline is mainly between cultural and human capital, which – given what has been earlier found out as regards the latter's status – means that at the very beginning of an analysis we are in a position to deem the concept under consideration as a misnomer of power to two. The situation is even worse, since – as in the case of its social counterpart – the concept in question is a multiple misnomer to the extent that it is closely tied not only to social and human capital, as has been shown above, but also to a term overlapping one being a true referent of the latter:

> For Bourdieu, capital acts as a social relation within a system of exchange, and the term is extended 'to all the goods material and symbolic, without distinction, that present themselves as rare and worthy of being sought after in a particular social formation (cited in Harker, 1990: 13) and cultural capital acts as a social relation within a system of exchange that includes the accumulated cultural knowledge that confers power and status. (Fowler 1997)

Overall, as the preceding shows, also for a plethora of his self-conscious and tacit followers as well as "for Bourdieu fields are not clearly demarcated; their boundaries are porous. The field is determined by the species of capital at stake" (Sanks 2007).

The principal explanatory concept being so fluid, it is small wonder that it, just as its equally slippery social counterpart, can be used for making over-blown claims on the basis of its putative relevance. Thus, a critic points to a rather dubious merit of cultural capital in the particular context in question:

> Ochiai is surely correct that the former slaves preferred farms of their own to working for wages and, when given the chance, sought to lessen their families' economic vulnerability by planting less cotton and more corn. Even so, there are other ways to explain such behavior than with reference to a deeply ingrained world view, as the author's own evidence makes clear. Sea Island blacks had every reason to be skeptical of the particular version of free labour introduced by their Yankee benefactors. Union troops looted black households and confiscated black property 'mercilessly' (p. 137). Government-managed plantations altered antebellum practices by increasing managerial control of the labour routine while decreasing traditional rations and privileges and paying labourers perpetually late, if at all. Supposedly sympathetic northern entrepreneurs reaped enormous profits on lands bought from the government at a pittance but reneged on pledges to assist African American employees in purchasing land of their own. It is small wonder that the former slaves were deeply suspicious of this alternative to slavery, but making inferences about their most fundamental cultural values in such a context is highly questionable (Goldman 2005).

But there is even more to the matter than that.

Bourdieu defines a field in more technical terms as: "a network, or configuration, of objective relations between positions. These positions are objectively defined, in their existence and in the determinations they impose upon their occupants, agents or institutions, by their present and potential situation (situs) in the structure of the distribution of species of power (or capital) whose possession commands access to the specific profits that are at stake in the field, as well as by their objective relation to other positions. [...] Bourdieu says, "In empirical work, it is one and the same thing to determine what the field is, where its limits lie, etc., and to determine what species of capital are active in it, within what limits, and so on" (1991: 98–9). [...] In any given field, there are players or actors who struggle to produce, distribute, appropriate, or control some form of capital. [...] each field is related to the larger field of social power. [...]" So, a field is an arena of competition for power or capital" (Sanks 2007).

As power is involved in social capital as well, it is fair to say that by the same token an additional misnomer implicated in the multiple capital framework has been disclosed (not to mention "profits" whose presence in a framework driven by an economic analogy is only natural).

Productiveness of the concept under consideration, unfortunately not in the positive sense of the word, manifests itself through its various applications, such as that by Emirbayer and Williams (2005) who employ Bourdieu's notion of fields and capital to examine the power relations in the field of social services, particularly homeless shelters. The scholars concerned identify the two distinct fields that operate in the same geographic location (the shelter) and the types of capital that are legitimate and valued in each. Specifically, they argue that homeless persons can possess "staff-sanctioned capital" or "client-sanctioned capital" (2005: 92) and claim that in the shelter, they are both at the same time, desirable and undesirable, valued and disparaged, depending within which of the two fields they are operating. Whilst their work shows certain minor differences as compared that one on which they draw (they assert that typically the resources that form the two aforementioned capitals are derived from a person's life rather than the family), their fertility or productivity, if you like, as regards capitals is nearly as impressive as that of their French master, and, let us add, the fruits of that blissful creativity are as sterile as those in Bourdieu's case.

Take, for instance, the following argument: "Most academics and administrators are not compensated at the level that their education, skills, and experience would garner in business or industry.

In the absence of sufficient real capital, the cultural capital of the academic world – recognition – is especially important. We live for and thrive on (whether we admit it to ourselves or not) the recognition of our colleagues, peers, disciplines, and institutions" (Olson 2006).

The first contention is perhaps true, but it does not follow that the same applies to its purported corollary – again, the point on the importance of recognition in the academic world is well put, only that it has nothing in common with the validation of a similar role pertaining to cultural capital. Why should professional recognition, respect or prestige, or even fame be regarded as a form of capital, if none of those phenomena possesses intrinsic attributes of real capital, as the author himself calls it, such as: alienability, exchangeability into other goods, etc. In other words, the alleged "proof" of cultural capital's relevance in the context in question hinges on applying a definite label to things without any inherent association with capital, and thus – surprise, surprise – on a misnomer.

To give the other side the benefit of the doubt, let us consider yet another definition of the concept in question by a scholar who on his part relies heavily on the master himself: "Cultural capital is like money in that it can be saved, invested, and used to obtain other resources (such as access to economic positions).

It has this currency because its "signals" are broadly accepted. Cultural capital "counts" because many people or, at least, key gatekeepers believe it should be rewarded" (Kingston 2001). Application of such economic notions as saving or investment to what is regarded as cultural capital is not only counter-intuitive, but falters in light of logical and substantive analysis. Indeed, this is the case even if the concept of cultural capital is restricted to one of its possible referents, i.e. labour power, although the latter is itself an economic, or more precisely, socio-economic concept, after all. And the association becomes even more untenable with reference to other possible meanings of cultural capital. The incongruity between the latter and the notion of capital (in the economic, that is, the only legitimate sense) becomes even more glaring in the case of other purported components of cultural capital. Even granted-what itself is extremely problematic, as shown in this chapter – that "cultural capital", or whatever is conceived as its object brings in its holder some benefits or rewards, it is immediately evident that the nature of those is vastly different from those yielded by capital *stricto sensu*. While an owner of fixed and variable capital may reasonably expect that it will bring him or her, a certain amount of profit (after selling the commodities produced by a given labour power), which expectations may of course fail, in the context of purported cultural capital no such process takes place. The connection between possessing a huge collection of books by one's parents and one's professional or business success is so distant, i.e. mediated by this many social and economic variables that no one can count on the attainment of the latter with a degree of certainty remotely close to that present in the capitalist situation.

Hence, the following attempt to defend the capital character of cultural capital: "As the word 'capital' implies, cultural capital is an asset that can be used to acquire other kinds of assets, such as educational credentials" (Wildhagen 2009) is abortive – nothing like a monetary transaction takes place there; moreover, the aforementioned scholar commits a chronic error of confounding two very different relations: direct and indirect one, that is to say, familiarity with high culture could be of assistance in acquiring education, but it is by no means an immediate means of this acquisition, and only then one could compare it with money as a medium of exchange (which, mind you, would still be a far cry from capital, since by any means every sum of money can be described as capital). Even more surprising, and inaccurate is the definition of cultural capital by Bourdieu himself as a "conventional, constant, legally-guaranteed value with respect to culture" (1986: 248). The phrase "surprising" as a matter of fact misses the point, as Bourdieu's flirtation with legal frameworks has been already mentioned Even so, this proclivity does not justify such overdone judgments on the alleged social relevance and efficacy of law.

To round off the present discussion of alleged affinity of cultural and real, economic capital, let us consider yet another argument made in favour of this similarity:

> It could be proposed that items of cultural capital are simply cultural goods which happen to be capital goods rather than consumption goods. Such a definition presupposes a definition of a cultural good. Although there has been some debate amongst cultural economists as to whether cultural goods and services can be differentiated from 'ordinary' economic goods and services, and, if so how, it is reasonable to suggest that a cultural good is one which has involved human creativity in its making, which conveys symbolic meaning (or multiple meanings) and which is identifiable, at least in principle, as embodying some intellectual property. Accepting these characteristics of a cultural good would allow us to substantiate the definition of cultural capital (Throsby 2001: 167).

Whilst Throsby's definition of "cultural good" is not unproblematic in its emphasis on creativity as allegedly pertaining only to cultural activities and in subsuming implicitly emotional into intellectual content of works of art, music, etc., the most objectionable is his justification of the applicability of the capital label on the grounds that the objects concerned constitute "capital" or investment goods, that is to say, means of production. Symptomatically, there are no specific examples that would illustrate this claim, which is not surprising for the sole category of objects that at least might be considered as a candidate for that role comprises intellectual means of production, such as software, industrial designs, etc. which can hardly be considered at the same footing as, say, Monet's paintings.

Bourdieu, to be sure, did not maintain that between economic and cultural capital there are no differences at all. However, in his view they boil down to the different modes of legitimation pertaining to the two respective dimensions of inequality. In the case of cultural capital, despite the fact that cultural capital is acquired in the home and the school via exposure to a given set of cultural practices – and therefore has a social origin – it is liable to be perceived as inborn "talent," and its holder "gifted," as a result of the fact that it is embodied in particular individuals. Moreover, because the school system transforms "inherited" cultural capital into "scholastic" cultural capital, the latter is predisposed to appear as an individual "achievement". For example, researchers have demonstrated that what they conventionally classify as middle-class parents typically talk more to infants and young children than do working-class or poor parents. As a result, middle-class children often have larger vocabularies when they enter school, and subsequently score more highly on standardised tests measuring verbal skills (Hart and Risley 1999; Lareau 2003). "Nevertheless, teachers, parents, and students themselves are likely to interpret the differences in test scores as a matter of natural talent or individual effort" (Lareau, Weininger 2003).

Pertinent as those observations are (barring the unfortunate terminology), they do not capture any unique feature of cultural, as distinct from economic inequalities. In the latter instance just as in the former one powerful class ideologies and rationalisations are at work to disguise the real socio-economic source of the disparities concerned, and among those, incidentally, individualistic myths of self-made men are and long have been salient in capitalism's economic life, notably in its stockholder, Anglo-Saxon variety.

An important source of all this confusion, and at the same time further misnomer hiding behind the construct under consideration, is revealed in the following statement: "Cultural capital (Bourdieu, 1986; Bourdieu & Passeron, 1977) includes culture-based factors and indicators of symbolic wealth that help define a person's class" (Wells 2008). What we have in mind is the term "symbolic wealth". Symbolic or not, wealth is closely related to property, as is, on its side, also the following statement "cultural "habits and dispositions" comprise a resource capable of generating "profits"; they are potentially subject to monopolisation by individuals and groups; and, under appropriate conditions, they can be transmitted from one generation to the next" (Lareau and Weininger 2003).

And there lies the rub. In various places in the book the concept of non-economic property relations as, in particular, underlying the units of social differentiation in the non-economic realm is highlighted. It also suggests that the inclusion of class in the above-mentioned particular context is – from the standpoint of socio-economic structuralism – misplaced, since although according to our approach classes may be involved in certain non-economic property relations, it is economic ownership that determines their location in the structure of societal differentiation.

Two other theorists put forward their case for the appropriateness of the term "capital" in conjunction with "cultural" in slightly different terms, but their argument is equally misguided: "since persons with the same credentials have a roughly equivalent worth on the labour market, educational degrees can be seen to be a distinct form of cultural capital" (Lareau, Weininger 2003). What this argument misses is that the credentials in question have some market value, or better – price because they can be relied upon as a testimony of holding a qualified labour power, and this could only be obscured by the term "capital", as amply demonstrated in Part I.

Given the battery of arguments in favour of this sort of "capitalisation", the reader may be forgiven for supposing that there are no others. But she would be mistaken; "render[ing] individuals interchangeable in this fashion, Bourdieu suggests that institutionalisation performs a function for cultural capital analogous to that performed by money in the case of economic capital" (Lareau, Weininger 2003). This is truly astonishing; the role of money the argument refers to is that of universal equivalent, a commodity having no intrinsic value, but exchangeable into all market goods. What educational credentials can be converted to? Between the moment of acquiring given qualifications and realising the value of given labour power there is a whole array of mediations, and the final market price received by a holder of given qualifications may be very different depending on concrete circumstances. There is not a shadow of resemblance between this process and the process of capital valorisation. The authors mentioned above also forget that in the economic case, it is capital itself, precisely – money capital that is employed to acquire all ingredients essential for setting in motion the process of material production and production of value, including surplus value. None of these applies to "cultural capital", therefore, one should perhaps employ the sociology of knowledge perspective to comprehend why the capital analogue exerts so powerful an influence on cultural capital proponents that they do not shy away from invoking value-loaded concepts, as Dunlap (1997) does, speaking of "the cultural capital of economic freedom".

Likewise, Sheridan-Rabineau (2010) joyfully proclaims, invoking another catchphrase: "Creativity is the cultural capital of the twenty-first century".

It is only for the sake of brevity that any broader review of misnomers that cultural capital and its derivative concepts can actually represent is not attempted at this point; to cite but one such example, however: "The capital (valued resource) at stake in the field of theology is the Christian symbol system [...] To further complicate matters, there are subfields with more specific forms of cultural capital, for example, biblical studies with the cultural capital of biblical languages and archeology, church history with its specific capital of historiography, medical ethics with its knowledge of medical science, etc." (Sanks 2007).

Since, as hinted above, Bourdieu's concept of field is ill-defined and thereby can be stretched out as one sees fit, in conjunction with the above thesis one can freely create new subvarieties of cultural capital, becoming-according to the above-mentioned definition-a cultural capital along the way.

This breadth allows its advocates to make equally exaggerated claims about cultural capital's purported importance, as in the following stunning assertion: "the crystallised capitalist profit structure cannot be obtained only with economic capital without the proper role of cultural capital" (Kim 2007). The only thinkable justification for this mind-boggling claim may be a kind of pseudo-dialectics in which everything connects with, and affects everything else. Otherwise, this stubbornly – despite scores of definitions – ambiguous term might be bring down to language without which not only profit-making but any form of economic, and indeed social interaction is inconceivable. But whether this or still some other meaning of the concept is at issue in the context in question, remains a puzzle.

Chapter 10
Cultural Capital as Labour Power

Thus, for example, the following quotation refers to knowledge, acquisition and possession of which constitutes part and parcel of financial employees' work (at transnational corporations, which accounts for the presence of the prefix in question), which, naturally, means that it is a component of their labour power. "an important function of transient professionals is also to network, and accumulate 'cultural capital'." (McDowell, 1997), "...as a part of their everyday expatriate experiences. Couched within the new economic geography" (Lee and Wills 1997), "...there has been a myriad of work discussing 'embedment', knowledge, expertise, and networks, as 'global' processes, which accumulate cultural capital within IFCs" (Amin and Thrift, 1997; Leyshon and Thrift 1997; McDowell 1997). "In this work, emphasis focuses towards investigating organisational cultures of professional staff, their knowledge, and the production/circulation of that knowledge. [...] the performance of a financial TNC is also very much linked to the success and speed with which their transient migrants, accumulate/circulate knowledge, expertise and 'intelligence' in, and out of, the institutional workplace. [...] they had, or could obtain, the specific knowledge, expertise, and skills required to ensure efficient operation of the financial system and global reach of the TNC." (Altintas 2003).

The intimate connection of the concept under consideration with that of labour power is clearly shown by the following review of Ghodsee's (2005) book, which even more underlines the reviewer's blunder in his persistent sticking to calling the country in question "communist", although the author of the volume under review employed such terms as "socialist" and "post-socialist". The first of the three terms cited above is, no doubt, one most widely used in the Western (as well as in newly sovereign nations, formerly dependencies of the Soviet Union) political science, journalism and common speech, but it is no justification whatsoever from the crucial socio-economic viewpoint. Now the American reviewer should know, and if he does not, it is to his peril, that communism according to Marx and Engels (who, even he should agree, are undeniably experts in the field under consideration) is a non-state, or more precisely-post-state order. Now, as another common term used to identify the group of countries concerned, i.e. "state socialism" indicates, there could be many shortages throughout the countries of Eastern and Central Europe, but the state wasn't exactly amongst those; nay, a common criticism against the said countries had been couched in terms of the state machine's overgrowth. How to account for this apparent hesitation on the part of Western public opinion to associate the socio-economic system under which the nations involved had lived after the Second World War? The question is rather easy to answer. Recall that for a considerable period of time that opinion was shaped or at least co-shaped by the left. Now left-wing, let alone leftist (commonly anti-Stalinist) intellectuals were reluctant to apply the label of (in their eyes) many noble connotations to what had been defined by their by no means the most radical wing as "the degenerated workers' state". And since nature abhors vacuum, as they say, another, this time round –pejorative or in the course of becoming one – term was at hand. And thus, to put it in a nutshell, communism in Eastern and Central Europe was born. Of course, stereotypes and myths can live long; nay, the aforementioned one lives even after its purported empirical referent passed away (vide: "post-communism" which, just as the term discussed above, is thus-in accordance with the general logic of the present work – a misnomer).

Be that as it may, let us come back to the aforementioned commentator:

> Many tourism workers were sent abroad for specialised training and deliberate exposure to Western ways to ensure the delivery of a better tourism product. Making use of Pierre Bourdieu's notion of social and cultural capital, Ghodsee shows that it was precisely the cultural capital represented by these experiences that benefited women in Bulgaria's transformation from a Communist to a privatised tourism economy. Just as high Communist Party officials used their political capital to secure ownership of newly privatised hotels, women working in tourism used their cultural capital to move into managerial positions or, at the very least, to maintain their jobs when everyone else around them – including their husbands, fathers, and brothers – was out of work. 'Privatization,' Ghodsee submits, 'was the key institutional change that unequivocally re-valued women's cultural capital in tourism to their benefit' (2005: 133).

> Today, women in Bulgaria make up the majority of the 161 workers in professions that under Communism were feminized. As in tourism, women predominate in law, medicine, banking, finance, and public administration, high-prestige professions in a capitalist society. Ghodsee's detailed and rigorous study of Bulgarian tourism provides important insights into this transformation, among them that 'Bulgarian tourism under communism created a labour force with high levels of general education, extended work experience with Westerners, and fluency in multiple foreign languages. Anyone with this package of cultural capital would have had the tools to adapt to the institutional changes that followed 1989' (p. 155) (Ballerino-Cohen 2008).

We do not want to torment further the commentator under consideration, but an awkward question arises: what kind of transformation was the collapse of the ancien regime and the transition to capitalism if he himself admits that one of the most salient features of the latter – the wide presence of women in what he calls "professions" in fact did not distinguish the new system at all, as under the former regime the occupations in questions had been equally, or even to a larger degree feminised.

Another research concerning socialist and post-socialist countries shows that cultural capital analysts ignore the concept of labour power to their peril. Eyal, Szelényi, and Townsley's (1998) examination of the class structure in Central Europe focuses exactly on cultural capital. They argue that members of the bureaucratic nomenclatura did not successfully exploit their authority under communism to appropriate large amounts state property during the privatisation process that marked the transition to capitalism.

Nor have the small-scale entrepreneurs who were tolerated in the final decades of state socialism managed to leverage their "head start" and become a full-blown capitalist class in the post-1989 period. Rather, in countries such as Czechoslovakia, Hungary, and Poland, a stratification system has emerged which can be characterised as a type of "capitalism without capitalists." In this system, cultural capital stands as the most important basis of power and privilege. Thus, the dominant class in these societies can be described as a "cultural bourgeoisie" rather than an economic bourgeoisie. This cultural bourgeoisie, which is a diverse group that includes former technocrats and dissident intellectuals, has largely monopolised the skills, know-how, and credentials (i.e., cultural capital) that have become critical to occupational success. The aforementioned authors argue that possession of cultural capital makes possible access to leading positions in the economy and the state and, conversely, that lack of cultural capital is a substantial barrier.

This argument testifies to a dramatic degree of ignorance of the socialist and post-socialist socio-economic realities. The present author has shown (1983; 1995; 2008) that what is commonly called the nomenklatura was in fact the ruling class. Under socialism it comprised many groups whose common denominator was their collective ownership of labour power and lumpen-ownership of the means of production, the former showing up in the shape of revolving door, a mechanism thanks to which a provincial party secretary could tomorrow become a managing director of a collective farm, and the day after tomorrow an editor-in-chief of a major daily. Far from being pushed to the margin in the wake of systemic breakthrough, it was also the nomenklatura members who were the principal beneficiaries of privatisation in the countries under consideration. Relatedly, it is interesting that the cultural capital adherents should invoke such phrases as "capitalism without capitalists". Not only it is contradiction in terms, but in using such a phrase the authors themselves dismiss their theoretical case for cultural capital which apparently turns out to be not a capital in the real sense of the word, one that would give rise to class relations. And this speaks volumes of the real value pertaining to the theoretical construct under consideration. Finally, many, albeit obviously not all, shopkeepers, small craftsmen or farmers became, after the capitalist restoration, full-blown capitalists. For instance, the rich Polish capitalist Jan Kulczyk inherited his first $1m from his father, a private entrepreneur.

That the concept in question does in fact refer largely to labour power is clearly shown also by the following passage:

...the job structure is bifurcated between jobs that offer pay and benefit packages sufficient to support a family and those offering insufficient remuneration. With the exception of the rapidly shrinking pool of skilled blue-collar or primary-sector unskilled blue-collar jobs, the majority of the desirable jobs generally require a college education. A full 31 percent of the available positions required advanced education, usually at an associate's- or bachelor's-degree level or above. Twenty-nine percent of the jobs called for either technical education in a skilled blue-collar trade or clerical skills. In these jobs employees are also expected to follow the cultural capital patterns of professional workplaces, including appropriate communication skills, the ability to think critically, willingness to work as a team, commitment to meeting deadlines, and readiness to take responsibility for the quality of the flexible hours. Most service-sector jobs – sales clerk, nursing assistant, restaurant worker, and others – call for reliability, willingness to work as part of a team, and the ability to communicate well, think critically, work in a high-pressure environment, and perform quality work. Most of these jobs seldom advanced educational skills, but many employers require a high-school diploma.

People like Sandy in service jobs need the highest level of bicultural skills to succeed in mainstream workplaces. While low-paying blue-collar jobs have lower expectations for communication skills, employers still want reliability, quality work, and the ability to work on a team. Many blue-collar workers develop these skills.

Skilled trades have always depended on critical thinking, creativity, and quality work. (Anderson 2000).

It is evident that the traits listed above refer not to any cultural capital whatsoever but simply to labour power. An ability to perform a specific type of work may require specific skills, including interactive ones. In an overwhelming number of cases, these are a product of social environment, including family setting, ties within one's peer groups and other social contacts and relationships, as well as training, inclusive of self-education. Why on earth one should "capitalise" this web of social relations?

The aforementioned reviewer goes on to state: "Welfare-to-work program experience among men hired at Quaker Residence illustrates the role of cultural capital appropriate for the workplace for blue-collar service-sector jobs. Quaker Residence's mission included creating opportunities for people in need for a variety of reasons, and many staff members were hired out of welfare-to-work programs or low-income neighborhoods. The maintenance jobs proved particularly appropriate for low-skilled and displaced workers with limited education because willingness to do the work, reliability, and honesty were the major prerequisites" (Anderson 2000).

The term of prerequisites highlights again that the concept in question refers to labour power, as the latter comprises exactly those manual and mental traits, skills and aptitudes that constitute essential preconditions of performing abstract or concrete labour. Further on, the author, inter alia, tells a story of a female employee:

> Several people failed to be hired by the agency out of the welfare-to-work program [...] . In most cases, these were individual failings, but sometimes individual behaviors combined with cultural values to limit long term opportunities. Blue-collar cultural capital skills held by many older workers often have very different patterns than the dominant service-sector employment soft-skills set. In her book on Kenosha, Katherine Dudley (1994) describes how line workers at 'the Motors' and similar employers deliberately regulated the timing of work. These line workers disdained higher education.

> Other people of colour from low-income, closed social capital communities experience clashes because they refuse to acquiesce to the power imbalances of low-skilled service-sector work. For example, Linda, a woman with limited work experience profiled in the next chapter, lost one job because she got into an argument with a customer:

> I got in a fight with a lady. We was cleaning up a room and this Chinese man, I thought he was already gone. It was after checkout. So I'm knocking – 'Housekeeping, housekeeping' – then nobody answers the door, so I take the key and I'm doing my work.

> Soon as I'm getting ready to leave, the man comes back askin' me, 'Why you just cleanin' my house? My room? It's going to take me five, ten minutes to get dressed. I ain't dressed.' I say, 'You look like you dressed to me.' So he's saying Chinese words. I don't know what he's saying but it sounds like he called me nigger. He say he going to go tell my [supervisor]. I cussed him out and I say, 'She going to believe you anyway. Who pay the money for the room?'

> So I told [the supervisor] I didn't cuss him. 'I didn't like this job anyway... you know? I quit. Before you even fire me, I quit...' 'If you had a problem you should've come down here and told me.' 'If I came down there and told you I had a problem you wouldn't believe me, 'cause I got an attitude.' So she was like, 'If that's the case, you can go home.' I say, 'If I do good on my job today and I go home then I quit.' Nobody talking to me and no Chinese cussing me out and I don't understand what you say. I cuss you right back out. I don't care.

> Linda quit because she anticipated that she would be fired for talking back to a customer. She relied on culture that had taught her that she had no rights in such a situation. The street culture of her community also put great importance on

being respected by the people around her. (Anderson 2000).' (Schneider 2004: 21)

The same story could be reinterpreted and couched in other terms, however. The female employee in question was required to possess important aspects of instrumentally particularistic labour power which, in fact, she did not hold. Her behaviour after the incident on the one hand flew from her class dignity that had been hurt by the hotel guest, and on the other-from the realistic recognition that she would have been fired anyway. One way or other, in both those respects her behaviour is accounted for by class rather than some general cultural considerations, not to mention capital!

The word "general" used in the above statement has been chosen deliberately, for in certain formulations or applications, if you will, the concept in question reaches indeed an incredible breadth. Take, for instance, the following assertion: "Change requires fostering bicultural practices that enable community residents and policy makers from different closed social capital networks to communicate productively" (Schneider 2004: 321).

The notion of cultural capital, or cultural practices is here understood so broadly that for all intents and purposes it becomes almost identical with that of society. Or, more precisely, the above-cited statement would permit as not to include into the concept only those actions that are not mediated by language, which is of course a cultural phenomenon or medium par excellence.

Similarly, another definition interprets "culture" as "cultural capital" in an entirely arbitrary and unfounded manner: "Culture becomes cultural capital when specific elements of a culture are used to identify someone as a member of a group. Cultural capital is a commodification of a particular culture or subculture that individuals or organisations can use through social capital to access resources of that group. These cultural capital cues can be subtle social patterns or clear symbols, such as speaking a particular dialect or reference to specific political beliefs" (Schneider 2004: 14).

Why a dialect or political belief should become a commodity commodities, remains a puzzle. The same applies to the use of the noun "capital"; even supposing – for the sake of argument – the broadest possible (and hence invalid) concept of capital equating it with any unspecified resources or advantages, the definition cited above does not hold water – "capital" is there understood merely as a means of accessing benefits, and not as a mechanism for their generation.

Another definition belonging to the same family enables us to pinpoint the source of the fallacy involved even more accurately: "Within the African American context, cultural capital can be defined as 'the sense of group consciousness and collective identity that serves as an economic resource to support collective economic or philanthropic efforts" (Ward 1992). Granted that the forms of consciousness indicated above may affect economic action, this still does not liken, let alone equate them to economic capital. To use a given thing in producing profit is not the same as this process being subject to some influence on the part of another thing; in other words, direct and indirect relationships should not be identified with each other.

A somewhat similar definitional case concerns the formulation in which the concept of cultural capital does not contribute anything to our understanding of what is at stake, is in fact utterly redundant: "Most coalition participants know the cultural capital cues expected by policy makers and can present their message effectively" (Schneider 2004:(323).

That the concept in question can be in many cases void is so evident that it attracts attention of others as well.

The term "cultural issues" is used where another, or even the same author, as he indeed does on other occasions, could use "cultural capital" instead – which indicates the latter's superfluous character: "As in development of any system, connecting employers to agencies or people needing work entails attention to all the social capital, cultural issues, skills, and supports needed to successfully link employers to a welfare-to-work system" (Schneider 2004: 365).

The relationship under consideration is also evident from conceptions of the sole father (in this the situation is here different than in two former cases where each concept was a child of many parents). Bourdieu's starting point was his exploration of the discrepancies in educational attainment from different social classes in France in the 1960s. For Bourdieu, the disparity in access to economic capital had not provided an adequate explanation for the educational discrepancies present there. Instead, the French sociologist proposed that, above and beyond economic factors, two other forms of capital – cultural capital and social capital – should be looked to as responsible for the reproduction of class privilege.

Within cultural capital Bourdieu (1986: 243) focuses on "physical capital" as consisting in "long-lasting dispositions of the mind and body" that carry with them particular social and cultural meanings that set parameters for individual action and serve to reproduce and legitimise structures of inequality. When class inequality is conceptualised in this way, the differences that establish the broadly defined categories of upper, middle, and lower class are more than just differences in access to material, cultural, and social resources. Instead, they are differences that are actually embodied. In other words, class inequality can find expression in embodied ways, such as physical appearance, pronunciation, stride, style, posture, Body language, diet, handwriting, and so on. For Bourdieu, then, the body itself is a marker of social class, as particular embodied properties exist as a consequence of specific class practices. In Bourdieu's view, for the body to be recognized as a signifier of class, some bodily properties must have attached to them more (or less) symbolic value than others. These different "valuations" attached to the size, shape, and appearance of the body mean that individuals possessing particular valued bodily traits are more able to "exchange" these physical properties for other valued resources. In this way, Bourdieu views the corporeal as a form of currency that results in the unequal accumulation of material resources and, by extension, an important contributor to class inequality (Perks 2012).

There are several problems with the conception laid out above. Firstly, it assumes a peculiar concept of the physical where both the body and mind are recognised at par as physical objects. This is all the more odd that Bourdieu points also to the symbolic nature of what he defines as cultural capital. To consider human consciousness as nothing more than as a set of energetic, at the end of the day material impulses of the brain is to indulge in a form of crude, naive materialism. This kind of vulgar materialism turns out to be infectious at that, as evidenced by the following statement by one of Bourdieu's followers: "the direct producers of the work in its materiality (artist, writer, etc.)" (Gracy 2007). Naturally, the fact that a painting, or a book appears in a material guise does by any means entail that the cultural objects in question are material, not ideal objects. For what matters in their case, the reason why a particular painting, or a poem are admired, is not their material form, but, conversely – ideal content. While indulging in this crude materialism or physicalism Bourdieu subscribes to the long tradition of French philosophy: consider, e.g., La Mettrie, this, needless to say constitute no justification for adopting this by no means just antiquarian doctrine – as it has been apparently galvanised by successes of neurology,[1] and at an another plane, genetics in recent years. This assessment of the Bourdieusian notion, of course, calls into question its interpretation as one which "represents the social-structural change from materialism to postmaterialism" (Kim, Kim 2007), which claim becomes less surprising given the same authors' subsumption of even "environment into "the mental sphere rather than the physical one".[2]

Besides, the definition referring to dispositions, etc. overlaps, to a degree that it becomes indistinguishable from, another Bourdieu's notion of habitus; after all, habitus is often defined as dispositions that are inculcated in the family but manifest themselves in different ways in each individual (Harker, 1990: 10; Webb, 2002: 37; Gorder, 1980: 226).[3] Moreover, there is yet another term overlapping the above-mentioned one. What Bourdieu (1986) terms *embodied cultural capital* is tightly linked to the dispositions of the habitus, and Bourdieu describes it as a

---

1   Indeed, its exponents, just as some other "hard scientists" claim, as BBC World Service's Forum in June, 2012 demonstrated, that the human being is a machine and nothing else or beyond that.

2   This claim, false as it is, suggest that an important reason for popularity of Bourdieu's notion (which, as is argued in the book, is not supported by its analytical quality) may be – paradoxically, considering Bourdieu's background – its appeal for anti-Marxists who are always fishing for new arguments. The authors in question (Kim, Kim 2007) use the concept in question to seemingly refute what they consider the Marxist view on the relationship of base and superstructure: "cultural capital, a byproduct of superstructure to some extent, contributes to reproducing the production relation and also to determining or continuing the unequal structure in capitalist societies".

3   In this context, a spectacular example of nearly supernatural powers ascribed to Bourdieusian constructs by his keen followers is the claim concerning financial, social, human and cultural capital that "each of these four forms of capital is consistently related to, and clearly shaped by, each individual's habitus" (Salisbury et al. 2001).

"corporeal hexis," a "style of expression," (1988: 56) "a durable way of standing, speaking, walking" (1990b: 70). Most importantly however, the attributes depicted above are actually aspects of labour power, especially – instrumentally particularistic labour power. For this reason, of course, their connection with class is a no-brainer. Last, but no means least, the promiscuous character of carelessness with which Bourdieu and/or his followers multiply one capital after another should to be condemned. The following researcher wins, in our humble opinion, a silver medal in that competition. Her list of capitals is impressive, to say the least, but what is really astonishing is the presence of one Karl Marx among those putatively supporting an idea of not shying away from unceremoniously christening virtually any phenomenon on earth by the name "capital". In her study she raises the questions:

> What are the key factors influencing the harmonious intercultural communication? Or going one step further, what are the important concepts which these factors reside in? In an early research [...] we developed a doxa model we find three factors, in which there are six basic variables, to understand the basic concepts of the international migration process as pull and push factors by a triangulation constituted by different forms of capital, i.e., political capital, cultural capital, social capital and symbolic capital as the intangible forms of capital (Bourdieu, 1998 [1986]); Bourdieu and Wacquant, 1992; Jacobs, 1961; Putnam, 1995; Coleman, 1994), and economic capital and natural capital as tangible forms of capital, (Smith, (1904[1776]); Marx, 1886[972]; von Boehm-Bawerk, 1959; Hawken, Paul; Amory Lovins & L. Hunter Lovins L.; Jansson, AnnMari; et al. 1994). [...]time and effort/energy are the necessary investment factors in all forms of capital. [...] Habitus, field and doxa are the fundamental variables for exploring and understanding the relationship among different forms of capital in a doxa model. These different forms of capital can build up habitus, which are functioned[4] in the different fields that we make use of, in an analysis of the communication in a harmonious way in an intercultural communication doxa. (Wang 2009)

The researcher's justification of her terminological choices is also remarkable, resting, as it does, on manipulating and stretching in an absolutely shameless way the meaning of such concepts as investment or gains: "'Capital, in our definition, not only refers to the economic capital, but also includes the non-economic forms of capital by our raising natural, political, cultural (including human capital), social, and symbolic capital, which, however, have the same properties as economic capital, i.e., the investment and the conversion character.' (Bourdieu 1986, Wang 2006). An understanding of capital should at first recognise the fact

---

4   Thus in original; the grammar and whole context of the sentence in question makes it difficult to figure out what is to function in the said fields: habitus or capitals.

that circulation is the premise for investment and the conversion of capital" (Wang 2009). And Wang continues to conjure up her analogies out of thin air:

> Capital can be invested in not only by its own form, but also by other forms of capital.

> Capital can be converted not only into its own form but also into other forms of capital.

> Capital can be converted into four different kinds of outcomes after being circulated, such as more/positive values, equal values, less/negative values and no values as zero. It is in this sense that I define capital in its fundamental form, which includes other subforms of capital, tangible or less tangible, as well as intangible, i.e., economic, cultural, social and symbolic capital, which includes their subforms (Wang, 2006: 18).

> We define forms of capital as communication resources/power/energy that are managed by the communicators' habitus in different fields in the process of intercultural communication. [...]The capacity of economic capital to produce a surplus value over its own value (cf. Marx, 1886[1972]) is what communicators intend to invest in and expect to convert to profits for communication. After the investment, an individual or an institution possesses forms of capital from the investment, but only in the conversion step does the investment have the opportunity to be realised in different returns (Wang 2009).

Wang's attitude towards Marx is quite different than Parsons', but the latter in his theory of symbolic communication media which, to be sure, has several shortcomings of its own (cf. Tittenbrun 2012) did not attempt to reduce economic capital to a form of communication, as the researcher being discussed at present does. At its core, this notion implies an idealistic conception of society reducing it to a set of communication relations.

Bourdieu himself defines cultural capital (committing along the way the fallacy of *ignotum per ignotum*) as "certain privileges afforded the cultural elite with linguistic, aesthetic, educational and physical capital. [...]many of the documentary filmmakers [...] inhabit Bourdieu's classical concept of the artistic habitus.[...] Even Dziga Vertov, socialist comrade though he was, is still positioned as the artist that uses his aesthetic disposition to frame the world around us to create art. The documentary filmmaker is involved in a habitus that denotes artistic privilege. Despite their actual class origins, their position as artist puts them into the class of the intelligentsia.[...] Thus, when Pare Lorentz investigates the sufferings of the working class in *The Plow that Broke the Plains* (1936), it is understood as a view of the working class through the eyes of the aesthetically privileged. The vein of cultural capital that I would like to juxtapose in the personality documentary is something of an inverse to this classical habitus of the artist. It is the denial of capital, and an adopting of the Average Joe persona. Here, to have cultural capital is negative. To be educated is detrimental. To be set apart as the intelligentsia is to be avoided at all costs. That is to say, in this mode, lack of capital becomes capital. To position oneself as Joe Schmoe who is completely unremarkable is to claim a populist capital and this is where the veracity of the documentary is derived." (Starowicz 2011).

The question of class is the subject of the subsequent chapter, so at this point let us draw the reader's attention to the author's dodge. First we are told that "to have cultural capital is negative". And then we are presented with a sophism: "Lack of capital becomes capital, a populist capital and this is where the veracity of the documentary is derived". Not only the first but also the second part of the aforementioned argument is illogical – however one defines populism, there are grounds to suppose that only those who are populists themselves will associate its meaning with veracity.

Our points made above regarding the Bourdieusian conception of cultural capital are supported also by the following statement by another Bourdieu's folower: "Cultural Reproduction refers to the process in which existing cultural values and norms are passed down from one generation to the next. Cultural Reproduction often results in Social Reproduction, or the process of transferring aspects of society (such as class) from one generation to the next.[...] Bourdieu defines three types of cultural capital: embodied, institutionalised, and objectified. Individuals may embody cultural capital through development of what Bourdieu calls 'long-lasting dispositions of the mind and body', meaning that through the process of enculturation individuals in a particular group (often a socioeconomic class) acquire and sustain a body of cultural knowledge and particular preferences in art, literature, and other aspects of culture. A person's particular embodied cultural capital is known as his or her habitus" (Gracy 2007).

What is worth noting in this context is that, his numerous protestations to the contrary notwithstanding, Bourdieu's much-trumpeted overcoming of the dilemma: subjectivism vs. objectivism, that precisely the just mentioned concept purportedly permits, is illusory. Bourdieu, who as most French Marxists, neo-Marxists and post-Marxists, whatever it would mean, is largely incapable of dialectical thinking, which demonstrates his dependence on the Althusserian formalism, style of thought that has exerted a huge influence on now already generations of especially French thinkers. Be that as it may, the Bourdieusian statement reproduced below is a blatant example of determinism, thinking along the lines of "iron laws".

> The passions of the dominated habitus, a somatised social relationship, the law of the social body converted into the law of the body, are not of a kind that can be suspended by a simple effort of will, founded on a liberatory awakening of consciousness (2000, 179–80).

Similarly, dialectics is conspicuous by its absence in the following over-deterministic definition: "habitus is necessity internalised and converted into a disposition that generates meaningful practices and meaning-giving perceptions" (www.newlearningonline).

A critic points out that "in Bourdieu›s accounts of bodily hexis, the body appears as a sort of physiological template that is «written by» culture and that reciprocally reproduces culture. [...] Bourdieu presents us with a sophisticated, yet deterministic, cycle of causation that runs from culture to the body, and back to culture" (Fries 2005). This results in culturalism as a form of idealism, a paradoxical bedfellow of crude materialism discussed in another context – "Capital gains value, or legitimacy, only if deemed acceptable by authorised social groups within a field" (Swartz 1997). This contention smacks of legal or quasi-juristic idealism, and bears little relationship with the real social world replete with informal and illegal relations, not to mention the fact that e.g. surplus value or profit belong to a quite other realm than legitimacy – a component of social consciousness. To be fair, it should be noted that some capital theorists implicitly distance themselves from the above view, as in this statement associating legitimacy with one form of capital only: "Various forms of capital have to be legitimised (i.e., socially accepted and valued) to translate in symbolic capital" (Adkins, Corurs 2009).

That the position identified above is shared by the founder and other members of cultural capital school may be illustrated by the following self-styled management guru, who gives us the following advice:

If you want to improve your results, then improve your cultural capital.

We have found from experience that the most successful formula for improving financial performance and shareholder value is to focus on:

Leadership development. The culture of an organisation is a direct reflection of the values of the leadership. There is a strong correlation between the values embraced by the leadership team and the strength and degree of values alignment found in the current culture. If you want to change the culture of your organisation, begin with the personal transformation of the leadership team (Barrett 2003).

Not only, in the manner of an idealistic emanationism, the corporate business performance is directly derived from the firm's cultural capital, but the latter hinges upon the value sets of a narrow group at the top of the organisation, which neglects a host of factors that may influence those personal attitudes.

While embodied cultural capital is often transmitted within the family environment, institutionalised capital is transmitted through schools, universities, and other educating bodies. Persons who possess institutionalised cultural capital have been academically sanctioned by legally guaranteed qualifications; that is, they have an earned degree or certification that grants them a particular status, and separates them from practitioners who do not have the qualifications. Thus, society has established a method to separate the physicians from the quacks, and the professors from the ardent amateurs. One may also apply this concept of institutionalised cultural capital to the institutions themselves, as society tends to recognize those cultural institutions that have affiliations with accrediting bodies (Gracy 2007).

In the final part of the above passage, just as in the quotation cited somewhat earlier, the concept in question is conceived of in a way that renders it yet another kind of misnomer (which in total means that we are dealing, too, with a multiple misnomer), referring to "cultural institutions in their role as the creators and sustainers of objectified cultural capital. In the future, moving image stewardship may no longer be the exclusive province of institutions such as archives and libraries" (Gracy 2007).

What is at stake here is simply culture as commonly, within the common-sense thought, understood,[5] and the adjective "capital" is utterly redundant, adding nothing to the content of the concept, and indeed, harmful in suggesting that ordinary books on library shelves or microfilms in archives are analogous to economic capital by virtue of being ideal, symbolic objects in question (as though, referring to an above-mentioned phrase, given institutions were linked to crediting rather than accrediting organisations). More specifically, and not in colloquial terms, cultural capital refers in that usage to products of activities comprising the ideational structure of society, as understood by socio-economic structuralism, i.e. theoretical framework developed by the author of this work. It may be added that from the viewpoint of the latter, as distinct from Bourdieu's notion which is focused on high-brow culture: high art, etc., (e.g. Kingston [2001] lists the following "persuasive understandings" of cultural capital: going to art museums or liking classical music.) there is no reason for limiting the scope of ideational products to, say, broadsheets as distinct from tabloids, Moore's sculptures, but not comics.

The second component of culture as conventionally considered refers to social consciousness, which, as it might have been expected, is also present in the cultural capital literature. A case in point is the following phrase referring to "the cultural capital of modernity and whiteness (Lattas 2011).[6] It is also to this kind of belief that the claim concerning "The White Eurocentric cultural capital imposed as the 'standard' or "mainstream" in US society" (Urrieta 2009) refers to.

---

5   As shown also by the following definition: "Objectified cultural capital refers to what is considered high art, and tends to be found in museums, concert halls, and the homes of the upper classes" (Dumais 2005). Also DiMaggio and Mohr (1985) conceived of the concept as attitude, activity, and knowledge about lofty culture.

6   For an extensive exposition, see (Tittenbrun 2012).

This kind of understanding is also presumably implicitly adopted in the following statement in which the word "capital" adds nothing in the way of understanding or explaining the process under consideration (couched in terms of another misleading analogy – the labour theory of value): "The investment in cultural capital is the quantity of "time devoted to acquiring" it (Bourdieu, 1986) and the investment of time is the period that a communicator offers to absorb a certain sort of culture in a society" (Wang 1999).

The aforementioned scholar attempts, to be sure, to defend the specific linguistic combination represented by the concept under consideration, yet her justification is singularly unconvincing; she refers to "cultural institutions in their role as the creators and sustainers of objectified cultural capital. [...] cultural heritage is a form of capital that can be accumulated, shared, transferred, and otherwise manipulated by both individuals and institutions, and that the control of significant amounts of cultural capital confers a certain power to the possessor" (Tracey 2007). Accumulation and transferability, as grounded in objectification also mentioned above) are precisely criteria commonly associated with the concept of culture in a usual anthropological sense,[7] and the world "manipulation" is so broad that it fits a variety of objects and phenomena, due to which it cannot be make use of in order to justify the phrase of cultural capital. Similar generality characterises the word "power" and it even less fits in the role of rational for the adoption and use of the concept of cultural capital. For instance, there is in currency the phrase "purchasing power" which means that each individual commanding a certain amount of money has the ability to enter into possession of a range of goods available in the market, but it does not follow that each such sum of money is a capital; money capital is something different from money used to purchase consumer goods.

Make no mistake, despite its language, the statement below at least alludes to – surprise, surprise – class, class mobility, class reproduction, and so on.

"It refers to the credentials and cultural assets embodied in individuals and their families. Cultural capital has been used in two contrasting directions. It is used to explain the reproduction of social hierarchy, as elite families endow their children with the cultural capital which enables them to succeed in maintaining their elite position. But it is also used to explain how some manage to use education to move from non-elite positions into elite positions" (Schuller 2001).

The fact of the matter is, the concept in question has been used, contrary to the above-cited writer, in more than two ways, not all of which are related to labour power, and even if this is the case, the relationship may be perverse, as in (Farkas

---

7   Which is almost literally reproduced by the explanation that "Bourdieu's concept of cultural capital refers to the cultural patterns passed on from generation to generation and includes ways of acting, speaking, dressing, eating, etc. (McLaren 1994), and a supplement to the effect that "and in the case of the U.S. it is that of Whites of the upper and middle class" (Urrieta 2009) only seeks to determine this consciousness' class nature, abstracting at this point from the particular notion of class (which in actual fact refers to social strata) used

et al. 1990) where Working hard (and by the same token the realisation of labour power rather than the latter per se) or in (Roscigno and Ainsworth-Darnell 1999; Teachman 1987) household educational resources like books and computers, and thus at best some means of acquiring some skills coming into the concept of labour power are defined as forms of cultural capital. In the specific case of Farkas et al., their particular choice appears to have been motivated by their willingness to bolster the central claim of cultural capital theory relating it to educational attainment, as the relevance of working hard to the latter is allegedly self-evident.

Chapter 11
Cultural Capital and Class

How Bourdieu's school of cultural capital conceptualises social class, has been partly discussed above. Given the relevance of this issue, however, it is well to consider the following statement:

> the structure of the distribution of the capital among the various directors (*dirigeants*) of the firm, that is, between owners and 'functionaries' – managers – and, among these latter, between the holders of different species of cultural capital: predominantly financial, technical or commercial, that is to say, in the French case, between the various elite corps and the schools where they received their training: the Ecole Nationale d'Administration, the Ecole Polytechnique or the Ecole des Hautes Etudes Commerciales (Bourdieu 2005).

Bourdieu's inability to recognise that in the above case various degrees of labour power are involved is, as a matter of fact, hardly surprising given his flawed understanding of ownership in general which stems, on the one hand, from his dependence on the juristic notion of property and, on the other, from the stance which may be dubbed "pandominationalism," i.e. transforming almost each relationship under investigation into one or another form of power or force, for that matter, which is clearly demonstrated, *inter alia*, by the following statement:

> The evolution of the relations of force between the major agents in the field of power within firms: most notably one sees, first, a pre-eminence of entrepreneurs with a mastery of new technologies, capable of assembling the funds required to exploit them, then the increasingly inevitable intervention of bankers and financial institutions, and finally the rise of managers. However, apart from the fact that one must analyze the particular form the configuration of the distribution of powers among firms assumes at each state of each field, it is by analysing, for each firm at every moment, the form of the configuration of powers within the field of power over the firm that one can fully understand the logic of the struggles in which the firm's goals are determined. It is, in fact, clear that these goals are stakes in struggles and that, for the rational calculations of an enlightened 'decision-maker,' we have to substitute the political struggle among agents who tend to identify their specific interests (linked to their position in the firm and their dispositions) with the interests of the firm and whose power can no doubt be measured by their capacity to identify, for better or for worse (as the Henry Ford example shows), the interests of the firm with their interests within the firm (Bourdieu 2005, 207).

And these conceptual drawbacks seem to express more general weaknesses pertinent to the general theory of society of Bourdieu. This notion lacks complexity, consequence and structure.

Somewhat similar objections may also be addressed towards the theory of class that Bourdieu employed. Declaratively, the French thinker distanced himself against Marxism, but in practice he took a considerable part of Marx's legacy in the field of class theory, using, for example, categories such as the petty bourgeoisie or working class. Curiously enough, capitalists are replaced by entrepreneurs, and, worse, the concepts of classes mingle with professional groups and strata such as the middle classes, higher classes etc. Meanwhile, the basic model, instead of making them more prominent, rather obliterates the boundaries between classes and estates (this concept, used by both Marx and Weber, is in socio-economic structuralism interpreted to refer to social groups grounded in non-economic property relations), which derives from its dependence on the concept of multiple capitals criticised above.

This much, up to a point, is evident from the following passage, despite its being split into two distinct parts, the first one containing the author's criticism of alleged similarity between cultural and economic capital; his Conclusion, though, is another matter – whilst it is indeed the case that the Bourdieusian class theory and Marxian one are difficult to reconcile, it does by any means follow that they constitute complementary approaches which always should both be used for the sake of gaining complete picture. True, Marx's class theory is no clear-cut body of ideas; since its inception it has been subject to many conflicting interpretations. One such a line of interpretation, drawing, as it does, on the notion of ownership is largely inconsistent with Bourdieu's scheme of social differentiation. The passage mentioned above reads:

> the kind of 'cultural capital' to which Savage et al., refer rests with the individual concerned, and cannot be stored or passed on in any direct sense (educational qualifications cannot be inherited). Its transmission is dependent upon the successful transmission of identity (or habitus). Objectively, winning the lottery might transform an individual (and their family) into rentier capitalists, but there are no tickets available for lotteries in cultural capital. In short, it is being argued that economic (e.g. Marx's) and cultural (e.g. Bourdieu's) class concepts cannot be seamlessly combined in a single theoretical 'approach' […].However, as they are not mutually exclusive, they may be used in combination with each other, and indeed, should be (Sayer 2005: 72).

> Bourdieu distinguishes the dominant class due to the size of the economic capital and cultural heritage. These include industrialists, managers of the private sector and university professors. At the opposite extreme is the working class including labourers and farm workers. Between these classes emerges the middle-class, i.e. small business owners, technicians, secretaries or primary school teachers. The French sociologist also divides the dominant class due to the predominance

of the capital. Industrialists and trade staff have a larger stock of economic capital compared to professors and artistic producers, but in turn those have a larger stock of cultural capital (Weininger 2002: 123–4).

The Bourdieusian conflation of stratification and class systems (Viinstra [2007], states with reference to Bourdieu's conception of capital that, e.g., "for Bourdieu, economic capital [is] deemed equal to income and wealth", which are, of course, typical criteria employed by a variety of stratification theories) has been already touched on earlier, but the above statement contributes somewhat to the picture; whilst it is still possible for the concept of middle class thus conceived to constitute a social stratum (should the concept be placed in a hierarchy – between upper and lower class, as it apparently does), the particular formulation above makes it clear how poor Bourdieu's understanding of social differentiation actually is.

To put in one bag "technicians, secretaries and primary school teachers" is not only to reveal one's lack of appreciation of labour power as a criterion of class identification, but also to confound class with non-class dimensions of social differentiation; primary school teachers, for instance, are a non-economic grouping that in terms of socio-economic structuralism is defined as a social estate. The term of secretaries is too general, lacking any sensible ground for determining their location in the structure of societal differentiation, since people designated by the term may function at a variety of social structures. Somewhat similar is the problem of technicians; even if one were to confine the category to industry (which is unfounded), a specific technician may perform an entirely different work, hold a different type of labour power, and thus to belong to a different class than his or her peer bearing the same occupational title; they can function as supervisors and lower-level managers, for instance, but also as producers of intellectual means of production. The remaining claims make equally little sense. It may, but also may not be the case that an industrialist possesses more economic capital than an artistic produce or even university professor, since in the latter case it depends only on concrete circumstances whether a given lecturer is, or is not an owner of a stockholding whose value may well be higher than the worth of capital held by a small factory owner, for instance. And there are many multimillionaire film producers. The concept of "trade staff" is, first, also broad, and second, the relation of particular individuals involved to capital ownership may be extremely different.

Add to this under-theorised treatment the class of intelligentsia mentioned in the previous chapter and the picture becomes even more hazy.

Weaknesses of Bourdieu's approach are evident for others as well; Kingston's (2001) assertion, however, which clearly shows this kind of awareness: "Bourdieu did not offer a fixed or operationally clear-cut class schema" is an understatement – the preceding suggests that the concept of class in Bourdieu's rendition is another misnomer.

Lumping together real socio-economic classes, social strata and social estates cannot be, moreover, justified as being accounted for by the following, allegedly:

'useful distinction between abstract (highly selective and one-sided) and concrete (many-sided) conceptions of class. Abstract concepts 'focus on a particular aspect of the social world, abstracting from others which may coexist with it'. (Sayer, 2005: 72).

Thus: "Marx's concepts of classes in capitalism, anchored in relations of production, is [...] highly abstract" (ibid.). Concrete concepts, such as, for example, are employed in Bourdieu's (1973) account of the French class structure, "...attempt...to synthesise diverse forms of differentiation" (Sayer, 2005: 73), that will include both economic resources and social behaviours (and even other axes of differentiation such as gender and race) (Marshall 1978).

This argument is based on a misunderstanding – or more precisely, shallow understanding – of the class concept. A specific definition of class must be viewed in its theoretical context, since it is only the latter that gives the terms mentioned concrete substance. In addition, class theory may be distinguished from class analysis, i.e. an application of concepts defined at the level of theory to concrete empirical phenomena. Within the latter, a given theoretical framework demonstrates its usefulness as a research tool, thus showing classes in action, as it were. This kind of analysis may be further refined, as mentioned elsewhere in the chapter, by differentiating between class characteristics strongly or weakly determined (by economic ownership relations). How useful such an analysis will turn out to be, and how rich its substantive results is a function of not employing "abstract" or "concrete" class definitions, as understood above, since the latter distinction should be redefined as one between productive and unproductive class concepts. It is their analytical value that determines the relevance, scope, etc. of research results. And we beg to differ with the aforementioned commentator, Bourdieu's concept of class should be defined not as much as concrete, but as an eclectic mixture of concepts belonging to a variety of theoretical frameworks, or indeed having no theoretical status whatsoever.

Equally erroneous is the following continuation of the argument outlined above:

> stratification theory entails the analysis of structured social inequality in all its aspects: material, social and cultural. Class analysis, however, with its focus on material inequality, has come to dominate stratification theory, generating models which see 'objective' economic conditions as logically prior to, and causative of, social relations. Conventional class analysis has been criticised for defining class in terms of employment relations, rather than as 'collectivities of people who share identities and practices' and for ignoring the influence of cultural and social resources on the micro processes by which classes are created and sustained over time and space (Devine 1998).

It is exceedingly difficult to imagine a single passage that would accumulate that many mistakes and misunderstandings. The praise of stratification theories glosses over the fact that usually each one of those rests on a particular criterion, or dimension of social differentiation – be it economic, political, subjective, and so on. And whilst there are multi-dimensional approaches to stratification, combining two or more such determinants, this circumstance can hardly count as their merit; quite the contrary, it exposes them to the charge of eclecticism and inconsistency. The scholar cited above happens, too, to entertain a rather narrow notion of class, betraying his intellectual parochialism, if one may say so; popular as Goldthorpe's class scheme is (as the term "employment relations" or "employment aggregates" indicates unequivocally that it is his and his associates' framework that is at stake), it is not the only one, and when one considers it to be superior, it is by no means a self-evident evaluation, which, accordingly, must be separately substantiated. In addition, economic relations are inherently social, and they do not need any special social coating to be such. As to culture, or more precisely what is put into this bag, the situation is only seemingly more complex; in actual fact, it is fairly simple. It is clear as day, and we only allow ourselves to repeat those commonplaces owing to the persistence of regrettable misunderstandings obscuring the matter. Of course, it is human beings who are engaged in economic relations and who perform economic actions. This necessarily means that human consciousness is part and parcel of those relationships and activities, too. But it is important not to jump on that basis to conclusions on the economic efficacy of this or that cultural element, or culture in general. This must be demonstrated case by case, and by any means cannot be taken for granted, as perennial debates over the so-called Weberian thesis may testify. Curiously enough, the author concerned at another occasion takes a rather similar view to that outlined above, as he notes that: A 'renewed' analysis would 'focus on how cultural processes are embedded within specific kinds of socio-economic practices" (Devine and Savage 2000: 193), "exploring how inequality is routinely reproduced through both cultural and economic practices" (2000: 196).

If some relations are embedded within other relations, then by definition both those kinds of relationships must be at least analytically distinct from each other. In other words, although this is a commonplace, it nevertheless apparently needs reiterating from time to time – there is a clear need for keeping distinct such concepts (and hence the respective adjectives) as society, economy and culture. Society is, of course, the broadest notion, as it is only within it that particular societal structures: ideational, political, economic and reproductive differentiate themselves.

Focusing again on the concept of cultural capital, on the other hand, apart from referring to labour power, it plays in the context of social differentiation a figurative role only.

This is also demonstrated by the heavy price in the form of arbitrariness paid by the cultural capital scholars for their desire to have the cake and eat it, that is to say, to employ the language and classificatory criteria of both class and stratification whose net result is no one can tell what their claims really refer to. Thus, Sherry Ortner (2003) provides a social analysis of the ways in which class mobility and cultural capital operated in the lives of her high-school class of 1958 at Weequahic High School in Newark. She aims to paint the picture of profound postwar social transformations.

Ortner is interested in understanding how the "Class of June '58" got from its modest, largely working-class and middle-class origins in the late 1950s to a situation in which, as she claims, there is virtually no recognizable working class left, and in which close to 60 per cent of the members of the class would now easily be described as part of America's wealthy "white overclass". It is rather unclear what the profits from the coinage of this neologism compared to the well-established in the theory of stratification term "upper class" are. But this is far from the end of the story. The core of the book is devoted to what is conceived of as discursive constructions of class – how class privilege and class "injuries" are understood by this cohort. She outlines her analytical and theoretical objectives as follows: "I am interested in understanding the workings of class in ordinary lives and in ordinary times. Specifically I pursue two questions broadly related to the two forms of class invisibility just discussed. First, I am interested in the ways that class as the general socioeconomic structure of U.S. society has undergone massive shape-changes since World War II, including specifically the vast enlargement of the middle class after the war and its almost equally massive shrinkage in the last few decades".

Thus, it turns out that the process of decline involves both the working and middle class. Should it imply that the US is no longer, as is commonly held, a middle-class society, but rather, an over-class one? After all, the elusive over-class is the only one whose perspectives appear to be bright, at least nothing is asserted to the contrary, in contrast to the two other classes.

So, if the book is advertised as "an ethnography of class consciousness and social change", one is far from being sure what classes, and how understood, are at stake, and thus, precisely what social changes are being described in this case.

And indeed, these shortcomings should be seen in a broader context of logical failings pertaining to the notion under consideration.

> For Bourdieu (1973: 101), objective classes are described as 'the set of agents who are placed in the homogeneous conditions of existence imposing homogenous conditionings and producing homogeneous systems of dispositions capable of generating similar practices+). Thus Bourdieu's account is [...] descriptive and tautological, as practices generate similar practices and the middle classes always win (Marshall 1998).

Given this kind of framework, it is small wonder that the above-mentioned reference to the concept of labour power is, in keeping with the misnomer rule, cryptic rather than explicit. In consequence, the Bourdieusian framework has attracted criticism levelled against its lack of consideration of gender. Kanter (in Robinson and Garnier, 1986) draws attention to the lack of interest in gender inequalities in the labour market in Bourdieu's work. This is indeed true, but it is important to see this criticism in a broader context, as this gap is directly related to the aforementioned lack of labour power in the conceptual armoury of the French sociologist. Investigating ownership of labour power in the context of labour power market, one arrives at the necessity of distinguishing ascriptive labour power whose one of important characteristics is the possibility of (negative and positive) discrimination as based on some attributes of a given labour power, such as gender. Given the evident relationship of labour power and class, the point just made permits to see that there is no contradiction between gender and class relations so that criticisms of Bourdieu for his neglect of gender inequalities as allegedly caused by his over-emphasis on class does not stand up to scrutiny.

In the relevant literature other implicit references to the notion of ascriptive labour power can be found, as e.g. in (Lareau and Horvat 1999) where being white is defined as a form of cultural capital.

Let us look at the relationship between what is dubbed cultural capital and the social structure from another angle. "Cultural capital refers to the role that distinctive kinds of cultural tastes, knowledge, and abilities play in relation to the processes of class formations in societies" (Vitae 2010).

Now it appears that the above argument is based on a major misunderstanding. Even abstracting from the otherwise deserving condemnation fact that, in line with the intellectual fluidity that characterises the cultural capital literature, there are several definitions that COUCH the relationship between it and e.g. taste quite differently, as in the following reference to "Bourdieu's notions of economic capital,[1] cultural capital and social capital [as[important forms of power in social space that potentially structure and define cultural tastes and practices" (Viinstra 2007).[2] Just like in the case of social capital where it was difficult, if not impossible, to pin down the boundary line between the phenomenon itself and its purported consequences, in the present instance it is not easy to grasp what ultimately determines what, as the following statement may illustrate: "there is a broad array of modes people use to listen to classical music. With respect to Bourdieu's theory of arts perception, in particular his notion of cultural capital, one can show empirically that the modes of cultural consumption in this case are determined by listeners' cultural capital" (Rössel 2011).

If one focuses on those aspects of what passes as cultural capital that come into the concept of labour power, then these, of course, by definition, are involved in

---

1 In addition, the formulation concerned illustrates the kind of dogmatism and narrow-mindedness typical of the French sociologist's adherents – the author somewhat forgets that there is a rich and voluminous tradition in political economy dealing with capital, as well that Bourdieu is by any means the only claimant to the title of the founding father of the social capital school of thought.

2 Another formulation of that sort makes it blatantly clear that the cultural capital literature, just like its social capital counterpart, finds it incredibly difficult precisely to specify what is a given form of capital, and what is its effects: "educational attainment and frequency of attendance at artistic/theatrical events [are] twin dimensions of cultural capital" (Viinstra 2007)

the formation of socio-economic classes; the remaining aspects, however, rather than form property relations, are conditioned by them, thus reversing the direction of dependence postulated in the above-cited passage.

To expand on this point, socio-economic structuralism, and precisely speaking, its theory of socio-economic class distinguishes two levels of social phenomena related to one's class position: class-determined and class-conditioned, or, to put it differently, primary and secondary class effects or outcomes. The former, such as income, are directly dependent on a given individual's class status, whereas in the latter case the dependence in question (which could therefore be termed weak) is indirect, i.e. it realises itself by medium of direct class effects. A collection of books or cultural participation would be appropriate examples. Roberts refers exactly to those class-conditioned phenomena (Roberts 2004) in defining cultural capital as participation in cultural activities – including leisure; as well as DiMaggio (1982) who defined it as participation in arts, music, and cultural events.

> In the classic work, *Distinction: A Social Critique of the Judgment of Taste,*
> *Bourdieu* (1984) studied members of French society, examining their preferences
> for and familiarity with types of music, art, and cinema. Bourdieu found that
> an individual's taste is conditioned strongly by his or her social status, in that
> members of higher social strata are more likely to prefer and be familiar with the
> music, art, and cinema associated with high culture and less likely to prefer and
> be familiar with more popular productions; similarly, the reverse is found for
> members of lower social classes. (Gamoran, Boxer 2005)

Notice the carelessness manifested in the interchangeable use of the terms: classes and strata (and the list is actually even more extensive – Gamoran and Boxer (2009) state: as follows: "The end result of differential socialisation of social classes is that social elites tend to pursue and attain higher levels of various cultural markers"), to which matter we come back below.

> In Bourdieu's model, those high in economic capital have more cultural and
> social capital (Sanks 2007).

> ...the extent of likely exposure to hardship (risk) is still largely dependent on
> the individuals' access to, and possession and maintenance of, various forms
> of capital. So despite some claims that class is increasingly irrelevant within
> these paradigms, and even though cultural capital has been extensively redefined
> within these transformations, we argue that recent social, economic, political and
> technological changes are engendering new forms of 'distinction' and inequality
> which 'still look a lot like class differences'. the individual's access to the space
> of flows, which contributes to one's possibility of successful practice, is still
> based on the individual's access to various forms of capital: economic, cultural
> and social (Beck 1992).

The scholars cited earlier go on to state that "As such, socialisation produces a form of capital, measured in terms of an individual's ability to engage in the culture of his or her society. Bourdieu called this cultural capital and defined it as the general cultural knowledge, skills, and background pertaining to the culture of the social elite. Appreciation of and ability to participate in high society, therefore, are developed by accumulating cultural capital through exposure to various cultural events and items. The more an individual immerses in society, the more he or she can develop cultural capital".

Bourdieu's *Distinction* (1984) focused on the greater cultural capital of social elites compared with non-elites in France, but other scholars have applied the concept to other populations as well; indeed, any culture or subset of a culture could be said to have its own cultural capital" (Gamoran, Boxer 2009).

While the second part of their argument corrects the shortcoming of too narrow a focus characteristic of the notion of cultural capital, laid out in the first part, it still does little to justify the combination of specific words used in the latter. Elsewhere (Tittenbrun 2011; 2012) the present author puts forward the concept of quasi-labour power as referring to the ability to perform a variety of non-work,[3] i.e. not gainful activities that is analogous to labour power. This concept seems to be a much better tool with which to approach cultural participation than the misleading term of cultural capital by virtue of which simple literacy would have to be classed as a form of capital, and, correspondingly, a literate person as a (cultural, to be sure, but however) capitalist. The cultural capital advocates go to such lengths in promoting their banner that they manage to find those capitalists even in the former socialist societies – concerning Czechoslovakia in particular, Wong (1988) argues "that socialist governments' efforts to improve educational opportunities for the disadvantaged and reduce the effects of social origins might paradoxically have increased the role of parental cultural capital in intergenerational inequality".

Along similar lines, but additionally over-stretching the concept, Sauceda (2009) depicts: "children with Latino ancestry tap into their lived experiences, history, background knowledge, and language skills – what Paulo Freire and Donaldo Macedo (1987) describe as cultural capital – while engaged in their classroom's literacy activities". In the same vein, Lareau and Weininger (2003) characterise Bourdieu's position as follows: "he emphasised that any 'competence' becomes a capital insofar as it facilitates of appropriation a society's 'cultural heritage'".

The above two dimensions of personality need to be kept relatively distinct, unlike in the statement whose author implicitly obliterates the distinction between the two – correctly pointing to the association of cultural with human capital, Throsby (2001: 167) fails to take account of those human characteristics that do not constitute essential components of work: "In sociology, the term is used,

---

3 The concept of quasi-work is somewhat similar to Rojek's (2001) construct of 'civil labour', which, in turn, is akin to Locke's (1963) notion of leisure as "refreshing labour".

following Pierre Bourdieu, to mean an individual's competence in high status culture. In economic terms, this characteristic of people can be construed as an aspect of their human capital".

The following passage refers to both labour power (in the case of managers) and quasi-labour power (defining the art of writing letters as an example of cultured behaviour manifested by the old bourgeoisie):

> Literary study has largely ceased to be a main avenue to success in modern society: The professional managerial class has made the correct assessment that, so far as its future profit is concerned, the reading of great works is not worth the investment of very much time or money. The perceived devaluation of the humanities curriculum is in reality a decline in its market value. Technical and professional knowledge have replaced the literary curriculum that formerly supplied the cultural capital that underwrote the rise of the bourgeoisie. Literary culture became 'culturally marginal to the social formation of modernity' (139). Guillory invites us to reflect on the 'historical category of literature' (265) and its complicated relation to the literary curriculum and hence the 'canon.'

> To review some of the history that Guillory analyzes, we need to go back to the eighteenth century when the study of literature in the vernacular provided the linguistic capital necessary to rise socially and was also instrumental in the unification of the ruling class. (Guillory refers to the 'immense social significance of polite letters as a transformative cultural force' [118].) Linguistic differentiation was always the point of a literary canon, says Guillory, with the schools functioning to reproduce social arrangements by distributing cultural capital unequally. The original rationale of a literary curriculum-used to justify its mission of producing a standard vernacular (Templin 1997).

And it must be added that the above is a fairly narrow understanding compared with some more extreme formulations in which cultural capital essentially takes over the entire personality: "skills that promote self-sufficiency (Ogbu 1978) are a form of cultural capital, a resource that includes linguistic style, patterns of behavior, modes of thinking, cultural awareness, academic competency, and general knowledge" (Swartz 1990).

As follows from our earlier analysis, two key concepts in the Bourdieusian framework – cultural capital and social class are misnomers, which significantly affect the most famous single thesis of the French sociologist.

Note that by reducing classes to strata and what he calls status groups Bourdieu apparently kills two birds with one stone. On the one side, he obtains an ambiguous and vague, to be sure, but at any rate some concept of class, and on the other, he bolsters his own notion of social hierarchy whose key property is reproduction. But this kind of substituting logic and semantics for empirics is bound to attract criticism.

A leading analyst of cultural capital objects nevertheless to its key application: "Although taste is differentiated by social status, there is no sign of discrete task classes with sharply segmented preferences...[and] although all research reports positive associations between measures of socioeconomic status and taste, the proportion of variance of these measures is low" (DiMaggio 1994: 59).

If one uses such notions as class, status and, of course, capital in such an under-theorised and loose way as the representatives of the cultural capital school do, then no wonder one must face the music.

The drawbacks discussed above pave the way for the following query which is to concern class, but in fact concerns stratification instead: "Do people actually use cultural concerns in making social distinctions, in deciding who is above and below them? Not significantly", answered Lamont (1992) on the basis of a series of qualitative interviews, probing the symbolic boundaries that the members of so-called upper-middle-class invoked to separate themselves from others and, reciprocally, to define their own sense of group identity.

It turns out that in constructing their own symbolic boundaries, these individuals "expressed little concern about cultural orientations – decidedly less than they did about moral and economic considerations. [...] Their accounts, then, directly challenge Bourdieu's argument that cultural distinctions play a significant role in social reproduction" (Kingston 2001).

> In 1970 the highly influential *Reproduction* (Bourdieu and Passeron 1977) developed this by offering a theory of how cultural reproduction fosters the social reproduction of the relations between groups and classes. The central but curiously ill-defined explanatory gambit of this text is the use of the concept of 'capital'. Different forms of capital appear through the book, each without proper definition: economic capital (implicitly), cultural capital, linguistic capital, scholastic capital, social capital. Cultural capital is the most developed of these, being used to explain how the cultural 'judgement' of the dominant group is presented as universal and selectively endowed, allowing it to legitimise its domination (Schuller, Baron, Field 2000).

The three above-mentioned authors state that "The contrast between sophisticated theoretical claims and weak empirical data is stark. Mechanisms of cultural reproduction and social reproduction are operationalised through the simple cross-tabulation of percentages of, for example, working/middle/upper class students by male/female by above/below twelve out of 20 in a particular test (Bourdieu and Passeron 1977: 81, Table 5). While statistical analysis later became more complex, the problem of operationalising non-tangible 'capitals' has remained significant" (Field, Schuller, Baron 2000).

Whether the theoretical apparatus employed by the French thinker is that sophisticated, is debatable; the authors of that judgment seem to conflate sophistication with elaboration, or, more precisely, over-elaboration. What is far less uncontroversial, however, is that the output of the said apparatus is not supported by empirical evidence:

> Bourdieu and Passeron (1977), in developing the concept of cultural capital and habitus sought to explain how schools, despite their relative autonomy from social structures, reproduced economic and social relations. As with the straight reproduction model, however, empirical evidence for this explanation is weak. Similarly, the treatment of the cultural capital of elites as unproblematically dominant without any attention to resistant other cultures means that we are still far from understanding how cultural capital works (Munn 2000).

This may be an under-statement, considering that:

> One influential social reproduction argument concerns the special importance of cultural capital (Bourdieu and Passeron 1970; Bourdieu 1997 [1983]): that the odds in school are stacked particularly heavily in favour of children and youth whose parents are the well-placed insiders in a society's educational and cultural institutions, the cultural elite. Not only can such parents urge their children on in school and help them with the schoolwork. Bourdieu's particular claim is that in order to succeed, especially in the selective stages of the system, you also need to be at ease with the life style which is taken for granted among those who have high status in this social field: the nuances of language, the aesthetic preferences, and other symbolic expressions which mark the insider against the outsider. Such elements are not just accoutrements of cultural privilege, according to Bourdieu; they serve as prerequisites for success. It would seem that the further one's origin is from a country's cultural elite, the fewer are one's chances of doing well in school. By this line of reasoning, immigrant children should be destined to fail in school.

> Very often, immigrant parents do not speak with ease the language of the country to which they have moved, let alone master its more socially exclusive nuances. Not being familiar with the education system from their own experience, immigrants should be at a disadvantage in helping their children navigate through it. Excepting those few who belong to a jet-setting international elite, the parents' grasp of the life-style subtleties of the form of cultural capital into whose ambit they have moved would be poor. Apart from the disadvantage due to having an immigrant background as such, the chances of failing in school are greater when the parents are poor, when parents secure menial jobs, and/ or had little schooling. Insofar as immigrant groups are disproportionately in these social categories, the educational prospects of youth from immigrant background should be dim.

Further, if the family belongs to a 'visible minority' typical of those who have migrated to 'the North' from a developing country, there is racist exclusion which could cause outright opposition to the 'white man's school' and channel immigrant youth towards a future in an ethnically distinct new 'underclass'. Social reproduction theory would also imply that among immigrants the principles of reproduction would broadly apply as among non-immigrants: that the relative educational success of children would mirror their family's social class and relative possession of cultural capital (Laugiq 2000).

Meanwhile, intuition or common-sense are not the best advisers in scholarly matters. So it is fully proper to query: "Does the weight of research evidence support such pessimistic hypotheses?"

Pre-empting the conclusion, which is that immigrant children are doing surprisingly well, before the data, let us consider the possible reason for this empirical failing. Now the Bourdieusian determinism discussed earlier means his approach is also mechanistic, and certainly anti-dialectic. Positing reproduction (which is merely one type of change) he kind of cannot grasp any counteracting tendencies and countervailing forces. The result is predictable:

> Findings of poor achievement are not dominant in international research literature on the educational achievement of immigrant youth. Sometimes immigrant youth from certain backgrounds lag behind others in school, but they typically do better than might be expected when account is taken of their parents' social class circumstances and level of schooling.

> The theme of 'trying hard' is common to the ethnographic studies on immigrants to the United States, reported in a compendium edited by Gibson and Ogbu (1991). Many of these studies fit Ogbu's (1991) distinction between immigrant minorities and 'involuntary' minorities. Youth from the former background do better in school. Quantitative survey research in the United States has corroborated the theme of immigrants trying harder and having high educational ambitions (Rumbaut 1997a; Fuligni 1997). In the UK, Tomlinson (1991) similarly claims that immigrant minority pupils show greater persistence and motivation than non-immigrants. An earlier Norwegian youth study (Laugiq 1996) found that, compared with ethnic Norwegians, immigrant youth of non-Western background did more homework and had more positive attitudes to school.

> Concerning educational performance and attainment, the consistency of positive results is less internationally complete. Before controlling for social class[4] and/or parental education, some immigrant groups match the native majority but others lag behind (Gillborn 1997 on the UK; Portes and MacLeod 1996 on the US;

---

4   This suggests a key role of class position as a determinant of academic attainment.

Engen, Kulbrandstad, and Sand 1997 on Norway; Lofgren 1991 on Sweden). In those studies that control for socio-cultural class conditions, the findings present a more optimistic view. In the case of American research, the focus has been on the predominantly Asian and Latin American nationalities in the new wave of immigration since the early 1980s. Most of the immigrant groupings examined outperform their peers (Fuligni 1997; Rumbaut 1997a, b; Portes and MacLeod 1996). Immigrant youth also seem to perform better than non-immigrant peers from the same ethnic background (Rumbaut 1995: 146).

Jon Laugiq notes that:

> European results are more mixed. British studies show that whilst Asians perform well after social class controls, youth of West Indian background do not perform as well as the majority white population (Gillborn and Gipps 1996). The few nationwide surveys which have been carried out elsewhere in Europe seem to show that performance differences from the majority grouping in secondary school achievement disappear once social class is controlled for.[5] Vallet and Caille (1996) found such results in France, and Laugiq (1996; 1999) in Norway. In Sweden, in a study of whole cohorts of people born in Sweden during 1953–70, Simila (1994) found that those of immigrant background obtained higher rates of upper academic-secondary schooling than those of non-immigrant parentage, after controlling for parental socioeconomic status (SES). Intriguingly the sole exceptions were those of Finnish, Norwegian and Danish parentage, groups which had come from just across the border (Laugiq 2000).

The aforementioned scholar thus summarises the evidence reviewed:

> A weakness of social reproduction theory is that it fails to explain such social fluidity and social advancement as does occur in a society. In particular, it offers little help in explaining educational success among individuals who lack the very class-related background resources which are deemed to be of decisive importance. Other conditions of social structure [...] also structure social action. In addition to the individual exceptions, it is also possible to trace particularly strong social ascent over generations by certain cultural groups. Social history is replete with examples concerning certain religious minorities as well as certain immigrant groups who in the space of two to three generations have risen from humble beginnings to a preponderance in middle-class professions: for example, Japanese Americans, Chinese Americans, immigrant Jews who started in the sweatshops of New York's garment district or in London's Spitalfields. Social reproduction is a reality, but so also are the forces that defy it (Laugiq 2000).

---

5   Which demonstrates again the preponderant impact of class.

To be sure, there is no logical reason for which cultural capital scholars should be prevented from accommodating social, including class mobility. Thus, Dunlap (1986) argues that "every class has its own cultural capital", concluding that "to move from one class to another, people must gain new cultural capital". Given the poor quality of class theory pertaining to the capital cultural literature and the spurious character of its central construct, the argument cited above is misleading. Reducing cultural capital to labour power, it is trivially true that different classes require distinct types of labour power, albeit this is by no means an universal regularity; a rentier, for example, does not work, and thus, does not own any labour power. Secondly, class mobility is driven by shifts in one's economic ownership, not cultural capital situation. Even granted, for the sake of argument (which is too crude an assumption) that every class is characterised by an unique bundle of behaviours linked to the notion of cultural capital, a *nouveau-riche* is not required to acquire habits and speech patterns of the bourgeois class to be its effective member, this being based on his or her ownership position.

This may suggests that as regards the Bourdieusian thesis, the bone of contention is not the fact of social reproduction as such but its mechanism. And there the Bourdieusian conception is at its weakest. "The Bourdieusian argument critically depends on the assumption that teachers value elite culture" (Kingston 2001).

Broderick and Hubbard (2000) examined this assumption, by investigating to what extent, if any, students' cultural capital is taken account of by teachers, thereby determining grades:

> None of the cultural capital variables that included 'household educational resources' was found to be significantly related to teachers' perceptions – and the addition of these variables to the model only slightly reduced the association between socioeconomic status (SES) and teachers' perceptions, which suggests that the alleged impact of cultural capital is spurious. Not only are teachers generally unimpressed by what researchers have regarded as cultural capital, but, the cultural capital variables had virtually no impact on the relationship between teachers' perceptions and students' grades and the former also accounted for only a small fraction of the substantial relationship between SES and grades.

This is not an isolated view; another study also concludes that "the association between parents' participation in high culture and children's educational attainment proves to be spurious. [...] The social background variable predicts both the lifestyle and the educational attainment of the family. This has very serious negative implications for Bourdieu's theory" (de Graaf 1986).

It may be surmised that those implications would have been somewhat mitigated had Bourdieu adopted a more robust conceptualisation of this "social background". This is also pointed out by McNeal (2001) in whose opinion sociologists of education encounter problems in applying the Bourdieusian notion of cultural capital because of their lack of "assessing the extent to which parent involvement differentially affects academic achievement by social class".

With that, the argument comes full circle, as the Bourdieusian and post-Bourdieusian sociology of education hinges on the notion of social differentiation.

This implies that to criticise Bourdieu's specific approach to social roots of educational inequalities is not to deny the need for this kind of research. To demonstrate this, it is useful to review again the main points that have emerged in the debate among educational sociologists.

Perhaps the most prominent issue surrounding cultural capital research is the empirical measurement of the concept. In one camp, researchers adhere closely to the measurement of cultural capital as outlined by Bourdieu, who used such items as one's taste in and knowledge of music and art to measure cultural capital. Many researchers follow his example, using similar measures, such as trips to museums, classical music concerts, and music and art classes (DiMaggio 1982; DiMaggio and Mohr 1985; Ganze-boom, DeGraaf, and Robert 1990; Kastillis and Rubenson 1990; Kalmijn and Kraaykamp 1996; Aschaffenburg and Maas 1997; Roscigno and Ainsworth-Darnell 1999; Sullivan 2001; Dumais 2002; Eitle and Eitle 2002). The other camp consists of those who argue that participation and interest in high-status art is irrelevant to school success in the American context. Farkas (1996) argues, for example, that what schools reward is not necessarily involvement in high-status culture, but certain "skills, habits, and styles," such as classroom deportment, that are valued by schools and teachers. In this view, cultural capital refers less to one's knowledge of and interest in high-status culture than one's tool kit of practical skills that can be put to use in school.

However, as Kingston (2001) points out, this turn in recent years toward expanding the measurement of cultural capital to include such things as household educational resources (e.g., books and computers) is inconsistent with a crucial aspect of the definition of cultural capital – that cultural capital is a high-status cultural signal used for the purposes of exclusion. Kingston (2001) writes that "such home practices represent the impact of 'culture,' even what may be called middle-class culture. But they do not represent exclusionary practices that are valued for their connection to a social group" (pp. 96–7). This is not to say that Kingston agrees neither with the measurement of cultural capital as participation in high-status cultural activities. Indeed, he argues that in the "highly pluralised and democratised" context of American culture, few "class-based exclusionary cultural practices" still exist (Kingston 2001: 91). Similarly, Lareau and Weininger (2003) argue that cultural divisions along social class lines have dissolved in the United States, which should lead to a diminished role of high-status cultural capital in perpetuating social class inequality in education.

It is true that "participation in high-status cultural activities is on the decline in the United States" (DiMaggio and Mukhtar 2004). Peterson and Kern (1996) found that individuals who are most interested in high-status culture have become more culturally omnivorous, expressing a wide variety of cultural interests, suggesting that elite rejection of popular culture has declined. However, the unequal distribution of high-status cultural participation across different levels of education persists, with highly educated people still more likely to participate in high-status cultural activities than are those with less education (DiMaggio and Mukhtar 2004). As long as high-status cultural participation is still disproportionately found among the socioeconomically advantaged, this means that there is some correlation between high-status cultural participation and social class.

We may even witness a resurgence of high-status cultural participation being wielded as a tool of exclusion in the name of securing academic advantage among the socioeconomically privileged. As Lucas (2001) argues, when access to a given level of education becomes universal, as has occurred with high school in the United States, the socioeconomically advantaged switch their focus from securing quantitative advantages (e.g., completing high school versus not) to seeking out qualitative advantages within that level of education. "As access to more years of education continues to widen, students' possession of high-status cultural capital could well assert itself as an important tool for the maintenance of socioeconomic inequality in high schools, with subtle differences in cultural experiences between students becoming increasingly consequential markers of distinction.

Therefore, there remains a place in educational research for examining the relationship between cultural capital, conceived as involvement in high-status culture, and educational outcomes. Indeed, as educational access has expanded to larger numbers of people, involvement in high-status culture may become a more important criterion for sorting students. It is in the spirit of measuring cultural capital such that it taps exclusionary class-based practices, along with an empirically supported belief that there do remain such exclusionary class-based practices in the United States, that the current study measures cultural capital as students' participation in high-status cultural activities" (Wildhagen 2009).

Intellectual Labour Power and Cultural Capital

Finally, let us consider an interesting view put forward by an American scholar; interesting insofar as its author is largely critical of Bourdieu's conception of cultural capital, but nevertheless considers it a useful and even necessary notion.

Steven Shapiro outlines the plan of his paper as follows: "we need to begin with an understanding of labour power's purchaser – capital – and turn to how intellectual labour power is a feature of cultural capital" (2009). Shapiro is aware of the potential dangers involved in the term of intellectual work; he rightly points out that each process of work has a more or less pronounced mental dimension to it. Characteristically enough, he does not on that basis defend the usefulness of the concept in question as a relative and contextualised one. Instead, he in effect abandons it for the benefit of a related concept – that of intellectual labour power, which he defines as "the process through which thought performance, which includes teaching, is commodified on the price-setting marketplace. For intellectual labour power cannot be anything but mysterious, until we analyze its delivery within the social formations based on restless accumulation for accumulation's sake via systematised exploitation" (Shapiro 2009). In short, the author is going to – and he indeed puts his idea into practice – employ the conceptual apparatus of Marxian political economy. How far he succeeds in his undertaking, however, is quite another issue. First, Shapiro without any theoretical reason restricts the concept of labour power to the capitalistic context. His entire discussion of the distinction between what he calls status and class societies (in which, again characteristically, the notion of feudalism never appears) is predicated on a peculiar conception of what he terms "social formation", and which properly should be termed rather "formation of society". But this does not really matter. What does matter, however, is his view of:

> the contrast between status and class forms of social organisation. Generally, a status-defined society is one in which power is seen as emerging from the right to manage consumption. Authority over consumption dominates in non-, pre-, or weakly capitalist ('premodern+) societies where power is instantiated, usually by warrior and priestly castes, through awe inspiring rituals of spectacular consumption, including the consumption of life through the repressive power of public terror, torture, and execution; the customary transfer of a body's integral labour, usually through slavery and serfdom; tributary redistribution of agricultural goods, typically within localised markets; and mercantile long-distance trades of precocities. The cultural aspect of status stratification is preeminently organised through differentiations of taste and the embodiment of consumer predispositions through life-passage rituals that so thoroughly incorporate the individual subject into social categories that these embodied distinctions become naturalised and unremarkable. Bourdieu captures this reification through his terms *hexis* and *habitus*, neologisms that capture the multidimensional social constructedness of habit and the habitation of an individual within relationally defined lifeworld hierarchies (Shapiro 2009: 252).

Now this argument suffers from many limitations. Although Shapiro refers repeatedly to Marx and other Marxist thinkers such as Gramsci, his above-cited conception owes much more to Beblen than Marx. To define an economic formation of society in terms of consumption rather than production relations (this common in the Marxist literature term should be taken to mean nothing other than ownership relations) is, parenthetically, alien to the spirit and letter of Marxian political economy – but what is pivotal, is not this departure from Marx, since "Capital" is naturally not a holy scripture, and should not be treated as such, but its highly problematic cognitive value; as a matter of fact, it obscures rather than sheds light on the fundamental property relations underlying each economic formation of society. In focusing on what he calls "authority over consumption", Shapiro fails to extend his favourite concept of power to the field of economic property relations; this would allow one to see that feudal lord's power over his or her serfs, and the "master's" control over his or her slave were in fact property relations, involving a dispossession of peasants and slaves from their labour power that was instead owned by the respective proprietary classes. Shapiro refers in passing to certain economic relations defining pre-capitalist formations, but, perhaps due to the lack of satisfactory notion of property, fails to see their ownership nature and implications, which are rather devastating for his conception of consumption-based economies and societies. Another price for this analytical gap is his lack of differentiating between particular pre-capitalist formations, such as: antic (mind you, not slave), feudal, Asiatic, not to mention the primitive one whose character was distinctive in that it was grounded in the common ownership of means of production and labour power, though in its late stage there emerged private semi-ownership, i.e. not involving the alienability of land, which constitutes one key form of deriving benefits from one's property).

Last but not least, his aforementioned conception, for which he cites Weber as his inspiration, is mistaken also owing to its very name. Weber's term "Stand" is chronically erroneously translated as "status" or "status group",[6] whereas in reality it refers to "estate", which makes a lot of difference. Not in Weber's original framework, to be sure, but within our socio-economic structuralism social estates are groupings based on non-economic ownership relations.[7]

For instance, Collins (1971: 1009) draws, according to his own testimony, on Weber's notion of status groups as clusters of people with similar consumption patterns and cultural styles, which groups are, in his view, the fundamental units of society. However, within the framework of socio-economic structuralism Shapiro's social estates are not the sole or even the single most important unit of social differentiation; they are units of such differentiation in the non-economic sphere. Concomitantly, the distinction between estate and class does not consist in the dependence of the former on consumption, and the latter on production relations, but economic property and extra-economic property relations, respectively. But it is a distinction nevertheless, contrary to Bourdieu who argues that "'status groups' based on a 'life-style' and a 'stylisation of life' are not, as Weber thought, a different kind of group from classes" (Bourdieu 1990: 139).

Relatedly, the conception discussed above is grounded in an equally queer view of the relationship between consumption and production:

> Of course, it is overly tendentious to insist on the separation of consumption from production, status from class, because capitalism vitiates the features of prior social systems only to reconfigure and reinstall them along capitalist lines. [...] There is little to be gained now, though, from an excessively fastidious and strict analytical separation of consumption from production because capitalism today does utilise consumer desire, especially after its reorientation in the early twentieth century with the rise of the mass consumer market (Shapiro 2009: 253).

---

6 As quotations in the body of the text amply show, these terms are used a lot in the cultural capital literature, which may be exemplified by DiMaggio and Mohr (1985), who argue that "prestigious status cultures are rooted in the historical classification projects of status groups, even if the present connection between cultural practice and group membership is weak.

7 See more in (Tittenbrun 2011; 2012).

There are several serious problems with this argument. First and foremost, there is no connection between the role of capitalist advertising and marketing policies rather than production per se (if anything, one should frame the issue as an effect of private capitalist ownership, since the need or even necessity for a mass industry engaged in the demand stimulation through shaping consumers' wants and tastes does not result from the requirements of mass production as such, but from its organisation on a capitalist, profit-oriented basis) as a force influencing consumers' attitudes and behaviour on the other hand and the alleged obliteration of the distinction between the spheres of consumption and production. Influence or even causative force are mistaken for belonging, which is, as a matter of fact, a fairly common error; in other words, even granted that production affects consumption (which in fact is, as argued above, a simplistic treatment), it does not by any means follow that production becomes consumption and/or vice versa (the latter might be said to be predicated on production's obvious dependence on consumption demand, which takes an extreme form under the customised production in the shape of "prosumption").

Small wonder that Shapiro's view of the second pole of his dichotomy is equally flawed:

> A class society is one in which power is now openly acknowledged as deriving from control over production, especially when its mode, the technical and social means of production, is driven by capitalist purposes of creating surplus value, the profit that can be used to expand production, and not merely reinstate it on the same scale as before. Class societies are typically ones controlled by the bourgeoisie, the third estate that does not define itself by its military brutality or theological shock and awe, but instead with the rationalisation of production separated from the caprices of priestly interpretations of spiritualised nature and the sanguinary codes of aristocratic honour and revenge (Shapiro 2009).

The assertion that under capitalism power is openly recognised as rooted in economic relations (not so much in production as such, but ownership – as mentioned above, in the Marxist literature the term of production relations in many, if not most, cases refers in fact to property relations) can raise some eyebrows. In each class formation its ruling classes are not particularly keen at the recognition of even the fact that they wield power in the first place, not to say its real source, which is usually masked and disguised by ideology).

In the above passage the term "bourgeoisie" appears, but Shapiro does not distinguish its historical and theoretical meaning. In class theory, at least Marxist class theory, the term does not simply refer to the third estate, as this is a concept pertaining to the feudal society, but to the capitalist ruling class. Moreover, the under-theorisation of the concept concerned is not an isolated event. On the contrary, it reflects some deeper-seated inconsistencies and ambiguities pertinent to Shapiro's view of social differentiation. His supposedly academic audience is told that:

Consider the enigmatic relation between bourgeois status in civil society and the economics of capitalist class. Few readers of this essay are likely to see themselves as participating in the capitalist exploitation of labourers for the purpose of profit. Yet, regardless of one's birth, just as few will be outside the sphere of the middle-class lifeworld. The link between social and economic forms is the institutional – in this case, the university that collates the profit of capitalist economy and state with bourgeois aspirations and the individualising competition of our students and ourselves (Shapiro 2009).

Now we have three, instead of to terms – the ranks of the capitalist class and the bourgeoisie have been joined by the middle class. Ironically, this concept, as repeatedly stressed throughout the book, pertains not to class, but rather stratification theory with which, in turn, the term "status" is often being associated. Thus, the term he applies to the capitalist formation appears from this point of view more appropriate to Shapiro's pre-capitalist formations, as it is them that are based on status. This hopeless mishmash is compounded by Shapiro's view of intellectual or academic labour power as, in his view, intrinsically involved in the relations of exploitation. Shapiro appears quite knowledgeable about Marxism so that his conceivable ignorance does not justify him in this instance. Exploitation is inseparably connected to surplus value. Meanwhile, services can only bring an owner of respective means of work put in motion by other people's labour power a share in the overall social pool of surplus value produced in such sectors of the economy as mining, manufacturing and transport, that is, where material labour affects use values of material goods. And this does not tell the whole story, for it is only to those institutions of higher education that are profit-oriented and privately owned that the former rule applies. Shapiro seems to imply that owing to the fact of public, or state funding even public universities and colleges are implicated in exploitation. But this is a gross misunderstanding. Tax collection only in some historic cases, as in the Asiatic economic formation, involves a private appropriation of surplus value, and even in the case mentioned above only in part. Otherwise, the mechanism concerned embodies in fact the opposite – that is, not private but social, public or common ownership. All other things being equal, after all, the state expends its revenues on public roads, bridges, museums and the like available to all members of society objects and spaces. Shapiro cannot pretend he is not aware of this, and perhaps this is the reason why he does recourse to a peculiar, rather idiosyncratic notion of surplus value purportedly pertaining to the academia, which is essential, if the rational for the concept of cultural capital as relying on the exploitation of intellectual labour power is to be maintained. Now the said labour power produces, in Shapiro's view, prestige. He writes, for instance: "If high-profile academics become engines of accelerated publication through serial slim volumes, the ensuing nimbus of prestige accrues not from the merit of ideas but from that individual's ability to summon continually the labour of presses and scarcity of its resources" (Shapiro 2009: 262). Shapiro is not joking; quite the contrary, he insists on the applicability of this particular framework in the case under consideration: "a high-prestige institution, which is so because it has already garnered unpaid labour, will find it easier to attract applicants willing to accept lower wages or work harder and longer in return for the noneconomic benefits of prestige" (Shapiro 2009).

In point of fact, however, his own statement just cited undermines the entire logic of his argument. It now appears that the bearers of academic labour power not only allegedly produce a form of surplus value appropriate for this particular setting, but partake of it, or benefit by the collective, institutional prestige, as couched by Shapiro himself, not to mention the fact – oddly enough, neglected by Shapiro – that whatever value they generate for their organisations, their academic output effects in their peers' recognition for their work in the first instance. Thus, the prestige game is not a zero-sum one, as would the above-mentioned exploitation analogy imply. And this seems to be the final nail in the coffin of untenable Shapiro's conception. His motivation appears to lie in his critical posture toward Bourdieu's notion of cultural capital, combined, though, with his equally strong wish to retain the, however redefined, concept.

Accordingly, he proclaims:

> My ensuing assertion is that the currently influential, if not standard, understanding of cultural and symbolic capital, largely derived from Pierre Bourdieu, is based on a set of false predicates, which often invokes Marx's terminology opportunistically, even while deflating the axiomatic definitions that give them analytical substance. The consequence of this elision means that many treatments of cultural capital unwittingly become reenactments, rather than distancing critiques thereof. In response, I propose the rudiments of a theory of cultural capital grounded in the exploitation of labour power through institutions of knowledge formation, and I name the form through which this value appears as prestige. Prestige is the social expression of the labour value given up by subjects to institutions and their agents in return for the perceived security of (occupational) privilege; it is the collective form of charisma. In this light, iconic figures become remunerated less for their individual work and its putative ingenuity than for how it attracts unpaid labour and its benefits for their institution to use in the congeries of bourgeois civil society. No discussion worth having about cultural capital, or so-called immaterial labour, can exist without foregrounding the material practices of the institution as a medium gaining and trading in labour value, rather than being seen as purely a place of positioning concepts (Shapiro 2009).

As argued above, Shapiro's conception of cultural capital, a corollary of which is, inter alia, the view of "academic remuneration as a local feature of cultural capital" (Shapiro 2009) is theoretically, logically and substantively untenable. Just one of its blunders lies in the applicability of the surplus value concept to the economy only, whereas the organisations concerned belong typically to the ideational rather than economic substructure of society at large; and those who do are indeed involved in some relationship with surplus value, but one that cannot be captured by the ill-conceived concept of cultural capital. Concomitantly, academic lecturers and researchers are, again in most cases, not members of any class but a social estate, and estates are involved in non-economic, instead of economic, property relations. Whilst it would take too much space to lay out the theory concerned in detail, let us merely draw attention to the use by Shapiro himself such concepts as privileges which refer precisely to this kind of ownership:

> For instance, mercantile interests work through the Enlightenment to disenchant medieval religious icons only to redirect their associated energy toward a new auratic idol, the capitalist commodity.

> Bourdieu's theoretical cartography needs redrawing not because it emphasises consumption, but because his treatment of the cultural field, as shaped by the indices of autonomy and heteronomy (terms that superficially correlate to production and consumption), depends on a premodern understanding of power as mainly exclusionary, rather than as a necessary traffic of gained surplus. (Shapiro 2009: 209).

The addition of the word "superficially" mitigates somewhat, but merely somewhat, blatantly undialectical mode of thinking – whilst consumption depends for production of material goods and services for objects satisfying consumer needs, this by any means entails that in this equation only consumption is a dependent variable, and production-independent one. In the US, abstracting at this point from the obvious absurdity of the mode of estimation of this most abused bourgeois statistics, i.e. GDP, the fact of the matter is, consumption accounts for two-thirds of their GDP. Besides, a given branch of production is obviously dependent on a plethora of others for raw materials, parts, machinery, tools; Shapiro would do well to study the enormous (only multiplied in the modern era of globalisation) interconnectedness of particular economic sectors as portrayed in the Leontief's input-output tables.

    This resuscitation of an earlier, no longer dominant form of power leads to the idealist return to the idea of a self-orienting social field, indicated by the relative positioning of abstract concepts, rather than a discussion of the field as a form of expression contoured by institutions as transistors of exploited labour power. In other words, the field is privileged more in relation to an idea of a static, cultural hoard, rather than one of dynamic cultural capital, which must continually be in motion to accumulate value, rather than rest in splendid isolation.

    The question of Bourdieu's idealism has been already considered above, similarly his treatment of power, so that without dwelling on these issues, we may turn to the subsequent paragraph, interesting owing to Shapiro's untypical direction of critique levied at the French scholar – whilst most frequent indictment against the French scholar are concerned with his determinism, he is rather rarely charged with voluntarism: "For Bourdieu, disciplines are relatively autonomous to the degree that they are free from the marketplace's monetarising pressures so that their practitioners seem to have the freedom and authority to define their own terms of evaluation and consecration. A field is heteronomous, subordinated, to the degree that it produces concepts in ways that are influenced by commercial pressures and the burden of bearing exchange value as a commodity" (Shapiro 2009: 210).

Inevitably, Shapiro draws on, but does not limit himself to Simmel's famous work on sociology and philosophy of money:

> This fantasy means that the hoarder imagines the only acceptable exchange to be the diachronic one across generations, through inheritance or status-confirming initiation rituals, rather than the synchronic one of social intercourse within an age cohort in a liberal marketplace. Yet the hoarder does not recognise that the seeming autonomy of his solitary pleasure is only possible because a social institution has established conventions that are either invisible or otherwise presented as unremarkable. In reality, all value comes from the institution's ability to accrue or transmit labour power, but the hoarder has tried to make these links opaque. In cultural terms, the hoarder's fetish of autonomy can be understood as analogous to the performative fallacy. Through the 1980s and 1990s, speech act theory was rehabilitated by writers claiming it as a tactic for local, identitarian rebellion against the power of authorities to nominate and classify subjects. Performative statements were said to enact through their declaration, rather than have recourse to an outside power. Yet, statements like 'I accuse' or 'I thee wed' are not self-enacting, since their social action is effective only if the speaker mediates an institution that enables and legitimises her or his statement with its authority. For 'I thee wed' to be successfully performative, the 'I' must be granted the power (by state or church) to perform matrimony. Otherwise, the statement is merely subjunctive:

> I would like to convey the privileges of marriage on you, but this can occur only if I have the institutional credentials to do so in a normative fashion. The performative statement appears to be self-enacting only because of the mystification of institutional power, which is transmitted through officiating statements (Shapiro 2009: 254).

Shapiro fails to see what has been hinted above; the term of culture, another holy cow of the social sciences, is actually a misnomer. In one of its senses it refers to some elements of social consciousness, such as morels, religion, law, ideology, humanities, etc. Worse still, in its all-encompassing meaning, common in anthropology (which, after all, is the native discipline of Pierre Bourdieu) it is – understood as a totality of human behaviours and their products – bordering on society:

> In like fashion, Bourdieu's notion of a field's relative autonomy has less to do with a discipline's ability to withstand the dictates of the marketplace than with

the relative power of its legitimising institution's ability to deliver the benefits of the marketplace in disguised fashion. Even as seemingly autonomous a field as theoretical math is usually so only because military financing flows through universities, which grant a perceived *cordon sanitaire* around the discipline. Without this institutional prophylactic, mathematics would be quickly recognised as always already heteronomised. Rather than illuminate these relations, the autonomy/heteronomy binary effectively mystifies the role of the state-influenced institution that provides the material resources for the production of mathematical knowledge. The modern relationship between consumption and production, status and class, has, therefore, to be understood as mediated by an institution that acts as the ostensibly neutral form of equivalence and evaluation. Like the money form that establishes the means of value between otherwise incommensurate commodities, the institutional form acts as the transistor between the sphere of consumption (status) and production (class). Consider the enigmatic relation between bourgeois status in civil society and the economics of capitalist class (Shapiro 2009: 255).

The relationship in question is indeed enigmatic, but for reasons that cannot be grasped by Shapiro's misconception As suggested above, the bourgeois and capitalist class refer in reality to the same entity; Shapiro ought also comprehensively to overview the long list of meanings pertaining to the tern of civil society, some of which, and by eminent thinkers at that, such as Hegel, are close exactly to what he associates with his "capitalist class". He goes on to say:

> Few readers of this essay are likely to see themselves as participating in the capitalist exploitation of labourers for the purpose of profit. Yet, regardless of one's birth, just as few will be outside the sphere of the middle-class lifeworld. The link between social and economic forms is the institutional – in this case, the university that collates the profit of capitalist economy and state with bourgeois aspirations and the individualising competition of our students and ourselves. Because Max Weber wrote within a Germany still struggling to achieve the middle-class subsumption of aristocratic elites, he inchoately perceived the broader role of institutionality and regarded the political party as the most intelligible nonstate institution (Shapiro 2009: 255).

Shapiro, who, as is clear from his essay, is a diligent disciple of Foucault, took over perhaps from the latter his well-known term of governmentality (elsewhere there function a structurally analogous term of functionality), and converted it – in accord with this fashionable, albeit not excessively beautiful linguistic pattern – to yet another word of the same family. But let us leave alone Foucault, and focus at the moment on Weber. Although there is a slight probability that the term of middle class appeared somewhere on the pages of Weber's voluminous work (similarly as it appears in Marx's writings), it does not really matter, for the concept does not truly belong to the theoretical framework of either of the two.

Freud's mode of production remains institutional with the slight modification being that the analyst's studio is linked to professional bodies through the publication of case reports and presentations to international conferences (Shapiro 2009: 256).

We have no interest, and no proclivity either, to defend Pierre Bourdieu, but to be fair, let us confront the above discussion with Shapiro's earlier criticism of idealism. Now, if not properly qualified, the notion of the founding father of psychoanalysis as a producer sounds somewhat bizarre; naturally, the intellectual movement in question turned out to be enormously productive in the field of literature, arts, film and last but not least, humanities, including psychology itself, although modern scholarship stresses rather its non-scientific nature.

> Foucault explicitly presented the production of disciplinary subjectivity through modern institutions and its hierarchies of professionalised experts as analogous to and simultaneous with the production of a modern proletarian subjectivity through the large-scale industrial factory with its hierarchies of managers and engineers. Just as the modern factory crosses a threshold as it requires the creation of an intermediary stratum of managers, who alone have a comprehensive and authoritative sense of the industrial operation, unlike the proletarian who only knows a fraction, the modern penal, judicial, and educational institutions create a stratum of knowledge workers. For Marx, the industrial factory was distinguished from the manufactory not by its new scale, technology, and managerial strata, but by its systematicity, its institutional ability to link with other social spheres to produce an expanding, interrelated map of capitalist relations that the now-dominant bourgeoisie would control as their domain. It was the nature of this institutional network that Gramsci was among the first to fully explain with his discussion of hegemony as constituted by the work of 'intellectuals.' (Shapiro 2009: 259).

Well, Shapiro, frankly, is not particularly well versed in the sociology of the economy. The socio-economic distinction between the manufacturing and factory modes of production is buried under the heap of generalities, whereas its core boils down to the machine as an application of science, being *differentia specifica* of the factory mode of production. This is by no means reducing the distinction in question to technological terms, since the machine entails a range of ownership relations, as is elucidated, amongst other things, in (Tittenbrun 2011: 2012). Secondly, the terminological blunder of middle class is even consistent with the notion of managers as a stratum; consistent, that is, equally false. The managerial class, megaclass, to be precise, has nothing in common with how it is conceived of in terms of the various steps in the stratification ladder.

> Power really comes from the ability to maintain a position of authority through social exchange within a mesh of mutually heteronomising institutions, and

Gramsci considers knowledge objects as sites of intellectual collabouration that locate a manifold articulation of common sense by a variety of dirigente. To call this relationality heteronomy is to apply a phobic predisposition to socialisation. (Shapiro 209: 259).

Let us turn a blind eye to the next irritating example of the language custom identified above, here showing up as "relationality"; far more important is the given scholar's definition of power that involves two fallacies – *idem per idem*: because power is defined by reference to authority which is no other that another form of power, and at the same time, *ignotum per ignotum*, since neither *definiens* of authority, nor that of social exchange, are specified so that the definition in this shape is, simply put, useless or empty. The state:

> functions as the preeminent broker of alliance because of its greater awareness of the social terrain as a result of its manifold official bureaus. These departments regularly interact with the broadest selection of dirigenti, who rely on the state's monopoly of certification as a prerequisite for insurance and credit mechanisms and seek to trade loyalty for the reward of the state's revenue gained from taxation.

> When dirigenti sense that their cultural authority is declining, they will often embrace what seems to be the magical discourse of others to bolster their own faltering position. Given the risk and intellectual investment costs of constituting new fields, many dirigenti, when faced with competition, simply search for what they think are the valorising elements that empower other dirigenti and clothe themselves with these terms. This strategy explains how certain words – such as period or stylistic names – suddenly arise, swiftly gain currency as groups, jealous of one another, and latch on to each other's manifestos, styles, or agendas. For the 'little French bourgeois' faced with insignificance, the name modern helps him believe that he has regained distinction (Shapiro 2009: 260).

This again shows all the perils of the modish current near Marxsisms, into one stream of which this Foucauldian–Bourdieusian thinker can be classed. The vague usage of the concept "bourgeoisie" with reference to state servants, lawyers, physicians, etc. most likely relies on the criterion of cultural capital as a class determinant with incredibly misleading results – some of the above may belong to the autocephalous class in the conventional parlance the petty bourgeoisie, a minority – to the (perhaps) rentier – bourgeoisie, or land-owning class, but the majority would belong to social estates. In addition, Shapiro's mention about the state is a good self-criticism of his own, mainly borrowed from Bourdieu, deliberations on cultural capital as well on power. The state, after all, as Weber whom Shapiro repeatedly quotes, but, it seems, scarcely draws on, defined as a legitimate monopoly of power.

What he sets out to prove instead is the relationship between academic salary and exploitation of labour power:

> Cultural capital emerges solely from a group's ability to attract 'students,' the formal and informal constituencies, the human supplements and replacements who give up unpaid labour power for the perceived rewards of inclusion within the imprimatur of one institution rather than another. Prestige is the precipitant of the consensual form of subordination that occurs when human agents 'gladly' give themselves over to the institutional formations that provide concepts and named subjectivities. This labour power is made to seem intangible and unremarkable but in reality involves work for the institution's necessary material operation. It is prestige, or more accurately the human labour informing it, that is the magnetic charm and implied currency that draws together different dirigenti into alliances or attracts one to the terms and behavioral styles of another. An institution and its representatives seem important only because they are the forms of appearance that represent the labour power that institutions have attracted and exploited.

> Prestige is the capitalist form of status and collective charisma, but unlike earlier forms of status, which often seek only to maintain the status quo, prestige is constantly circulated to gain more profit. So while employees in separate corporations might have the same titular rank, one that

> works for a high-prestige company will have confidence in the future and the reliability of job security, if not promotion. In return, she or he may give over more unpaid time to the firm in order to rest in the institution's glow. The other may suffer a crisis of confidence about his or her firm as potentially becoming obsolete in ways that require layoffs. Consequently, the low-prestige worker may work to the minimum and seek to join a higher prestige company. In turn, a high-prestige institution, which is so because it has already garnered unpaid labour, will find it easier to attract applicants willing to accept lower wages or work harder and longer in return for the noneconomic benefits of prestige.

The preceding passage confirms the author's capacity to confuse – it is not clear if his propositions refer to labour, or work, one in an economic, or in an non-economic sense, and so on; in relation to companies, for example, more appropriate seems to be the term of reputation or brand rather than prestige. All this confusion stems directly from the unfortunate striving for extending the economic framework into the non-economic domain, as a result of which it is difficult, if not impossible, to respect the distinctiveness of specific non-economic structures, such as the ideational one, or its substructures, such as academic or educational ones. The author under consideration violates the latter sphere's specificity in ascribing it "material operation". To be sure, upon closer scrutiny material production may indeed occur within the aforementioned institutions (e.g. boilers), but such nuances are perhaps too subtle in terms of Shapiro's crude opposition: production-consumption.

He ends his essay on a high note:

> In the university setting, the presence of a high-reputation individual, concentration, or journal attracts graduate students who seem to validate the importance of new research in ways that help the institution, in turn, gain cultural and monetary capital in the form of grants from the state and donations from private sources, seeking to sanitise gains made disreputably elsewhere. Most important in the current dispensation, graduate students provide the main source of exploitable labour as underpaid teachers.

> The same is true of junior researchers who compete for employment in otherwise low-prestige locations. If one scholar receives a higher salary than another, it is not primarily due to any neutral consideration of a work's immanent quality; rather, it's due to the way the scholar's work represents labour transfers hidden from view and how these glue together institutional alliances. If high-profile academics become engines of accelerated publication through serial slim volumes, the ensuing nimbus of prestige accrues not from the merit of ideas but from that individual's ability to summon continually the labour of presses and scarcity of its resources. In a case of a winner's win, an editor who secures a prestige scholar similarly benefits, so that a cross-institutional strata of actors can emerge through a shared theme or discourse. This felt 'newness' is never anything other than a means for a cartel-like arrangement to capitalise on labour transfers through a shared circulation of prestige, which – precisely because it is shared among institutions – no longer seems produced by any institution at all but is simply an innocent, spontaneous creation of personalised 'genius.' Academic celebrity simply registers the degree to which individual actors participate within the surplus gained from exploitation reaped by institutions that buttress their aura. The end of cultural capital, which must be a core demand of any emancipatory ethic, will come only with the dismantling of the current kind of bourgeois institutions that generate this form of capital. Let none of us naively participate. or rest easily in our own. (Shapiro 2009: 108)

In spite of Shapiro's radical, stylistics the revolutions, unfortunately, do not arise from lofty appeals, but from good science, and the latter is somewhat missing; the concept of capital (irrespective of the source of their funding) – in the only permissible, i.e. economic sense, with reference to universities is only plausible in the case of private, profit-oriented institutions. In all other instances, that is, communal, state, charitable, etc. institutions of higher education the notion of capital is by definition ruled out. This has implications for the notion of exploitation, for where is no capital, there cannot be economic exploitation in the sense of obtaining surplus value, albeit there may be oppression, and many other abject behaviours.

> What lies at the root of academic remuneration in a culture of professionalised celebrity? I take this question as an opportunity to reconsider the notion of cultural capital. Discounting the idea that 'intellectual labour' exists, I argue that we need instead to discuss 'intellectual labour power,' the process through which thought performance, which includes teaching, is commodified on the price-setting marketplace. When viewed in this light, Pierre Bourdieu's influential definitions of cultural capital will be found wanting, as they do not account for the social differences that capitalist practices make as they reconfigure status societies into contract ones. Instead, I propose the rudiments of a theory of cultural capital grounded in the exploitation of labour power through institutions of knowledge formation, and I nominate the form through which this value appears as prestige. Prestige is the social expression of the labour value given up by subjects to institutions and their agents in return for the perceived security of (occupational) privilege; it is the collective form of charisma. In this light, iconic figures become remunerated, less for their individual work and its putative ingenuity than for how it attracts unpaid labour and its benefits for their institution to use in the congeries of bourgeois civil society. (Shapiro 2009: 257–64)

The topic discussed above has been analysed by us already earlier, so that at this point we shall restrict ourselves to the remark that with all its failings, the Bourdieusian concept of cultural field had at least that merit that did not blurred the line between it and the marketplace; quite the contrary, Bourdieu was at pains to demonstrate the specificity of the field. Whilst obviously capitalist market relations function in some areas of, notably the so-called hard sciences, the scholar as an university lecturer or an author of papers published in professional journals bears a remote, if any, resemblance, to a capitalist. Indeed, oftentimes, if anything, Shapiro's notion of exploitation would apply, as many journals charge under a variety of pretext substantial fees from rather poorly remunerated scholars. But this is quite another story.

Conclusion
The Unholy Trinity

Let us begin this final reckoning with the statement of a fairly typical view of purported merits credited to the French social scientist whose name has figured prominently throughout the book.

One of Bourdieu's significant contributions to social theory [...] is his notion of "capital". He distances himself from Marx, Swartz observes, by extending the idea of capital from the merely economic "to all forms of power, whether they be material, cultural, social, or symbolic (Sanks 2007).

Even leaving aside the conflation of capital with power criticised above, the only thing in the above passage that we can agree on, is Bourdieu's indeed undebatable departure from Marx; this, however, by itself, is neither a plus, nor minus. Meanwhile, our analyses throughout the book unequivocally show that there is little to celebrate; Bourdieu and others subscribing to the idea of multiple capitals by forcefully "capitalising" a whole gamut of social, non-capital relations convert them into economic ones, on paper only, to be sure, which, though, does not diminish the harm being done. First and foremost, the conceptual framework of Bourdieu and other theorists – who, with all their differences, agree on the suitability of its underlying assumption for social analysis – consists in point of fact of misnomers. As argued above, none of the three notions concerned has much in common with capital in the true sense, referring instead to a diversity of phenomena whose socio-economic significance – like that of labour power – is in fact opposite[1] rather than identical to capital.

Typical of the kind of conceptual hypertrophy and promiscuity indulged in by the theorist of the school of thought under consideration is the following argument: MacGillivray and Walker (2002: 198) speak about a precursor to social capital theory Jane Jacobs whose pragmatism, as they reckon, shows in her early identification (1961: 83) of social networks as a form of capital: "Lowly, unpurposeful and random as they may appear, sidewalk contacts are the small change from which a city's wealth of public life may grow."

The phrase 'social capital' unites a term from sociology and anthropology with another from economics to produce a concept which seems to integrate two approaches traditionally treated as opposed. At the heart of the concept

---

1 Although frankly, this caveat appears to be too sophisticated in relation to the non-economic capital literature, it is fair to qualify that statement by pointing to the legitimate presence of such concepts as variable capital.

of capital is a latent power to generate new production. 'Social' is harder to specify by abstract definition, without invoking a variant of the term itself, but it is easy enough to use – perhaps too easy. It evokes linkages, associations whether of family, friends, or other interest groups. The cognate phrase 'human capital' clearly seeks to play off the classic distinction between capital and labour, but does so in such a way as to make us appreciate the sense of skilled human beings in a workforce as being as vital to successful production as are investment funds, machines and raw materials. 'Social capital' points away from the issue of material production of goods and market-led services towards wider issues of societal integration. Scarcity of economic capital is the main brake on development in the poorest societies. Human capital through education is a critical issue for societies which seek to compete effectively with their rivals.

If productivity is more easily secured, but economic competitiveness leads to unemployment, we often find a low-pay sector and problems of political and social alienation among the have-nots. Radical redistribution of capital and employment opportunities no longer appear to northern electorates as a persuasive political option because, in Galbraith's term, there is a dominant 'culture of contentment' (Galbraith 1993). Differences in social capital access offer themselves to centre-ground politicians as helping those who are a post-industrial awkward class, needing much, but hard to help in ways which the rest of the electorate will accept. (IQIZOS 2002: 125)

Useful as this argument is (in indicating a vital ideological reason for the popularity of social capital), it also vividly shows how over-flexible and vague the definitional premises of the framework under consideration are. The tentacles of those new species of octopus are spread so widely that almost anything can find itself in their range.

What all those extra-economic forms of capital focus on is "investment in social relations with expected returns in the marketplace" (Nan Lin 2001; cited in: Simmons 2011).

This tends to create a false image of the social life as populated by various types of capitalists busily making their investments in order to gain – suffice it to insert here utility to clearly bring out that this is economism writ large, based on orthodox neoclassical microeconomics, as can be seen from what follows:

On the micro-level, economic capital is a resource for the actor. On the macro-level, societal economic capital improves the opportunity structure for the individual under certain conditions. Thus, economic capital on both levels positively affects the perceived chances of fulfilling aspirations. As long as the latter remain unchanged life satisfaction will increase. Social and cultural factors partially follow the same logic, as indicated by the terms social and cultural capital. Under a set of assumptions, the hypotheses derived are that personal and societal economic capital, national pride and national integration, religiosity, and societal religious integration, all positively affect the life satisfaction of the individual. (Jagodzinski 2001)

Those who subscribe to the multiple capitals framework over-generalise the concept of capital and detach it from its economic background, generating what may be dubbed "The unholy trinity", for its components are anything but god-like; as a matter of fact, they should be termed more properly theoretical pests, as they do more harm than good in the cognitive process, obscure rather than illuminate. Indeed, being misnomers they do so by definition. If, however, the use of the three concepts concerned in research cannot reveal any new, hitherto obscure aspects of social reality, this raises a question of rationale. When the capital concepts seem so blatantly flawed – what can account for their astonishing popularity across the social sciences?

The clue is to be sought in the sociology of knowledge, where the re-labelling of the various phenomena as "capital" should be rendered as a form of "structural adjustment": "Where terms like 'neighbourhood', 'club', and 'network' do not carry the same charge because they do not lit the desiderata of economic rationality. The term 'capital' has all the right connotations for a culture in which economic rationality is hegemonic" (Schuller 1997).

This is an understatement. In more precise terms, the supremacy in question refers to capitalism, and indeed the spread and expansion of capitalistic market relations have taken unprecedented proportions; as manifested in the language itself, children in some US schools are "incentivised" to read books, and they are also paid money for good grades.

Or is it not fair to say, following one Elizabeth Anderson, (cited in Sandel 2012) that surrogate motherhood "commodifies" children and women's labour.

His book, *What Money Can't Buy: The Moral Limits of Markets* takes on what the author calls, in accord with our own argument above, the "imperialism" of economic ideas. He reckons we are in thrall to markets and use them to answer questions that markets aren't meant to answer.

According to Sandel, "We are in the grip of a way of looking at the world and social life and even personal relations that is dominated by economic ways of thinking. That's an impoverished way of looking at the world."

He asks what it says about us that we employed more mercenaries than US soldiers in Iraq and Afghanistan? Sandel is also worried at the idea that his government should sell immigration rights, as that would in his opinion cheapen the idea of citizenship.

The above comments must not, however, be regarded as a vindication of the multiple capitals framework as purportedly reflecting the phenomena and processes of the sort mentioned above. The said framework is, however, expressive rather than reflective of those realities; the concepts of non-economic forms of capital are indeed badly suited for their analysis, as the former, in particular, are very vague about the notion of property central to the expansion of capital and commodity-money economy.

In this light, the sole merit that we are able to see regarding the conceptual framework under consideration is the aforementioned signalling significance – its success in a variety of non-economic realms expresses the expansion of real capital and market into those other spheres of life.

Finally, a word is due regarding the goals and expected impact of the book. The purpose has been clear – an in-depth analysis of a triad of enormously popular concepts. This has been a critical examination, making use of the working hypothesis treating all three constructs as misnomers. This supposition has been repeatedly confirmed in the course of analysis; moreover, what is worthy of mention in this context is the fact of multiple positive verification, which rules out any possibility that the results were obtained by accident. The specific character of particular misnomers at issue as well as of the procedure of conceptual extension involved in particular cases have been extensively discussed above, and there is no need to reiterate here relevant insights and arguments. What, if any, impact the book can have? It is reasonable to practise modesty in that regard and do not hold out for pie in the sky – it of course would be wildly unrealistic to expect the demise of research on human, cultural and social capital as a result of the present book. On the other hand, it still may have some influence, perhaps on the growth rate of the relevant literature due to the fact that certain scholars will think twice prior to commencing or working out their research.

Arguably, the human, social and cultural capital literature put a spell on us all (with some exceptions, to be sure), and whilst the best tool for fighting off black magic seems to be its white counterpart rather than scholarly analysis, out of necessity the latter must be considered the second best option. To the present author, like to the child in Andersen's parable, the situation seemed simple enough; yet, considering the widespread recognition of the concepts concerned, it seems not enough to have one's eyes wide open and to be outspoken, as these characteristics pertain to many adherents of the very framework at issue. In this context the merit of our study seems to lie in its comprehensiveness; whilst there are a range of publications criticising here and there the notion of social capital, cultural capital, or human capital, to our knowledge there are no works available of such a wide-ranging scope.[2] This broad perspective has made it possible to identify and take on some methodological issues shared by all three conceptual frameworks concerned.

---

2 Barring our own monograph to be published by Brill which was already mentioned above.

Bibliography

Aaronson, D. and Sullivan, D. (2001), *Growth in Worker Quality*. Human Capital Externalities and Growth. Federal Reserve Bank of Chicago 25(4).

Abbott, A. (1988). Transcending General Linearity. *Sociological Theory*, 6: 169–86.

Abraham, K. and Farber, H. (1987), Job Duration, Seniority, and Earnings. *American Economic Review*, 278–97.

Abramovitz, M. (1986), Catching Up, Forging Ahead, and Falling Behind. *Journal of Economic History* 46(2): 358–406.

Adam, F. and Roncevic, B. (2003), Social Capital: Recent Debates and Research Trends. *Social Science Information* 42(2): 155–83.

Addison, P. (1975), *The Road to 1945*. London: Quartet.

Adkins, N.R. and Corus, C. (2009), Health literacy for improved health outcomes: effective capital in the marketplace. *Journal of Consumer Affairs* 43(2): 199–222.

Adler, P.S. and Seok-Woo, K. (2002), Social Capital: Prospects For a New Concept. Academy of Management. *The Academy of Management Review* 27: 17–40.

Adonis, A. and Pollard, S. (1997), *A Class Act: The Myth of Britain's Classless Society*. London: Hamish Hamilton.

Agelopoulos, G. (1997), From Bulgarievo to Nea Krasia, from "Two Settlements" to "One Village": Community Formation, Collective Identities and the Role of the Individual, in *The Development of a Greek Macedonian Cultural Identity*, edited by P. Mackridge and E. Yanakakis. New York: Berg, pp. 133–51.

Ahern, M., Hendryx, M. and Siddarthan, K. (1996), The Importance of Sense of Community on People's Perceptions of their Health Care Experience. *Medical Care* 34: 911–23.

Ainley, P. (1991), *Young People Leaving Home*. London: Cassell.

Akerlof, G. in R. Swedberg (1990), (ed.), *Economics and Sociology, Redefining Their Boundaries: Conversations with Economists and Sociologists*. Princeton: Princeton University Press, pp. 61–77.

Akerlof, G. (1970), The Market for "Lemons": Quality Uncertainty and the Market Mechanism. *Quarterly Journal of Economics* 54: 345–64.

Alchian, A.A. and Demsetz H. (1972), Production, Information Costs, and Economic Organization. *American Economic Review* 62: 777–95.

Aldridge, S., Halpern, D. and Fitzpatrick, S. (2002), *Social Capital: A Discussion Paper*. London, England: Performance and Innovation Unit.

Ali, S.M. (1985), Contribution of education towards labour productivity. *Pakistan Economic and Social Review* 23(1), 41–54.

Allan, D. (1993), *Virtue, Learning and the Scottish Enlightenment.* Edinburgh: Edinburgh University Press.

Almond, G. and Verba, S. (1963), *The Civic Culture.* Princeton: Princeton University Press.

Althusser, L. (1971), *Lenin and Philosophy and Other Essays.* London: New Left Books.

Altintas, H. (2003), Globalization, migration and global city hypothesis. *International Journal of Economic Development.* October.

Altonji, J. and Shakotko, R. (1987), Do Wages Rise with Job Seniority? *Review of Economic Studies* 54(3): 437–59.

American Management Association (1995), *1995 AMA Survey on Downsizing and Assistance to Displaced Workers.* New York: American Management Association.

Amin, A. and Thomas, M.D. (1996), The Negotiated Economy: State and Civic Institutions in Denmark. *Economy and Society* 25(2): 255–81.

Anderson, B. (1983, 1991), *Imagined Communities: Reflections on the Origins and Spread of Nationalism.* London: Verso.

Anderson, C.L., Locker, L. and Nugent, R. (2002), Microcredit, Social Capital, and Common Pool Resources. *World Development* 30: 95–105.

Anheier, H. and J. Kendall. (2002), Interpersonal Trust and Voluntary Associations. *British Journal of Sociology* 53: 343–62.

Antikainen, A., Houtsonen, J., Kauppila, J. and Houtelin, N. (1996), *Living in a Learning Society: Life-histories, Identities and Education.* London: Falmer Press.

Aoki, M. (1984), *The Co-operative Game Theory of the Firm.* Oxford: Clarendon Press.

Applebaum, E. and Berg, P. (2000), High-Performance Work Systems: Giving Workers a Stake, in M.M. Blair and T.A. Kochan (eds), *The New Relationship: Human Capital in the American Corporation.* Washington, D.C.: Brookings Institution, pp. 205–38.

Appleby, A. (1978), *Famine in Tudor and Stuart England.* Liverpool: Liverpool University Press.

Arbuckle, J.L. (1995), *AMOS,* ver. 3.5. Chicago: SmallWaters Corporation.

Arendt, H. (1948), *The Origins of Totalitarianism.* New York: Harcourt & Brace.

Argyle, M. (1992), Benefits Produced by Supportive Social Relationships, in Hans O.F. Veiel and Urs Baumann (eds), *The Meaning and Measurement of Social Support.* New York: Hemisphere, pp. 13–31.

Armstrong, D. (1997), *Status 0: A Socio-economic Study of Young People on the Margin.* Belfast: Training and Employment Agency.

Arnstein, S.R. (1969), A Ladder of Citizen Participation. *AIP Journal* July 1969.

Arrow, K. (1970), *Essays in the Theory of Risk Bearing.* Amsterdam: North-Holland.

Arrow, K. (1973). Higher education as a filter. *Journal of Public Economics* 2(3): 193–216.

Arrow, K. (1974), *The Limits of Organization.* New York: Norton & Co.

Arrow, K. (1999), Observations on Social Capital, in P. Dasgupta, and I. Serageldin (eds), *Social Capital: A Multifaceted Perspective.* Washington: World Bank, pp. 3–5.

Arrow, K.J. (1985), The Economics of Agency, in J.W. Pratt and R. Zeckhauser (eds), *Principals and Agents: The Structure of Business.* Boston: Harvard Business School Press, pp. 37–51.

Arthur, W.B. (1989), Competing Technologies, Increasing Returns, and Lock-ins by Historical Events. *Economic Journal* 99: 116–31.

Asadi, A., Akbari, M., Fami, H.S., Iravani, H., Rostami, F. and Sadati, A. (2008), Poverty alleviation and sustainable development: The role of social capital. *Journal of Social Sciences* (4)3: 202–15.

Aschaffenburg, K. and Maas, I. (1997), Cultural and Educational Careers: The Dynamics of Social Reproduction. *American Sociological Review* 62(4): 573–87.

Ashton, D. and Green, F. (1996), *Education, Training and the Global Economy.* Cheltenham: Edward Elgar.

Aspinwall, B. (1984), *Portable Utopia: Glasgow and the United States, 1820–1920.* Aberdeen: Aberdeen University Press.

Assensoh, A. and Yvette, M. (2002), Social Capital, Civic Engagement, and the Importance of Context, in S.L. McLean, D.A. Schultz, and M.B. Steger (eds), *Social Capital Critical Perspectives on Community and "Bowling Alone"* New York and London: New York University Press, pp. 203–17.

Axelrod, R. (1981), The Emergence of Co-operation among Egoists. *American Political Science Review* 75(2): 306–18.

Bagde, S. (2008) *Human Capital and Economic Development in India.* Dissertation.

Baicai, S. and Xingjian, X. (2010) Why Ethnic Minority Children Are More Likely to Drop Out of School: A Cultural Capital Perspective. *Chinese Education & Society* 43(5): 31.

Baier, A. (1994). *Moral Prejudices.* Cambridge, MA: Harvard University Press.

Bain, K. and Hicks, N. (1998), "Building social capital and reaching out to excluded groups: The challenge of partnerships." Paper presented at CELAM meeting on *The Struggle Against Poverty Towards the Turn of the Millennium.* Washington D.C.

Baker, G., Gibbons, R. and Murphy, K. (1996), "Implicit Contracts and the Theory of the Firm." Working Paper, April.

Baker, W. (1990), Market Networks and Corporate Behavior. *American Journal of Sociology* 96: 589–625.

Ballester, M., Livnat, J. and Sinha, N. (1999), *Labour Costs and Investments in Human Capital.* SSRN-id218893.

Bandura, A. (1996), *Self-efficacy in Changing Societies.* Cambridge: Cambridge University Press.

Banfield, E.C. (1958), *The Moral Basis of a Backward Society.* Glencoe: Free Press.

Banks, M., Bates, I., Breakwell, V., Bynner, J., Emler, N., Jamieson, I. and Roberts, K. (1991), *Careers and Identities*. Milton Keynes: Open University Press.

Bankston, C.L, and Zhou, M. (2002), Social Capital as a Process: The Meanings and Problems of a Theoretical Metaphor. *Sociological Inquiry* 72: 285–317.

Baptiste, Ian. (2002) Educating Lone Wolves: Pedagogical Implications of Human Capital Theory. *Adult Education Quarterly* 51(3): 184–201.

Barber, B. (1983), *The Logic and Limits of Trust*. New Brunswick, NJ: Rutgers University Press.

Barber, B. (1984), *Strong Democracy: Participatory Politics for a New Age*. Berkeley: University of California Press.

Barnes, M. (1997), *Care, Communities and Citizens*. London: Longman.

Barney, J. (1991), Firm Resources and Sustained Competitive Advantage. *Journal of Management,* 17: 99–120.

Baron, J. and Hannan, M. (1994), The Impact of Economics on Contemporary Sociology. *Journal of Economic Literature,* 32: 1111–46.

Baron, S. and Dumbleton, P. (2001), *The Politics of Learning Disability*. Basingstoke: Macmillan.

Barrett, R. (2003), Improve Your Cultural Capital. *Industrial Management*, September/October 45(5): 20–24.

Barro, R. (1991), Economic Growth in a Cross-Section of Countries. *Quarterly Journal of Economics* 106(2): 407–43.

Bartel, A. (1995), Training, Wage Growth, and Job Performance: Evidence from a Company Database. *Journal of Labour Economics* 13(July): 401–25.

Bartel, A. and Borjas, G. (1981), Wage Growth and Job Turnover: An Empirical Analysis, in S. Rosen (ed.), *Studies in Labour Markets*. New York: National Bureau of Economic Research, pp. 65–90.

Bassi, L.J., Gallagher, A.L. and Schroer, E. (1996), *The ASTD Training Data Book*. Alexandria, VA: American Society for Training and Development.

Bassi, L.J. and McMurrer, D.P. (1998), Training and Investment Can Mean Financial Performance. *Training and Development* 52(May): 40–42.

Baum, F. (1999), The Role of Social Capital in Health Promotion: Australian Perspectives. *Health Promotion Journal of Australia* 9(3): 171–8.

Baum, F.E., and Ziersch, A.M. (2003), Social Capital. *Journal of Epidemiology & Community Health* 57: 320–3.

Bauman, Z. (1998), *Work, Consumerism and the New Poor*. Buckingham: Open University Press.

Baumgartner, F.R. and Walker, J.L. (1988), Survey Research and Membership in Voluntary Associations. *American Journal of Political Science* 32: 908–27.

Baumgartner, F.R. and Walker, J.L. (1996), *Accounting for Tastes*. Cambridge, MA: Harvard University Press.

Bay Area Community Council, (2002), Understanding Social Capital & How it Works in *Our* Community A Project of the Bay Area Community Council.

Beall, J. (1998), Social Capital in Waste – A Solid Investment? *Journal of International Development* 9(7): 951–61.

Beck, U. (1992), *Risk Society: Towards a New Modernity.* London: Sage.

Becker, G. (1962), Investment in Human Capital: A Theoretical Analysis. *Journal of Political Economy* (70)5: 9–49.

Becker, G. (1964, 1993), *Human Capital: A Theoretical and Empirical Analysis, with Special Reference to Education, 3rd Edition.* Chicago: University of Chicago Press.

Becker, G. (1975), *Human Capital: A Theoretical and Empirical Analysis, with Reference to Education, 2nd edition.* New York: National Bureau of Economic Research.

Becker, G. (1976), *The Economic Approach to Human Behavior.* Chicago: University of Chicago.

Becker, G. (1985), Human capital, effort, and the sexual division of labor. *Journal of Labour Economics* 3(1), S33–S58.

Becker, G. (1990), Gary S. Becker, in Swedberg, R. (ed.), *Economics and Sociology, Redefining Their Boundaries: Conversations with Economists and Sociologists.* Princeton: Princeton University Press, 27–46.

Becker, G. (1992), The Adam Smith address: Education, labour force quality, and the economy. *Business Economics* 27(1): 7–12.

Becker, G. (1996). *Accounting for Tastes.* Cambridge, MA: Harvard University Press.

Becker, G. and Tomes, N. (1986), Human capital and the rise and fall of families. *Journal of Labour Economics* 4(3): S1–S39.

Beckford, G. (1972), *Persistent Poverty: Underdevelopment in Plantation Economies of the Third World.* New York: Oxford University Press.

Beeker, C., Guenther Gray, C. and Raj, A. (1998), Community Empowerment Paradigm and the Primary Prevention of HIV/AIDS. *Social Science and Medicine* 46(7): 831–42.

Bell, F. and Millward, R. (1998), Public Health Expenditures and Mortality in England and Wales 1870–1914. *Continuity and Change* 13(2): 221–40.

Belliveau, M.A., OReilly III, C.A. and Wade, J.B. (1996), Social Capital at the Top: Effects of Social Similarity and Status on CEO Compensation. *Academy of Management Journal* 39: 1568–93.

Bender, T. (1978), *Community and Social Change.* New Brunswick: Rutgers University Press.

Ben-Ner, A.W.A., Burns, G.D. and Putterman, L. (2000), Employee Ownership: An Empirical Exploration, in M. Blair and T.A. Kochan (eds), *The New Relationship: Human Capital in the American Corporation.* Washington D.C.: Brookings Institution, pp. 194–232.

Bennett, W.L. (1998), The Uncivic Culture: Communication, Identity, and the Rise of Lifestyle Polities. *PS: Political Science and Politics* (31)4: 741–61.

Ben-Porath, Y. (1967), The Production of Human Capital and the Lifecycle Model of Earnings. *Journal of Political Economy* 75(4): 352–65.

Berg, I. (1970), *Education and Job: The Great Training Robbery.* New York: Praeger.

Berkes, F. and Folke, C. (1994), Investing in cultural capital for sustainable use, in A.M. Jansson, et al. (eds), *Investing in Natural Capital: The Ecological Economics to Sustainability.* Washington, D.C.: Centre for Resource Economics.

Berkman, L. (1995), The Role of Social Relations in Health Promotion. *Psychosomatic Medicine,* 57(3): 245–54.

Berle, A.A. and Means, G.C. (1932, 1991), *The Modern Corporation and Private Property.* New Brunswick, NJ: Transaction Publishers.

Berlin, I. (1969), *Four Essays on Liberty.* Oxford: Oxford University Press.

Berman, S. (1997), Civil Society and the Collapse of the Weimar Republic. *World Politics* 49(April): 401–29.

Berman, S. (1997), Civil Society and Political Institutionalization. *American Behavioral Scientist* (40)5: 562–74. (Special Edition: Social Capital, Civil Society and Contemporary Democracy).

Bernhardt, D. and Scoones, D. (1993), Promotion, Turnover and Pre-Emptive Wage Offers. *American Economic Review* 83(4): 771–91.

Bernstein, R.J. (1985), Introduction, in R.J. Bernstein (ed.), *Habermas and Modernity.* Cambridge: Polity Press, pp. 1–32.

Berry, C.J. (1997), *Social Theory of the Scottish Enlightenment.* Edinburgh: Edinburgh University Press.

Bishop, J.H. (1994), The Impact of Previous Training on Productivity and Wages, in L.M. Lynch (ed.) *Training and the Private Sector: International Comparisons,* pp. 161–200. Chicago, IL: University of Chicago Press.

Bjørnskov (2006), The Multiple Facets of Social Capital. *European Journal of Political Economy* 22(1): 22–44.

Blair, M.M. (1995), *Ownership and Control: Rethinking Corporate Governance for the Twenty-First Century.* Washington, D.C.: The Brookings Institution.

Blair, M.M., and Kruse, D.L. (1999), Giving Employees an Ownership Stake. *Brookings Review* 17(4) Fall.

Blair, M.M., and Kochan, T.A. (2000a), Introduction, in M.M. Blair and T.A. Kochan, *The New Relationship. Human Capital in the American Corporation.* Washington, D.C.: Brookings Institution, pp. 1–27.

Blair, M.M., and Stout, L.A. (1999), A Team Production Theory of Corporate Law. *Virginia Law Review* 85(2): 247–328.

Blair, M.M. and Stout, L.A. (1998), A Team Production Theory of Corporate Law in *Corporate Governance Today,* pp. 233–88. Sloan Project on Corporate Governance, Columbia University Law School.

Blair, M.M. (1999), *Firm-Specific Human Capital and Theories of the Firm.* Georgetown University Law Center Business, Economics and Regulatory Policy Working Paper No. 167848. Social Science Research Network Electronic Paper Collection at: http://papers.ssrn.com/abstract=167848

Blair, M.M. (1999), Firm-Specific Human Capital and Theories of the Firm, in M.M. Blair and M.J. Roe (eds), *Employees and Corporate Governance.* Washington, D.C.: Brookings Institution.

Blair, T. (1998), *The Third Way: New Politics for the New Century.* London: Fabian Society.

Blasi, J.R., and Kruse, D.L. (1991), *The New Owners: The Mass Emergence of Employee Ownership in Public Companies and What It Means to American Business.* New York: HarperCollins.

Blau, J.L. (1963), Introduction, in F. Wayland [1835], *The Elements of Moral Science,* edited by J.L. Blau. Cambridge, MA: Harvard University Press, ix–xlix.

Blaug, M. (1970), *An Introduction to the Economics of Education.* London: Penguin.

Blaug, M. (1972), The correlation between education and earnings: What does it signify? *Higher Education* 1(1): 53–76.

Blaug, M. (1976), The empirical status of human capital theory: A slightly jaundiced survey. *Journal of Economic Literature* 24(3): 827–55.

Blaxter, L. and Hughes, C. (2001), Social Capital: a Critique, in *The Politics and Practice of Widening Participation in Higher Education,* edited by J. Thompson. Leicester: National Institute of Adult Continuing Education.

Bloch, A.B. and Levy, C. (1999), *Refugees, Citizenship and Social Policy in Europe.* Basingstoke: Macmillan.

Block, F. (1990), *Post-Industrial Possibilities.* Berkeley, CA: University of California Press.

Bluestone, B. (1977), Economic theory and the fate of the poor, in J. Karabel and A.H. Halsey (eds), *Power and Ideology in Education.* New York: Oxford University Press, pp. 335–40.

Boggs, C. (2001), Social capital and political fantasy: Robert Putnam's 'Bowling Alone'. *Theory and Society* 30(2): 281–97.

Boggs, C. (2002) Social Capital as Political Fantasy, in S.L. McLean, D.A. Schultz, and M.B. Steger (eds), *Social Capital Critical Perspectives on Community and 'Bowling Alone'.* New York and London: New York University Press, pp. 183–202.

Bogle, J. (1999), Creating Shareholder Value for Mutual Fund Shareholders. *Corporate Board* 20 (January–February).

Boix, C. and Posner, D. (1996), *Making Social Capital Work: A Review of Robert Putnam's Making Democracy Work: Civic Traditions in Modern Italy* (Working Paper No. 94). Cambridge, MA: Center for International Affairs, Harvard University.

Boix, C. and Posner, D. (1998), Social Capital: Explaining its Origins and Effects on Government Performance. *British Journal of Political Science* (29)3: 686–93.

Bollen, K.A. (1989), A New Incremental Fix Index for General Structural Equation Models. *Sociological Methods and Research* 17(3): 303–16.

Bollen, K.A. (1989a), *Structural Equations with Latent Variables.* New York: Wiley.

Borgatti, S.P. and Foster, P.B. (2003), The network paradigm in organizational research: A review and typology. *Journal of Management* 29(6): 991–1013.

Botma, G.J. (2008), Poles apart: mapping the field of arts journalism in South Africa. *Critical Arts.* DOI: 10.1080/02560040802166284, ISSN 0256–0046/ Online 1992–6049, pp. 83–100.

Bott, E. (1957), *Family and Social Network.* London: Tavistock.

Boud, D. and Garrick, J. (1999), *Understanding Learning at Work.* London: Routledge.

Bourdieu, P. (1977), Cultural Reproduction and Social Reproduction, in J. Karabel and A.H. Halsey (eds), *Power and Ideology in Education.* New York: Oxford University Press, pp. 487–511.

Bourdieu, P. (1977), *Outline of a Theory of Practice.* Cambridge: Cambridge University Press.

Bourdieu, P. (1980), Le capital social: notes provisoires. *Actes de la Recherche en Sciences Sociales,* 31(2): 2–3.

Bourdieu, P. (1984), *Distinction.* Richard Nice (trans.). Cambridge, MA: Harvard University Press.

Bourdieu, P. (1984), *Distinction: A Social Critique of the Judgement of Taste.* London: Routledge and Kegan Paul.

Bourdieu, P. (1986), The Forms of Capital, in J.G. Richardson (ed), *Handbook of Theory and Research for the Sociology of Education.* Westport: Greenwood Press, pp. 241–60.

Bourdieu, P. (1988), *Homo Academicus.* Cambridge: Polity Press.

Bourdieu, P. (1991d?), *The Craft of Sociology: Epistemological Preliminaries.* New York: Walter de Gruyter & Co.

Bourdieu, P. (1993), *Sociology in Question.* London: Sage.

Bourdieu, P. (1996), *Language and Symbolic Power.* Cambridge: Polity Press.

Bourdieu, P. (1997), The Forms of Capital, in A.H Halsey, H. Lauder, P. Brown, and A.S. Wells (eds), *Education: Culture, Economy, Society.* Oxford: Oxford University Press, pp. 46–58.

Bourdieu, P. (2000), *Pascalian Mediations.* Stanford, CA: Stanford University Press.

Bourdieu, P. and Passeron, J.C. (1970), *La reproduction.* Paris: Les Editions de Minuit.

Bourdieu, P. and Passeron. J.C. (1977), *Reproduction in Education, Society and Culture.* Richard Nice (trans.). Beverly Hills, CA: Sage.

Bourdieu, P. and Wacquant, L. (1992), *An Invitation to Reflexive Sociology.* Chicago: University of Chicago Press.

Bowles, S. and Gintis, H. (1975), The Problem with Human Capital Theory – A Marxian Critique. *American Economic Review* 65(2), pp. 74–82,

Bowles, S. (1998), Endogenous Preferences: The Cultural Consequences of Markets and Other Economic Institutions. *Journal of Economic Literature* 36(1): 75–111.

Bowles, S. (1999), Social Capital and Community Governance *Focus: Newsletter for the Institute for Research on Poverty* 20(3): 6–10.

Bowles, S. and Gintis, H. (1976), *Schooling in Capitalist America*. London: Routledge and Kegan Paul.

Bowles, S., and Gintis, H. (1975), The problem with human capital theory: A Marxian critique. *The American Educational Review* 65(2), 74–82.

Bowles, S. and Gintis, H. (2002), Social Capital and Community Governance. *The Economic Journal* 112(483): 419–36.

Boxman, E.A.W., De Graaf, P.M. and Flap, H.D. (1991), The Impact of Social and Human Capital on the Income Attainment of Dutch Managers. *Social Networks* 13: 51–73.

Boyarin, J. (1991), *Polish Jews in Paris: The Ethnography of Memory.* Bloomington: Indiana University Press.

Boyte, H. (1995), *Beyond Deliberation: Citizenship as Public Work* in PEGS conference, edited by Civic Practices Network.

Braudel, F. (1973), *The Mediterranean World in the Age of Philip II.* London: HarperCollins.

Breen, K. (1996), Board Focus Charts Varied Terrain of Corporate Governance Abroad. *Corporate Governance Bulletin* 13 (July–September): 15–16.

Breen, T.H. (1993), The Meanings of Things: Interpreting the Consumer Economy in the Eighteenth Century, in *Consumption and the World of Goods*, edited by J. Brewer and R. Porter. London: Routledge, pp. 249–60.

Brehm, J. and Rahm, W. (1997), Individual-Level Evidence for the Causes and Consequences of Social Capital. *American Journal of Political Science* 41(3): 999–1023.

Brehm, J. and Rahn, W. (1997), Individual-Level Evidence for the Causes and Consequences of Social Capital. *American Journal of Political Science* 41(3): 999–1023.

Breiger, R. (1974), The Duality of Persons and Groups. *Social Forces* 53: 181–90.

Brewer, G.A. (2003), Building Social Capital: Civic Attitudes and Behavior of Public Servants. *Journal of Public Administration Research and Theory* 13(1): 5–26.

Brewer, J. (1989a), Conjectural History, Sociology and Social Change in Eighteenth-Century Scotland: Adam Ferguson and the Division of Labour, in D. McCrone, S. Kendrick, and P. Straw (eds), *The Making of Scotland*. Edinburgh: Edinburgh University Press, pp. 13–30.

Brewer, J. (1989b), *The Sinews of Power: War, Money and the English State, 1688–1783*. London: Routledge.

Briggs, A. (1968), *Victorian Cities*. Harmondsworth: Penguin.

Briggs, V.M. Jr. (1987), Human resource development and the formulation of national economic policy. *Journal of Economic Issues* 21(3), 1207–40.

Broderick, M. and Hubbard, R. (2000), "Teachers Perceptions of Students: The Missing Link in Connecting Cultural Capital and Student Success?" Paper presented at the annual meeting of the Southern Sociological Society, New Orleans.

Brown, A. and Galligan, Y. (1993), Changing the Political Agenda for Women in Scotland and Ireland. *West European Politics*, (16)2: 165–89.

Brown, A.J. (1997), *Becoming Skilled during a Time of Transition: Observations from Europe*. Paper to Sixth National Career Development Association Conference, Daytona Beach, Florida.

Brown, C.G. (1987), *The Social History of Religion in Scotland, 1780–1914*. London: Methuen.

Brown, J. (1989), Why Do Wages Increase with Tenure? On-the-Job Training and Life-Cycle Wage Growth Observed Within Firms. *American Economic Review* 79(5): 971–91.

Brown, L.D. and D. Ashman. (1996), Participation, Social Capital, and Intersectoral Problem Solving: African and Asian Cases. *World Development* 24(9): 1467–79.

Brown, P. (1987), *Schooling Ordinary Kids*. London: Tavistock Press.

Brown, P. and Lauder, H. (1997), Education, Globalization and Economic Development, in *Education: Culture, Economy, Society*, edited by A.H. Halsey, H. Lauder, P. Brown and A. Stuart Wells. Oxford: Oxford University Press, pp. 172–92.

Brown, P. and Lauder, H. (2000), Child Poverty, Education and Collective Intelligence, in *Key Papers in the Sociology of Education*, edited by S. Ball. London: Routledge.

Brown, P. and Lauder, H. (2001), *Capitalism and Social Progress*. Basingstoke: Macmillan.

Brown, P., Lauder, H. and Scase, R. (1994), *Higher Education and Corporate Realities*. London: UCL Press.

Brown, S.J. and Fry, M. (1993), *Scotland in the Age of the Disruption*. Edinburgh: Edinburgh University Press.

Browne, M. and Cudeck, R. (1993), Alternative Ways of Assessing Model Fit, in *Testing Structural Equation Models*, edited by K.A. Bollen and J.S. Long. Newbury Park, CA: Sage, pp. 136–62.

Bruner, J. (1990), *Acts of Meaning*. Cambridge, MA: Harvard University Press.

Bukowitz, W.R., Williams, R.L. and Mactas, E.S. (2004), Research-Technology Management Human capital measurement: the centrality of people to knowledge-intensive organizations makes it important to measure the ROI on human capital. A new metric is designed to help. May 1, 2004 *Research-Technology Management*.

Bullen, P. and Onyx, J. (1998), *Measuring Social Capital in Five Communities in NSW*. Centre for Australian Community Organisations and Management CACOM Working Paper Series (41): 49.

Burchell, J., Day, D, Hudson, M., Ladipo, D., Mankelow, R., Nolan, J., Reed, H., Wichert, I. and Wilkinson, F. (1999), *Job Insecurity and Work Intensification*. York: Joseph Rowntree Foundation.

Bureau of Labor Statistics (1996a), *BLS Reports on the Amount of Employer-Provided Formal Training.* USDL 96–268. Washington (July 10).

Bureau of Labor Statistics. (1996b), *BLS Reports on the Amount of Formal and Informal Training Received by Employees.* USDL 96–515. Washington.

Burke, E. (1987), *Reflections on the Revolution in France.* Indianapolis: Hackett.

Burt, R. (1992), *Structural Holes: The Social Structure of Competition.* Cambridge, MA: Harvard University Press.

Burt, R. (1997), The Contingent Value of Social Capital. *Administrative Science Quarterly* 42(2): 339–65.

Burt, R. (1998), The gender of social capital. *Rationality and Society* 10(1): 5–46.

Burt, R. (2000), The Network Structure of Social Capital, in Sutton, R. and Staw, B. (eds), *Research in Organizational Behavior* 22. Greenwich: JAI Press, 345–423.

Burt, R. (2001), Structural Holes Versus Network Closure as Social Capital, in *Social Capital: Theory and Research*, edited by R. Burt. New York: Aldine de Gruyter, pp. 31–56.

Buys, L. and Bow, V. (2002), The impact of privacy on social capital, in *Social Change in the 21st Century Conference.* Brisbane: Queensland University of Technology.

Bynner, J. (1989), *Transition to Work: Results from a Longitudinal Study of Young People in Four British Labour Markets* (ESRC 16–19 Initiative Occasional Papers No. 4). London: City University.

Calhoun, C. (1997), *Habermas and the Public Sphere.* Cambridge, MA: MIT Press, p. 268.

Campbell, A. (1992), Community Participation: A New Frontier in Land Management, in *International Conference on Sustainable Land Management*, edited by R.P. Henriques. Napier NZ: Hawkes Bay Regional Council, pp. 18–27.

Campbell, C. and Mzaidume, Y. (1999), *Social Capital and Grassroots Participation in Community Health Projects.* Paper presented to First International Conference on Critical and Qualitative Approaches to Health Psychology. St Johns, Canada, July.

Campbell, C. and Mzaidume, Y. with Wood, R., and Kelly, M. (1999), *Social Capital and Health.* London: Health Education Authority.

Caplan, N, Whitmore, J.K., and Choy, M.H. (1989), *The Boat People and Achievement in America: A Study of Family, Hard Work and Cultural Values.* Ann Arbor: University of Michigan Press.

Cappelli, P. (1997), *Change at Work.* Oxford University Press.

Carnoy, M. (1977), Education and economic development: The first generation. *Economic Development and Cultural Change,* 25(Suppl.): S428–S448.

Carroll, M.C. and Stanfield, J.R. (2003), Social capital, Karl Polanyi, and American social and institutional economics. *Journal of Economic Issues* 37(2): 397–404.

Carter, A.P. (1994), *Measuring the Performance of a Knowledge-based Economy* (Working Paper No. 337). Waltham, MA: Department of Economics, Brandeis University.

Castells, M. (1996), *The Information Age, Volume 1: The Rise of the Network Society.* Oxford: Basil Blackwell.

Castells, M. (1997), *The Information Age, Volume 2: The Power of Identity.* Oxford: Basil Blackwell.

Castle, E.N. (2002), Social capital: An interdisciplinary concept. *Rural Sociology* 67(3): 331–49.

Cavaye, J. (2004), *Social Capital: A Commentary on Issues, Understanding and Measurement.* Australia: Obersatory PASCAL – Place Management, Social Capital and Learning Regions, p. 27.

Ceridian UK Ltd. (2007) (PDF). *Human Capital White Paper.* Retrieved 2007–02–27.

Cernea, M. (1993), The sociologist's approach to sustainable development. *Finance Development* 30(4): 11–15.

Chambers, (1997), *Whose Reality Counts?* London: Intermediate Technology Publications.

Chandler, A.D. (1992), Organizational Capabilities and the Economic History of the Industrial Enterprise. *Journal of Economic Perspectives* 3(6): 79–100.

Chandler, A.D.J. (1962), *Strategy and Structure: Chapters in the History of the Industrial Enterprise.* Cambridge: MIT Press.

Chastaing, M. (1954), Reid, la philosophie du sens commun et la probleme de la connaissance dautrui. *Revue philosophique,* 144: 352–99.

Checkland, O. (1980), *Philanthropy in Victorian Scotland: Social Welfare and the Voluntary Principle.* Edinburgh: John Donald.

Cherry, S. (1980), The Hospitals and Population Growth: The Voluntary General Hospitals, Mortality and Local Populations in the English Provinces in the Eighteenth and Nineteenth Centuries. *Population Studies,* 34(1): 59–75, 251–6.

Chhibber, A. (1999), Social capital, the state, and development outcomes, in *Social Capital: A Multifaceted Perspective,* edited by I. Serageldin. Washington, D.C.: World Bank, pp. 296–310.

Chitnis, A.C. (1986), *The Scottish Enlightenment and Early Victorian English Society.* London: Croom Helm.

Church of Scotland (1989), *The Government of Scotland,* reprinted in L. Paterson (ed.) (1998). *A Diverse Assembly: The Debate on a Scottish Parliament.* Edinburgh: Edinburgh University Press, pp. 183–8.

Clark, C., Dyson, A., Millward, A. and Robson, S. (1999), Theories of Inclusion, Theories of Schools: Deconstructing and Reconstructing the "Inclusive" School. *British Educational Research Journal* 25(2): 157–77.

Clark, M.M. and Munn, P. (1997), *Education in Scotland: Policy and Practice from Preschool to Secondary.* London: Routledge.

Clarke, P.F. and Trebilcock R.C. (1997), *Understanding Decline: Perceptions and Realities of British Economic Performance.* Cambridge: Cambridge University Press.

Coase, R.H. (1937), The Nature of the Firm. Reprinted in *The Nature of the Firm*, edited by O. Williamson and S. Winter. Cambridge: Cambridge University Press.

Coase, R.H. (1937), The Nature of the Firm. *Economica*, 4(16): 386–405.

Coats, A. (1996), Special Issue: The Post-1945 Internationalization of Economics. *History of Political Economy*, 28 (Supplement).

Coburn, D. (2000), Income Inequality, Social Cohesion and the Health Status of Populations: The Role of Neo-Liberalism. *Social Science and Medicine* 51(1): 135–46.

Coffee, J.C. Jr. (1999), The Future as History: The Prospects for Global Convergence in Corporate Governance and Its Implication. *Northwestern University Law Review* 93 (Spring): 641–70.

Coffield, F. (2000), The Structure Below the Surface: Reassessing the Significance of Informal Learning, in *The Necessity of Informal Learning*, edited by F. Coffield. Bristol: Policy Press, 1–11.

Cohen, A. (1969), *Custom and Politics in Urban Africa: A Study of Hausa Migrants in Yoruba Towns.* London: Routledge and Kegan Paul.

Cohen, A. (1996), Personal Nationalism: A Scottish View of Some Rites, Rights, and Wrongs. *American Ethnologist* 23(4): 802–15.

Cohen, C.B. (2008) Women, Cultural Capital, and Tourism in Bulgaria. *Current Anthropology* 49(1): 160–61

Cohen, J.L. and Arato, A. (1992), *Civil Society and Political Theory.* Cambridge, MA: MIT Press.

Cohen, R. and Hughes, M. with Ashworth, L. and Blair, M. (1994), *Schools Out: The Family Perspective on School Exclusion.* London: Barnardos and Family Service Unit.

Cohen, S., Doyle, W., Skoner, D., Rabin, P. and Gwaltney, J. (1997), Social Ties and Susceptibility to the Common Cold. *Journal of the American Medical Association* 277: 1940–4.

Cohen, S., Doyle, W., Skoner, D., Rabin, P. and Gwaltney, J. and Fields, G. (1999), *Social Capital and Capital Gains, Or Virtual Bowling in Silicon Valley: An Examination of Social Capital in Silicon Valley.* Berkeley: Berkeley Round Table on the International Economy (BRIE), University of California.

Coleman, J. (1988), Social Capital in the Creation of Human Capital. *American Journal of Sociology* 94 (Suppl.): S95–S120.

Coleman, J. (1990), *Foundations of Social Theory.* Cambridge, MA: The Belknap Press of Harvard University Press.

Coleman, J. (1991), *Social Theory for a Changing Society.* Oxford: Westview Press.

Coleman, J. (1998), *The Nature and Location of Religious Social Capital.* Unpublished paper presented at the Religion, Social Capital and Democratic Life Conference, Calvin College, Grand Rapids, MI, October.

Coleman, J.S. (1961), *Adolescent Society.* New York: Free Press.

Coleman, J.S. (1984), Introducing Social Trust into Economic Analysis. *American Economic Review*, 74(2): 84–8.

Coleman, J.S. (1988), Social Capital in the Creation of Human Capital. *American Journal of Sociology* 94: S95–S12O.

Coleman, J.S. (1988b), The Creation and Destruction of Social Capital: Implications for the Law. *Notre Dame Journal of Law, Ethics and Public Policy* 3: 375–404.

Coleman, J.S. (1990a), *Foundations of Social Theory.* Cambridge, MA: Harvard University Press.

Coleman, J.S. (1990b), James S. Coleman, in R. Swedberg (ed.), *Economics and Sociology, Redefining Their Boundaries: Conversations with Economists and Sociologists.* Princeton: Princeton University Press, pp. 47–60.

Coleman, J.S. (1990c), *Equality and Achievement in Education.* Boulder, CO: Westview Press.

Coleman, J.S. (1991), Prologue: Constructed Social Organisation, in *Social Theory for a Changing Society*, edited by P. Bourdieu and J.S. Coleman. Oxford: Westview Press, 1–14.

Coleman, J.S. (1994), *Foundations of Social Theory.* Cambridge, MA: Belknap Press.

Coleman, J.S. (1997), Social Capital in the Creation of Human Capital, in *Education, Culture, Economy and Society*, edited by A.H. Halsey, H. Lauder, P. Brown, and A. Stuart Wells. Oxford: Oxford University Press, pp. 80–95.

Coleman, J.S. (2002), Social capital and poverty: a microeconomic perspective. in *The Role of Social Capital in Development*, edited by T. Van Bastelaer. Melbourne: Cambridge University Press, pp. 19–41.

Coleman, J.S. and Hoffer, T. (1987), *Public and Private Schools: The Impact of Communities.* New York: Basic Books.

Coleman, J.S. (1997), *Foundations of Social Theory.* Cambridge, MA: Harvard University Press.

Coles, (2010), Can effective human capital management lead to increased firm performance? SSRN-id1024549.pdf IE Working Paper WP 15 / 02 15/02/2002

Collier, P. (1998), *Social Capital and Poverty* (Social Capital Initiative Working Paper No. 4). Washington, D.C.: World Bank.

Collier, P. (1998), *Social Capital and Poverty.* Washington D.C.:World Bank.

Collier, P. and Gunning, J.W. (1999), Explaining African economic performance. *Journal of Economic Literature* 37: 64–111.

Collins, J.C. and Porras, J.I. (1994), *Built to Last: Successful Habits of Visionary Companies.* London: Century.

Collins, M. (1991), *Adult Education as Vocation: A Critical Role for Adult Educators.* New York: Routledge.

Collins, R. (1971), Functional and Conflict Theories of Educational Stratification. *American Sociological Review* 36(6): 1002–19.

Collins, R. (1979), *The Credential Society: An Historical Sociology of Education and Stratification*. New York: Academic Press.

Commission for Racial Equality (1996), *Exclusion From School: The Public Cost*. London: Commission for Racial Equality.

Contractor, F.J., Mudambi, S. (2008), The influence of human capital investment on the exports of services and goods: an analysis of the top 25 services outsourcing countries. *Management International Review* 48(4): October.

Cook, K.S., Emerson, R.M., Gilmore, M.R. and Yamagishi, T. (1983), The Distribution of Power in Exchange Networks: Theory and Experimental Results, *American Journal of Sociology* 89(2): 275–305.

Cooper, H., Arber, S., Fee, L., and Ginn, J. (1999), *The Influence of Social Support and Social Capital on Health: A Review and Analysis of British Data*. London: Health Education Authority.

Coplestone, F.C. (1955), *Aquinas*. Harmondsworth: Penguin.

Coté, S. (2001), The Contribution of Human and Social Capital. *ISUMA*, 2(1), [Online] Available at: www.isuma.net.

Coulthard, M., Walker, A. and Morgan, A. (2001), *Assessing people's perceptions of their neighbourhood and community involvement (Part I)* London: Health Development Agency.

Cox, E. (1995), *A Truly Civil Society*. Sydney: ABC Books.

Cox, E. (1997), Building Social Capital. *Health Promotion Matters* 4: 1–4.

Cox, E. and Caldwell, P. (2000), Making policy social, in *Social Capital and Public Policy in Australia*, edited by Ian Winter. Melbourne: National Library of Australia, pp. 43–73.

Crafts, N.F.R. (1995), The Golden Age of Economic Growth in Western Europe, 1950–1973. *Economic History Review*, 48(3): 429–47.

Cressy, D. (1993), Literacy in Context: Meaning and Measurement in Early Modern England, in *Consumption and the World of Goods*, edited by J. Brewer and R. Porter. London: Routledge, 305–19.

Cross, K.P. (1981), *Adults as Learners*. San Francisco: Jossey-Bass.

Crowther, J., Martin, I., and Shaw, M. (1999), *Popular Education and Social Movements in Scotland Today*. Leicester: National Institute of Adult and Continuing Education, 270 References

Cullingford, C. and Morrison, J. (1995), Bullying as a Formative Influence: The Relationship Between the Experience of School and Criminality. *British Educational Research Journal* 21(5): 547–60.

Cunningham, L.A. (1999), Commonalities and Prescriptions in the Vertical Dimension of Global Corporate Governance. *Cornell Law Review* 84 (July): 1133–94.

Curry, N. (1993), Rural development in the 1990s: does prospect lie in retrospect?, in *Rural Development in Ireland: a Challenge for the 1990s*, edited by J Greer. Avebury: Aldershot.

Cusack, T. (1999), Social Capital, Institutional Structures, and Democratic Performance: A Comparative Study of German Local Governments. *European Journal of Political Research* 35(1): 1–34.

Daft, R.L. and Lewin, A. (1990), Can Organization Studies Begin to Break Out of the Normal Science Straitjacket? An Editorial Essay, *Organization Science* 1(1): 1–9.

Dahl, R. (1965), *Modern Political Analysis.* Englewood Cliffs, NJ: Prentice Hall.

Dalum, B., Laursen, K., and Villumsen, G. (1998), Structural Change in OECD Export Specialisation and Stickiness. *International Journal of Applied Economics* 13(3): 423–43.

Daniere, A., Takahashi, L.M. and NaRanong, A. (2002a), Social capital and environmental management: culture, perceptions and action among slum dwellers in Bangkok, in *Social Capital and Economic Development: Well-being in Developing Countries*, edited by S. Ramaswamy. Cheltenham, UK: Edward Eglar.

Daniere, A., Takahashi, L.M. and NaRanong, A. (2002b), Social capital, networks, and community environments in Bangkok, Thailand. *Growth and Change* 33: 453–84.

Darling, J. (1989), The Moral Teaching of Frances Hutcheson. *British Journal of Eighteenth-Century Studies*, 12: 165–74.

Dasgupta, P. (1988), Trust as a Commodity, in *Trust: Making and Breaking Cooperative Relationships*, edited by Diego Gambetta. New York: Basic Blackwell, pp. 49–72.

Dasgupta, P. (2000), Economic Progress and the Idea of Social Capital, in *Social Capital: A Multifaceted Perspective*, edited by P. Dasgupta and I. Serageldin. Washington, D.C.: World Bank, pp. 325–424.

David, P.A. (1985), Clio and the Economics of QWERTY. *American Economic Review*, 75(2): 332–7.

Davie, G. (1986), *The Crisis of the Democratic Intellect: The Problem of Generalism and Specialism in Twentieth-Century Scotland.* Edinburgh: Edinburgh University Press.

Davie, G. (1991), *The Social Significance of the Scottish Philosophy of Common Sense.* Edinburgh: Polygon.

Davis, J. (1982), Achievement Variables and Class Cultures: Family, Schooling, Job, and Forty-nine Dependent Variables in the Cumulative CSS. *American Sociological Review* 47(5): 189–201.

Davis, J.A. and Smith, T.W. (1994), *General Social Surveys, 1972–1994* (MRDF). Chicago: National Opinion Research Center.

Day, R.E. (2002), Social capital, value, and measure: Antonio Negri's challenge to capitalism. *Journal of the American Society for Information Science and Technology* 53(12): 1074–82.

De Berry, J. (1999), *Life After Loss: An Anthropological Study of Post-War Recovery, Teso, East Uganda, with Special Reference to Young People.* Ph.D. thesis, London School of Economics.

De Bresson, C. (1996), *Economic Interdependence and Innovative Activity.* Cheltenham: Edward Elgar.

De Graaf, N., De Graaf, P. and Kraaykamp, G. (2000), Parental Cultural Capital and Educational Attainment in the Netherlands: A Refinement of the Cultural Capital Perspective. *Sociology of Education* 73(2): 92–111.

De Graaf, P.M. (1986), The impact of financial and cultural resources on educational attainment in the Netherlands. *Sociology of Education* 59 (October): 237–46.

De Plahhol, X. (1968), *Les Fondements Geographiques de l'Histoire de Islam.* Paris: Flammarion.

De Souza Briggs, X. (1997) Social Capital and the Cities: Advice to Change Agents. *National Civic Review* 86(2): 111–17 19. *INGENIO* (CSIC-UPV) Working Paper Series 2009/02.

De Tocqueville, A. (1969), *Democracy in America*, ed. J. P. Mayer. New York: Harper Perennial.

DeFilippis, J. (2001), The Myth of Social Capital in Community Development *Housing Policy Debate* 12(4): 781–806.

Dei Ottati, G. (1996), Trust, Interlinking Transactions and Credit in the Industrial Districts. *Cambridge Journal of Economics*, 18(6): 529–46.

Dekker, P. and Uslaner, E.M. (2001), Introduction. pp. 1–8 in *Social Capital and Participation in Everyday Life*, edited by E.M. Uslaner. London: Routledge.

Demsetz, H. (1991), The Theory of the Firm Revisited, in *The Nature of the Firm*, edited by O. Williamson and S. Winter. Cambridge University Press.

Denison, E. (1962), *The Sources of Economic Growth in the United States.* New York: Committee for Economic Development.

Denison, E.F. (1967), *Why Growth Rates Differ.* Washington, D.C.: Brookings Institution.

Denkenberger, A. (1998), Shareholders Speculate on Implementation of Dutch Governance Reforms. *Corporate Governance Bulletin* 15 (January–March): 21–2.

Department for Education and Employment. (DfEE) (1997), *Education Action Zones: An Introduction.* London: DfEE.

Department of Trade and Industry. (1998), *Our Competitive Future: Building the Knowledge Driven Economy.* London: Department of Trade and Industry.

Derrida, J. (1976), *Of Grammatology.* Baltimore: Johns Hopkins University Press.

Devine, F., Savage, M., Crompton, R. and Scott, J. (eds) (2004), *Rethinking Class, Identities, Cultures and Lifestyles.* Basingstoke: Palgrave.

Dewar, D. (1988), *Williamson lecture.* Stirling University, 21 October, reprinted in L. Paterson (ed.) (1998). A Diverse Assembly: The Debate on a Scottish Parliament. Edinburgh: Edinburgh University Press, pp. 169–73.

Dewey J. (1916), *Democracy and Education.* New York: Free Press.

Dickens, W.T., and Lang, K. (1993), Labour Market Segmentation Theory: Reconsidering the Evidence, in *Labour Economics: Problems in Analyzing Labour Markets*, edited by W. Darity Jr. Boston: Kluwer Academic, pp. 141–80.

Dierickx, I. and Cool, K. (1989), Asset Stock Accumulation and Sustainability of Competitive Advantage. *Management Science* 12(35): 1504–13.

DiMaggio, P. (1982), Cultural Capital and School Success: The Impact of Status Culture Participation on the Grades of U.S. High School Students. *American Sociological Review* 47(2): 189–201.

DiMaggio, P. (1994), Social Stratification, Life-Style, and Social Cognition, in *Social Stratification: Class, Race, and Gender in Sociological Perspective*, edited by D.B. Grusky. Boulder, CO: Westview Press, pp. 458–65.

DiMaggio, P. (2002), *Taking the Measure of Culture. A meeting at Princeton University*, June 7–8, 2002, Meeting prospectus, http://www.Princeton.edu/*artspol/ moc_prospectus.html.

DiMaggio, P. and Mohr, J. (1985), Cultural Capital, Educational Attainment, and Marital Selection. *American Journal of Sociology* 90(6): 1231–61.

DiMaggio, P. (1979), On Pierre Bourdieu. *American Journal of Sociology* 84(6): 1460–74.

Doeringer, P.B. and M.J. Piore. (1971), *Internal Labour Markets and Manpower Analysis.* Lexington, MA: D.C. Heath.

Dolfsma, W. and Dannreuther, Ch. (2003), Subjects and boundaries: Contesting social capital-based policies. *Journal of Economic Issues* 37(2): 405–13.

Dolfsma, W. and Dannreuther, Ch. (2003), Subjects and boundaries: Contesting social capital-based policies. *Journal of Economic Issues* 37(2).

Domar, E. (1966), The Soviet Collective Farm as a Producer Cooperative. *American Economic Review* 56: 734–57.

Donaldson, W. (1986), *Popular Literature in Victorian Scotland.* Aberdeen: Aberdeen University Press.

Doran, B.M. (2004), Long-term attachments and long-run firm rates of return. *Southern Economic Journal* 71(2).

Dow, G.K. (1993), Why Capital Hires Labor: A Bargaining Perspective. *American Economic Review* 83 (March): 118–34.

Dow, G. and Putterman, L. (1999) Why Capital (Usually) Hires Labor: An Assessment of Proposed Explanations, in *Employees and Corporate Governance*, edited by M. Blair and M.J. Roe. Washington D.C.: Brookings Institution.

Dube, Y., Howes, J., and McQueen, D. (1957), *Housing and Social Capital.* Toronto: Royal Commission on Canada's Economic Prospects.

Dumais, S.A. (2002), Cultural capital, gender, and school success: The role of habitus. *Sociology of Education*, 75(1): 44–68.

Dumais, S.A. (2005), Children's cultural capital and teachers' assessments of effort and ability: the influence of school sector. *Catholic Education* Jun 1.

Dunlap, K.M. (1997), Family Empowerment: One Outcome of Cooperative Preschool Education. *Child Welfare*, Jul/Aug. 76(4).

Durkheim, E. (1933), *Division of Labour in Society*, trans. G. Simpson. New York: Macmillan.

Durkheim, E. (1976), *The Elementary Forms of the Religious Life, trans.* J.W. Swain. London: Allen & Unwin.

Durkheim, E. (1982), *The Rules of Sociological Method and Selected Texts on Sociology and its Method*, ed. S. Lukes. London: Macmillan.

Durlauf, S. (1999), The case "against" Social Capital *Focus: Newsletter for the Institute for Research on Poverty* 20(3): 1–5.

Durlauf, S. (2002), On the Empirics of Social Capital. *The Economic Journal* 112(November) F459–F479.

Durlauf, S.N. (2002b), Symposium on social capital: Introduction. *The Economic Journal* 112: 417–418.

Dyos, H.J. and Reeder, D.A. (1973), Slums and Suburbs, in *The Victorian City: Images and Realities*, edited by H.J. Dyos and M. Wolf. London: Routledge and Kegan Paul, pp. 359–86.

Easterly, W. (2000), *Happy societies: the middle class consensus and economic development.* Washington, DC: World Bank, Development Research Group.

Eastis, C.M. (1998), Organizational Diversity and the Production of Social Capital. *American Behavioral Scientist,* 42(1), *66–77.*

Eccles, R.G., and Mavrinac, S.C. (1995), Improving the Corporate Disclosure Process. *Sloan Management Review* 36(4): 11–25.

Economic and Social Research Council (ESRC) (1994), *The Learning Society: Knowledge and Skills for Employment Research Programme.* Swindon: ESRC.

Editors Note. 2001. Americas Cultural Capital: Recommendations for Structuring the Federal Role. *The Journal of Arts Management, Law, and Society* 182(31): 3. Fall.

Edwards, B. and Foley, M. (1997), Social Capital and the Political Economy of our Discontent. *American Behavioural Scientist* 40(5(): 669–78.

Edwards, B. and Foley, M. (1998), Civil Society and Social Capital Beyond Putnam. *American Behavioural Scientist* 42(1): 124–39.

Edwards, B. and Foley, M. (1997), Escape From Politics? Social Theory and the Social Capital Debate. *American Behavioral Scientist* 40(5), 550–61.

Edwards, O.D. (1989), A *Claim of Right for Scotland.* Edinburgh: Polygon.

Ehrenholt, A. (1995), No Conservatives Need Apply. *New York Times,* November 19.

Ekeh, P. (1974), *Social Exchange Theory: The Two Traditions.* Cambridge, MA: Harvard University Press.

Ekins, P. (1992), A Four-Capital Model of Wealth Creation, in *Real Life Economics: Understanding Wealth Creation*, edited by P. Ekins and M. Max-Neef. London: Routledge, pp. 147–55.

Ellerman, D.P. (1986), Horizon Problems and Property Rights in Labor-Managed Firms. *Journal of Comparative Economics* 10(4): 62–78.

Elster, J. (1989), Social Norms and Economic Theory. *Journal of Economic Perspectives* 3(4): 99–117.

Emirbayer, M., and Williams, E. (2005), Bourdieu and Social Work. *Social Service Review* 79(4): 689–725.

Eng, E. and Parker, E. (1994), Measuring Community Competence in the Mississippi Delta: The Interface between Programme Evaluation and Empowerment. *Health Education Quarterly*, 21(2): 199–210.

Engen, T.O., Kulbrandstad, L.A., and Sand, S. (1997), *Til keiseren hva keiserens er? Om minoritetselevenes laeringsstrategier og skoleprestasjoner. Sluttrapport fra prosjektet Minoritetselevenes skoleprestasjoner.* Hamar: Oplandske Bokforlag.

Enright, M.J. (1998), Regional Clusters and Firm Strategy, in *The Dynamic Firm*, edited by A.D. Chandler, P. Hagstróm, and O. Solvell. Oxford: Oxford University Press, pp. 315–42.

Epstein, R.A. (1985), Agency Costs, Employment Contracts, and labour Unions. in *Principals and Agents: The Structure of Business*, edited by J.W. Pratt and R. Zeckhauser, pp. 127–48. Harvard Business School Press.

Eraut, M. (2000), Non-Formal Learning, Implicit Learning and Tacit Knowledge in Professional Work, in *The Necessity of Informal Learning*, edited by F. Coffield. Bristol: Policy Press, 12–31.

Ernst and Young Center for Business Innovation (1997a), *Measures that Matter.* Cambridge, MA: Ernst and Young LLP.

Ernst and Young Center for Business Innovation (1997b.) *Twenty Questions on Knowledge in the Organization.* Cambridge, MA: Ernst and Young LLP.

Ernst and Young Center for Business Innovation. (1998), *Measuring Business Performance, 11–15 (comment by Steven M. Ji. Wallman).* Cambridge, MA: Ernst and Young LLP.

Eskelinen, H., Hannibalsson, I., Malmberg, A., and Vatne, E. (1998), *Competitiveness, Localised Learning and Regional Development: Specialisation arid Prosperity in Small Open Economies.* London: Routledge.

Etzioni, A. (1996), The Responsive Community: A Communitarian Perspective. *American Sociological Review*, 61(1): 1–11.

Evans, P. (1992), The state as problem and solution: Predation, embedded autonomy, and structural change, in *The Politics of Economic Adjustment: International Constraints, Disruptive Conflicts and the State*, edited by R. Kaufman. Princeton: Princeton University Press.

Evans, P. (1995), *Embedded Autonomy: States and Industrial Transformation.* Princeton: Princeton University Press.

Evans, P. (1996), Government action, social capital and development: Reviewing the evidence on synergy. *World Development* 24(6): 1119–32.

Eyal, G., Szelényi, I, and Townsley, E. (1998), *Making Capitalism without Capitalists: The New Ruling Elites in Eastern Europe.* London and New York: Verso.

Falk, I. and Guenther, J. (1999), *Role of Situated Trust in Rural Sustainability: Levels of Trust Community Profile.* Launceston: Centre for Research and Learning in Regional Australia, p. 17.

Falk, I. and Harrison, L. (1998), *Indicators of Social Capital: Social Capital as the Product of Local Interactive Learning Processes.* Launceston: Centre for Research and Learning in Regional Australia, p. 23.

Falk, I. and Kilpatrick, S. (1999), *What is Social Capital? The Study of Interaction in a Rural Community.* Launceston: Centre for Research and Learning in Regional Australia, p. 27.

Fama, E.F., and Jensen, M.C. (1983), Separation of Ownership and Control. *Journal of Law and Economics* 26 (June): 301–25.

Farkas, G., Grobe, R., Sheehan, D. and Shuan, Y. 1990. Cultural Resources and School Success: Gender, Ethnicity and Poverty Groups Within an Urban School District. *American Sociological Review* 55: 127–42.

Fatton, R. Jr. (1995), Africa in the Age of Democratization: The Civic Limitations of Civil Society. *African Studies Review* 38(2): 67–99.

Favell, A. (1993), James Coleman: Social Theorist and Moral Philosopher. *American Journal of Sociology* 99(3): 590–613.

Felkins, P.K. (2002), Linked communities and social capital, in *Community at Work: Creating and Celebrating Community in Organisational Life.* New Jersey: Hampton Press Inc.

Ferguson, A. (1966), *An Essay on Civil Society*, ed. D. Forbes. Edinburgh: Edinburgh University Press.

Fernandez Kelly, M.P. (1995), Social and Cultural Capital in the Urban Ghetto: Implications for the Economic Sociology of Migration, in *The Economic Sociology of Immigration*, edited by A. Portes. New York: Russell Sage Foundation, pp. 213–47.

Fevre, R. (1989), Informal Practices, Flexible Firms and Private Labour Markets. *Sociology* 23(1): 91–109.

Fevre, R. (1990), Sub/contracting and Industrial Development, in *Interpreting the Past, Understanding the Present*, edited by S. Kendrick, P. Straw and D. McCrone. Basingstoke: Macmillan, pp. 196–216.

Fevre, R. (1992), *The Sociology of Labour Markets.* Hemel Hempstead: Harvester Wheatsheaf.

Fevre, R. (1998), *Spirits of the Hive: Different Visions of Economic Rationality and Morality in Late Modernity.* Paper to Work Employment and Society Conference, Cambridge, 14–16 September.

Fevre, R. (2000), Socializing social capital: Identity, the transition to work, and economic development, in *Social Capital: Critical Perspectives*, edited by Tom Schuller. Oxford: Oxford University Press, pp. 94–110.

Fevre, R., Gorard, S., and Rees, G. (2000), Necessary and Unnecessary Learning: The Acquisition of Knowledge and "Skills" In and Outside Employment in South Wales in the Twentieth Century, in *The Necessity of Informal Learning*, edited by F. Coffield. Bristol: Policy Press, pp. 64–80.

Field, J. (1999), Schooling, Networks and the Labour Market: Explaining Participation in Lifelong Learning in Northern Ireland. *British Journal of Educational Research* 24(4): 501–15.

Field, J., Schuller, T. and Baron, S. (2000), Social Capital and Human Capital Revisited in *Social Capital: Critical Perspectives*, edited by T. Schuller. Oxford: Oxford University Press, pp. 243–64.

Fielding, M. (1996), Beyond Collaboration: On the Importance of Community, in *Consorting and Collaborating in the Market Place*, edited by D. Bridges and C. Husbands. London: Falmer, pp. 149–67.

Fine, B. (1997), The New Revolution in Economics. *Capital and Class* 61: 143–8.

Fine, B. (1999), The Developmental State is Dead – Long Live Social Capital? *Development Change* 30(1): 1–19.

Fine, B. (1999a), From Becker to Bourdieu: Economics Confronts the Social Sciences. *International Papers in Political Economy* 5(3): 1–49.

Fine, B. (1999b), *The World Bank and Social Capital: A Critical Skinning*, mimeo. London: School of Oriental and African Studies.

Fine, B. (1999c), A Question of Economics: Is it Colonizing the Social Sciences? *Economy and Society* 28(3): 403–25.

Fine, B. (2000), Endogenous Growth Theory: A Critical Assessment. *Cambridge Journal of Economics* 24(2): 245–65.

Fine, B. (2001), *Social Capital versus Social Theory: Political Economy and Social Science at the Turn of the Millennium*. London: Routledge.

Fine, B. (2002), They F**k You Up Those Social Capitalists *Antipode* 34(4): 796–99.

Fine, B. and Green, F. (2000), Economics, Social Capital and the Colonization of the Social Sciences, in *Social Capital*, edited by Baron, S., Field, J. and Schuller, T. Oxford: Oxford University Press.

Firth, R.W. (1967), *The Work of the Gods in Tikopia (2nd edn)*. London: Athlone Press.

Fischer (2005) Bowling Alone: Whats the Score? *Social Networks* 27(2): 155–67.

Fisher, C., Hout, M., Jankowski, M., Lucas, S., Swidler, A., and Voss, K. (1996), *Inequality by Design: Cracking the Bell Curve Myth*. Princeton: Princeton University Press.

Fisher, I. (1906), *The Nature of Capital and Income*. New York: Macmillan.

Fishman, R. (1987), *Bourgeois Utopias: The Rise and Fall of Suburbia*. New York: Basic Books.

Fitzenz, J. (2000), *The ROI of Human Capital*. New York: American Management Association.

Floud, R. and McCloskey, D. (eds) (1994), *The Economic History of Britain Since 1700 (2nd edn)*. Cambridge: Cambridge University Press.

Foley M.W. and Edwards, B. (1997), Editors' Introduction: Escape from Politics? Social Theory and the Social Capital Debate. *American Behavioral Scientist* 40(5): 550–61 (Special Edition: Social Capital, Civil Society and Contemporary Democracy.)

Foley M.W. and Edwards, B. (1998), Beyond Tocqueville: Civil Society and Social Capital in Comparative Perspective: Editors' Introduction. *American Behavioral Scientist* 42(1): 5–20. (Special Edition: Beyond Tocqueville: Civil Society and Social Capital in Comparative Perspective.)

Foley, M. and Edwards, B. (1999), Is it time to disinvest in social capital? *Journal of Public Policy* 19(2): 141–73.

Foley, M. and Edwards, B. (1999), Is it Time to Disinvest in Social Capital? *Journal of Public Policy* 19(2): 199–231.

Foley, M.W. and Edwards, B. (1997), Escape from Politics: Social Theory and the Social Capital Debate. *American Behavioral Scientist* 40(5): 550–61.

Foley, M., McCarthy, J.D. and Chaves, M. (2001), Social Capital, Religious Institutions and Poor Communities, in *Social Capital and Poor Communities*, edited by S. Saegert, J.P. Thompson, and M. Warren. New York: Russell Sage Foundation.

Forbes, D. (1966), Introduction, in A. Ferguson (1966) [1767], *An Essay on Civil Society*, edited by D. Forbes. Edinburgh: Edinburgh University Press, pp. xiii–xli.

Forsman, M. (2005), *Development of Research Networks: The Case of Social Capital.* Åbo: Åbo Akademi University Press University Press.

Foss, N.J. and Loasby, B.J. (1998), *Economic Organization, Capabilities and Co-ordination.* London and New York: Routledge.

Foucault, M. (1997), *Discipline and Punish: The Birth of the Prison.* London: Allen Lane.

Fowler, B. (1997), *Pierre Bourdieu and Cultural Theory.* London: Sage Publications Inc.

Fox, A. (1974), *Beyond Contract: Work Power and Trust Relations.* London: Faber and Faber.

Fox, J. (1992), Democratic Rural Development: Leadership accountability in rural peasant organisations. *Development Change* 23(2): 1–36.

Fox, J. (1994), The difficult transition from clientelism to citizenship: Lessons from Mexico. *World Politics* 46: 151–84.

Fox, J. (1996), How does civil society thicken? The political construction of social capital in rural Mexico. *World Development* 24(6): 1089–1103.

Fox, J. (1997), The World Bank and social capital: contesting the concept in practice. *Journal of International Development* 9(7): 963–71.

Fox, J. and Gershman, J. (2000), The World Bank and social capital: Lessons from ten rural development projects in the Philippines and Mexico. *Policy Sciences* 33(3/4): 399–419.

Fox, J. and Brown, L.D. (1998) *The Struggle for Accountability: The World Bank, NGOs and the Grassroots Movement.* Cambridge: MIT Press.

Francis, P.A., Milimo J.T., Njobvu, C.A., and Tembo, S.P.M. (1997), *Listening to Farmers: Participatory Assessment of Policy Reform.* World Bank Africa Region Series, Washington, D.C.

Frank, A.G. (1984), The unequal and uneven historical development of the world economy. *Contemporary Marxism* 9, 71–95.

Frank, A.G. (1989), The development of underdevelopment. *Monthly Review* 41(2): 37–51.

Frank, K.A. and Yasumoto, J.Y. (1998), Linking action to social structure within a system: Social capital within and between subgroups. *The American Journal of Sociology* 104(3): 642.

Frazis, H., Gittleman, M. and Joyce, M. (2000), Correlates of training: An analysis using both employer and employee characteristics. *Industrial and Labour Relations Review* 53(3): 443–62.

Freire, P. (1970/1993), *The Pedagogy of the Oppressed.* London: Penguin.

Friedman, M. (1953), *Essays in Positive Economics.* Chicago: University of Chicago.

Friedman, M. (1962), The role of government in education, in *Capitalism and Freedom*, edited by M. Friedman. Chicago: University of Chicago, pp. 3–43.

Fries, C.J. (2005), Ethnocultural space and the symbolic negotiation of alternative as "cure". *Canadian Ethnic Studies Journal* 37(1): 87–100.

Fry, M. (1987), *Patronage and Principle: A Political History of Modern Scotland.* Aberdeen: Aberdeen University Press.

Fukuyama, F. (1992), *The End of History and the Last Man.* New York: Free Press.

Fukuyama, F. (1995), Social Capital and the Global Economy. *Foreign Affairs* 74(5): 89–103.

Fukuyama, F. (1995), *Trust: the social virtues and the creation of prosperity.* London: Hamish Hamilton.

Fukuyama, F. (1995), *Trust: The Social Virtues and the Creation of Prosperity.* New York: The Free Press.

Fukuyama, F. (1997), Social capital and the modern capitalist economy: Creating a high trust workplace. *Stern Business Magazine* 4.

Fukuyama, F. (1999), Social Capital and Civil Society. *IMF Conference in Second Generation Reforms.* [Online], Available: www.imf.org/external/pubs/ft/seminar/1999/reforms/fukuyama.htm

Fukuyama, F. (1999), *The Great Disruption: Human Nature and the Reconstitution of Social Order.* New York: The Free Press.

Fukuyama, F. (1999), *Social Capital and Civil Society.* Prepared for delivery at the IMF Conference on Second Generation Reforms.

Fukuyama, F. (2001), Social capital, civil society and development. *Third World Quarterly* 22(1): 7–20.

Fukuyama, F. (2002), Social capital and development: The coming agenda. *SAIS Review* 22(1): 23–37.

Fuligni, A.J. (1997), The Academic Achievement of Adolescents from Immigrant Families: The Roles of Family Background, Attitudes and Behavior. *Child Development*, 68(2): 351–63.

Furubotn, E.G., and Pejovich, S. (1974), Property Rights and the Behavior of the Firm in a Socialist State: The Example of Yugoslavia, in *The Economics of Property Rights*, edited by E.G. Furubotn and S. Pejovich. Cambridge, MA: Ballinger.

Galbraith J.K. (1993), *The Culture of Contentment.* Harmondsworth: Penguin.

Galston, W.A. and Levine, P. (1997), Americas Civic Condition: A Glance at the Evidence. *The Brookings Review*, 15(4): 23–6.

Gamarnikov, E. and Green, A. (1999), Developing Social Capital: Dilemmas, Possibilities and Limitations in Education, in *Tackling Disaffection and Social Exclusion*, edited by A. Hayton. London: Kogan Page, pp. 46–64.

Gambetta, D. (1988), "Can We Trust Trust?" in *Trust: Making and Breaking Cooperative Relationships,* edited by Diego Gambetta. New York: Basic Blackwell, pp. 213–37.

Gambetta, D. (1988), *Trust: Making and Breaking Co-operative Relations.* Oxford: Basil Blackwell.

Gamm, G. and Putnam, R.D. (1999), The Growth of Voluntary Associations in America, 1840–1940. *Journal of Interdisciplinary History* 29: 511–57.

Gamoran, A. and Boxer, M. (2005), Religious participation as cultural capital development: sector differences in Chicago's Jewish schools. *Catholic Education* June.

Gant, J., Ichniowski, C. and Shaw, K. (2002). Social capital and organisational change in high-involvement and traditional work organisations. *Journal of Economics and Management* 11(2): 289–328.

Gardner, H. (1993), *Frames of Mind: The Theory of Multiple Intelligences* (2nd edn). London: Fontana.

Gathmann, C and Schönberg, U. (1985) General Is Specific Human Capital? IZA Discussion Paper No. 2485 December 2006.

Gellner, E. (1995), The Importance of Being Modular, in *Civil Society*, edited by J.A. Hall. Cambridge: Polity Press, pp. 32–55.

General Accounting Office (USA) (1994), *Elementary School Children: Many Change School Frequently, Harming Their Education: Report to the Hon. Marcy Kaptur*. Washington, D.C.: House of Representatives.

Ghodsee, K. (2005), *The Red Riviera: Gender, Tourism, and Postsocialism on the Black Sea*. Durham, NC: Duke University Press.

Gibbons, R. and Katz, L. (1991). Layoffs and Lemons. *Journal of Labour Economics* 9(4): 351–80.

Gibson, A. (1979), *People Power.* Harmondsworth: Penguin.

Gibson, M.A. and Bhachu, P.K. (1991), The Dynamics of Educational Decision Making: A Comparative Study of Sikhs in Britain and the United States, in *Minority Status and Schooling: A Comparative Study of Immigrant and Involuntary Minorities*, edited by M.A. Gibson and J.U. Ogbu. New York: Garland, pp. 63–96.

Giddens, A. (1990), *The Consequences of Modernity.* Stanford, CA: Stanford University Press.

Giddens, A. (1991), *Modernity and Self Identity: Self and Society in the Late Modem Age.* Cambridge: Polity Press.

Gillborn, D. (1997), Ethnicity and Educational Performance in the United Kingdom: Racism, Ethnicity, and Variability in Achievement. *Anthropology and Education Quarterly* 28(3): 351–74.

Gillborn, D. and Gipps, C. (1996), *Recent Research on the Achievements of Ethnic Minority Pupils.* London: HMSO (Ofsted Reviews of Research Series), p. 274 References.

Gillies, P. (1998), The Effectiveness of Alliances and Partnerships for Health Promotion. *Health Promotion International* 13(1): 1–21.

Gilligan, C. (1982), *In a Different Voice.* Cambridge, MA: Harvard University Press.

Gilsenan, M. (1973). *Saint and Sufi in Modern Egypt: An Essay in the Sociology of Religion.* Oxford: Clarendon Press.

Gilson R.J. and Mnookin, R.H. (1985), Sharing Among the Human Capitalists: An Economic Inquiry into the Corporate Law Firm and How Partners Split Profits, 37 *Stan L Rev* 313.

Gilson, R.J. (1997), *Globalizing Corporate Governance: Convergence of Form or Function.* Working Paper. Columbia University Law School.

Gintis, H. (1971), Educational production relationships: Education, technology, and the characteristics of worker productivity. *The American Educational Review* 61(2): 266–79.

Giroux, H. (1983), *Theory and Resistance in Education: A Pedagogy for the Opposition.* South Hadley, MA: Bergin & Garvey,

Glaeser, E.L., Laibson, D.I., Scheinkman, J.A. and Soutter, Ch.L. (2000), Measuring trust. *The Quarterly Journal of Economics* 115(3): 811–46.

Glaeser, E.L., Laibson, D. and Sacerdote, B. (2002), An economic approach to social capital. *The Economic Journal* 112(483): 437–58.

Glaeser, E.L., Laibson, C.L., Scheinkman, J.A., and Soutter, C.L. (1999), *What Is Social Capital? The Determinants of Trust and Trustworthiness* (Working Paper No. 7216). Cambridge, MA: NBER.

Godwin, R.K. (1988), *One Billion Dollars of Influence.* Chatham House, NJ: Chatham House.

Goffman, E. (1975), *Frame Analysis.* Harmondsworth: Penguin.

Goldman, R.M. (2005), ReWriting White: Race, Class, and Cultural Capital in Nineteenth-Century America. *The Journal of American History* 84.

Goldsmith, A.H., Veum, J.R. and Darity, W. (1997), The impact of psychological and human capital on wages. *Economic Inquiry*, October: 815–828.

Goldstein, T. (2003), Contemporary Bilingual Life at a Canadian High School: Choices, Risks, Tensions, and Dilemmas. *Sociology of Education* 76(3): 247–64.

Goldthorpe, J. (1996), The Uses of History in Sociology: Reflections on Some Recent Tendencies, in *Citizenship Today: The Contemporary Relevance of T.H. Marshall*, edited by M. Bulmer and G. Rees. London: UCL Press, pp. 101–24.

Goleman, D. (1996), *Emotional Intelligence.* London: Bloomsbury.

Good, R. (2000), Social Capital and Policy Development. *Social Policy Journal of New Zealand.* 185.

Goodman, R., Speers, M., McLeroy, K., Fawcett, S., Kegler, M., Parker, E., Smith, S., Sterling, T., and Wallerstein, N. (1998), Identifying and Defining the Dimensions of Community Capacity to Provide a Basis for Measurement. *Health Education and Behaviour* 25(3): 258–78.

Gorard, S., Rees G., and Fevre, R. (1999a), Patterns of Participation in Lifelong Learning: Do Families Make a Difference? *British Educational Research Journal* 25(4): 517–32.

Gorard, S., Rees G., and Fevre, R. (1999b), Two Dimensions of Time: The Changing Social Context of Lifelong Learning. *Studies in the Education of Adults*, 31(1): 35–48.

Gorard, S., Rees G., and Fevre, R. and Furlong, J. (1997), *Learning Trajectories: Some Voices of Those in Transit* (Working Paper No. 11). Cardiff: School of Education, University of Cardiff.

Gordon, D., Shaw, M., Dorling, D., and Davey Smith, G. (1999), *Inequalities in Health: The Evidence Presented to the Independent Enquiry into Inequalities in Health*. Bristol: Policy Press.

Gordon, L.A., Pound, J. and Porter, T. (1994), *High-Performance Workplaces: Implications for Investment Research and Active Investing Strategies*. Waban, MA: Gordon Group.

Gough, I. (1996), Justifying Basic Income? *Imprints* 1: 82–3.

Gould, S. (1981), *The Mismeasure of Man*. London: Pelican.

Gow, D. and Vansant, J. (1983), Beyond the rhetoric of rural development participation: How can it be done? *World Development* 11: 427–443.

Gracy, K.F. (2007), Moving image preservation and cultural capital. *Library Trends* 56(1).

Granovetter, M. (1973), The Strength of Weak Ties. *American Journal of Sociology*, 78(4): 1350–80.

Granovetter, M. (1974), *Getting a Job: A Study of Contracts and Careers*. Cambridge, MA: Harvard University Press.

Granovetter, M. (1985), Economic action and social structure: the problem of embeddedness. *American Journal of Sociology* 91(3) (November): 481–510.

Granovetter, M. (1994), Business Groups, in N.J. Smelser and R. Swedberg (eds), *The Handbook of Economic Sociology*. Princeton: Princeton University Press, 453–75.

Granovetter, M. (1973), The Strength of Weak Ties. *American Journal of Sociology* 78(4): 1350–80.

Granovetter, M. (1985), Economic Action and Social Structure: The Problem of Embeddedness. *American Journal of Sociology* 91: 481–510.

Granovetter, M. (1985), Social Structures and Economic Action: The Problem of Embeddedness. *American Journal of Sociology*, 91(3): 481–510.

Grave, S.A. (1960), *The Scottish Philosophy of Common Sense*. Oxford: Oxford University Press.

Gray, P. and Noakes, J. (1993), Reintegration of Children with Challenging Behaviours into the Mainstream School Community in *Silent Conspiracies: Scandals and Success in the Care and Education of Vulnerable Young People*, edited by A. Miller and D. Lane. Stoke: Trentham Books, 47–74.

Gray, R., et al. (1995), The Greening of Enterprise: An Exploration of the (Non) Role of Environmental Accounting and Environmental Accountants in Organizational Change. *Critical Perspectives on Accounting* 6 (April): 211–36.

Green, D. (1994), *Re-inventing Civil Society.* London: Institute of Economic Affairs.

Green, D. (1995), *Community Without Politics.* London: Institute of Economic Affairs.

Green, F., Ashton, D., and Sung J. (1999), The Role of the State in Skill Formation: Evidence from the Republic of Korea, Singapore, and Taiwan. *Oxford Review of Economic Policy* 15(1): 82–96.

Greenwald, B. (1986), Adverse Selection in the Labor Market. *Review of Economic Studies* 53(3): 325–47.

Grimble, R. and Chan, M. (1995), Stakeholder analysis of natural resource management in developing countries: some practice guidelines for making management more participatory and effective. *Natural Resources Forum* 19: 113–24.

Groot, W., Hartog, J. and Oosterbeek, H. (1994), Returns to Within-Company Schooling of Employees: The Case of the Netherlands in *Training and the Private Sector: International Comparisons*, edited by L.M. Lynch. Chicago: University of Chicago Press, pp. 299–308.

Grootaert, C. (1997), *Social Capital: The Missing Link?* (Social Capital Initiative Working Paper No. 3). Washington, D.C.: World Bank.

Grootaert, C., Narayan, D., Jones, V. N. and Woolcock, M. (2003), *Measuring Social Capital. An Integrated Questionnaire.* World Bank Working Paper 18.

Grootaert, Ch. (1998), *Social Capital, Household Welfare and Poverty in Indonesia.* World Bank, photocopy.

Grootaert, Ch. (2001), Social capital: the missing link, in *Social Capital and Participation in Everyday Life*, edited by E.M. Uslaner. London: Routledge, pp. 9–29.

Grootaert, Ch. and Van Bastelaer, T. (2002a), Conclusion: measuring impact and drawing policy implications, in *The Role of Social Capital in Development*, edited by Thierry Van Bastelaer. Melbourne: Cambridge University Press, pp. 341–50.

Grootaert, Ch. and Van Bastelaer, T. (2002b), Introduction and Overview. pp. 1–7 in *The Role of Social Capital in Development*, edited by T. Van Bastelaer. Melbourne: Cambridge University Press.

Grootaert, Ch. and Van Bastelaer, T. (2002c), *The Role of Social Capital in Development: An Empirical Assessment.* New York: Cambridge University Press.

Grootaert, Ch., Van Bastelaer, T. and World Bank (2002), *Understanding and measuring social capital: a multidisciplinary tool for practitioners.* Washington, D.C.: World Bank.

Grossman, S.J., and Hart, O.D. (1986), The Costs and Benefits of Ownership: A Theory of Vertical and Lateral Integration. *Journal of Political Economy* 94 (August): 691–719.

Guenther, J. and Falk, I. (1999), *Measuring trust and community capacity: social capital for the common good.* Launceston: Centre for Research and Learning in Regional Australia, p. 90.

Guest, A.M., and Orpesa, R.S. (1986), Informal Social Ties and Political Activity in the Metropolis. *Urban Affairs Quarterly* 21: 550–74.

Habermas, J. (1984) [1981], *The Theory of Communicative Action I. Reason and the Rationalisation of Society.* London: Heinemann.

Habermas, J. (1987a), [1968], *Knowledge and Human Interests.* Cambridge: Polity Press.

Habermas, J. (1987b), *The Philosophical Discourse of Modernity*, trans. F. Lawrence. Cambridge, MA: MIT Press.

Habermas, J. (1989), *The Structural Transformation of the Public Sphere: An Inquiry into a Category of Bourgeois Society.* Cambridge, MA: MIT Press.

Habermas, J. (1990), *The Taming of Chance.* Cambridge: Cambridge University Press.

Hackett, B. (1996), *The New Deal in Employment Relationships.* New York: The Conference Board.

Hacking, I. (1975), *The Emergence of Probability.* Cambridge: Cambridge University Press.

Hagan, J., MacMillan, R. and Wheaton, B. (1996), New Kid in Town: Social Capital and the Life Course Effects of Family Migration on Children. *American Sociological Review* 61: 368–85.

Hagen, E.E. (1964), *On the Theory of Social Change.* Homewood, IL: Dorsey Press.

Halebsky, S. (1976), *Mass Society and Political Conflict: Toward a Reconstruction of Theory.* Cambridge: Cambridge University Press.

Hall, J.A. (1995), In Search of Civil Society, in *Civil Society*, edited by J.A. Hall. Cambridge: Polity Press, 1–31.

Hall, J.A. and Lindholm, C. (1999), *Is American Breaking Apart?* Princeton: Princeton University Press.

Hall, P. (1997), Social Capital in Britain. Paper prepared for Bertelsmann Stiftung Workshop on Social Capital, Berlin, June 1997.

Hall, P. (1999), Social Capital in Britain. *British Journal of Political Science* 29(3): 417–61.

Hall, P.D. (1999), Vital Signs: Organizational Population Trends and Civic Engagement in New Haven, Connecticut, 1850–1998. In *Civic Engagement in American Democracy*, edited by T. Skocpol and M.P. Fiorina. Washington, DC: Brookings.

Hall, R.E. and Jones, C.I. (1999), Why Do Some Countries Produce So Much More Output Per Worker Than Others? *Quarterly Journal of Economics,* 114(1): 83–116.

Hall, S. and Held, D. (1989), Citizens and Citizenship, in S. Hall and M. Jacques (eds), *New Times*. London: Lawrence and Wishart, pp. 173–88.

Halpern, D. (1998), *Social Capital, Exclusion and the Quality of Life: Towards a Causal Model and Policy Implications*. London: Nexus.

Halpern, D. (1999), *Social Capital, Exclusion and the Quality of Life*. London: Institute for Public Policy Research.

Halpern, D. (2001), Moral values, social trust and inequality: can values explain crime? *British Journal of Criminology* 41.

Halpern, D. and Young, M. (1997), The Family and Social Justice, in *Education: Culture, Economy and Society*, edited by A.H. Halsey, H. Lauder, P. Brown, and A. Stuart Wells. Oxford: Oxford University Press, pp. 784–98.

Halsey, A.H., Lauder, H., Brown, P., and Stuart Wells, A. (eds) (1997), *Education: Culture, Economy and Society*. Oxford: Oxford University Press.

Halsey, A.H. (1972), *Educational Priority: EPA Problems and Policies*. London: HMSO.

Hammersely, M. (1997), Educational Research and Teaching: A Response to David Hargreaves TTA Lecture. *British Educational Research Journal* 23(2): 141–62.

Hancock, T. (1993), The Healthy City from Concept to Application, in J. Kelley and M. Davies (eds), *Healthy Cities: Research and Practice*. London: Routledge, pp. 14–24.

Hanifan L.J. (1920), *The Community Center*. Boston: Silver, Burdett and Co.

Hanifan, L.J. (1916), The Rural Community Center. *Annals of the American Academy of Political and Social Science* 67: 130–38.

Hanifan, L.J. (1920), *The Community Center*. Boston: Silver, Burdette & Co.

Hannan, C. (1999), *Beyond Networks: Social Cohesion and Unemployment Exit Rates* (Discussion Paper No. 99/28). Colchester: Institute for Labour Research, University of Essex. 276. References.

Hansen, W.L. (1970), *Education, Income and Human Capital*. New York: Columbia University Press for National Bureau of Economic Research.

Hansmann, H. (1988), Ownership of the Firm. *Journal of Law, Economics, and Organization* 4 (Fall): 267–305.

Hansmann, H. (1996), *The Ownership of Enterprise*. Harvard University Press. Belknap Press.

Hansmann, H., and Kraakman, R. (1999), *The End of History for Corporate Law?* Working Paper.

Hanushek, E. and Woessmann, L. (2008), The role of cognitive skills in economic development, *Journal of Economic Literature* 46(3), pp. 607–68.

Haq, M. (1996), *Reflection on Human Development*. Delhi: Oxford University Press.

Haque, N. (1999), Incentives and human resource management in the design of public sector reform. *Pakistan Development Review* 38(4).

Hardwig, J. (1991), The Role of Trust in Knowledge. *Journal of Philosophy* 88: 693–708.

Hargreaves, A. (1980), Synthesis and the Study of Strategies: A Project for the Sociological Imagination, in P. Woods (ed.), *Pupil Strategies: Explorations in the Sociology of the Secondary School*. London: Croom Helm, pp. 162–97.

Hargreaves, D. (1996), *Teaching as a Research-based Profession*. London: Teacher Training Agency.

Hargreaves, D. (1997), In Defence of Research for Evidence-based Teaching: A Rejoinder to Martyn Hammersley. *British Educational Research Journal* 23(4): 405–20.

Harker, R. (1990), Education and Cultural Capital in *An Introduction to the Work of Pierre Bourdieu: The Practice of Theory*, edited by Harker, R., Mahar, C., and Wilkes, C. Macmillan Press, London.

Harrison, B. (1992), Industrial Districts: Old Wine in New Bottles? *Regional Studies*, 26: 469–83.

Harrison, R. (1993), Disaffection and Access, in J. Calder (ed.), *Disaffection and Diversity: Overcoming Barriers to Adult Learning*. London: Falmer, pp. 2–18.

Harriss, J. and De Renzio, P. (1997), An Introductory Bibliographic Essay. *Journal of Development Studies* 9(7): 919–37 (Special Issue, ed. J. Harriss: Policy Arena: "Missing Link" or "Analytically Missing": The Concept of Social Capital).

Hart, B., and Risley, T.R. (1995), *Meaningful differences in the everyday experiences of young American children*. Baltimore: Brooks Publishing.

Hart, O. (1989), An Economist's Perspective on the Theory of the Firm. *Columbia Law Review* 89: 1757–74.

Hart, O. and Moore, J. (1990), Property Rights and the Nature of the Firm. *Journal of Political Economy* 98(6): 1119–58.

Harvie, C. (1977), *Scotland and Nationalism: Scottish Society and Politics, 1707–1977*. London: Allen and Unwin.

Harvie, C. (1981), *No Gods and Precious Few Heroes*. London: Edward Arnold.

Harvie, C. (1990), Gladstonianism, the Provinces, and Popular Political Culture, 1860–1906, in R. Bellamy (ed.), *Victorian Liberalism*. London: Routledge, pp. 152–74.

Hashimoto, M. (1981), Firm-Specific Human Capital as a Shared Investment. *American Economic Review* 71 (June): 475–82

Hashimoto, M. and Yu, B. (1980), Specific Capital, Employment Contracts and Wage Rigidity. *Bell Journal of Economics* 11: 536–49.

Hawe, P., and Shielle, A. (2000), Social capital and health promotion: a review. *Social Science Medicine* 51: 871–885.

Hawken, P., Lovins, A., and Lovins, L. (1999), *Natural Capitalism: The Next Industrial Revolution*. London: Earthscan.

Hayes, M.T. (1986), The New Group Universe, in A.J. Cigler and B.A. Loomis (eds), *Interest Group Politics* (2nd edn). Washington, D.C.: Congressional Quarterly Press, pp. 133–45.

Haynesa P. (2009), Before Going Any Further With Social Capital: Eight Key Criticisms To Address. Institute of Innovation and Knowledge Management, INGENIO (CSIC–UPV). Working Paper Series 2009/02.

Healy, K. and Hampshire, A. (2002), Social capital: a useful concept for social work? *Australian Social Work* 55: 227–38.

Hean, S., Cowley, S. and Forbes, A. (2003), The M-C-M cycle and social capital. *Social Science Medicine* 56: 1061–72.

Heard, J. (1998), Global Governance Reform Is Key to Global Finance. *Directors Monthly* 22 (October): 18–19.

Hearn, J. S. (1998), The Social Contract: Re-Framing Scottish Nationalism. *Scottish Affairs* 23/Spring: 14–26.

Hearn, J.S. (forthcoming). Introduction, in J.S. Hearn (ed.), *Taking Liberties: Contesting Visions of the Civil Society Project* (Special Issue of Critique of Anthropology).

Hechter, M. (1987), *Principles of Group Solidarity.* Berkeley: University of California Press.

Heffron, J.M. (2000), Beyond community and society: The externalities of social capital building. *Policy Sciences* 33: 477–94.

Heiner (2008), Relevance of education and intelligence at the national level for the economic welfare of people, *Intelligence,* 36: 127–42.

Helland, H. (1997), *Etnisitet ogskoletilpasning. En undersOkelse av norske, pakistanske ogkonfusianske Osloungdommers skoleprestasjoner.* Magistergradsavhandling. Institutt for sosi-ologi og samfunnsgeografi, Universitetet i Oslo.

Heller, P. (1996), Social capital as a product of class mobilization and state intervention: Industrial workers in Kerala, India." *World Development* 24: 1055–1071.

Hennock, E.P. (1973), *Fit and Proper Persons: Ideal and Reality in Nineteenth-Century Urban Government.* London: Edward Arnold.

Hennock, E.P. (1987), *British Social Reform and German Precedents: The Case of Social Insurance 1880–1914.* Oxford: Clarendon Press.

Herrnstein, R. and Murray, C. (1994), *The Bell Curve: Intelligence and Class Structure in American Life.* New York: Free Press.

Higgins, J. (1999), Closer to Home: The Case for Experiential Participation in Health Reforms. Canadian *Journal of Public Health* 90(1): 30–4.

Hill, M. (1993), *The Policy Process: A Reader.* New York: Harvester Wheatsheaf.

Hirsch, F. (1977), *The Social Limits to Growth.* London: Routledge and Kegan Paul.

Hirschman, A.O. (1984), *Getting Ahead Collectively: Grassroots Experiences in Latin America.* New York: Pergamon Press.

Hirschon, R. (1989), *Heirs of the Greek Catastrophe: The Social Life of Asia Minor Refugees in Piraeus.* Oxford: Clarendon.

Hirschon, R. (2000), The Creation of Community: Well-Being without Wealth in an Urban Greek Refugee Locality, in *Risks And Reconstruction: Experiences of*

Resettlers and Refugees, edited by M. Cernea and C. McDowell. Washington D.C.: World Bank, 393–411.

Hirst, P. (1993), *Associative Democracy*. Cambridge: Polity Press.

Hitt, M.A., Ho-Uk, L., and Yucel, E. (2002), The importance of social capital to the management of multinational enterprises: Relational networks among Asian and Western firms. *Asia Pacific Journal of Management* 19: 353.

Hobbes, T. [1658](1968), *Leviathan*. New York: Penguin.

Hodgson, G. M. (1988), *Economics and Institutions*. Cambridge: Polity Press.

Hodkinson, P., Sparkes A., and Hodkinson, H. (1996), *Triumph and Tears: Young People, Markets and the Transition from School to Work*. London: David Fulton.

Hoffer, T., Greeley, A., and Coleman, J.S. (1985), Achievement and Growth in Public and Catholic Schools. *Sociology of Education* 58(2): 74–97.

Hogwood, B.W. and Gunn, L.A. (1984), *Policy Analysis for the Real World*. Oxford: Oxford University Press.

Hollis, M. (1988), *The Cunning of Reason*. Cambridge: Cambridge University Press.

Holmstrom, B. (1982), Moral Hazard in Teams. *Bell Journal of Economics* 13 (Autumn): 324–40.

Holmstrom, B. and Milgrom, P. (1991), Multi-Task Principal-Agent Analyses: Incentive Contracts, Asset Ownership, and Job Design. *Journal of Economics and Organization* 7 (Special Issue): 24–52.

Holmstrom, B. and P. Milgrom. (1994), The Firm as an Incentive System. *American Economic Review* 84 (September): 972–91.

Homans, G. (1961), *Social Behaviour: Its Elementary Forms*. New York: Harcourt, Brace and World.

Hopmann, S. and Konzali, R. (1997), Close our Schools! Against Trends in Policy-Making, Educational Theory and Curriculum Studies. *Journal of Curriculum Studies* 29(3): 259–66.

Hopper, T., and P. Armstrong. (1991), Cost Accounting, Controlling Labour and the Rise of Conglomerates. *Accounting, Organization, and Society* 16: 405–37.

Hornbeck, D.W., and Salamon, L.M. (eds.). (1991), *Human Capital and America's Future: An Economic Strategy for the Nineties*. Baltimore: Johns Hopkins University Press.

Hughes, D. and Lauder, H. (1991), Human Capital Theory and the Wastage Of Talent. *New Zealand Journal of Educational Studies* 26: 5–20.

Hume, D. (1978), *A Treatise of Human Nature*, ed. L.A. Selby-Brigge and P.H. Nidditch. Oxford: Oxford University Press.

Hunter, B. (2000), *Social exclusion, social capital and Indigenous Australians: Measuring the social costs of unemployment*. Canberra: Centre for Aboriginal Economic Policy Reserach, ANU.

Huntoon, L. (2001), Government use of nonprofit organizations to build social capital. *The Journal of Socio-Economics* 30: 157.

Hutton, W. (1996), *The State We're In* (revised edn). London: Vintage.

Hyden, G. (1997), Civil Society, Social Capital and Development: Dissection of a Complex Discourse. *Studies in Comparative International Development* 32(1): 3–30.

Imich, A. (1994), Exclusions from School: Current Trends and Issues. *Educational Research* 36(1): 3–11.

Inglehart, R. (1997), *Modernization and Post-modernization: Cultural, Economic and Political Change in 43 Societies.* Princeton: Princeton University Press.

Ingram, R.W., and Frazier, R.B. (1980), Environmental Performance and Corporate Disclosure. *Journal of Accounting Research*: 614.

Inkeles, A. (2000), Measuring social capital and its consequences. *Policy Sciences* 33: 245–68.

Institute of Cultural Affairs International (1998), *Beyond Prince and Merchant: Citizen Participation and the Rise of Civil Society.* New York: Pact Publications.

Investopedia "Human Capital: The most overlooked Asset Class".

Israel, B., Checkoway, B., Schulz, A., and Zimmerman, M. (1994), Health Education and Community Empowerment: Conceptualising and Measuring Perceptions of Individual, Organisational and Community Control. *Health Education Quarterly* 21(2): 149–70.

Israel, G., Beaulieu, L. and Hartless, G. (2001), The influence of family and community social capital on educational achievement. *Rural Sociology* 66: 43–68.

Jack, G., and Jordan, B. (1999), Social capital and child welfare. *Children and Society* 13: 242–56.

Jackman, R.W. and Miller, R.A. (1998), Social Capital and Politics. *Annual Review of Political Science* 1: 47–73.

Jacobs, J. (1961), *The Death and Life of Great American Cities: The Failure of Town Planning.* New York: Random House.

Jacobson, L., LaLonde, R. and Sullivan, D. (1993), Earnings Losses of Displaced Workers. *American Economic Review* 83(4): 685–709.

Jacoby, S.M. (1990), The New Institutionalism: What Can It Learn from the Old? *Industrial Relations* 29 (Spring): 316–59.

Jagodzinski, W. (2010), Economic, Social, and Cultural Determinants of Life Satisfaction: Are there Differences Between Asia and Europe? *Soc Indic Res* 97: 85–104. DOI 10.1007/s11205–009–9555–1.

James, W. (1997), The Names of Fear: Memory, History and the Ethnography of Feeling among Uduk Refugees. *Journal of the Royal Anthropological Institute,* 13(1): 115–31.

Jencks, Ch. and Phillips, M. eds. (1998), *The Black–White Test Score Cap.* Washington, D.C.: Brookings Institution Press.

Jensen, M.C., and Meckling, W.H. (1976), Theory of the Firm: Managerial Behavior, Agency Costs and Ownership Structure. *Journal of Financial Economics* 3 (October): 305–60.

Jensen, M.C., and Meckling, W.H. (1979), Rights and Production Functions: An Application to Labor-Managed Firms and Codetermination. *Journal of Business 52* (October): 469–506.

Jodha, N.S. (1998), Poverty and environmental resource degradation: An alternative explanation and possible solutions. *Economic and Political Weekly* 23(36/7): 2384–90.

Johnson, M. and Roebuck, C. (2008), Nurturing a new kind of capital. *Financial Executive*.

Johnson, T. (1972), *Professions and Power*. London: Macmillan.

Johnston, R. and Soroka, S.N. (2001), Social capital in a multicultural society: the case of Canada, in *Social Capital and Participation in Everyday Life*, edited by Eric M. Uslaner. London: Routledge, pp. 30–36

Jones, R.R. (1998), *Conceptualizing Social Capital, Civil Society, and Democratic Consolidation*. Paper presented at the Western Political Science Association Annual Meeting, Los Angeles, California, 19–21 March.

Jordan, G. and Maloney, W.A. (1997), *The Rise of the Protest Business: Mobilizing Campaign Groups*. Manchester: Manchester University Press.

Joreskog, K.G., and Sorbom, D. (1986), *LISREL 6: Analysis of Linear Structural Relationships by Maximum Likelihood and Least Square Methods*. Mooresville, IN: Scientific Software.

Joreskog, K.G., and Sorbom, D. (1993), *LISREL 8: Users Reference Guide*. Chicago: Scientific Software International.

Jovanovic, B. Firm-Specific Capital and Turnover. (1984), Matching, Turnover, and Unemployment. *Journal of Political Economy* 108–22.

Jovanovic, B. Firm-Specific Capital and Turnover. (1979), *Journal of Political Economy* 1246–60.

Kaestle, C.F. (1983), *Pillars of the Republic: Common Schools and American Society, 1780–1860*. New York: Hill and Wang.

Kalmijn, M. and Kraaykamp, G. (1996), Race, Cultural Capital, and Schooling: An Analysis of Trends in the United States. *Sociology of Education* 69(1): 22–34.

Kandel, D.B. (1999), Coleman's Contributions to Understanding Youth and Adolescence, in *James S. Coleman*, edited by J. Clark. London: Falmer, pp. 33–45.

Katz, E. and A. Ziderman (1990), Investment in General Training: The Role of Information and Labour Mobility. *Economic Journal*, 100: 1147–58.

Katz, L.F., and Summers, L.H. (1989), *Industry Rents: Evidence and Implications*. Brookings Papers on Economic Activity: Microeconomics, 209–75.

Katzenstein, P.J. (1985), *Small States in World Markets: Industrial Policy in Europe*. New York: Cornell University Press.

Kavanaugh, A.L. and Patterson, S.J. (2001), The impact of community computer networks on social capital and community involvement." *The American Behavioral Scientist* 45: 496–509.

Kawachi, I. and Kennedy, B. (1999), Income Inequality and Health: Pathways and Mechanisms. *Health Services Research* 34(1): 215–278. References.

Kawachi, I., Kennedy, B.P. and Glass, R. (1999b), Social capital and self-rated health: a contextual analysis. *American Journal of Public Health* 89: 1187–1193.

Kawachi, I., Kennedy, B.P. and Wilkinson, R.L. (1999a), Crime: social disorganization and relative deprivation. *Social Science & Medicine* 48: 719–731.

Kawachi, I., Kennedy, B., and Wilkinson, R. (1999b), *The Society and Population Health Reader: Income Inequality and Health*. New York: The New Press.

Kay, J.A. (1993), *Foundations of Corporate Success: How Business Strategies Add Value*. Oxford: Oxford University Press.

Kazee, T.A. and Roberts, S.L. (1998), *Eroding Political Trust in America: An Assessment of Its Nature and Implications*. Paper to American Political Science Association Annual Conference, Boston, 3–6 September.

Keane, J. (1998), *Civil Society: Old Images, New Visions*. Cambridge: Polity Press.

Keeley, B. (2007), *OECD Insights: Human Capital*. OECD.

Keep, E. (1997), "There's No Such Thing as Society…": Some Problems with an Individual Approach to Creating a Learning Society. *Journal of Educational Policy* 12(6): 457–71.

Kelley, J. and Davies, M. (1993), Healthy Cities: Research and Practice, in *Healthy Cities: Research and Practice*, edited by J. Kelley and M. Davies. London: Routledge, pp. 1–13.

Kennedy, B., Kawachi, I., and Brainerd, E. (1998), The Role of Social Capital in the Russian Mortality Crisis. *World Development*, 26(11): 2029–43.

Kenworthy, L. (1997), Civic Engagement, Social Capital, and Economic Cooperation. *American Behavioral Scientist* 40(5): 645–56.

Kerr, C., Dunlop, J., Harbison., F., and Meyer, C. (1973), *Industrialism and Industrial Man*. Harmondsworth: Penguin.

Kidd, C. (1993), *Subverting Scotland's Past*. Cambridge: Cambridge University Press.

Kilby, P. (2002), *Social capital and civil society*. Canberra: National Centre for Development Studies at ANU, pp. 1–15.

Kilpatrick, S. (2000), *How social capital facilitates learning outcomes for small family businesses*. University of Tasmania.

Kilpatrick, S., Bell, R. and Falk, I. (1998), *Groups of Groups: the role of group learning in building social capital*. Launceston: Centre for Research and Leaning in Regional Australia, p. 13.

Kimberly L., and Prothrow-Smith, D. (1997), Social Capital, Income Inequality and Mortality. *American Journal of Public Health* 87(9): 1491–8.

Kinder, K. and Wilkin, A. (1998), *With All Respect: Reviewing Disaffection Strategies*. Slough: National Foundation for Educational Research.

Kingston, P. (2000), *The Classless Society*. Stanford, CA: Stanford University Press.

Kingston, Paul W. (2001), The Unfulfilled Promise of Cultural Capital Theory. *Sociology of Education* Extra Issue: 88–99.

Kinsley, J. (1968), *Commentary*, Vol. III of J. Kinsley (ed.), *The Poems and Songs of Robert Burns*. Oxford: Clarendon Press.

Klees, S. (1986), Planning and Policy Analysis in Education: What Can Economics Tell Us? *Comparative Education Review*, 30: 574–607.

Klein, B., Crawford, R.A. and Alchian, A.A. (1978), Vertical Integration, Appropriable Rents, and the Competitive Contracting Process. *Journal of Law and Economics* 21 (October): 297–326.

Klein, B. (1988), Vertical Integration as Organizational Ownership: The Fisher Body–General Motors Relationship Revisited, 4 *J.L. Econ. & Organization*.

Knack, S. (1999), *Social Capital, Growth and Poverty: A Survey of Cross-Country Evidence* (Social Capital Initiative Working Paper No. 4). Washington, D.C.: World Bank.

Knack, S. (2002), Social capital and the quality of government: Evidence from the states. *American Journal of Political Science* 46: 772–85.

Knack, S. and P. Keefer (1997), Does Social Capital Have an Economic Payoff? A Cross-Country Investigation. *Quarterly Journal of Economics* 62(4): 1251–88.

Knack, S. and Keefer, P. (1997), Does Social Capital Have an Economic Payoff? A Cross-Country Investigation. *Quarterly Journal of Economics* 52(4), 1251–87.

Knoke, D. (1999), Organizational networks and corporate social capital in *Corporate Social Capital and Liability*, edited by S.M. Gabbay. Boston: Kluwer, pp. 17–42.

Knoke, D. and Kukliński, J. (1991), Network Analysis: Basic Concepts, in *Markets, Hierarchies and Networks: The Coordination of Social Life*, edited by G. Thompson, J. France, R. Levacic, and J. Mitchell. London: Sage, pp. 173–82.

Koike, K. (1990), Intellectual Skill and the Role of Employees as Constituent Members of Large Firms in Contemporary Japan, in *The Firm as a Nexus of Treaties*, edited by M. Aoki, B. Gustafsson, and O.E. Williamson.Newbury Park, CA: Sage Publications, pp. 185–208.

Kolankiewicz, G. (1996), Social Capital and Social Change. *British Journal of Sociology* 47(3): 427–41.

Kontogiorgi, E. (1996), *The Rural Settlement of Greek Refugees in Macedonia, 1923–30*. D.Phil thesis, University of Oxford.

Krange, O. and Bakken, A. (1998), Innvandrerangdoms skoleprestasjoner: Tradisjonelle klasseskiller eller nye skillelinjer? *Tidsskrift for samfunnsforskning* 39(3): 381–410.

Kreps, D.M. (1990), Corporate Culture and Economic Theory, in *Perspectives on Positive Political Economy*, edited by J.E. Alt and K.A. Shepsle. Cambridge: Cambridge University Press, pp. 90–143.

Kreps, D.M. (1996), Markets and Hierarchies and (Mathematical) Economic Theory. *Industries and Corporate Change* 5(2): 561–95.

Kreuter, M. (1997), *National Level Assessment of Community Health Promotion Using Indicators of Social Capital, WHO/EURO Working Group Report.* Atlanta: CDC.

Krishna, A. (1999), Creating and Harnessing Social Capital, in *Social Capital: A Multifaceted Perspective*, edited by I. Serageldin. Washington, DC: World Bank, pp. 71–93.

Krishna, A. and Uphoff, N. (2002), Mapping and measuring social capital through assessment of collective action to conserve and develop watersheds in Rajasthan, India, in *The Role of Social Capital in Development*, edited by T. Van Bastelaer. Melbourne: Cambridge University Press, pp. 85–88, 115–124.

Krishna, A. and Uphoff, N. (1999), *Mapping and Measuring Social Capital: A Conceptual and Empirical Study of Collective Action for Conserving and Developing Watersheds in Rajasthan, India.* Forthcoming as a publication of the Social Development Department, The World Bank.

Krueger, A.B. and Summers, L.H. (1988), Efficiency Wages and Inter-Industry Wages Structure. *Econometrica* 56 (March): 259–93.

Kuznets, S. (1971), *Economic Growth of Nations: Total Output and Population Structure.* Cambridge, MA: MIT Press.

Labonte, R. (1999), Social capital and community development. *Australian and New Zealand Journal of Public Health* 23: 430–433.

Lacey, C. (1988), The Idea of a Socialist Education, in *Education in Search of a Future.* Basingstoke, edited by H. Lauder and P. Brown. Falmer Press, 91–8.

Ladas, S.P. (1932), *The Balkan Exchange of Minorities: Bulgaria, Greece and Turkey.* New York: Macmillan.

Ladd, E.C. (1996), The Data Just Don't Show Erosion of America's Social Capital. *Public Perspective* 7: 1–30.

Ladd, E.C. (1996), The Data Just Don't Show Erosion of America's Social Capital. *The Public Prospect* 7(4): 7–16.

Lamont, M. (1992), *Money, Morals, and Manners: The Culture of the French and the American Upper-Middle Class.* Chicago: University of Chicago Press.

Lamont, M. and Lareau A. (1988), Cultural Capital: Allusions, Gaps, and Glissandos in Recent Theoretical Developments. *Sociological Theory* 6: 153–68.

Landry, R., Amara, N. and Lamari, M. (2002), Does Social Capital Determine Innovation? To What Extent? *Technology Forecasting and Social Change* 69, 681–701.

Langford, C. (1989), *A Polite and Commercial People: England 1727–83.* Oxford: Oxford University Press.

Lappe, F., Moore Du Bois, K. and Martin, P. (1997), Building social capital without looking backward. *National Civic Review* 86: 119.

Lareau, A. (2003), *Unequal Childhoods: Class, Race, and Family Life.* Berkeley, CA: University of California Press.

Lareau, A. and McNamara H.E. (1999), Moments of Social Inclusion and Exclusion: Race, Class, and Cultural Capital in Family–School Relationships. *Sociology of Education* 72: 37–53

Lareau, A. and Weininger, E.B. (2003), Cultural Capital in Educational Research: A Critical Assessment. *Theory and Society* 32(5/6): 567–606.

Lasch, C. (1991), *The Culture of Narcissism.* New York: Norton.

Lash, S. and Urry, J. (1993), *Economies of Signs and Space.* London: Sage.

Latour, B. (2005), *Reassembling the Social* Oxford: Oxford University Press.

Lattas, A. (2011), Violence and Pleasure: neoliberalism, civil society and corporate governance in West New Britain. *Oceania.* March 1.

Lauder, H. and Hughes, D. (1990), Social Origins, Destinations and Educational Inequality, in J. Codd, R. Harker, and R. Nash (eds), *Political Issues in New Zealand Education.* Palmerston North: The Dunmore Press.

LAUGIQ, J. (2000), Social Capital Trumping Class and Cultural Capital? Engagement in School among Immigrant Youth. in *Social Capital: Critical Perspectives*, edited by T. Schuller. Oxford: Oxford University Press.

Lauglo, J. (1996), *Motbakke, men mer driv? Innvandrerungdom i norsk skole.* UNGforskrapport 6/96. Oslo: NOVA.

Lauglo, J. (1999), Working Harder to Make the Grade. Immigrant Youth in Norwegian Schools. *Journal of Youth Studies,* 2(1): 77–100.

Lave, J. and Wenger, E. (1991), *Situated Learning: Legitimate Peripheral Participation.* Cambridge: Cambridge University Press.

Lawrence, B. and Hayden, C. (1997), Primary School Exclusions. *Educational Research and Evaluation* 3(1): 54–77.

Laybourn, K. (1990), *Britain on the Breadline: A Social and Political History of Britain Between the Wars.* Gloucester: Alan Sutton.

Lazear, E.P. (1998), *Personnel Economics for Managers.* New York: John Wiley.

Lazega, E. and Pattison, P.E. (2001), Social capital as social mechanisms and collective assets: The example of status auctions among colleagues, in *Social Capital: Theory and Research*, edited by R. Burt. New York: Aldine de Gruyter, pp. 185–208.

Leana, C.R., and Van Buren, H.J. III. (1999), Organisational social capital and employment practices. *Academy of Management Review* 24: 538–55.

Lee, B.A., Oropesa, R.S., Metch, B.J. and Guest, A.M. (1984), Testing the Decline-of-Community Thesis: Neighborhood Organizations in Seattle, 1929–1979. *American Journal of Sociology* 89: 1161–88.

Lee, F. and Harley, S. (1998), Peer Review, the Research Assessment Exercise and the Demise of Non-Mainstream Economics. *Capital and Class*, 66: 23–51.

Leeder, S. and Dominello, A. (1999), Social capital and its relevance to health and family policy. *Australian and New Zealand Journal of Public Health* 23: 424–9.

Lehman, E. (1987), The Crisis of Political Legitimacy: What Is It; Who's Got It; Who Needs It. *Research in Political Sociology* 3: 203–21.

Lemann, N. (1996), Kicking in Groups. *Atlantic Monthly* 277(4): 22–6.

Lemmel, L. (2001), The dynamics of social capital: Creating trust-based relationships and trustworthy environments. *National Civic Review* 90: 97–103.

Lenman, B. (1981), *Integration, Enlightenment and Industrialisation: Scotland 1746–1832.* London: Edward Arnold.

Lester, G. (1998), Careers and Contingency. *Stanford Law Review* 51(1).

Levi, M. (1996), Social and Unsocial Capital: A Review Essay of Putnam's "Making Democracy Work". *Politics and Society*, 24(1): 45–55.

Levi, P. (1959), *Survival in Auschwitz: The Nazi Assault on Humanity.* New York: Orion Press.

Lévi-Strauss, C. (1969), *The Elementary Structures of Kinship.* Boston: Beacon Press.

Levitt, I. (1988), *Government and Social Conditions in Scotland, 1845–1919.* Edinburgh: Scottish History Society.

Li, Y., Savage, M. and Pickles, A. (2003), Social capital and social exclusion in England and Wales (1972–1999). *British Journal of Sociology* 54: 497–526.

Light, I. and C. Rosenstein, (1995), *Race, Ethnicity, and Entrepreneurship in Urban America.* New York: Aldine de Gruyter.

Light, I. and Bonacich, E. (1988), *Immigrant Entrepreneurs.* Berkeley, CA: University of California Press,

Light, I., Bhachu, P. and Karageorgis, S. (1993), Migration Networks and Immigrant Entrepreneurship, in *Immigration and Entrepreneurship. Culture, Capital and Ethnic Networks*, edited by I. Light and P. Bhachu. New Brunswick, NJ: Transaction Publishers, pp. 25–49.

Lin, N. (1976), *Foundations of Social Research.* New York: McGraw-Hill.

Lin, N. (1999), Building a network theory of social capital *Connections* 22(1): 28–51.

Lin, N. (2000), Inequality in Social Capital *Contemporary Sociology* 29(6) 785–795.

Lin, N., Cook, K.S. and Burt, R.S. (2001a), *Social Capital: Theory and Research.* New York: Aldine de Gruyter.

Lin, X. (2007), Small Business and Entrepreneurship. *Journal of Small Business and Entrepreneurship.*

Lippman, S.A. and Rumelt, R.P. (1982), Uncertain Imitability: An Analysis of Interfirm Differences in Efficiency under Competition. *Bell Journal of Economics* 12: 418–38.

Lipset, S.M., and Schneider, W. (1983), *The Confidence Gap: Business, Labor, and Government in the Public Mind.* New York: Free Press.

Lipset, S. M., Trow, M.A. and Coleman, J.S. (1956), *Union Democracy: The Internal Politics of the International Typographical Union.* Glencoe, IL: Free Press.

Llewllyn, C., and Payne, C. (1980), *Social Mobility and Class Structure in Modern Britain.* Oxford: Clarendon Press.

Loasby, B.J. (1992), Market Co-ordination, in B.J. Caldwell and S. Boehm (eds), *Austrian Economics: Tension and New Directions.* Boston: Kluwer, pp. 137–56.

Locke, J. (1947), *On Politics and Education.* Roslyn, NY: Black.

Locke, J. (1963), Some thoughts concerning education, in *The Works of John Locke*, Vol. 9. Aalen, Germany: ScientiaVerlag.

Lockwood, D., Bechofer, R, and Piatt, J. (1968–9), *The Affluent Worker, 3 vols.* Cambridge: Cambridge University Press.

Loizos, P. (2000). Are Refugees Social Capitalists? in *Social Capital: Critical Perspectives*, edited by T. Schuller. Oxford: Oxford University Press, pp. 132–49.

Lomas, J. (1998), Social Capital and Health: Implications for Public Health and Epidemiology. *Social Science and Medicine* 47(9): 1181–88.

Looker, E.D. (1994), Active Capital: The Impact of Parents on Youths' Educational Performance and Plans, in *Sociology of Education in Canada: Critical Perspectives on Theory, Research, and Practice*, edited by L. Erwin and D. MacLennan. Toronto: Copp Clark Longman, pp. 164–87.

Lopez, L. and Stack, C. (2001), Social Capital and the Culture of Power: Lessons from the Field, in *Social Capital and Poor Communities*, edited by S. Saegert, J. Phillip Thompson, and M. Warren. New York: Russell Sage Foundation.

Lorensen, M. (2002), Building social capital. *Journal of Family and Consumer Sciences* 94: 80.

Loury, G. (1977), A Dynamic Theory of Racial Income Difference, in *Women, Minorities, and Employment Discrimination*, edited by P.A. Wallace and A. LeMund. Lexington, MA: Lexington Books.

Loury, G. (1977), A Dynamic Theory of Radical Income Differences, in *Women, Minorities, and Employment Discrimination*, edited by A. LeMund. Lexington, MA: Lexington Books.

Loury, G. (1992), The economics of discrimination: Getting to the core of the problem. *Harvard Journal for African American Public Policy* 1: 91–110.

Lowndes, V., Stoker, G., Pratchett, L., Leach, S., and Wingfield, M. (1998), *Enhancing Public Participation in Local Government.* London: Department of the Environment, Transport and Regions.

Luhmann, N. (1979), *Trust and Power.* Chichester: Wiley.

Luhmann, N. (1988), Familiarity, Confidence, Trust: Problems and Alternatives. in *Trust: Making and Breaking Cooperative Relationships,* edited by D. Gambetta. New York: Basic Blackwell, pp. 94–107.

Lundvall, B. (1992), *National Systems of Innovation: Towards a Theory of Innovation and Interactive Learning* London: Pinter.

Lundvall, B.A. and Maskell, P. (2000). Nation States and Economic Development: From National Systems of Production to National Systems of Knowledge Creation and Learning, in *The Oxford Handbook of Economic Geography*, edited by Clark G.L., Feldman, M.P and Gertler M.S. New York: Oxford University Press.

Lynch, L.M., and Black, S.E. (1998), Beyond the incidence of employer-provided training. *Industrial and Labour Relations Review* 52: 64–81.

Lyons, M. (2000), Non-profit organisations, social capital and social policy in Australia, in *Social capital and public policy in Australia*, edited by I. Winter. Melbourne: National Library of Australia. pp. 165–91.

Lyons, M. (2001), *Third Sector: The Contribution of Nonprofit and Cooperative Enterprises in Australia* London: Allen and Unwin, p. 20.

MacGillivray, A., Weston, C., and Unsworth, C. (1998), *Communities Count: A Step by Step Guide to Community Sustainability Indicators.* London: New Economics Foundation.

Macintyre, S. and Ellaway, A. (1999), *Local Opportunity Structures, Social Capital and Social Inequalities in Health: What Can Central and Local Government Do?* Paper presented at the 11th Australian Health Promotion Conference, Perth, May.

Mackintosh, J.P. (1968), *The Devolution of Power.* Harmondsworth: Penguin.

MacIntyre, A. (1985), *After Virtue.* London: Duckworth.

Macnaghten, P., Grove-White, R., Jacobs, M., and Wynne, B. (1995), *Public Perceptions and Sustainability in Lancashire: Indicators, Institutions and Participation.* Lancaster: Centre for the Study of Environmental Change, Lancaster University for Lancashire County Council.

MacRae, D. (1969), Adam Ferguson, in *The Founding Fathers of Social Science* edited by T. Raison. Harmondsworth: Penguin, pp. 17–26.

Madden, E.H. (1968), *Civil Disobedience and Moral Law in Nineteenth Century American Philosophy.* Seattle: University of Washington Press.

Madden, E.H. (1998), Common Sense School, in E. Craig (ed.), *Encyclopaedia of Philosophy*. London: Routledge, pp. 446–8.

Maglen, L.R. (1990). Challenging the human capital orthodoxy: The education-productivity link re-examined. *The Economic Record* 66(195): 281–94.

Malmberg, A. and Maskell, P. (1997), Towards an Explanation of Industry Agglomeration and Regional Specialization. *European Planning Studies* 5(1): 25–41.

Maloney, W.A. (1999), Contracting Out the Participation Function: Social Capital and Checkbook Participation, in *Social Capital and European Democracy* edited by J. van Deth, M. Maraffi, K. Newton, and P. Whiteley. London: Routledge, pp. 108–19.

Maloney, W.A. and Jordan, G. (1997), The Rise of Protest Businesses in Britain, in *Private Groups and Public Life: Social Participation, Voluntary Associations, and Political Involvement in Representative Democracies*, edited by J.W. van Deth. London: Routledge, pp. 107–24.

Maloney, W.A., Smith, G., and Stoker, G. (1998), *Social Capital and Urban Governance: Adding a More Contextualized "Top-Down" Perspective.* Paper presented to Political Studies Association Workshop, University of Bath Jean Monnet Centre of Excellence, 6 November.

Manns, J.W. (1994), *Reid and his French Disciples.* Leiden: Brill.

Mansur, F. (1972), *Bodrum: A Town in the Aegean.* Leiden: Brill.

Maraffi, M. (1994), Making Democracy Work [book review] *American Journal of Sociology* 99(5): 1348–49.

Maraffi, M. (1998), Voluntary Associations, Political Culture and Social Capital in Italy: A Complex Relationship. *European Consortium for Political Research News* 9: 15–17.

Marginson, S. (1993), *Education and public policy in Australia.* New York: University of Cambridge Press.

Marquand, D. (1988), *The Unprincipled Society.* London: Jonathan Cape.

Marr, A. (1995), *Ruling Britannia: The Failure and Future of British Democracy.* London: Michael Joseph.

Marsden, P. V. (1990), Network Data and Measurement. *Annual Review of Sociology*, 16: 435–63.

Marshall, A. [1890] (1930), *Principles of Economics* (8th edn). London: Macmillan.

Marshall, G. (1998), *Goldthorpe Class scheme. A Dictionary of sociology* http://www.encyclopedia.com accessed June 2, 2010.

Marshall, G., Newby, H., Rose, D., and Vogler, C. (1989), *Social Class in Modern Britain.* London: Routledge.

Marshall, R. and Zarkin, G. (1987), The Effect of Job Tenure on Wage Offers. *Journal of Labour Economics* 5: 301–24.

Marshall, T.H. (1950), *Citizenship and Social Class, and Other Essays.* Cambridge: Cambridge University Press.

Marwick, A. (1964), Middle Opinion in the Thirties: Planning, Progress, and Political "Agreement". *English Historical Review* 79: 285–98.

Marx, K. (1961), The Material Forces and the Relations of Production, in *Theories of Society: Foundations of Modern Sociological Theory*, edited by T. Parsons, E. Shils, K.D. Naegele, and J.R. Pitts. New York: Free Press, pp. 136–8.

Marx, K. (1976), *Capital* (Vol. 1, E. Mandel, ed.). Harmondsworth, UK: Penguin. (Original work published 1867).

Marx, K. (1981), *Capital* (Vol. 3, E. Mandel, ed.). Harmondsworth, UK: Penguin. (Original work published 1894).

Marx, K. *Capital,* volume III, ch. 29 pp. 465–6 of the International Publishers edition.

Maskay, F. (1996), *Women and Representation: Discourses of Equality and Difference.* Edinburgh: University of Edinburgh.

Maskell, P. (1997), Learning in the Village Economy of Denmark: The Role of Institutions and Policy in Sustaining Competitiveness, in *Regional Innovation Systems: The Role of Governance in a Globalized World*, edited by H.J. Braczyk, P. Cooke, and M. Heidenreich. London: UCL Press, pp. 190–213.

Maskell, P. (1998), Successful Low-Tech Industries in High-Cost Environments: The Case of the Danish Furniture Industry. *European Urban and Regional Studies* 5(2): 99–118.

Maskell, P. (2000), Social Capital, Innovation and Competitiveness, in *Social Capital: Critical Perspectives*, edited by Baron, S., Field, J. and Schuller, T. Oxford: Oxford University Press, pp. 111–23.

Maskell, P. and Tornqvist, G. (1999), *Building a Cross-Border Learning Region: The Emergence of the Northern European Oresund Region.* Copenhagen: Copenhagen Business School Press.

Masten, S.E., Meehan, J.W. and Snyder, E.A. (1989), Vertical Integration in the U.S. Auto Industry: A Note on the Influence of Transaction Specific Assets. *Journal of Economic Behavior and Organization* 12 (October): 265–73.

Matarosso, F. (1997), *Use or Ornament?: The Social Impact of Participation in the Arts.* London: Comedia.

Maxwell, S. (1982), The Secular Pulpit: Presbyterian Democracy in the Twentieth Century, in *Scottish Government Yearbook 1982*, edited by H.M. Drucker and N. Drucker. Edinburgh: Unit for the Study of Government in Scotland, University of Edinburgh, pp. 181–98.

Mayanja, M.K. (2002), *Graduate employment: Investing in the service mandate of the African university.* Paper presented at the Symposium on the African Universities in the 21st Century. Dakar, Senegal.

Maynard, R.A. and Mcgrath, D.J. (1997), Family Structure, Fertility and Child Welfare, in *The Social Benefits of Education*, edited by J. Behrman and N. Stacey. Detroit: University of Michigan Press, pp. 125–74.

McChesney, R.W. (1997), "The Global Media Giants: The Nine Firms that Dominate theWorld," *Extra* 10.6 (November/December), http://www.fair.org/extra/9711/ gmg.html.

McChesney, R.W. (2001), "Global Media, Neoliberalism, and Imperialism," *Monthly Review* 52.10 (March): http://www.monthlyreview.org/301rwm.html.

McCrone, D. (1992), *Understanding Scotland: The Sociology of a Stateless Nation.* London: Routledge.

McCrone, D., and Paterson, L. (1998), *Politics and Society in Scotland (2nd edn).* London: Macmillan.

McCrone, D., Paterson, L. and Surridge, P. (1999), *The Scottish Electorate: The 1997 General Election and Beyond.* London: Macmillan.

McLaren, P. (1994), *Life in schools, an introduction to critical pedagogy: the foundations of education* (2nd edn). London, UK: Longman.

McLean, S.L., Schultz, D.A. and Steger, M.B. (2000), Introduction, in *Social Capital Critical Perspectives on Community and "Bowling Alone"* edited by S.L. McLean, D.A. Schultz, and M.B. Steger. New York and London: New York University Press, pp. 1–20.

McMahon, W. (1998), Conceptual Framework for the Analysis of the Social Benefits of Lifelong Learning. *Education Economics* 6(3): 309–46.

McMillan, D. and Chavis, D. (1986), Sense of Community: A Definition and Theory. *Journal of Community Psychology* 14(1): 6–23, 282 References.

McMillan, J. (1997), *Losing Sight of Tinkerbell*. The Herald, 16 August: 32, reprinted in L. Paterson (ed.) (1998). *A Diverse Assembly: The Debate on a Scottish Parliament*. Edinburgh: Edinburgh University Press, pp. 296–8.

McNeal Jr., R.B. (2001), Differential effects of parental involvement on cognitive and behavioral outcomes by socioeconomic status. *Journal of Socio-Economics* 30(2).

McNeely, C.L.; Figueroa-Garcia, A. (2003), U.S. educational outcomes and the new Latino immigrant. *International Journal of Economic Development*. October 1.

McPherson, J.M. (1982), Hypernetwork Sampling: Duality and Differentiation among Voluntary Associations. *Social Networks* 3: 225–49.

McQueen, H. (2011), *Fictitious Capital*. Workers Bush Telegraph. Workers Bush Telegraph MPRA Paper No. 11761, posted 14 January 2009. 12: 29

Mead, G.H. (1967), *Mind, Self and Society,* Chicago: Chicago University Press.

Meade, J.E. (1972), The Theory of Labor-Managed Firms and of Profit Sharing. *Economic Journal* 82 (March supplement): 402–28.

Mellor, A. (1999), Victims of Bullying, in *Good Practice in Working with Victims of Violence*, edited by H. Kemshall and J. Prichard. London: Jessica Kingsley, pp. 75–88.

Menzel, U. (1980), *Der entwicklungsweg Danemarks (1880–1940) Ein Beitrag zum konzept autozentrierter entwickhing.* Projekt Untersuchung zur grundlegung einer praxisorientierten theorie autozentrierter entwicklung. Forschungsbericht No. 8. Bremen: Bremen Universitat.

Merton, R.K. (1964), *Social Theory and Social Structure*. New York: Free Press.

Meyerson, E.M. (1994), Human Capital, Social Capital and Compensation: The Relative Contribution of Social Contacts to Managers Incomes. *Acta Sociologica* 37: 383–99.

Michaelowa, K. (2000), *Returns to education in low income countries, evidence for Africa.* Retrieved 15 October, 2003, from http://hwwa.de/projectsRes/RP

Milbank, D. (2001), "Needed: Catchword for Bush Ideology," *Washington Post* (February 1): Al.

Milburn, K. (1995), A Critical Review of Peer Education with Young People with Special Reference to Sexual Health. *Health Education Research: Theory and Practice* 10(4): 407–20.

Miles M.B. and Huberman, A.M. (1994), *Qualitative Data Analysis*. Thousand Oaks, CA: Sage Publications.

Milgrom, P. and Roberts, J. (1992), *Economics, Organization and Management*. Englewood Cliffs, NJ: Prentice-Hall.

Mill, J.S. (1831), (1975), *Three Essays*. Oxford: Oxford University Press.

Mill, J.S. [1859] (1956), *On Liberty* (C. Shields, ed.). New York: Macmillan.

Miller, C. (1998), *Developing and Newly Industrializing Countries*. Cheltenham: Edward Elgar.

Mills, C.W. (1959), *The Sociological Imagination*. Harmondsworth: Penguin.

Mincer, J. (1974), *Schooling Experience and Earnings.* New York: Columbia University Press.

Mincer, J. and Jovanovic, B. (1981), Labor Mobility and Wages, in *Studies in Labor Markets,* edited by S. Rosen. New York: National Bureau of Economic Research, 21–63.

Mishel, L., Bernstein, J. and Schmitt, J. (2001), *The State of Working America 2000–2001.* Ithaca, NY: Cornell University Press.

Mittelman, J.H. (2000), *The Globalization Syndrome: Transformation and Resistance.* Princeton: Princeton University Press.

Mohan, G. and Mohan, J. (2002), Placing Social Capital, *Progress in Human Geography,* 26(2): 191–210.

Molina F. X. (2005), The Territorial Agglomerations of Firms: A Social Capital Perspective from the Spanish Tile Industry. *Growth and Change* 35(1) 74–99.

Molina F.X., Martinez, M.T., Ares, M.A., and Hoffmann, V.E. (2008), *La Estructura y Naturaleza del Capital Social en las Aglomeraciones Territoriales de Empresas* Bilbao: Fundación BBVA.

Molina, J.A., Ortega Grossman, R. and Robert, J. (2005), Blind investment: if people are a company's biggest asset, why don't Wall Street analysts pay more attention to them? *HR Magazine.*

Mondak, J. (1998), Editors Introduction, in *Political Psychology* 199(3): 434–40 (Special Issue: Psychological Approaches to Social Capital).

Mondal, A. Hye. (2000), Social capital formation: the role of NGO rural development programs in Bangladesh. *Policy Sciences* 33: 459–75.

Monteverde, K. and Teece, D.J. (1982a) Supplier Switching Costs and Vertical Integration in the Automobile Industry. *Bell Journal of Economics* 13 (Spring): 206–13.

Monteverde, K. and Teece, D.J. (1982b), Appropriable Rents and Quasi-Vertical Integration. *Journal of Law and Economics* 25 (October): 321–28.

Montgomery, J.D. (2000), Social capital as a policy resource. *Policy Sciences* 33: 227–43.

Moody, J. and Bearman, P.S. (1997), *Shaping School Climate: School Context, Adolescent Social Networks, and Attachment to Schools.* Manuscript. University of North Carolina at Chapel Hill, Department of Sociology.

Morgan, A. (1999), *Developing an Index of Social Capital: Experience from the Health Education Authority, England.* Paper presented to the 11th Australian Health Promotion Conference, Perth, May.

Morlino, L. (1995), Italy's Civic Divide *Journal of Democracy* 6(1): 173–77.

Morris, M. (1998), "Social Capital and Poverty in India." Working Paper, Institute of Development Studies, Sussex.

Morris, R.J. (1990), Scotland 1830–1914: The Making of a Nation Within a Nation, in W.H. Fraser and R.J. Morris (eds), *People and Society in Scotland,* Vol. II: 1830–1914. Edinburgh: John Donald, pp. 1–7.

Morrow, V. (1999), Conceptualising social capital in relation to the well-being of children and young people: a critical review. The Editorial Board of The *Sociological Review*: 744–65.

Morrow, V. (1999), Conceptualising Social Capital in Relation to Health and Well-Being for Children and Young People: A Critical Review. *Sociological Review* 47(4): 744–65.

Mortimore, P. and Whitty, G. (1999), School Improvement: A Remedy for Social Exclusion?, in A. Hayton (ed.), *Tackling Disaffection and Social Exclusion*. London: Kogan Page, pp. 80–94.

Morton, G. (1996), Scottish Rights and "Centralisation" in the Mid-Nineteenth Century. *Nations and Nationalism* 2: 257–79.

Morton, G. (1998a), Civil Society, Municipal Government and the State: Enshrinement, Empowerment and Legitimacy. Scotland, 1800–1929. *Urban History*, 25: 348–67.

Morton, G. (1998b), What If? The Significance of Scotlands Missing Nationalism in the Nineteenth Century, in *Image and Identity: The Making and Re-Making of Scotland Through the Ages*, edited by D. Broun, R. J. Finlay, and M. Lynch. Edinburgh: John Donald, pp. 157–76.

Morton, G. (1999), *Unionist Nationalism*. East Linton: Tuckwell.

Moser, C. (1998), The Asset Vulnerability Framework: Reassessing Urban Poverty Reduction Strategies. *World Development* 26(1): 1–19.

Moser, C. and Holland, J. (1997), *Urban Poverty and Violence in Jamaica*. World Bank Latin American and Caribbean Studies Viewpoints Series, Washington, D.C.

Moshe, A.B and Morikawa, T. (1990), "Estimation of Travel Demand Models from Multiple Data Sources," submitted to the Eleventh International Symposium on Transportation and Traffic Theory. Yokohama, Japan.

Mosris, C.T. and Adelman, I. (1988), *Comparative Patterns of Economic Development 1850–1914*. Baltimore: John Hopkins University Press.

Mouque, D. (1999), *Sixth Periodic Report on the Social and Economic Situation and Development of the Regions of the European Union*. Brussels: European Commission.

Mundo, P.A. (1992), *Interest Groups: Cases and Characteristics*. Chicago: Nelson Hall.

Munkirs, J. (1985), *The Transformation of American Capitalism*. Armonk, NY: M.E. Sharpe.

Munn, P. (1999a), The Darker Side of Pupil Culture, in J. Prosser (ed.), *School Culture*. London: Paul Chapman, pp. 111–21.

Munn, P. (2002), Social Capital, Schools, and Exclusions, in *Social Capital: Critical Perspectives*, edited by T. Schuller. Oxford: Oxford University Press.

Munn, P. Cullen, M.A., Johnstone, M., and Lloyd, G. (1997), *Exclusions from School and In-School Alternatives*. Edinburgh: Scottish Office (Interchange No. 47).

Munn, P., Lloyd, G., and Cullen, M.A. (2000), *Alternatives to Exclusion from School*. London: Sage.

Munn, P. (1999b), *Promoting Positive Discipline in Scottish Schools*. Edinburgh: Faculty of Education, University of Edinburgh.

Muntaner, C. and Lynch, J. (1999), Income Inequality, Social Cohesion and Class Relations: A Critique of Wilkinsons Neo-Durkheimian Research Program. *International Journal of Health Sendees* 29(1): 59–81.

Murnane, R. and Levy, F. (1999), *Teaching the New Basic Skills*. New York: Free Press.

Muthen, B.O. (1989), Latent Variable Modeling in Heterogeneous Populations. *Psychometrika* 54: 557–85.

Nahapiet, J. and Ghoshal, S. (1998), Social capital, intellectual capital, and the organizational advantage. *Academy of Management Review* 23: 242.

Nairn, T. (1977), *The Break-Up of Britain*. London: Verso.

Nairn, T. (1997), *Faces of Nationalism*. London: Verso.

Naphapiet, J. and Ghoshal, S. (1997), *Social Capital, Intellectual Capital and Organisational Advantage*, Management Research Papers 97(6). Oxford: Oxford Centre for Management Studies.

Narayan, D. (1997), *Voices of the Poor: Poverty and Social Capital in Tanzania, Environmentally and Socially Sustainable Development Studies and Monographs Series* 20. Washington, D.C.: World Bank.

Narayan, D. (1999), *Bonds and Bridges: Social Capital and Poverty* (Policy Research Working Paper 2167). Washington: World Bank.

Narayan, D. (2002), Bonds and bridges: social capital and poverty. in *Social Capital and Economic Development: Well-being in Developing Countries*, edited by S. Ramaswamy. Cheltenham: Edward Elgar.

Narayan, D. and Cassidy, M.F. (2001), A dimensional approach to measuring social capital: development and validation of a social capital inventory. *Current Sociology* 49: 59–102.

Narayan, D. and Pritchett, L. (1997), *Cents and Sociability: Household Income and Social Capital in Rural Tanzania* (Social Development Policy Research Working Paper No. 1796). Washington, D.C.: World Bank.

Narayan, D. and Pritchett, L. (1999), Social capital: Evidence and implications. pp. 269–96 in *Social Capital: A Multifaceted Perspective*, edited by I. Serageldin. Washington, D.C.: World Bank.

Nauck, B. (2000), Social Capital and Intergenerational Transmission of Cultural Capital Within a Regional Context, in *Adversity and Challenge in Life in the New Germany and in England*, edited by J. Bynner and R.K. Silbersen. London: Macmillan, pp. 212–38.

Neal, D. (1995), Industry-Specific Human Capital: Evidence from Displaced Workers. *Journal of Labour Economics* 13(4): 653–77.

Neal, D. (1997), The Effects of Catholic Secondary Schooling on Educational Achievement. *Journal of Labour Economics* 15(1): 98–123.

Nelson, J. M. (1994), Labour and Business Roles in Dual Transitions: Building Blocks or Stumbling Blocks? in *Intricate Links: Democratization and Market Reforms in Latin America and Eastern Europe*, edited by J.M. Nelson. New Brunswick, NJ: Transaction Publishers, pp. 147–94.

Nelson, R.R., and Winte, S.G. (1982), *An Evolutionary Theory of Economic Change*. Cambridge, MA: Belknap Press.

Newton, K. (1976), *Second City Politics*. Oxford: Oxford University Press.

Newton, K. (1997), Social Capital and Democracy. *American Behavioral Scientist* 40(5): 575–86. (Special Edition: Social Capital, Civil Society and Contemporary Democracy).

Nielsen, K. and Pedersen, O.K. (1988), The Negotiated Economy. Ideal and History. *Scandinavian Political Studies* 2(11): 79–101.

Norris, P. (1996), Does Television Erode Social Capital? A Reply to Putnam. *Political Science and Politics*, 29: 474–79.

North, D. (1990), *Institutions, Institutional Change and Economic Performance*. New York: Cambridge University Press.

Norton, A. (2001), The market for social capital. *Policy* Autumn 2001: 40–44.

Norton, H.S. (1985), *The Quest for Economic Stability: Roosevelt to Reagan*. Columbia: University of South Carolina Press.

Novos, I. (1995), Imperfections in labour Markets and the Scope of the Firm. *International Journal of Industrial Organization* 13(3): 387–410.

Novos, I. and Waldman, M. (1995), *Returns to Tenure: Conceptual and Empirical Issues*. Mimeo, Cornell University.

Nye, D.E. (1998), *Consuming Power: A Social History of American Energies*. Cambridge, MA: MIT Press.

Nye, J.S. (1997), In Government We Don't Trust. *Foreign Policy*, 108/Fall: 99–111.

Obstfeld, D. (2005), Social Networks, the Tertius Lungens Orientation, and Involvement in Innovation. *Administrative Science Quarterly* 50, 100–130.

O'Connell, M. (2003), Anti Social Capital. Civic Values versus Economic Equality in the EU. *European Sociological Review* 19(3): 241.

Ogbu, J.U. (1991), Immigrant and Involuntary Minorities in Comparative Perspective, in M.A. Gibson and J.U. Ogbu (eds), *Minority Status and Schooling: A Comparative Study of Immigrant and Involuntary Minorities*. New York: Garland, pp. 3–36.

Oh, H., Kilduff, M. and Brass, D.J. (1999), "Communal social capital, linking social capital, and economic outcomes." in paper presented at the annual meeting of the Academy of Management. Chicago.

Oi, W. (1962), Labour as a Quasi-Fixed Factor of Production, *Journal of Political Economy,* 70(6): 538–55.

Oliver, P.E. and Marwell, G. (1988), The Paradox of Group Size in Collective Action: A Theory of the Critical Mass, II. *American Sociological Review* 53(1), 1–8.

Olson, G. (2006), Appraising You as We Should. *Chronicle of Higher Education* 52(39).

Olson, M. (1982), *The Rise and Decline of Nations: Economic Growth, Stagflation and Social Rigidities.* New Haven: Yale University Press.

Omori, T. (2001), Balancing Economic Growth With Well Being: Implications Of The Japanese Experience. *ISUMA* 2(1), [Online], Available: www.isuma.net.

ONeill, B.J. (1987), *Social Inequality in a Portuguese Hamlet: Land, Late Marriage and Bastardy 1870–1978.* Cambridge: Cambridge University Press.

Onyx, J. and Bullen, P. (1997), *Measuring Social Capital in Five Communities in New South Wales: An Analysis* (Working Paper 41). Sydney: Centre for Australian Community Organisations and Management, University of Technology, Sydney.

Onyx, J. and Bullen, P. (2000), Sources of social capital, in I. Winter (ed.) *Social Capital and Public Policy in Australia.* Australian Institute of Family Studies, Melbourne, pp. 105–34.

Organisation for Economic Co-operation and Development (OECD), (1998), *The Knowledge–Based Economy.* Paris: OECD, p. 284, References.

Organisation for Economic Co-operation and Development (OECD), (1999), *Managing National Innovation Systems.* Paris: OECD.

Organization for Economic Co-operation and Development. (1985), *Education in Modern Society.* Paris: Author.

Organization for Economic Co-operation and Development. (1986a), *Education and effective economic performance: A preliminary analysis of the issues.* Paris: Author.

Organization for Economic Co-operation and Development. (1986b), *Productivity in industry.* Paris: Author.

Organization for Economic Co-operation and Development. (1986c), *OECD science and technology indicators, no. 2: R&D, inventions and competitiveness.* Paris: Author.

Organization for Economic Co-operation and Development. (1987), *Structural adjustment and economic performance.* Paris: Author.

Organization for Economic Co-operation and Development. (1990), *OECD in figures.* Paris: Author.

Orphanides, A. and Zervos, D. (1998), Myopia and Addictive Behaviour. *The Economic Journal* 108(446): 75–91.

Ortner, S. (2003), *New Jersey Dreaming: Capital, Culture, and the Class of '58.* Durham: Duke University Press.

Osier, A. and Hill, J. (1999), Exclusion from School and Racial Equality: An Examination of Government Proposals in the Light of Recent Research Evidence. *Cambridge Journal of Education* 29(1): 33–62.

Ostrom, E. (1994), Consituting social capital and collective action. *Journal of Theoretical Politics* 6: 527–562.

Ostrom, E. (2000), Social Capital: A Fad or a Fundamental Concept? in *Social Capital: A Multifaceted Perspective, edited by* P. Dasgupta and I. Serageldin. Washington, D.C.: World Bank, 172–214.

O'Toole, T. (1990), *The Economic History of the United States.* Minneapolis: Lerner Publications.

Paci, M. (1977), Education and the capitalist labour market. In J. Karabel and A.H. Halsey (Eds.), *Power and Ideology in Education.* New York: Oxford University Press, pp. 340–55.

Pahl, R. and Spencer, L. (1997), The Politics of Friendship. *Renewal* 5(3/4): 100–107.

Paldam, M. and Tinggaard Svendsen, G. (2000), An essay on social capital: looking for the fire behind the smoke. *European Journal of Political Economy* 16: 339–66.

Pantoja, E. (1999), "Exploring the concept of social capital and its relevance for community based development: the case of minin areas in Orissa, India." South Asia Infrastructure Unit, World Bank.

Parcel, T.L. and Menaghan, E.G. (1994), Early Parental Work, Family Social Capital and Early Childhood Outcomes. *American Journal of Sociology* 99(4): 972–1009.

Park, R. (1928), Human Migration and the Marginal Man. *American Journal of Sociology* 33: 881–93.

Parker, M. (1990), *Creating Shared Vision.* Illinois: Dialog International Ltd.

Parry, G., Moyser, G. and Day, N. (1992), *Political Participation and Democracy in Britain.* Cambridge: Cambridge University Press.

Parsons, C. (1996), Permanent Exclusions from School in England: Trends, Causes and Responses. *Children and Society* 10: 177–86.

Parsons, C. (1999), *Education, Exclusion and Citizenship.* London: Routledge.

Parsons, D. (1972), Specific Human Capital: An Application to Quit Rates and Layoff Rates. *Journal of Political Economy* 1120–43.

Parsons, T. (1959), The School Class as a Social System: Some of its Functions in American Society. *Harvard Educational Review,* 29: 297–318.

Pateman, C. (1989), *The Disorder of Women: Democracy, Feminism and Political Theory.* Cambridge: Polity Press.

Paterson, L. (1994), *The Autonomy of Modern Scotland.* Edinburgh: Edinburgh University Press.

Paterson, L. and Wyn Jones, R. (1999), Does Civil Society Drive Constitutional Change? The Cases of Wales and Scotland, in *Wales and Scotland: Nations Again?* edited by B. Taylor and K. Thomson. Cardiff: University of Wales Press, pp. 169–97.

Pattie, S.P. (1997). *Faith in History: Armenians Rebuilding Community.* Washington and London: Smithsonian Institution Press.

Paul, S. (1987), *Community Participation in Development Projects.* Washington, D.C.: World Bank, Discussion Paper No. 6.

Paxton, P. (1998), "Capitalizing on Community: Social Capital and the Democratic Society." PhD. dissertation. University of North Carolina at Chapel Hill, Department of Sociology.

Paxton, P. (1999), Is Social Capital Declining in the United States? A Multiple Indicator Assessment. *The American Journal of Sociology* 105(1) (July), 88–127.

Pena, M.V.J. and Lindo-Fuentes, H. (1998), *Community Organization, Values and Social Capital in Panama*. Central America Country Management Unit Economic Notes No. 9, The World Bank, Washington, D.C.

Pennar, K. (1997), The tie that leads to prosperity: The economic value of social bonds is only beginning to be measured. *Business Weekly*: 153–155.

Pentzopoulos, D. (1962), *The Balkan Exchange of Minorities*. The Hague: Mouton.

Perkin, H. (1969), *The Origins of Modern English Society 1780–1880*. London: Routledge and Kegan Paul.

Perks, T. (2012), Physical capital and the embodied nature of income inequality: gender differences in the effect of body size on workers incomes in Canada. *Canadian Review of Sociology* 49(1).

Perreault, T. (2003), Social Capital, Develpment, and Indigenus Politics in Ecuadorian Amazonia. *Geographical Review* 93(3): Jul.

Perreira, K.M., Mullan-Harris, K. and Lee, D. (2006), Making it in America: High School completion by Immigrant and Native Youth. *Demography* 43(3) August: 511–36.

Petersen, D. M. (2002), The Potential of Social Capital Measures in the Evaluation of Comprehensive Community-Based Health Initiatives. *The American Journal of Evaluation* 23: 55–64.

Peterson, R.A., and Kern, R.M. (1996), Changing Highbrow Taste: From Snob to Omnivore *American Sociological Review* 61, 900–907.

Peterson, R., and Simkus, A. (1992), How Musical Taste Groups Mark Occupational Status Groups, in *Cultivating Differences: Symbolic Boundaries and the Making of Inequality*, edited by Lamont, M., and Fournier, M. University of Chicago Press, Chicago, pp. 152–86.

Phelps Brown, H. (1988), *Egalitarianism and the Generation of Inequality.* Oxford: Clarendon Press.

Phillips, M., Brooks-Gunn, J., Duncan, G., Klebanov, P. and Crane, J. (1998), Family Background, Parenting Practices, and the Black–White Test Score Gap, in *The Black–White Test Score Cap*, edited by C. Jencks and M. Phillips. Washington, DC: Brookings Institution Press, pp. 103–48.

Phillipson, N. (1969), Nationalism and Ideology, in J.N. Wolfe (ed.), *Government and Nationalism in Scotland*. Edinburgh: Edinburgh University Press, pp. 167–88.

Phillipson, N. (1983), The Pursuit of Virtue in Scottish University Education, in N. Phillipson (ed.), *Universities, Society and the Future*. Edinburgh: Edinburgh University Press, 87–109.

Piachaud, D. (1999), Progress on Poverty: Will Blair Deliver on Eliminating Child Poverty? *New Economy*, 6(3): 154–60.

Piatt, S. and Treneman, A. (1997), *The Feel Good Factor: A Citizens Handbook for Improving your Quality of Life*. London: Channel 4 Television. Politics and Society (1996). Special section of critical assessments of Making Democracy Work, with articles by Ellis Goldberg, Filippo Sabetti, Margaret Levi and Daniela Gobetti. *Politics and Society*, 24(1): 3–82.

Piazza-Georgi, B. (2002), The role of human and social capital in growth: Extending our understanding. *Cambridge Journal of Economics* 26: 461–79.

Pierson, C. (1991). *Beyond the Welfare State?* Cambridge: Polity Press.

Pigou, A.C. (1928), *A Study in Public Finance*. London: Macmillan, p. 29.

Pilkington, P. (2002), Social capital and health: measuring and understanding social capital at a local level could help to tackle health inequalities more effectively. *Journal of Public Health Medicine* 24: 156–59.

Polanyi, K. (1944), *The Great Transformation*. Boston: Beacon Press.

Popay, J. (2000), "Social capital: The role of narrative and historical research." *Journal of Epidemiology and Community Health* 54: 401.

Pope J. (2003), *Social capital and social capital indicators: A reading list*. Working Paper Series No. 1. Public Health Information Development Unit, Adelaide.

Porter Liebeskind, J. (2000), Ownership, Incentives, and Control in New Biotechnology Firms, in *The New Relationship. Human Capital in the American Corporation* edited by M.M. Blair and T.A. Kochan, pp. 299–326.

Portes A. (1998), Social Capital: Its Origins and Application in Contemporary Sociology, *Annual Review of Sociology* 24: 1–24.

Portes, A. (1987), The Social Origins of the Cuban Enclave Economy of Miami. *Sociological Perspectives* 30: 340–72.

Portes, A. (1995), Economic Sociology and the Sociology of Immigration: A Conceptual Overview, in A. Portes (ed.), *The Economic Sociology of Immigration*. New York: Russell Sage Foundation, pp. 1–41.

Portes, A. (1995), *The Economic Sociology of Immigration: Essays on Networks, Ethnicity and Entrepreneurship*. New York: Russell Sage Foundation.

Portes, A. (1998), Social Capital: Its Origins and Applications in Modern Sociology. *Annual Review of Sociology* 24: 1–24.

Portes, A. and A. Stepick (1993), *City on the Edge: The Transformation of Miami*. Berkeley: University of California Press.

Portes, A. and Sensenbrenner, L. (1993), Embeddedness and Immigration: Notes on the Social Determinants of Economic Action. *American Journal of Sociology* 98(6): 1320–50.

Portes, A. and MacLeod, D. (1996), Educational Progress of Children of Immigrants: The Roles of Class, Ethnicity, and School Context. *Sociology of Education* 69: 255–75.

Portes, A. and Landolt, P. (1996), The Downside of Social Capital. *The American Prospect* 26: 18–21.

Portes, A. and Sensenbrenner, J. (1993), Embeddedness and immigration: Notes on the social determinants of economic action. *American Journal of Sociology* 98: 1320–50.

Portney, K. E. and J. M. Berry, (1997), Mobilizing Minority Communities: Social Capital and Participation in Urban Neighborhoods. *American Behavioral Scientist* 40(5), 632–44.

Prahalad, C.K. and Hamel, G. (1990), The Core Competence of the Corporation. *Harvard Business Review*, 3: 79–91.

Prasad, L. (2007), *Role of cognitive social capital in sustainable irrigation management: some observations from Western Tarai.* Contributions to Nepalese Studies Nepal.

Preece, J. (2002), *"Supporting community and building social capital."* Association for Computing Machinery. Communications of the ACM 45: 37–39.

Prendergast, C. (1993), The Role of Promotion in Inducing Specific Human Capital Acquisition. *Quarterly Journal of Economics 108* (May): 523–34.

Pretty, J. and Frank, B.R. (2000), *"Participation and social capital formation in natural resource management: Achievements and lessons."* in Plenary paper for International Landcare 2000 Conference. Melbourne, Australia.

Pretty, J. and Ward, H. (2001), Social capital and the environment. *World Development* 29: 209–227.

Price, B. (2002), Social capital and factors affecting civic engagement as reported by leaders of voluntary associations. *Social Science Journal* 39: 119–127.

Pruijt, H. (2002), Social capital and the equalizing potential of the Internet. *Social Science Computer Review* 20: 109–115.

Psacharopoulos, G. (1988), Education and development: A review. *Research Observer, 3,* 99–116.

Putnam, R.D. (1936), The Prosperous Community: Social Capital and Public Life. *The American Prospect*, 4/13: 11–18.

Putnam, R.D. (1993), "The Prosperous Community – Social Capital and Public Life." *American Prospect* (13, 35–42).

Putnam, R.D. Leonardi, R. and Nanetti R.Y., (1993), *Making Democracy Work: Civic Traditions in Modern Italy.* Princeton: Princeton University Press.

Putnam, R.D. (1995), Bowling Alone: America's Declining Social Capital. *Journal of Democracy* 6: 65–78.

Putnam, R.D. (1996), The Strange Disappearance of Civic America. *American Prospect* 24: 34–48.

Putnam, R.D. (1996), Who Killed Civic America? *American Prospect*, March: 66–72.

Putnam, R.D. (1998a), *The Distribution of Social Capital in Contemporary America.* Plenary Address to Michigan State University International Conference on Social Capital, 20–2 April.

Putnam, R.D. (1998b), *Foreword.* Housing Policy Debate, 9: i–viii.

Putnam, R.D. (2000), *Bowling Alone: The Collapse and Revival of American Community.* New York: Simon & Schuster.

Putterman, L. (1984), On Some Recent Explanations of Why Capital Hires Labor. *Economic Inquiry* 22 (April): 171–87.

Putterman, L. and Kroszner, R.S. (1996), The Economic Nature of the Firm: A New Introduction, in *The Economic Nature of the Firm: A Reader, 2d ed.*, edited by Putterman and Kroszner, 1–31. Cambridge: Cambridge University Press.

Putzell, J. (1997), Accounting for the "Dark Side" of Social Capital: Reading Robert Putnam on Democracy. *Journal of International Development,* 9/7: 939–49 (Special Issue on the Concept of Social Capital).

Quibria, M.G. (2003), The Puzzle of Social Capital. A Critical Review, *Asian Development Review,* 20(2): 19–39.

R.H. (1967), *Robert E. Park: On Social Control and Collective Behavior.* Chicago: University of Chicago Press.

Rajan, R.G., and Zingales, L. (1998), Power in a Theory of the Firm. *Quarterly Journal of Economics* 113(2): 387–432.

Randolph, B. and Judd, B. (1999), *Social exclusion, neighbourhood renewal and large public housing estates.* Paper presented to the Social Policy Research Centre Conference, "Social Policy for the 21st Century: Justice and Responsibility". University of New South Wales, July 1999.

Ranson, S. (1993), Markets or Democracy for Education. *British Journal of Educational Studies* 41(4): 333–52.

Ranson, S. and Stewart, J. (1994), *Management for the Public Domain.* London: Macmillan.

Ray, D. (2002), Preface. in *Social Capital Critical Perspectives on Community and "Bowling Alone"*, edited by S.L. McLean, D.A. Schultz, and M.B. Steger, pp. XI–XVI,

Read, D. (1961), *Press and People 1790–1850.* London: Arnold.

Real Vision. (2000), "Facts and Figures about our TV Habit." http://www.tv–turnoff.org. 280 M.B. Steger.

Reed, R. and DeFillippi, R.J. (1990), Causal Ambiguity, Barriers to Imitation and Sustainable Competitive Advantage. *Academy of Management Review*, 1(15): 88–102, 286 References.

Rees, G. (1997), Making a Learning Society: Education and Work in Industrial South Wales. *Welsh Journal of Education* 6(2): 4–16.

Rees, G., and Gorard, S. (1999), Some Sociological Alternatives to Human Capital Theory and their Implications for Research on Post-compulsory Education and Training. *Journal of Education and Work* 12(2): 117–40.

Rees, G., Fevre, R., Furlong, J., and Gorard, S. (1997), History, Place and the Learning Society. *Journal of Education Policy* 12(6): 485–97.

Rees, G., Fielder, S., and Rees, T. (1992), *Employees Access to Training Opportunities: Shaping the Social Structure of Labour Markets.* Paper to Seminar on Training and Recruitment, Royal Society of Arts, London.

Rees, G., Williamson, H., and Istance, D. (1996), "Status Zero": A Study of Jobless School-Leavers in South Wales. *Research Papers in Education*, 11(2): 219–35.

Reich, R. (1991), *The Work of Nations.* London: Simon & Schuster.

Reid, T. (1969), *Essays on the Intellectual Powers of Man.* Cambridge, MA: MIT Press.

Reiman, J. (1990), *The Rich Get Richer and the Poor Get Prison*, 3d edn. New York: Macmillan.

Renold, E., and Furlong, J. (1998), A Gendered Appraisal of the Transition to a Learning Society, in R. Benn (ed.), *Research, Teaching and Learning: Making Connections in the Education of Adults.* Leeds: SCUTREA, 62–7.

Rhodes, R.A.W. (1996), The New Governance: Governing Without Government. *Political Studies* 44(4): 652–67.

Richardson, G.B. (1953), Imperfect Knowledge and Economic Efficiency. *Oxford Economic Papers*, 5(2): 136–56.

Richardson, G.B. (1972), The Organisation of Industry. *Economic Journal* 82: 883–96.

Richardson, J. (1986), The Forms of Capital, in *Handbook of Theory and Research for the Sociology of Culture*, edited by J.G. Richardson. New York: Greenwood Press, pp. 241–58.

Riddell, S. (1997), *The Concept of a Learning Society for Adults with Learning Difficulties.* Professorial Lecture, Napier University, Edinburgh, June.

Riddell, S. (1999b), Supported Employment in Scotland: Theory and Practice. *Journal of Vocational Rehabilitation* 12(3): 181–95.

Riddell, S. (2000), The Meaning of the Learning Society for Adults with Learning Difficulties: Bold Rhetoric and Limited Opportunities, in F. Coffield (ed.), *Differing Visions of the Learning Society: Research Findings, ii.* Bristol: Policy Press.

Riddell, S., and Wilson, A. (1998), The Best Burgers? The Person with Learning Difficulties as Worker, in T. Shakespeare (ed.), *The Disability Reader.* London: Cassell, pp. 94–109.

Riddell, S., and Wilson, A. (1999), The Secret of Eternal Youth: Identity, Risk and Learning Difficulties. *British Journal of the Sociology of Education* 20(4): 483–99.

Riddell, S., Baron, S., and Wilson, A. (1999a), Captured Customers: People with Learning Difficulties in the Social Market. *British Educational Research Journal* 25(4): 445–61.

Rifkin, J. (1996), *The End of Work.* New York: Tarcher/Putnam.

Rissel, C. (1994), Empowerment: The Holy Grail of Health Promotion? *Health Promotion International* 9(1): 39–45.

Ritchie, M. (2000), Social capacity, sustainable development, and older people: lessons from community –based care in Southeast Asia. *Development in Practice* 10: 638–51.

Ritzen, J. (2001), "Social Cohesion, Public Policy, and Economic Growth: Implications for oecd Countries," keynote address presented at Symposium on the Contribution of Human and Social Capital to Sustained Economic Growth and Well Being, Quebec.

Roberts, J.M. (1976), Liberté, Egalité, Fraternité: Sources and Development of a Slogan. *Tijdschrift voor de Studie Van de Verlichting* 4(3/4): 329–69.

Roberts, K. (2004), Leisure inequalities, class divisions and social exclusion in present-day Britain. *Cultural Trends* 13(2), 57–71.

Robertson, J. (1990), The Legacy of Adam Smith: Government and Economic Development in the Wealth of Nations, in R. Bellamy (ed.), *Victorian Liberalism*. London: Routledge, pp. 15–41.

Robertson, R. (1992), *Globalization: Social Theory and Global Culture.* London: Sage.

Robinson, D. (1997), *Social Capital And Policy Development.* Wellington, New Zealand: Institute of Policy Studies, Victoria University of Wellington.

Robinson, D. (2000), Social Capital in Action. *Social Policy Journal of New Zealand*: 185.

Robison, Lindon J., Schmid, A.A. and Siles, M.E. (2002), Is social capital really capital? *Review of Social Economy* 60: 1–24.

Rodrik, D. (1998), *Where did all the growth go? External shocks, social conflict and growth collapses.* Cambridge: National Bureau of Economic Research.

Rojek, C. (2001), Leisure and life politics. *Leisure Sciences* 23, 115–25.

Romano, R. (1996), *Corporate Law and Corporate Governance.* Paper prepared for Conference on Firms, Markets and Organizations, University of California at Berkeley, Haas School of Business.

Romer, P.M. (1987), *Growth Based on Increasing Returns Due to Specialization.* Papers of the American Economic Association, 2(77): 56–62.

Roscigno, V. and Ainsworth-Darnell, J. (1999), Race, Cultural Capital, and Educational Resources: Persistent Inequalities and Achievement Returns. *Sociology of Education* 72: 158–78.

Rose, R. (1998), "Getting Things Done in an Anti-Modern Society: Social Capital and Networks in Russia." Social Capital Initiative Working Paper No. 6. The World Bank, Washington, D.C.

Rose, R. (1999), *What Does Social Capital Add to Individual Welfare? An Empirical Analysis of Russia*, Social Capital Initiative Working Paper No. 15, The World Bank, Washington DC. http://www.worldbank.org/poverty/scapital/wkrppr/wrkppr.htm

Rose, R. (2000), How much does social capital add to individual health? A survey study of Russians, *Social Science and Medicine* 51(9): 1421–35.

Rosen, S. (1985), Implicit Contracts: A Survey. *Journal of Economic Literature* 23 (September): 1144–75.

Rosen, S. (1987), "Human capital," in *The New Palgrave Dictionary of Economics, Vol. 2*, pp. 681–90, edited by S.N. Durlauf and L.E. Blume. Palgrave.

Rosenberg, M. (1956), Misanthropy and Political Ideology. *American Sociological Review* 21: 690–95.

Rosenberg, N. (1972), Technology and American Economic Growth. White Plains, NY: Sharpe. Rothstein, B. (forthcoming), Sweden – The Rise and Decline of Organized Social Capital, in R.D. Putnam (ed.), *A Decline of Social Capital?*

Political Culture as a Precondition for Democracy. Guterslöh: Bertelsmann Verlag.

Rosow, S.J. (2000), Globalization as Democratic Theory, *Millennium* 29(1): 27–45.

Rössel, J. (2011), Cultural capital and the variety of models of cultural consumption in the opera audience. *Sociological Quarterly* 52(1): 83–103.

Rossilah J. (2004), Human Capital: A Critique. *Jurnal Kemanusiaan* ISSN 1675–1930.

Rossman G.B. and Wilson B.L. (1984), Numbers and words: Combining quantitative and qualitative methods in a single large-scale evaluation study. *Evaluation Review* 9(5): 627–43.

Rossman G.B. and Wilson B.L. (1991), Numbers and words revisited: Being shamelessly eclectic. *Evaluation Review* 9(5): 627–43.

Rothman, H. (1999), The Editors and Authors of Economics Journals: A Case of Institutional Oligopoly *Economic Journal* 109(453): 1165–86.

Rothstein, B. (2003), Social capital, economic growth and quality of government: The causal mechanism. *New Political Economy* 8: 49–71.

Routledge, B.R. and von Amsberg, J. (2003), Social capital and growth. *Journal of Monetary Economics* 50: 167–93.

Rowthorn, B. (1992), Government Spending and Taxation in the Thatcher era, in J. Michie (ed.), *The Economic Legacy 1979–92*. London: Academic Press, 261–95.

Rubinstein, W.D. (1986), *Wealth and Inequality in Britain*. London: Faber & Faber.

Rudd, M.A. (2000), Live long and prosper: collective action, social capital and social vision. *Ecological Economics* 34: 131–44.

Rule, J. (1992), *The Vital Century. Englands Developing Economy 1715–1814*. Harlow: Longman.

Rumbaut, R.G. (1995), The New Californians: Comparative Research Findings on the Educational Progress of Immigrant Children, in *California's Immigrant Children: Theory, Research and Implications for Educational Policy*, edited by R.G. Rumbaut and W.A. Cornelius. San Diego: Center for U.S.–Mexican Studies, University of California.

Rumbaut, R.G. (19976), Assimilation and its Discontents: Between Rhetoric and Reality. *International Migration Review*, 31(4): 923–60.

Rumbaut, R.G. (1997a), *Passages to Adulthood: The Adaptation of Children of Immigrants in Southern California*. Report to the Russell Sage Foundation Board of Trustees from the project Children of Immigrants: The Adaptation Process of the Second Generation. Project Site: San Diego, California.

Runciman, W.G. (1998), *The Social Animal*. London: HarperCollins.

Rutherford, M. (2011), The Social Value of Self-Esteem. *Society* 48(5): 407–12.

Rutter, M., Maugham, B., Mortimore, P. and Ouston, J. (1979), *Fifteen Thousand Hours: Secondary Schools and Their Effects on Children*. London: Paul Chapman.

Ryan, A. (1995), *John Dewey and the High Tide of American Liberalism.* New York: Norton.

Sabetti, F. (1996), Path Dependency and Civic Culture: Some Lessons from Italy about Interpreting Social Experiments. *Politics and Society*, 24(1): 19–44.

Sahel, C. (1982), *Work and Politics.* Cambridge: Cambridge University Press.

Salamone, S. (1987), *In the Shadow of the Holy Mountain: The Genesis of a Rural Greek Community and its Refugee Heritage.* Boulder, CO: East European Monographs.

Salamone, S. and Stanton, J.B. (1986), Introducing the Nikokyra: Ideality and Reality in Social Process, in J. Dubisch (ed.), *Gender and Power in Rural Greece.* Princeton: Princeton University Press, pp. 97–120.

Sammons, P., Stoli, L., Lewis, D., and Ecob, R. (1988), *School Matters: The Junior Years.* London: Paul Chapman.

Sammons, P., Thomas, S., and Mortimore, P. (1997), *Forging Links: Effective Schools and Effective Departments.* London: Paul Chapman.

Samoff, J. (1994) (ed.), *Coping with crisis: Austerity, adjustment and human resources.* New York: UNESCO/ILO.

Sampson, R.J., Morenoff, J.D. and Earls, F. (1999), Beyond Social Capital: Spatial dynamics of collective efficiency for children. *American Sociological Review* 64: 633–60.

Sampson, R.J., Raudenbush, S.W. and Felton, E. (1997), Neighborhoods and Violent Crime: A Multilevel Study of Collective Efficacy. *Science* 277: 918–24.

Sandefur, R. and Laumann, E. (1998), A Paradigm for Social Capital. *Rationality and Society* 10(4): 481–501.

Sandel, M.J. (2011), *What Money Can't Buy. The Moral Limits of Markets.* Farrar, Straus & Giroux.

Sander, T.H. (2002), Social capital and new urbanism: leading a civic horse to water. *National Civic Review* 91: 213–21.

Sanders, J.M., and Nee, V. (1996), Immigrant Self-Employment: The Family as Social Capital and the Value of Human Capital. *American Sociological Review* 61: 231–49.

Sanderson, M. (1972), Literacy and Social Mobility in the Industrial Revolution in England. *Past and Present* 56: 75–104.

Sanks, H.T. (2007), Homo theologicus: toward a reflexive theology (with the help of Pierre Bourdieu). *Theological Studies* 68(3).

Sassoon, D. (1996), *One Hundred Years of Socialism.* London: I.B. Tauris.

Sauceda Curwen, M. (2009), Visiting Room 501. *Phi Delta Kappan* June.

Saxenian, A. (1994), *Regional Advantage: Culture and Competition in Silicon Valley and Route 128.* Cambridge, MA: Harvard University Press.

Sayer, A. (2005), *The Moral Significance of Class.* Cambridge: Cambridge University Press.

Schaefer-McDaniel, N.J. (2004), Conceptualizing Social Capital among Young People: Toward a New Theory. *Children, Youth and Environments* 14(1): 140–50.

Schaeffer, R.K. (1997), *Understanding Globalization: The Social Consequences of Political, Economic, and Environmental Change.* Lanham, MD: Rowman & Littlefield.

Schayegh, C. (2007), The social relevance of knowledge: Science and the formation of modern Iran, 1910s–40s. *Middle Eastern Studies* 43(6): 941–60.

Schiff, M. (1992), Social Capital, Labour Mobility, and Welfare. *Rationality and Society* 4: 157–75.

Schipani, C.A., Dworkin, T.M.; Kwolek-Folland, A. and Maurer, V.G. (2009), Pathways for women to obtain positions of organizational leadership: the significance of mentoring and networking. *16 Duke Journal of Gender Law & Policy* 89.

Schlozman, K.L., and Brady, H. (1995), *Voice and Equality: Civic Voluntarism in American Politics.* Cambridge, MA: Harvard University Press.

Schlozman, K.L., and Brady, H. (1997), The Big Tilt: Participatory Inequality in America. *The American Prospect* 32/May–June: 74–80.

Schmid, A.A. (2000), Affinity as social capital: its role in development. *The Journal of Socio-Economics* 29: 159.

Schmid, A.A. (2002), Using motive to distinguish social capital from its outputs. *Journal of Economic Issues* 36: 747–768.

Schneider, M., Teske, P., Marschall, M., Mintrom, M. and Roch, Ch. (1997), Institutional Arrangements and the Creation of Social Capital: The Effects of Public School Choice. *American Political Science Review* 91(1): 82–93.

Schofield, R.S. (1972), Crisis Mortality. *Local Population Studies*, 9: 9–22.

Schofield, R.S. (1981), Dimensions of Illiteracy in England 1750–1850, in H.J. Graff (ed.), *Literacy and Social Development in the West: A Reader.* Cambridge: Cambridge University Press, 201–13.

Scholte, J.A. (2000), *Globalization: A Critical Introduction.* New York: St. Martins Press.

Schudson, M, (1996), What If Civic Life Didn't Die? *The American Prospect*, 25/March–April: 17–20.

Schuller, T. (1995), is There Less Adult Learning in Scotland and Northern Ireland? A Quantitative Analysis. *Scottish Journal of Adult and Continuing Education*, 2(2): 71–80.

Schuller, T. (1997), Building Social Capital: Steps Towards a Learning Society. *Scottish Affairs*, 19/Spring: 77–91.

Schuller, T. (1999), Is There Divergence between Initial and Continuing Education in Scotland and Northern Ireland? *Scottish Journal of Adult and Continuing Education,* 5(2): 61–76.

Schuller, T. (2000), Human and Social Capital: The Search for Appropriate Techno-methodology. *Policy Studies*, 21(1): 25–35.

Schuller, T. (2000), Networks, Norms and Trust: Explaining Patterns of Lifelong Learning in Scotland and Northern Ireland, in F. Coffield (ed.), *Differing Visions of the Learning Society: Research Findings, ii*. Bristol: Policy Press.

Schuller, T. (2001), The Complementary Roles of Human and Social Capital. *ISUMA*, 2(1), [Online], Available: www.isuma.net.

Schuller, T. and Bamford, C. (2000), A Social Capital Approach to the Analysis of Continuing Education: Evidence from the UK Learning Society Research Programme. *Oxford Review of Education* 26(1): 5–20.

Schuller, T. and J. Field (1998), Social Capital, Human Capital and the Learning Society. *International Journal of Lifelong Education* 17(4): 226–35.

Schuller, T., Baron, S. and Field, J. (2000), Social capital: A Review and Critique, in Baron, S., Field, J. and Schuller, T. (eds). *Social Capital. Critical Perspectives,* Oxford: Oxford University Press, 1–3821. INGENIO (CSIC–UPV) Working Paper Series 2009/02.

Schutz, A. (1967), *The Phenomenology of the Social World*. London: Heinemann.

Schultz, A. (1995), Empowerment as a Multi-Level Construct: Perceived Control at the 288 References Individual, Organisational and Community Levels. *Health Educational Research: Theory and Practice* 10(3): 309–27.

Schultz, Ch.L. (2000), Has Job Security Eroded for American Workers? in *The New Relationship. Human Capital in the American Corporation*, edited by M.M. Blair and T.A. Kochan. McQueen, Humphrey, pp. 28–65.

Schultz, D.A. (2002), The Phenomenology of Democracy: Putnam, Pluralism, and Voluntary Associations, in *Social Capital Critical Perspectives on Community and "Bowling Alone"* edited by S.L. McLean, D.A. Schultz, and M.B. Steger. New York and London: New York University Press, pp. 74–98.

Schultz, T.W. (1959), Investment in man: An economist view. *The Social Service Review* 33(2): 109–17.

Schultz, T.W. (1960), Capital formation by education. *Journal of Political Economy* 68(6): 571–83.

Schultz, T.W. (1961), Investment in human capital. *American Economic Review, 51(1),* 1–17.

Schultz, T.W. (1975), The value of the ability to deal with disequilibrium. *Journal of Economic Literature, 13(3),* 827–846.

Schultz, T.W. (1989), Investment in people: Schooling in low income countries. *Economics of Education Review* 8(3): 219–23.

Schulz, T.W. (1961b), *Investment in Human Beings*. Chicago: Chicago University Press.

Schumpeter, J. (1934), *The Theory of Economic Development*. Cambridge, MA: Harvard University Press.

SCIG. (2000), Short papers from the April, 1998 Social Capital Conference at Michigan State University. *The Journal of Socio-Economics* 29: 579.

Scott, H. and Bolzman, C. (1999), Age in Exile: Europes Older Refugees and Exiles, in A. Bloch and C. Levy (eds), *Refugees, Citizenship and Social Policy in Europe*. New York: St. Martins Press, pp. 168–86.

Scott, J. (1991), *Social Network Analysis: A Handbook*. Thousand Oaks, CA: Sage.

Scott, P.H. (1989), *Cultural Independence*. Edinburgh: Scottish Centre for Economic and Social Research.

Scottish Consultative Committee on the Curriculum (SCCC). (1999), *Guidelines for the Curriculum of Secondary Schools*. Dundee: SCCC.

Scottish Office (1998), *Guidance on Issues Concerning Exclusion from School*, Circular No. 2/98. Edinburgh: Scottish Office.

Seely, J., Sim, A. and Loosely, E. (1956). *Crestwood Heights: a study of the culture of suburban life*. New York: Basic Books.

Sehr, D.T. (1997), *Education for Public Democracy*. New York: State University of New York Press.

Seligman, A.B. (1992), *The Idea of Civil Society*. New York: The Free Press.

Senghaas, D. (1982), *Von Europa lemen, Frankfurt am Main: Suhrkamp*. Translated by K.H. Kimmig (1985) as *The European Experience: A Historical Critique of Development Theory*. Leamington Spa and Dover: Berg Publishers.

Sennett, R. (1970), *The Uses of Disorder: Personal Identity and City Life*. New York: W.W. Norton.

Sennett, R. (1998), *The Corrosion of Character: The Personal Consequences of Work in the New Capitalism*. New York: W.W. Norton.

Sennett, R. and Cobb, J. (1977), *The Hidden Injuries of Class*. Cambridge: Cambridge University Press.

Serageldin, I. (eds) (2000) *Social Capital: A Midtifaceted Perspective*. Washington D.C.: World Bank.

Seymour W. Itzkoff (2003), *Intellectual Capital in Twenty-First-Century Politics*. Ashfield, MA: Paideia.

Shaffer, H.G. (1961), Investment in human capital: Comment. *The American Economic Review* 51(5), 1026–35.

Shaffer, H.G. (1999), *American Capitalism and the Changing Role of Government*. Westport, CT: Praeger.

Shapiro, M.J. (2002), Post-Liberal Civic Society and the Worlds of Neo-Tocquevillean Social Theory in *Social Capital Critical Perspectives on Community and "Bowling Alone"*, edited by S.L. McLean, D.A. Schultz, and M.B. Steger. New York and London: New York University Press, pp. 99–126.

Shapiro, S. (2009), Intellectual Labor Power, Cultural Capital, and the Value of Prestige. *South Atlantic Quarterly* 108: 2, Spring DOI 10.1215/00382876–2008–032

Shearmur, J. and Klein, D.B. (1997), Good Conduct in the Great Society: Adam Smith and the Role of Reputation, in D.B. Klein (ed.), *Reputation: Studies in the Voluntary Elicitation of Good Conduct*. Ann Arbor: University of Michigan Press, pp. 29–45.

Sher, R.B. (1985), *Church and University in the Scottish Enlightenment*. Edinburgh: Edinburgh University Press.

Sherrod, L. (2005), Work Your Cultural Capital, *Essence* 36(8).

Shiell, A. and Hawe, P. (1996), Health Promotion Community Development and the Tyranny of Individualism. *Health Economics* 5: 241–7.

Shimada, H. (1988), *Hyuman Wea No Keizaigaku: Amerika No Naka No Nihon Kigyo (Economics of Humanware)*. Tokyo: Iwanami Shoten.

Shleifer, A. and Summers, L.H. (1988), Breach of Trust in Hostile Takeovers, in *Corporate Takeovers: Causes and Consequences*, edited by A.J. Auerbach, University of Chicago Press, pp. 33–56.

Sicherman, N. and Galor, O. (1990), A Theory of Career Mobility. *Journal of Political Economy* 98(1): 169–92.

Silvey, R., and Elmhirst, R. (2003), Engendering Social Capital: Women Workers and Rural–Urban Networks in Indonesias Crisis. *World Development* 31: 865–79.

Simila, M. (1994), Andra generationens innvandrare i den svenska skolan, in R. Erikson and J.O. Jonsson (eds), *Sorteringen i skolan*. Stockholm: Carlssons.

Simmel, G. (1903), The Metropolis and Mental Life, in *The Sociology of Georg Simmel*, translated and edited by Kurt H. Wolff. New York: Free Press, pp. 409–24.

Simmel, G. (1971), *On Individuality and Social Forms*. Chicago: University of Chicago Press.

Simmons, O.S. (2011), Lost in transition: the implications of social capital for higher education access. *87 Notre Dame Law Review*, 284.

Sinclair-Desgagne, B., and Cadot, O. (1997), *"Career Concerns and the Acquisition of the Firm-Specific Skills."* Discussion Papers. Wissenschaftszentrum Berlin.

Sirianni, C, and L. Friedland. (1997), *"Civic innovation and American democracy."* Civic Practices Network.

Skinner, B.F. (1971), *Beyond Freedom and Dignity.* New York: Bantam.

Skocpol, T. (1984), *The Theory of Moral Sentiments*, ed. D.D. Raphael and A.L. Macfie. Vol. I of the Glasgow Edition of the Works and Correspondence of Adam Smith (Indianapolis: Liberty Fund, 1982).

Skocpol, T. (1984) *Vision and Method in Historical Sociology*. New York and Cambridge: Cambridge University Press

Skocpol, T. (1996), Unravelling From Above. *The American Prospect* 25/March–April: 20–5.

Skocpol, T. (1997), Americas Voluntary Groups Thrive in a National Network. *The Brookings Review* 15(4): 16–19.

Skrabski, A., Kopp, M. and Kawachi, I. (2003), Social capital in a changing society: Cross sectional associations with middle aged female and male mortality rates. *Journal of Epidemiology and Community Health* 57: 114.

Slack, P. (1988), *Poverty and Policy in Tudor and Stuart England*. Harlow: Addison Wesley Longman.

Slangen, L.H.G., van Kooten, G.C. and Suchanek, P. (2004), Institutions, social capital and agricultural change in central and eastern Europe. *Journal of Rural Studies* 20(2): 245–56.

Sloan, D. (1971), *The Scottish Enlightenment and the American College Ideal.* New York: Teachers College Press.

Small, M.L. (2002), Culture, cohorts, and social organization theory: Understanding local participation in a Latino housing project. *The American Journal of Sociology* 108: 1–54.

Smith P., Morita Y., Junger-Tas J., Olweus D., Catalanot E., and Slee P. (eds) (1999), *The Nature of School Bullying: A Cross Cultural Perspective.* London: Routledge.

Smith, A. [1776](1937), *An Enquiry into the Nature and Causes of the Wealth of Nations.* New York: Random House.

Smith, G. (1998), A Very Social Capital: Measuring the Vital Signs of Community Life in Newham, in B. Knight et al. (eds), *Building Civil Society: Current Initiatives in Voluntary Action.* West Malling: Charities Aid Foundation, pp. 51–73.

Smith, M.H., Beaulieu, L.J. and Seraphine, A. (1995), Social Capital, Place of Residence, and College Attendance. *Rural Sociology* 60: 363–80.

Smith, S.S.R. and Kulynych, J. (2002), Liberty, Equality, and ... Social Capital? in *Social Capital: Critical Perspectives on Community and "Bowling Alone"*, edited by S.L. McLean, D.A. Schultz, and M.B. Steger. New York and London: New York University Press, pp. 127–46.

Smith, S. Samuel, and J. Kulynych. (2002), It may be social, but why is it capital? The social construction of social capital and the politics of language. *Politics & Society* 30: 149–86.

Smith, T.W. (1981), "Can We Have Confidence in Confidence: Revisited," pp. 119–89 in *Measurement of Subjective Phenomena,* edited by D.F. Johnston. Washington, D.C.: U.S. Department of Commerce, 126.

Smith, T.W. (1990), Trends in Voluntary Group Membership: Comments on Baumgartner and Walker" *American Journal of Political Science* 34: 646–61.

Smith, T.W. (1994), Is There Real Opinion Change? *International Journal of Public Opinion Research* 6: 187–203.

Smith, T.W. (1997), Factors Relating to Misanthropy in Contemporary American Society. *Social Science Research* 26: 170–96.

Snijders, T.A.B. (1999), Prologue to the measurement of social capital. *The Tocqueville Review* 20: 27–44.

Sobel, I. (1978), The human capital revolution in economic development: Its current history and status. *Comparative Educational Review*, 22(2), 279–308.

Sobel, J. (2002), Can We Trust Social Capital? *Journal of Economic Literature* 40(1): 139–54.

Sobels, J., Curtis, A. and Lockie, S. (2001), The role of Landcare group networks in rural Australia: exploring the contribution of social capital. *Journal of Rural Studies* 17: 265–76.

Social Exclusion Unit (1998), *Truancy and School Exclusion Report.* London: Stationery Office, cm 3957.

Social Exclusion Unit (1999), *Social Exclusion Unit: What It's All About?* www. cabinet–office.gov.uk/seu.

Solomon, W.S. (2000), More Form than Substance: Press Coverage of the WTO Protests in Seattle, *Monthly Review* 52(1) (May). http://www.monthlyreview. org/500solo.html.

Solomos, J. and Back, L. (1995), *Race, Politics and Social Change.* London: Routledge.

Solow, R. (2000), Notes on Social Capital and Economic Performance, in P. Dasgupta and I. Serageldin (eds), *Social Capital: A Multifaceted Perspective.* Washington, D.C.: World Bank, pp. 6–10.

Somers, M. (1994), The Narrative Constitution of Identity: A Relational and Network Approach. *Theory and Society*, 23: 605–49.

Soubeyran, A., and S. Weber. (2002), District formation and local social capital: a (tacit) co-opetition approach. *Journal of Urban Economics* 52: 65–92.

Spellerberg, A. (1997), Towards a framework for the measurement of social capital, in D. Robinson (ed.) *Social Capital and Policy Development*, Institute of Policy Studies, Victoria University of Wellington, Wellington NZ.

Spence, L. (2000), Social Capital and Informal Learning, in F. Coffield (ed.) *The Necessity of Informal Learning.* Bristol: Policy Press, pp. 32–42.

Spence, M. (1973), Job Market Signalling. *Quarterly Journal of Economics,* 873: 355–74.

Spender, J. C. (1996), Making Knowledge the Basis of a Dynamic Theory of the Firm. *Strategic Management Journal*, 17: 45–62.

Stalker, K., Baron, S., Riddell, S., and Wilkinson, H. (1999), Models of Disability: The Relationship between Theory and Practice in Non-Statutory Organisations. *Critical Social Policy* 19(1): 5–31.

Stalker, K., Wilkinson, H., and Riddell, S. (1998), The Learning Society: The Highest Stage of Human Capitalism?, in F. Coffield (ed.), *Learning at Work.* Bristol: Policy Press, 49–57.

Stanton-Salazar, R., and Dornbusch, S. (1995), Social capital and the reproduction of inequality: Information networks among Mexican-origin High School students. *Sociology of Education*, 68(2): 116–35.

Starowicz, K. (2011), *The American personality documentary: fetishization, nostalgia and the working class.* 2011 CineAction.

Staveren, I. Van. (2003), Beyond social capital in poverty research. *Journal of Economic Issues* 37: 415–24.

Steger, M.B. (1993), *The Collapse of Real Socialism in Poland.* London; New York: Janus Publishing.

Steger, M.B. (2002), Robert Putnam, Social Capital, and a Suspect Named Globalizationin: *Social Capital Critical Perspectives on Community and "Bowling Alone"* edited by S.L. McLean, D.A. Schultz, and M.B. Steger. New York and London: New York University Press, pp. 260–80.

Steiger, J.H., and J.M. Lind. (1980), *Statistically Based Tests for the Number of Common Factors.* Paper presented at the annual meeting of the Psychometric Society, Iowa City, Iowa.

Stein, M. (1960), *The Eclipse of Community: An Interpretation of American Studies.* New York: Harper & Row.

Steinberg, L. (1997), *Beyond the Classroom.* New York: Simon & Schuster.

Sternberg, R. (1996), Myths, Countermyths, and Truths about Intelligence. *Educational Research*, March: 11–16.

Stigler, G.J., and G.S. Becker. (1977), De Gustibus Non Est Disputandum. *American Economic Review* 67: 76–90.

Stirling, M. (1992), How Many Pupils Are Being Excluded? *British Journal of Special Education* 19(4): 128–30.

Stockdale, J. (1995), The Self and Media Messages: Match or Mismatch?, in I. Markova and R. Farr (eds), *Representations of Health, Illness and Handicap.* London: Harwood, pp. 31–48.

Stoker, G. (1997), Local Government Reform in Britain after Thatcher, in J. Lane (ed.), *Public Sector Reform.* London: Sage, pp. 74–87.

Stoker, G. (1998), Governance as Theory: Five Propositions. *International Social Sciences Journal* 155: 17–28.

Stoker, G. and Young, S. (1993), *Cities in the 1990s.* Harlow: Longman.

Stolle, D. (1998), *Making Associations Work: Group Characteristics, Membership and Generalized Trust.* Paper presented at the 1998 meeting of the American Political Science Association, Boston, September 3–6.

Stolle, D. and Rochon, T. (1998), Are All Associations Alike? (forthcoming) in Edwards and Foley (eds.), *Beyond Tocqueville: Civil Society and Social Capital in Comparative Perspective.* Thematic Issue of the *American Behavioral Scientist.*

Stone, W and Hughes, J. (2002), *Social capital: empirical meaning and measurement validity.* Melbourne: Australian Institute of Family Studies, pp. 64.

Stone, W. (2001), Measuring social capital: Towards a theoretically informed measurement framework for researching social capital in family and community life. *Family Matters* Autumn: 38.

Stone, W. (2001), Measuring Social Capital. *Australian Institute of Family Studies,* Research Paper No. 24. [Online], Available: www.aifs.org.au/

Streeck, W. (1989), Skills and the Limits of Neo-Liberalism: The Enterprise of the Future as a Place of Learning. *Work, Employment and Society* 3(1): 89–104.

Sturgess, G. (1997), Taking Social Capital Seriously, in A. Norton, M. Latham, and S.G. Sturgess (eds), *Social Capital: The Individual, Civil Society and The State.* Sydney: Centre for Independent Studies, pp. 49–83.

Sturgess, G. (1997), Taking Social Capital Seriously, in Norton, A. Latham, M. Sturgess, G. and Stewart-Weekes, M. (eds) *Social Capital: The Individual, Civil Society and the State* St. Leonards: Centre for Independent Studies. 49–83.

Suarez-Orozco, M.M. (1991), Immigrant Adaptation to Schooling: A Hispanic Case, in M.A. Gibson and J.U. Ogbu (eds), *Minority Status and Schooling: A Comparative Study of Immigrant and Involuntary Minorities*. New York: Garland, pp. 37–62.

Subramanian, S.V., Kimberly A. Lochner, and Kawachi, I. (2003), Neighborhood differences in social capital: a compositional artifact or a contextual construct? *Health & Place* 9: 33–44.

Sullivan, A. and Sheffrin, S.M. (2003), *Economics: Principles in action*. Upper Saddle River, New Jersey: Pearson Prentice Hall.

Sullivan, J.L., Borgida, E., Jackson, M.S. and Riedel, E. (2002), Social capital and community electronic networks: For-profit versus for-community approaches. *The American Behavioral Scientist* 45: 868–86.

Swartz, D. (1990), Pierre Bourdieu: Culture, education, and social inequality, in K.J. Dougherry and F.M. Hammack (Eds.), *Education and Society: A Reader*. Ft. Worth, TX: Harcourt Brace Jovanovich, pp. 70–80.

Swedberg, R. (ed.) (1990), *Economics and Sociology, Redefining Their Boundaries: Conversations with Economists and Sociologists,* Princeton: Princeton University Press.

Szreter, S. (1997a), Economic Growth, Disruption, Deprivation, Disease and Death: On the Importance of the Politics of Public Health. *Population and Development Review*, 23: 693–728, 290 References.

Szreter, S. (1997b), British Economic Decline and Human Resources, in P.F. Clarke and R.C. Trebilcock (eds), *Understanding Decline: Perceptions and Realities of British Economic Performance*. Cambridge: Cambridge University Press, pp. 73–102.

Szreter, S. (1999), A New Political Economy for New Labour: The Importance of Social Capital. *Renewal* 7(1): 30–44.

Szreter, S. (2000), Social capital, the economy, and education in historical perspective. pp. 56–77 in *Social Capital: Critical Perspectives*, edited by T. Schuller. Oxford: Oxford University Press.

Szreter, S. and Mooney, G. (1998), Urbanisation, Mortality and the Standard of Living Debate: New Estimates of the Expectation of Life At Birth in Nineteenth-Century British Cities. *Economic History Review* 50: 84–112.

Tabarrok, A. (2000), An Economic Theory of Avant-Garde and Popular Art, or High and Low Culture. *Southern Economic Journal*.

Tanaka, J.S. (1993), Multifaceted Conceptions of Fit in Structural Equation Models, in *Testing Structural Equation Models*, edited by K.A. Bollen and J. Scott Long. Newbury Park, Calif.: Sage Publications, pp. 10–39.

Tannen, D. (1990), *You just Don't Understand: Women and Men In Conversation*. London: Virago.

Tarrow, S. (1996), Making Social Science Work Across Space and Time: A Critical Reflection on Robert Putnam's Making Democracy Work. *American Political Science Review*, 90(2): 389–97.

Tawil, O., Verster, A. and O'Reilly, K. (1995), *Enabling Approaches for HIV/AIDS Promotion: Can We Modify the Environment and Minimise the Risk?* AIDS, 9: 1299–306.

Tawney, R. (1982), *The Acquisitive Society.* Brighton: Wheatsheaf.

Taylor, M. (1997), *The Impact of Local Government Changes on the Voluntary and Community Sectors: New Perspectives on Local Government.* London: Joseph Rowntree Foundation.

Taylor, M. (2000), Communities in the lead: Power, organisational capacity and social capital. *Urban Studies* 37: 1019–35.

Taylor, S. and Spencer, L. (1994), *Individuals Attitudes: Individual Commitment to Lifetime Learning: Report on Qualitative Phase, Research Series No. 31.* Sheffield: Employment Department.

Teachman, J. (1996), Intellectual Skill and Academic Performance: Do Families Bias the Relationship? *Sociology of Education* 69: 35–48.

Teachman, J., K. Paasch, and K. Carver, (1997), Social Capital and the Generation of Human Capital. *Social Forces* 75 (4): 1343–59.422.

Teachman, J (1987*),* Family Background, Educational Resources and Educational Attainment. *American Sociological Review* 52: 548–57.

Temple, J. (1999), Initial Conditions, Social Capital, and Growth in Africa. *Journal of African Economics* 7(3): 309–47.

Temple, J. and P.A. Johnson, (1998), Social Capability and Economic Growth. *Quarterly Journal of Economics* August, 965–990.

Templin, Ch. (1997), *Canons, class, and the crisis of the humanities.* College Literature, Vol. 22, Issue 2.

Tendler, J., and S. Freedheim. (1994), Trust in a rent-seeking world: Health and environment transformed in northeast Brazil. *World Development* 22: 1771–92.

Terman, L. (1923), *Intelligence Tests and School Reorganisation.* New York: World Book Co.

Thane, P. (1982), *The Foundations of the Welfare State.* Harlow: Longman.

Thomas, C. Y. (1996), Capital markets, financial markets and social capital. *Social and Economic Studies* 45: 1–23.

Thompson, E. P. (1967), Time, Work-Discipline and Industrial Capitalism. *Past and Present* 38: 56–97.

Thrift, N. (1999), The Place of Complexity, *Theory Culture and Society* 16(3): 31–69.

Throsby, D. (1999), Cultural capital, *Journal of Cultural Economics* 23: 3–12.

Throsby, David (2001), *Economics and Culture,* Cambridge: Cambridge University Press.

Thurow, L.C. (1974), Measuring the economic benefits of education, in *Higher Education and the Labour market,* edited by M.S. Gordon, New York: McGraw-Hill, pp. 373–418.

Thurow, L.C. (1977). Education and economic equality, in *Power and Ideology in Education*, edited by J. Karabel and A.H. Halsey. New York: Oxford University Press, pp. 325–35.

Thurow, L.C. (1982), The failure of education as an economic strategy. *The American Economic Review* 72(2): 72–6.

Thurow, L.C. (1983), *Dangerous Currents: The State of Economics*. Oxford: Oxford University Press.

Tiryakin, E. (1998), *is There a Future for Sociology in the Global Age?* Paper to British Association Conference, Cardiff University, September.

Titmuss, R.M. (1950), *Problems of Social Policy*. London: HMSO.

Tittenbrun, J. (1995), The Managerial Revolution Revisited: The Case of Privatisation in Poland. *Capital and Class* 55: 21–328.

Tittenbrun, J. (2008), Z deszczu pod rynnę *[From the Frying Pan into the Fire]*. Poznan: Zysk and Co.

Tittenbrun, J. (2009a), Two Capitalism, in: J. Tittenbrun (ed.), *Capitalism of Capitalisms?* Szczecin: My Book.

Tittenbrun, J. (2011), Shareholder Capitalism vs. Stakeholder Capitalism, in *Humanities and Education*, edited by W. Bondareva, Samara.

Tocqueville de, A. [1835, 1840], (1990), *Democracy in America*. New York: Vintage.

Tolley, K., and Wolstenholme, J. (1996), *Is AIDS a Disease of Poverty?* AIDS Care, 8(3): 351–63.

Tomer, J. (1987), *Organisational Capital: The Path to Higher Productivity and Well-Being*. Westport, CT: Praeger.

Tomlinson, S. (1991*)*, Ethnicity and Educational Attainment in England: An Overview. *Anthropology and Education Quarterly* 22: 121–39.

Tonnies, F. (1887, 1957), *Community and Society – Gemeinschaft und Gesellschaft*, translated and supplemented by C.P. Loomis. East Lansing: Michigan State University Press.

Topel, R. (1986), Job Mobility, Search, and Earnings Growth: A Reinterpretation of Human Capital Earnings Functions, in *Research in Labour Economics, Vol. 8*, edited by R. Ehrenberg. Greenwich, CN: JAI Press, pp. 199–223.

Topel, R. (1991), Specific Capital, Mobility, and Wages: Wages Rise with Job Seniority. *Journal of Political Economy* 99(1): 145–76.

Topel, R.H. (1990), Specific Capital and Unemployment: Measuring the Costs and Consequences of Job Loss, in *Studies in Labor Economics in Honor of Walter Y. Oi*, edited by A.H. Meltzer and C.I. Ploser. Amsterdam: North Holland, pp. 181–214.

Topel, R.H. (1991), Specific Capital, Mobility, and Wages: Wages Rise with Job Security. *Journal of Political Economy* 99 (February): 145–76.

Topel, R.H. (2000), "Managing the workplace," Lecture Notes for Topic 1: Labour markets and human capital. Lecture notes for Business 343, The University of Chicago.

Torpe, L. (2003), "Social capital in Denmark: a deviant case?" *Scandinavian Political Studies* 26: 27–48.

Toumarkine, A. (1995), *Les Migrations des Populations Musulmanes Balkaniques en Anatolie (1876–1913)*. Istanbul: ISIS.

Trigilia, C. (2001), "Social Capital and Local Development." *European Journal of Social Theory* 4: 427–42.

Tsai, W. and Ghoshal, S. (1998), Social Capital and Value Creation: The Role of Intrafirm Networks, *Academy of Management Journal* 43(4): 464–76.

Tsouros, A. (ed.) (1990), *WHO Healthy Cities Project: A Project Becomes a Movement (Review of Progress 1987 to 1990)*. Copenhagen: WHO/FADL.

Turner, J.H. (1999), The formation of social capital, in *Social Capital: A Multifaceted Perspective*, edited by I. Serageldin. Washington, D.C.: World Bank, pp. 94–147.

Uphoff, N. (1996), *Learning from Gal Oya*. London: Intermediate Publications.

Uphoff, N. (1999), Understanding social capital: Learning from the analysis and experience of participation. pp. 215–253 in *Social Capital: A multifaceted perspective*, edited by I. Serageldin. Washington, DC: World Bank.

Uphoff, N. and Wijayaratna, C.M. (2000), Demonstrated Benefits from Social Capital: The Productivity of Farmer Organizations in Gal Oya, Sri Lanka. *World Development* 28: 1875–90.

Urban Task Force (1999), *Towards an Urban Renaissance: Final Report of the Urban Task Force (Lord Rogers of Riverside, Chair)*. London: Department of the Environment, Transport and the Regions.

Urrieta, L.Jr. (2005), *Heritage charter school: a case of conservative local white activism through a postmodern framework*. Educational Foundations.

Uslaner, E.M. 2001. Volunteering and social capital: how trust and religion shape civic participation in the United States, in *Social Capital and Participation in Everyday Life*, edited by E.M. Uslaner. London: Routledge, pp. 104–17.

Uzzi, B. (1996), The Sources and Consequences of Embeddedness for the Economic Performance of Organizations: The Network Effect. *American Sociological Review* 61: 674–98.

Vallet, L-A. and Caille, J-P. (1996), *Les Eleves Etrangers dans l'Ecole et le College Français*. Les dossiers d'Éducation et Formations, 67, Ministère de l'Éducation nationale, DEP, 153.

Van Deth J.W. (1998), Introduction: Social Involvement and Democratic Polities, in J.W. van Deth (ed.), *Private Groups and Public Life: Social Participation, Voluntary Associations, and Political Involvement in Representative Democracies*. London: Routledge, 1–23.

Van Deth J.W. and Kreuter, F. (1998), Membership of Voluntary Associations, in J.W. van Deth (ed.), *Comparative Politics: The Search for Equivalence in Comparative Politics*. London: Routledge, 135–55.

Van Deth, J.W. (2003), Measuring social capital: orthodoxies and continuing controversies. *International Journal of Social Research Methodology* 6: 79.

Vanek, J. (1970), *The General Theory of Labor-Managed Market Economies.* Ithaca, NY: Cornell University Press.

Vanek, J. (1977), The Basic Theory of Financing of Participatory Firms, in *The Labor-Managed Economy: Essays by Jaroslav Vanek.* Ithaca, NY: Cornell University Press.

Veenstra G. (2001), Social Capital and Health. *Isuma* 1(2): 72–81.

Veenstra, G. (2002), Explicating social capital: trust and participation in the civil space. *Canadian Journal of Sociology* 27: 547–74.

Veenstra, G. (2007), Who the Heck is Don Bradman? Sport Culture and Social Class in British Columbia, Canada. *Canadian Review of Sociology & Anthropology* 44(3): 319–44.

Verba, S. and Nie, N. (1972), *Participation in America: Political Democracy and Social Equality.* New York: Harper & Row.

Verba, S., Kay Lehman S., and Brady, H.E. (1995), *Voice and Equality: Civic Volunteerism in American Politics.* Cambridge, MA: Harvard University Press.

Verba, S., Nie, N.H. and Jae-On, K. (1978), *Participation and Political Equality: A Seven-nation Comparison.* Cambridge: Cambridge University Press.

Vincent, C. and Tomlinson, S. (1997), Home–School Relationships: The Swarming of Disciplinary Mechanisms? *British Educational Research Journal* 23(3): 361–77.

Vitae, M. (2010), *Social and Cultural Capital in Education. International Encyclopedia of Education* (Third Edition) http://dx.doi.org/10.1016/B978–0–08–044894–7.00571–6.

Wachter, K., and Gregory, A. (1990), *Height, Health and History: Nutritional Status in the United Kingdom, 1750–1980.* Cambridge: Cambridge University Press.

Waldinger, Roger. 1995. The Other Side of Embeddedness: A Case-Study of the Interplay of Economy and Ethnicity. *Ethnic and Racial Studies* 18(3): 555–80.

Waldman, M. (1984), Job Assignments, Signalling and Efficiency. *Rand Journal of Economics* 15(2): 255–67.

Waldman, M. (1990), Up-or-Out Contracts: A Signaling Perspective. *Journal of Labor Economics* 8(2): 230–50.

Walker, G. and Kogut, B. (1997), Social Capital, Structural Holes and the Formation of an Industry Network. *Organization Science: A Journal of the Institute of Management Sciences* 8: 109.

Walker, J (1991), *Mobilizing Interest Groups in America: Patrons, Professions and Social Movements.* Ann Arbor: University of Michigan Press.

Wall, E., Ferrazzi, G. and Schryer, F. (1998), Getting the goods on social capital. *Rural Sociology* 63: 300–322.

Wallis, A. (1998), Social capital and community building (Building Healthier Communities: Ten Years of Learning) (part 2). *National Civic Review* 87: 317–19.

Wallis, A., Crocker, J.P. and Schechter, B. (1998), Social capital and community building, part 1. *National Civic Review* 87: 253–72.

Walsh, J.R. (1935), Capital concept applied to man. *Quarterly Journal of Economics* 49(2), 255–85.

Walters, P.B., and Rubinson, R. (1983), Educational expansion and economic output in the United States, 1890–1969: A production function analysis. *American Sociological Review* 48, 480–93.

Walters, W. (2002), Social capital and political sociology: Re-imagining politics? *Sociology: The Journal of the British Sociological Association* 36: 377–97.

Wang, Y-H. (2009), *An Analysis of the Harmonious Process in Intercultural Communication.* China Media Research.

Ward, A. (1992), "The African American Struggle for Education in Columbus, Ohio: 1803–1913" (Masters thesis, The Ohio State University, Columbus, OH).

Ward, B. (1958), The Firm in Illyria: Market Syndicalism. *American Economic Review* 48: 566–89.

Warde, A., Tampubolon, G., Longhurst, B. and Ray, K. (2003), Trends in social capital: Membership of associations in Great Britain, 1991–98. *British Journal of Political Science* 33: 515.

Warde, A., Martens, L., and Oben, W. (1999), Consumption and the Problem of Variety: Cultural Omnivorousness, Social Distinction and Dining Out. *Sociology* 33(1): 105–27.

Warner, M. (1999), Social capital construction and the role of the local state. *Rural Sociology* 64: 373–93.

Wasserman, S. and Faust, K. (1994), *Social Network Analysis: Methods and Applications.* Cambridge: Cambridge University Press.

Watson, G.W., and Papamarcos, S.D. (2002), Social capital and organizational commitment. *Journal of Business and Psychology* 16: 537–52.

Watson, S., Waslander, S., Thrupp, M., Strathdee, R., Simiyu, I., Dupuis, A., McGlinn, J. and Hamlin, J. (1999), *Trading in Futures: Why Markets in Education Don't Work.* Buckingham: Open University Press.

Watts and Shrader (1998), December. The genogram. A new tool for documenting patterns of decisionmaking, conflict and vulnerability within households. *Health Policy and Planning* 13(4): 459–64.

Wayland, F. (1963), *The Elements of Moral Science*, ed. J.L. Blau. Cambridge, MA: Harvard University Press.

Weatherly, L.A. (2003), The Value of People. *HR Magazine*, 10473149, 48(9).

Weil, S.W. (1986), Non-Traditional Learners within Traditional Higher Education Institutions: Discovery and Disappointment. *Studies in Higher Education*, 11(3): 219–35.

Weininger E.B. (2010), *Foundations of Class Analysis in the work of Bourdieu, in: Alternative Foundations of Class, 2002.* http://www.ssc.wisc.edu/~wright/Found-all.pdf.

Weininger, E.B. (2005), Foundations of Pierre Bourdieus Class Analysis, in Wright, E.O. (ed.), *Approaches to Class Analysis.* Cambridge University Press, Cambridge, UK.

Weiss, A. (1990), *Efficiency Wages: Models of Unemployment, Layoffs, and Wage Dispersion.* Princeton University Press.

Weisskopf, T.E. (1987), The Effect of Unemployment on Labour Productivity: An International Comparative Analysis. *International Review of Applied Economics* 1(1): 129–51.

Wellman, B., A. Quan Haase, A., Witte, J. and Hampton, K. (2001), Does the Internet increase, decrease, or supplement social capital? Social networks, participation, and community commitment. *The American Behavioral Scientist* 45: 436–55.

Wellman, B., Carrington, P.J. and Hall, A. (1988), Networks as Personal Communities. pp. 130–84 in *Social Structures: A Network Approach*, edited by B. Wellman and S.D. Berkowitz. Cambridge: Cambridge University Press.

Wells, R. (2008), The Effects of Social and Cultural Capital on Student Persistence: Are Community Colleges More Meritocratic?, *Community College Review* 36(1).

Welsh, T, and M. Pringle. (2001), Social capital. Trusts need to recreate trust. *BMJ* [Clinical Research Edn] 323: 177–8.

Westlund, H. and Nilsson, E. (2005), Measuring Enterprises Investments in Social Capital: A Pilot Study. *Regional Studies,* 39(8): 1079–94.

Whetstone, A.E. (1981), *Scottish County Government in the Eighteenth and Nineteenth Centuries.* Edinburgh: John Donald.

White, L. (2002), Connection matters: exploring the implications of social capital and social netowrks for social polcy. *Systems Research and Behavioral Science* 19: 255–69.

Whitehead, A. (1996), *Exit Voice and Loyalty in City Communities, Southampton Institute Professorial Lecture.* Southampton: Southampton Institute.

Whiteley, P. (1999), The Origins of Social Capital, in J. van Deth, M. Maraffi, K. Newton and P. Whiteley (eds), *Social Capital and European Democracy.* London: Routledge, 3–24.

Whittington, K.E. (1998), Revisiting Tocquevilles America. *American Behavioral Scientist*, 42/1: 21–32 (Special Edition: Beyond Tocqueville: Civil Society and Social Capital in Comparative Perspective).

Widén-Wulff, G. (2007), *The Challenges of Knowledge Sharing in Practice: A Social Approach.* Oxford: Chandos.

Wiggins, S.N. (1991), The Economics of the Firm and Contracts: A Selective Survey. *Journal of Institutional and Theoretical Economics* 147 (December): 603–61.

Wildhagen, T. (2009), The Cultural Capital Effect. *The Sociological Quarterly* 50: 173–200.

Wilkinson, R. (1996), *Unhealthy Societies: The Affliction of Inequality.* London: Routledge.

Wilkinson, R. (1999), Putting the Picture Together: Prosperity, Redistribution, Health, and Welfare, in M. Marmot and R.G. Wilkinson, *Social Determinants of Health.* Oxford: Oxford University Press, pp. 256–74.

Williams, B., Campbell, C., and MacPhail, C. (1999), *Managing HIV/AIDS in South Africa: Lessons from Industrial Settings*. Johannesburg: CSIR.

Williams, C. and Gulati, G. (2007), Social Networks in Political Campaigns Facebook and the 2006 midterm Elections, 2007 Annual Meeting of the American Political Science Association, Chicago, September.

Williamson, J. (1994), Coping with City Growth, in R. Floud and D. McCloskey (eds), *The Economic History of Britain Since 1700 (Vol. 1: 1700–1860)* (2nd edn). Cambridge: Cambridge University Press, pp. 332–56.

Williamson, O.E. (1975), *Markets and Hierarchies: Analysis and Antitrust Implications*. New York: Free Press.

Williamson, O.E. (1985), *The Economic Institutions of Capitalism: Firms, Markets, Relational Contracting*. New York: Free Press.

Williamson, O.E. and Bercovitz, J. (1996), The Modern Corporation as an Efficiency Instrument: The Comparative Contracting Perspective, in *The American Corporation Today*, edited by C. Kaysen. Oxford: Oxford University Press.

Williamson, O.E., Wachter, M.L. and Harris, J.E. (1975), Understanding the Employment Relation: The Analysis of Idiosyncratic Exchange. *Bell Journal of Economics* 6 (Spring): 250–80.

Willis, P. (1977), *Learning to Labour*. Farnborough: Saxon House.

Wilson, J. and Musick, M. (1997), Who Cares? Toward an Integrated Theory of Volunteer Work. *American Sociological Review* 62: 694–713.

Wilson, P.A. (1997), Building Social Capital: A Learning Agenda for the Twenty-first Century. *Urban Studies* 34: 745–760.

Wilson, W.J. (1987). *The Truly Disadvantaged: The Inner City, The Underclass and Public Policy*. Chicago: Chicago University Press.

Wilson, W.J. (1987), *The Truly Disadvantaged: The Inner City, The Underclass and Public Policy*. Chicago: Chicago University Press.

Winter, I. (2000a), Major themes and debates in the social capital literature: The Australian connection, in *Social capital and public policy in Australia*, edited by I. Winter. Melbourne: National Library of Australia, pp. 17–42.

Winter, S.G. (1987), Knowledge and Competence as Strategic Assets, in D.J. Teece (ed.), *The Competitive Challenge: Strategies for Industrial Innovation and Renewal*. Cambridge, MA: Ballinger, pp. 159–83.

Wirth, L. (1938), Urbanism as a Way of Life, in *On Cities and Social Life*, edited by A.J. Reiss, Jr. Chicago: University of Chicago Press, pp. 60–83.

Withrington, D.J. (1988), A Ferment of Change: Aspirations, Ideas and Ideals in Nineteenth-Century Scotland, in D. Gifford (ed.), *The History of Scottish Literature: Volume 3, Nineteenth Century*. Aberdeen: Aberdeen University Press, pp. 43–63.

Wolfe, A. (1998), *One Nation AfterAll*. New York: Viking.

Wolfinger, R. and Rosenstone, S. (1980), *Who Votes?* New Haven, CN: Yale University Press.

Wolfstetter, E., Brown, M. and Meran, G. (1984), Optimal Employment and Risk Sharing in Illyria: The Labour Managed Firm Reconsidered. *Journal of Institutional and Theoretical Economics* 140: 655–68.

Wollebaek, D. and Selle, P. (2003), Participation and social capital formation: Norway in a comparative perspective. *Scandinavian Political Studies* 26: 67–91.

Woolcock, G. (2002a), "Social capital and community development: Fad, friend or foe?" in Queensland Local Government Community Services Association Annual Conference. Rockhampton.

Woolcock, M. (1998), Social Capital and Economic Development: Towards a Theoretical Synthesis and Policy Framework. *Theory and Society* 27: 151–208.

Woolcock, M. (2000), *Using Social Capital: Getting the Social Relations Right in the Theory and Practice of Economic Development.* Princeton: Princeton University Press.

Woolcock, M. and Narayan, D. (2000), Social capital: Implications for development theory, research, and policy. *The World Bank Research Observer* 15: 225–49.

World Almanac and Book of Facts. New York, 2006, World Almanac Books.

World Bank (1997), *Expanding the Measure of Wealth: Indicators of Environmentally Sustainable Development.* Washington, D.C.: World Bank.

World Bank (2000), *World Development Report.* Washington, D.C.: World Bank.

Wozniak, G. (1984), The adoption of interrelated innovations: A human capital approach. *Review of Economics and Statistics* 66(1), 70–79.

Wrigley, E.A. (1987), *People, Cities and Wealth: The Transformation of Traditional Society.* Blackwell: Oxford.

Wrigley, E.A. (1988), *Continuity, Chance and Change: The Character of the Industrial Revolution in England.* Cambridge: Cambridge University Press.

Wuthnow, R. (1997), "The Changing Character of Social Capital in the United States." Working paper. Princeton University, Department of Sociology.

Wuthnow, R. (1998), *Loose Connections: Joining Together in Americas Fragmented Communities.* Cambridge, MA: Harvard University Press.

Yamamoto, Y. and Brinton, M.C. (2010), Cultural Capital in East Asian Educational Systems: The Case of Japan. *Sociology of Education* 83(1): 67–83.

Yap, J.Y.C. (1986), *Refugee Trauma and Coping: A Study of a Group of Vietnamese Refugee Children Attending School in Southern England,* unpublished Ph.D. thesis. London: Institute of Education, University of London.

Yli-Renko, H., Autio, E. and Tontti, V. (2002), Social Capital, Knowledge, and the International Growth of Technology-Based New Firms, *International Business Review* 11: 279–304, 22.

Zhao, Y. (2002), Measuring the social capital of laid-off Chinese workers. *Current Sociology* 50: 555–71.

Zhou, M. and Bankston, C.L. III (1994), Social Capital and the Adaptation of the Second Generation: The Case of Vietnamese Youth in New Orleans. *International Migration Review*, 23(4): 821–45.

Zhou, Min, and Bankstron III, C. (1994), Social Capital and the Adaptation of the Second Generation: The Case of Vietnamese Youth in New Orleans. *International Migration Review* 28: 841–45.

Zuboff, S. (1988), *In the Age of the Smart Machine.* New York: Basic Books.

Index

For Product Safety Concerns and Information please contact our EU
representative GPSR@taylorandfrancis.com Taylor & Francis Verlag GmbH,
Kaufingerstraße 24, 80331 München, Germany

Printed and bound by CPI Group (UK) Ltd, Croydon, CR0 4YY
01/05/2025
01858461-0003

.